First published in Great Britain in 2015 by Unkant Publishers
2 Pascoe Road, London SE13 5JB

Designed by Keith Fisher and Andy Wilson
Cover illustration by Andy Wilson

British Library Cataloguing-in-Publication Data
A CIP catalogue record for this book is available from the
British Library
A Paperback Original

ISBN 978-0-9926509-4-0
1 3 5 7 9 10 8 6 4 2

Set in Unkant Jensen
www.unkant.com

Yealm

a sorterbiography

Sheila Lahr

Unkant Publishers

London

Contents

Sheila Lahr

Sheila Lahr was born in 1927 to an anarchist father who had left rural Germany behind him, and a Jewish mother whose parents had made the journey from Poland to London's East End. She grew up in a flurry of contradictions: left politics leavened with literary liberalism versus the strict Catholicism of her convent school, Germans versus Jews. After growing up with evacuation, her parents' internment and the free-wheeling atmosphere of war-time London, Sheila became a political activist, joining the Trotskyists in criticising the Communist Party and fighting the fascists in Dalston. In the the late 40s, she met and married George Leslie (1918-2012), a comrade in the Revolutionary Communist Party, with whom she had four children. In later years, Sheila took an degree in Humanities and trained as a teacher, but was dismayed by the repressive regime in 70s schools. She worked for the campaigning body Fair Play for Children and for the National Association of Women's Clubs, always writing stories and poems and painting. After some decades of minuting meetings for pension campaign groups, *Revolutionary History* and other grouplets, she now spends her days in North Finchley doing crosswords, sketching and reading. Sheila is always delighted if young activists call for Sunday dinner.

A Yealm of long straw is normally reckoned to be approximately sixteen or seventeen inches wide and about five inches thick. This treatment is known as 'yealming' and the tight wet bundles of straw, when they are gathered together for thatching, are known as 'yealms'. the ends of the individual straws in the yealms are made as level as possible.
Michael Billett, *Thatching and Thatched Buildings*

Chronos was the god of time of ancient Greeks; a god devoted to devouring his own children, as he multiplied them from the future and swallowed them into the past. A fable of time. A fabulous creature of change.
Dr. R.L. Worrall, *Time and Lifetime*

This 'sorterbiography'—a word coined by Ivy Litvinov to mean memoirs which are a mixture of fact and fiction—is dedicated to the following: my son Mark; my daughters Georgina, Adelaide and Esther and their children; and in memory of the Our Lady's Convent Hostel at 97 Attimore Close, Welwyn Garden City during World War Two: I always promised to write a book and dedicate it to the children with whom I had lived for two years!

In memory of my late husband, George Leslie.

Ian Patterson: Foreword

Anybody might be troubled by wondering what their life is for, what its purpose might be, or might have been. Anybody might wonder how to make sense of it, as I do as I look at the triumph of the rapacity, greed, selfishness and cruelty of those with power and capital here in the UK and all over the world. In recent years there has been a spate of autobiographies and autobiographical fictions retelling often in meticulous detail the small and not so small events of personal lives, but in most cases they don't manage to make much of a connection to the world beyond the personal context. The personal may theoretically be the political, but it isn't if there isn't any politics.

Sheila Lahr's memoir is different. As I read it I experienced the narrative, perhaps oddly now I come to write it down, as a sort of figure of eight, shifting all the time under the pressure of time and history, but at the same time resilient enough to resist buckling under its weight. Here's a flavour of what I mean—early on in the book we read this:

> And so I am born into a world of cruelty, compromise, murder, mayhem, megalomania, paranoia, politics as power, tactics as betrayal. But the dustbins of history are not yet full and may yet be emptied and scattered, for as Walter Benjamin writes, revolution interrupts and breaks up the heap, providing for humankind a new beginning.

But such direct commentary is not the only way history provides a backdrop for this story of a child growing towards womanhood in the 1930s and 40s, though the occasional reminders of national and world events that are woven into it provide a kind of extra dimension.

> *In spite of ourselves we pass through time, or time passes through us, and the events recorded in this book for the most part took place fifty years ago and more.*

The past is shadowed by its future, the present by both. The dramatic present of the narrative is full of the moment, of course, but also shaped by pasts and pregnant with futures, as another passage from the book makes clear. No. 41 Wilton Road is about to be bombed, and four of its occupants to die, buried under earth in the Anderson shelter in their garden, but we don't know that yet:

> *At No. 41, in the upstairs flat, live the Pearces, husband and wife. That is the old No. 41, not the postwar house which replaced it. And sometimes I wonder whether the present residents feel the presence of the former home, the rooms at times seeming to take on different sizes and altered shapes. Do they lose their way down a passage, or find themselves in the wrong room? Or conversely, had the old No. 41 ever felt insubstantial to the Pearces, the new house shaking it apart as it grew up in its midst? Or had Mrs. Pearce ever sensed the children of later generations making their home in the space of her flat—the children longed for by her, but denied?*

This sense of the whole of time in the present moment is what gives *Yealm* its extraordinary quality. It is a wonderfully full and detailed account of a childhood and adolescence, like an old-fashioned novel, in which a cast of hundreds is brought to life and lost again. Some of the characters are well-known, at least to a 1930s literary nerd like me: Sheila's unlucky father Charlie Lahr, James Hanley (who had an affair with her mother), Rhys Davies, Valentine Ackland and Sylvia Townsend Warner, and plenty of others. But they come and go, according to the ways they impinge on Sheila's life and consciousness. And the reason it works is because of her consciousness, which is both created with hindsight and recreated with complete presentness. The two books which it calls to my mind are in many ways quite different, being written with a profoundly literary sense of form and shaped into artifice in order to get at their truth: Proust's *In Search of Lost Time*, and Edward Upward's *The Spiral Ascent*. But *Yealm* has a comparable fluency, evocativeness, detail and reflectiveness. And it's very well-written and a real pleasure to read. The world it portrays is one familiar to me at one remove, as it's close to the world my mother (born eight years before Sheila) grew up in, but which I never knew. The personal becomes generalisable. People's lives and their often brief intersections with other lives create the fabric of another role history plays in the book, which I haven't mentioned so far. It's hardly there but it's felt throughout and becomes briefly explicit near the end. By this time we've read so much about Sheila and her family, her fears and her troubles, about the house in Muswell Hill, and the aspirations and limitations of friends, acquaintances, neighbours, enemies, teachers and the like that we have a deep and nuanced sense of a community and the limits placed on its freedom. We cheer, therefore, with Sheila, when the liberating effect of the war gives this community real importance, and when that sense of importance is made tangible in the election of a Labour government in 1945, even though the founding pillars of the welfare state are shadowed by the attack that is to be launched on them seventy years later by a resentful Tory government. As she says, *"Radio, newspapers and government all tell us what wonderful people we are, us, the British working class. How will we be pictured once the war is ended?"*

Not often enough like this, is my answer. If you want to know not just about one set of individual lives, not just about the local history of part of North London, not just about the awfulness of education, or the intransigence of bureaucracy, or even coming of age during the war, but if you want to get a sense of what it all might actually mean, to us as readers, as inheritors, as future components of the dustbin of history, then this book that you're holding in your hands is one of the things you should read. I've just finished it and I want to read it again.

Ian Patterson
Queens College, Cambridge
2015-vii-14

Beginnings: I Am Born Into a Certain Family History

At times when reading I meet my father Charles Lahr in one of his many guises. Perhaps in 1907 when together with Guy Aldred he trundles a wheelbarrow through London's streets 'broad and narrow'. The wheelbarrow is weighted down by a second-hand platen machine, bought for ten shillings borrowed from an acquaintance who has been convinced by Aldred of the necessity for the Bakunin press. My father is aged twenty-two, having been born in Wendelsheim and named Carl on 27th July, 1885. He is of middle height, his brown hair stands up on his head, his nose and ears are prominent and his green eyes look out in surprise at the drab urban world through which he is passing. He has been in London for two years, but still finds difficult the transition from the villages of the Rhine to an environment in which every sign of growing life has been bulldozed.

My father struggles with the wheelbarrow, while his companion ambles along by his side, talking most of the time, expounding his ideas, waving his arms. But occasionally, when a kerb proves too high, or a hill too steep, he puts out a hand to the barrow as if to pat it on its way.[1]

I have met my father also in a greasy spoon cafe, some time after the First World War. He sits at a wooden table, surrounded by a few cronies, one with a flat, large-brimmed black hat, a

---

1. John Taylor Caldwell, *Come Dungeons Dark—The Life and Times of Guy Aldred, Glasgow Anarchist*, Luath Press, Barr, Ayrshire, 1988.

second wearing a suit so shiny that it appears polished, a third wrapped about in a long, black Mackintosh. They are watched over by a fat man dressed in a greasy off-white apron, who stands behind the wooden counter next to the yellow cakes and curling sandwiches. My father wears a Kaiser moustache, its ends waxed, and as he speaks its points move up and down in a kind of dance. In contrast to his companions he wears a stiff collar, tie and well pressed black suit. He is telling the story of how, before the war, he was followed for several days by two detectives who suspected him of plotting to shoot the Kaiser. This in 1907, when the Kaiser was on a State visit to Britain. A story my father is to tell many times and which, is referred to briefly by William Fishman in *East End Jewish Radicals 1875-1914*.

The years pass and in 1927 my father and friends are wandering through a Rhine village. I am at home with my mother. It is August 1927 and I was born earlier in the year, on the 56th Anniversary of the Paris Commune: 18th March.

> *For hours she has been struggling to escape, through the dry canal which at one moment opens before her and then closes in upon itself and her, bringing pain in its wake now that the protecting waters have drained away. In her nostrils, and unidentified by her, is the stink of blood, but she accepts it as part of what is, as she has her present journey and all that has gone before, the imprisonment, the sudden forced movements without any apparent origin, the daily changes in her physical condition—all are received by her without thought for she has no earlier experience as a source of reference. Now the canal opens once more and she responds with one final effort, launching herself forward, pushing and pulling with both hands and feet, so that at last she scrambles out of the canal and, with a cry of triumph, into the light.*

My father is trudging up the hill to Hof Iben, occupied by his widowed sister-in-law, Anna. The day is cool and our companions, several young writers and an artist all of whom my father has brought from England, shiver, and hunch their shoulders. H.E. Bates, Rhys Davies and the artist William Roberts are among this group and later Bates is to write a short story about the difficulties met with in obtaining a bath in these villages. Bates take careful note, for one day he will be an important writer and remark upon this journey in his autobiography *The Blossoming World*.[2]

The way is long and surrounded by fields of grape vines, the ripening grapes to be harvested in September. Hof Iben stands on the summit and is a building the colour of sandstone. My father stops a little way before it to tell our companions that here once stood the gates against which his brother, Fritz, bruised and bloody, his earth-stained hands covering his blond head, was trampled by the horse and crossed by the wheels of the cart. And we see Fritz as a small boy in Bad Nauheim coming upon Elizabeth, Empress of Austria, who is living there incognito. As she walks through the village Fritz approaches her *"Good morning, Your Majesty"* he says politely, giving a little bow. The Empress is nonplussed. *"You must not call me that!"* she tells him. He stamps his foot. *"Yes, I must"* and holds out his hand to receive a small coin. This, happening again and again.

Fritz, the brother who was said to have stolen Hof Iben from his thirteen siblings, following their parents' deaths; buying out his brothers and sisters with money which during the inflationary period following the First World War had no value. But my father does not concern himself with this, for he is a man without desire for property or possessions.

Anna, the sister-in-law, a plain, dumpy, young woman dressed in a dark shapeless garment and wearing her mousy hair screwed back into a bun, waits at the door, the small blond boy Werner clinging to her skirts. Somewhere in the background is a camp in Gillingham, Dorset for Second World War German prisoners. And further away hovers the war memorial on which Werner is to execute himself by hanging, first smoking a cigar, which he places on the left side of the horizontal stone cross in the cemetery.

In some confusion Anna kisses my father and glances slyly at his companions about whose crazy demands for constant hot water and regular baths she has been informed by local gossip.

Sadly, I am unlikely to meet between the covers of books my mother, Esther Lahr, née Argeband, known as Archer, born on 10th December 1897 at 32 Stanhope Street in the Sub-district of Regent's Park.

---

2. H.E. Bates, *The Blossoming World*, Michael Joseph, 1971.

"There's a number of mentions of your father in books" says my mad cousin Cecil (whose name I mentally translate into 'Gabriel') *"but your mother hardly gets a mention and never more than the fact that she was Charlie's wife."* *"It's because she's a woman"* I explain and Cecil is satisfied.

However, I have met my mother once during the First World War, speaking from a platform in Victoria Park in the East End, her red curly hair acting as a beacon to draw the crowds around her, to the warmth of her anger at ruling classes which send their youth to kill each other. Her bright blue eyes flash and she grasps the top of the stand which because of her small stature puts her into the position of a child peering over a wall. This glimpse of my mother was given me by Ken Weller in *Don't Be A Soldier,* published by Journeyman 1985.

Time passes and yet in itself is static. It is we who pass through time and use as signposts our inventions of seconds, minutes, hours, days, weeks, months, years, so as to place our temporary existence in context and to mark our physical decay. And we invent also high days and holidays as extra markers to reassure ourselves that our journey is worthwhile. Behind us the discarded past builds up into an ever-increasing mountain of decay and this rubbish heap is known by us as history—as was first perceived by Walter Benjamin who on breaking his journey to glance behind saw clearly for the first time a wasting, withering, rotting pile. And as he stood observing, the heap spilled forward to encompass him and mark his grave: as it will for all of us.

And yet we find these signposts consoling. Therefore, I boast of my accidental connection to the Paris Commune on a day when in the Mother's Home, 396 Commercial Road, in the District of Stepney, I am born. My tiny mother heavily pregnant is accompanied to the Home by my grandmother, Rachel Argeband (née Wanderman), through the East End streets, past the terraces of one-storey houses whose front doors open directly onto a room; through the grey, deserted streets and the market place, empty except for a few forgotten cabbage leaves and specky apples left to rot in the gutter, across the Commercial Road where my grandmother is to be killed by a lorry in 1938 while returning home from the synagogue. But on this day she looks away, intent upon the coming birth and refuses to see herself lying stilly in the roadway, the killer lorry now stationary, while a curious group of sightseers observe her dying body. Instead, she hurries my labouring mother onwards, my mother, with pride, carrying all before her.

Elsewhere, and far away, in Shanghai, execution squads stalk through the town, for 1927 is the year of the Chinese Civil War, or as Harold Isaacs calls it 'The Tragedy of the Chinese Revolution', and so, during the month of my birth, the newspapers exhibit pages of photographs of events 'as they unfolded'. 2,000 British troops sent out to Shanghai to defend British financial interests, while the terror rages, let loose by the garrison commander General Li-Pao-Chang, the police of the International Settlement and the French concession. The executioner himself bears a broad-sword and is surrounded by soldiers. Those who are wise run for cover, but not all are so quick, especially at the beginning, before it is understood that such things can happen. The squad watches sharply for those distributing or holding up a leaflet to read, or to identify a striker or student, whereupon such a one is seized and marched to a street corner. Forced to bend over by soldiers he is neatly decapitated by the Executioner who has raised the sword high to bring it down to slice through the exposed neck of the victim. Then, triumphantly, the head, caught up with its expression in death of terror, or disbelief, is placed upon a sharp pointed bamboo and paraded to the next scene of execution. There are rumours in Shanghai that the terror will soon end, for General Chiang Kai-shek of the Nationalist armies, supported by the Communist Party, is no more than twenty-five miles away. But cunningly, he does not come. He waits until General Li has destroyed all left-wing political opposition, trade unionists, socialists and communists.

Then, when I am eight days old and lying peacefully asleep, Chiang enters the town to proclaim victory. Chiang rewards Li by making him Commander of the 8th Division of the Nationalist Army.

In the meantime, my mother lies on a hard labour bed, oblivious to the noise around her of the clatter and bangs made by hospital procedure and the screams and groans of fellow inmates. She is there by courtesy of donations collected by appeals for finances in the national press and from wealthy benefactors intent upon absolution with the added advantage of tax relief. It is in this manner that the working population is reduced to beggary. However, largesse stopping short of all but the plainest of fare, the lockshen soup, gefüllter fish and latkas are provided by my grandmother, Rachel, who makes a daily pilgrimage to our bed-side.

Here I should record that Rupert Croft-Cooke, author of a number of books among which is *The Last Spring* in which he writes of my father and his coterie,[3] at the time of my birth wrote for me an eight page *Natal Ode*, published by E. Archer.

Verses which start with the poet's remark:

> *'A child is born, unborn before'*
> *As Archibald Y Campbell sings,*
> *I find the lines not only poor*
> *but little information brings,*
> *Since even for the sake of rhymes*
> *Kids are not born a dozen times...*

And so I am born into a world of cruelty, compromise, murder, mayhem, megalomania, paranoia, politics as power, tactics as be-trayal. But the dustbins of history are not yet full and may yet be emptied and scattered, for as Walter Benjamin writes, revolution interrupts and breaks up the heap, providing for humankind a new beginning.

I find it interesting that the debris of those past years before my birth stand out more sharply in my mind than the detritus collected immediately afterwards. For the latter form a disor-dered crazy paving of memory. For instance, I am in my father's arms. We are in a street and it is dusk. He shows me his cut and bloody thumb, holding it up for my inspection. Then, I am lying on a hard bed in a white room. I am alone and perhaps I scream or cry out, for suddenly women dressed in white bustle towards me. They speak to one another and not to me, but I am given a wrist-watch to hold. Then again I am alone. I run my fingers over the glass on the face of the watch and the hard metallic back and throw it away across the room with as much force as I can muster.[4]

I am in a garden where there is a square of grass around which I pedal a small tricycle, concentrating furiously to complete the square, pushing down hard on each rising pedal for it is impera-

---

3. Rupert Croft-Cooke, *The Last Spring*, Putnam, 1964.
4. My father and I were in a car accident in which Rhys Davies was also a passenger in the car. D.H. Lawrence refers to this incident in one of the letters in the *Collected Edition*.

tive that each journey be finished. Perhaps even then I suffered from compulsions.

I am in a garden and faces hang above me over a garden gate. Children older than myself. I know that they want to walk me up the road, but I am frightened that they will take me away and I will never return to my mother.

I am in a room and my baby sister is lying in a pram. I stand on tip-toes to place near to her head a sea-shell, so that she too may listen to the sound of the sea. My mother comes into the room and is angry. I am guilty. Guilt, guilt, mea culpa, the predominant emotion of my childhood.

My father and I are in a park. On the ground and covering the path in front of me are brown, fallen leaves. Stiffly, I stand still. I cannot pass over them. *"Come on"* urges my father *"they're only dead!"* I cry out in terror.

I am in a house empty of furniture. I walk up the stairs, to spy through an open door a floor fascinating in its gleaming darkness. My mother calls to me, but I run onto the floor to fall and be stained by its blackness. Of course, it is no accident that I remember this fall onto the darkened floor at 9 Wilton Road—the domicile of my childhood—for its black stain which then covered my hands, limbs and dress, subsequently, under the tutelage of the nuns, penetrated into my soul which throughout my childhood I see as a black sole-shaped image occupying my body.

However, these are my earliest memories and I have held on to them for more than half of a century, although I must have forgotten events of much greater moment. Perhaps these recordings have persisted because they form the very basis of my memory and so take up what space they please. It is the memories, which follow, that have been forced to fit in where they can and have become increasingly compacted over the years.

The house at 9 Wilton Road is detached and the first house to be built in that road. It was built and occupied by a Master Builder, W. Piddington Esq., who had also badly designed it. He lived there, until his death, with two spinster daughters who waited upon his every want, but as soon as they were free, happily they sold up and fled. In later years the Builder had become blind and so when we moved into the house the garden was a jungle. Of course, at times the blind Builder had forgotten that the neatly laid out lawn, the carefully cultivated shrubs and the straight rows of border plants were overcome and lost beneath bramble, bracken, waist-high grass, tangled weeds and self-seeded trees, for in his mind's eye he saw still his neat suburban paradise. Then, he would step out into its rank disorder, stumbling and cursing and hitting out with his white stick at the vegetation which he could feel, but not see. His two daughters shrieking at him from the doorway *"Be careful! Be careful!"*

My father soon tamed the savage growth and planted rows of cabbages, potatoes, tomatoes, beans, peas, fruit bushes and trees, and other edibles, for having come from peasant stock he saw this as the appropriate use for a piece of ground. However, my mother led him to compromise by introducing borders of flowers and allowing my sister and me a very small piece of grass on which to play, although it was never adequate and I longed for a lawn large enough for me to practice the long-jump, at which I rather fancied my chances. But, for the most part, admonitions not to step on beans, potatoes, tomatoes and so on continually interrupt my childhood.

Now, many years later, the wilderness has reclaimed that garden and once again the blind man stumbles through its maze thrashing about him with his white stick, but his daughters no longer call to him, while the shade of my father grits his teeth at such waste of land.

When she first moves into Wilton Road, Muswell Hill, London, N10 my mother is happy for she has arrived at an important milestone on her way up the heap. An indicator which shows her and my father as the proud possessors of a mortgage for a three-bedroomed house, all mod cons, in a delectable suburb. Certainly a progression from whence she had come—the East End with its crowded tenements and its concreted-over fields and verdure.

My mother's life had begun long, long ago, before she was born, when the persecuted Jews fled from Russia and Poland in response to edicts, pogroms and expulsions which made them set sail in whatever craft was available. Sometimes a scene in my mind's eye shows me people waiting patiently on a dock, watching the black, uninviting water and tossing ships. The men dressed in broad-brimmed black hats and the women in shawls which cover their bewigged heads. Their faces are pale and they clutch at each other for support. The children, their eyes big and round, hang on to their mother's skirts.

But perhaps, because human beings are so resilient, the picture should be one of bustling activity, shouting and arguing, persons with waving arms running back and forth yelling instructions and admonitions at one another and at playing children who chase each other and ignore their parents' commands. However, whatever it was like, my mother was born out of this turmoil to be a first generation Englishwoman.

It must be remembered that early immigrants from Eastern Europe, heirs to the Anarcho-Communist tradition, fought for an improving quality of life; fought against the sweater, the slum landlord and against discrimination, throwing off also the restrictions of a culture brought from a foreign land. And for my mother, this culminated in a detached three-bedroomed house in Muswell Hill which, on her part, was a compromise for in the absence of the overthrow of existing society and the building of the new, she must accept a substitute and settle for what was, 'bettering herself' in the only recognised manner.

But this did not prevent her in later years, when she no longer worked in the bookshop which was hers, but which had become my father's, from lamenting her isolation in this dull, conventional suburb. By then she was marooned, largely by poverty, at the edge of which we coped for the next few years because by the end of 1929, in common with business generally, the book trade slumped. Later, his business might have recovered, but in my father's unbusiness-like hands this became more and more unlikely.

When my mother was overcome by the pain of living she screamed against the four walls between which she was trapped and her voice bounded off each wall and hit us, her children, buffeting us into corners, driving us from room to room. My father is never there to be caught in her desperate anger for he is a man who comes home for an evening meal only and to sleep.

Sometimes my mother, as if in memory of the former occupant, the Builder, blindfolds herself with a dark band as the only way to escape; protesting all the while that she is only resting her eyes. I sit on the edge of a chair, watching and listening to her, the tears running down my face, for I am convinced that this temporary blindness is permanent and that her maiming is mine also. I weep and wail and my mother becomes angry and declares that she wants to die. At this I shake with fright and terrified that I will lose her, I invent a headache or stomach-ache so that I do not go to school. Then, all day long I watch over her waiting for her mood to lighten and for us to be once again happy.

But those are the bad times and when we first move into Wilton Road its sunless rooms are filled by a rosy glow and the house itself is enclosed in a rainbow. But it is only a month later, in October 1929, that the recession whirls like a tornado around the globe, whipping up and obliterating numerous small and large businesses and investors. There had been a harbinger in the previous year when in May 1928 panic selling had hit Wall Street, but this had been regarded as a hiccup. Other harbingers during that year bore no direct reference to the coming slump, but they joined the heap of history and bided their time, for events have a habit of forming themselves into a pattern, into a gestalt.

In China, where confusion had so marked the year of my birth, the Kuomintang has murdered at least 140,000 dissidents during a terror which laid waste the countryside. In the USSR in January 1928 Stalin exiled all key opposition figures, Leon Trotsky exiled to Alma-Ata on the Russian Chinese frontier.

On 27th August Britain signs a Treaty renouncing war to which representatives of fifteen countries meeting in the French Foreign Ministry append their signatures. Amidst cheers, the first to sign, is Gustav Stresemann, the German foreign Minister.

Almost a year later, on 9th June, two days after my sister's birth in 1929, it is decided, under a plan named for an American Banker, Owen Young, that the German reparations debt for the First World War, paid to the allies and chiefly to America, will not be cleared until 1988. The Stalhelm (soldiers' private army) hold demonstrations to pressurise the Reichstag against this plan.

Perhaps, even then, the figure of my father hovered at Potters Bar, some time in the years 1936-38, holding the hands of two small girls. We are standing at the edge of a large crowd of German veterans from World War I, veterans now living in the UK. From somewhere above us comes the voice of the speaker at this Remembrance Ceremony, the Nazi Herr von Ribbentrop, German Ambassador to England. *"Für die, die für's Vaterland gefallen sind"* he thunders (for those who have fallen for the Fatherland) *"und für die, die Sie ermordet haben!"* shouts back my brave father (and for those you have murdered!) Hiding in the shadows are the death and destruction of the Second World War, the Holocaust and the threat of nuclear annihilation.

Of course, the recession of 1929, announced by panic and riot on Wall Street, police dispersing hysterical investors, should not have taken my mother by surprise, for had she not made an assiduous study of Marxist economics? Was she not fully conversant with its theory of capitalism's cycles, culminating every few years in commercial crisis? Or did she, as an ex-pupil of a Board school, where learning by rote was the order of the day, see Marxism as merely another lesson which remained firmly between the covers of a text-book? Or did she hope, as we all do, that disaster is something that happens to other people?

My mother found her changed circumstances especially galling, because when she had first moved into Wilton Road, she had boasted to her family of the bookshop's success. My grandmother, my mother's available siblings and various other members of the extended family, had been invited to view and praise this suburban house. *"Look at me!"* my mother's deportment said *"I am not the* shlemiel *you thought! In spite of what you call my mad socialist ideas and a gentile husband! I've got a pretty little house and two well-kept children, even if they are only girls."*

There is no record of what my grandmother Rachel said, but she arrived at this non-kosher household carrying her own food and her own pots and pans, the latter tied together on a string and slung about her neck. As for my Aunt Becky, she was peeved, yet proud, of these symbols of her sister's success, but she murmured to her husband and to other family members *"We know they're both* meshigeneh, *so let's hope they can pay for all this!."*

And yet, and yet, and yet. Perhaps even then in those tidy rooms with their bookshelves and prints upon the walls, could be spied the ghosts of our future tenants who for some years rented the three upstairs rooms, while my parents, sister and I crowd into the rest of the house.

However, at the time of the first visit to the house, my mother must have regretted that her father had died on 30th January, 1926 and so never saw the house, nor her children, for of all her family he was the person she most wanted to please and impress. It was my grandfather, Samuel Argeband, whom I never knew, who inculcated in my mother a love of learning. Whereas my grandmother was not literate, my grandfather had been educated in his native Poland, both at school and, as a male, at the Shul. Therefore, he was able to translate this knowledge into learning to speak, read and write good English, and so help his children with their school work. Esther, as the youngest, coming in for much of his attention.

In those days, Esther flew on winged feet along the streets of the seaside town, the smell of ozone in her dainty nostrils. At about the same time and at another place, my father-to-be, Carl, sniffs also at the sea as he leans over the side of a ship bringing him to England. No passport, no papers—for as he was in the future to say often, *"two world wars for freedom and freedom lost!"* But, my mother-to-be skims over the pavements oblivious of Carl's ship tossing on the water, passing sailors sipping their pints outside street corner pubs and doing her best to avoid knocking into women carrying shopping baskets, some of whom pause for a moment to wonder why a small ginger-haired girl is running like the clappers.

"Dad" she shouts, running through the open front door of the Portsmouth house. The father, a thickset man of medium height whose drooping moustache gives his face a melancholy aspect, rises from his chair with an effort. *"What now!"* he mutters, but puts on his father face for his pretty, bright, youngest child as Esther opens the living-room door. The Father has been sitting all morning in a large, shabby armchair, drawing life into his lungs, while his wife works at their market stall, for he is struggling with asthma, bronchitis and emphysema. Since moving away from London smogs and giving up barbering (on my mother's birth certificate his occupation is given as 'Master Hairdresser') his health has improved, but he continues to suffer occasional attacks. Now he stoops forward to catch his breath. *"Stop, Esther"* he wheezes, *"don't be so noisy."* She stands still, her eyes wide. *"Dad,"* she says earnestly, *"my teacher says we're to find out the countries of the British Empire. All of them. She's going to ask us this afternoon, can we look in the book?"* 'The Book' is an old encyclopaedia picked up from a junk stall. The Father smiles proudly at this daughter who thirsts so for knowledge, and takes down a thick tome from a shelf built into a recess. Then, gladly he sits down again, Esther beside him on the arm of the chair. They turn the pages, Aa, Ab and so on to the Ba, Be... at last Br, British, British Empire. The Father shows Esther a map of the world—green, yellow, mauve, orange, but mostly pink. *"all the pink countries are the British Empire"* he tells Esther and they both marvel. Esther seeing them all covered in pink grass, pink skies, pink trees, pink houses; India (the Jewel in the Crown), British West Africa, British Central Africa, British South Africa, Ceylon, British West Indies, British East Indies, British Guiana, Gibraltar, Malta, Falkland Islands, Brit-

ish New Guinea, Singapore, Hong Kong, Sudan, Canada, Australia, New Zealand, Ireland.

Truly, this is magnificent, for here they are, a formerly subject people, dispossessed, driven out of lands where they had been ghettoized, restricted, enacted against and murdered. And now, not only are they free, but they are the heirs to an Empire on which the sun never sets! Esther finds paper and pencil and quickly copies out from the encyclopaedia her new-found knowledge, certain of returning to school triumphant.

This is the same man who is to say to my mother three or four years before my birth *"you'll never have children, it takes guts to bring up a family."* That is why I owe my being directly, as well as indirectly, to my grandfather, for my mother, anxious to prove herself to him, decides to become pregnant. This was with 'Poppy' who was to be stillborn on, or about, 11ᵗʰ November, some two years before my birth. 11ᵗʰ November, Armistice Day, on the eve of which in 1938 my grandmother Rachel is to die. 'Poppy', a pale child with dark hair and bright blue eyes. My mother's stories bring Poppy back to life and for years my sister and I play that we have an older sister and include her in our games. Now, my mother, desperate to produce a live child, embarks upon a further pregnancy, but by the time I am born my grandfather, Samuel Argeband, is dead at the age of fifty-six years, in the East End of London; his occupation once more barbering, his heart worn out by the constant struggle to breathe and the complications which followed.

My mother once told me that she wanted neither of her children to grieve for her in the desperate way she mourned her father. But this was not within her gift.

The Father is lying in the high double bed, its brass bedstead dull in the half-light, for the curtains are drawn although it is day. He is propped up high on pillows and his chest rises and falls with his effort to breathe, each rasping breath cutting through the silence of the room. His daughter Becky, a plump young woman whose skin hangs on her heavily, is there to watch over him while her mother is at the market. Restlessly she is thinking about all she has to do at home and awaits impatiently her mother's return. *"Florrie's frock is only half-sewn, the sleeves to be put in. I'll do it this evening. Blue should be a good colour for her not too light to get dirty quick Woolfie's gone through his socks again get some at the market when the Mother comes home soon I hope or Esther looks in about time*

she looked in." She gets up and twitches the curtain back to look
out into the street for a moment, then shrugs and sits down again,
glancing across at the Father as she does so.

*Always sick Mother's had a hard life we've all had to take on his
burdens nice to be ill could I be ill with Gussy and the children at
my back all day and night? Now I'm expecting again the powder
didn't do any good just as well Gussy would have been suspicious
all right for the men they don't have to bear 'em or care for 'em
I was really sick this morning really heaved could I sit down let
alone lie in bed? No, it's Mum this, Mum that, Becky, Becky,
Becky, what did Sam say Becky at beck and call well he was right
he was a nice boy married that Bloomfield girl not good looking
and running to fat what'll I give Gussy for dinner tonight the
children can have bread and jam they had fish at dinner they ate
well that Esther's a smart one all right no babies lives like a lady.*

The Father coughs and she looks towards him.

*He gave her one hundred pounds to start that shop a hundred
pounds all that money they'll never get it back what's she ever
done for him and it's me who's given them grandchildren hers was
born dead and who knows the reason for that and they'll never
be brought up Jewish not proper grandchildren they've only got
me but they can't see it Esther's too busy acting the grand lady in
that dusty bookshop with her goy friends and Charlie lit-er-ary
they call it I call it littery (she smiles to herself) Wolfe was educated calls himself Wilfred disappeared somewhere in America
no one knows where Mark's a shlemiel now his boxing's over
never fight again he needs a woman behind him one who's got her
head screwed on right too fond of shiksas never do him any good
took his money Esther was spoilt since she was little I won't make
more of one than the other 'tho Gussy makes a fuss of Florrie I
hope that's not an unlucky name terrible for poor Flora dying like
that by fire and the children they take me for granted.*

The Father coughs again and Becky gets up from the chair and
goes to him. *"How are you Dad?"* He closes his eyes without answering. *"Don't tell me then!"* Resentment bubbles up inside her
and explodes in bitter words. *"You want to pull yourself together!"*
His eyes remain closed and he gives no indication that he has
heard her. Maddened by what she sees as his indifference she
finds words shouted at the Father by the Mother over the years

when little money was coming into the house and there were hungry mouths to feed and bills to pay. *"You're lazy!"* she taunts the dying man, leaning over him, this man who has controlled her during her growing years and is now within her power. *"You're lazy—even Esther says you're lazy!"*

Esther, who in the light of her Father's illness has decided not to go to the shop, catches these last words as she opens the bedroom door and for a moment it is as if she has been hit by a physical force which knocks all the breath from out of her body. She stands in the doorway unable to move. Becky, at her sister's entrance, has turned away in confusion, but decides to brazen it out. *"Oh, you've come then at last!"* she hectors. *"Not before time!"* Esther ignores her and goes to the Father, taking one of his unresisting hands into her own. He turns his head, opening his eyes to look at her and within them she senses reproach. *"It's not true Dad"* she half whispers *"I never said that. She's lying,"* her voice breaks and the Father looks away without giving any sign that he believes in her.

This scene haunts my mother to the end of her life for she had forgiven him long ago for hurts for which she had never blamed him.

Proud of her cleverness, he had promised that when the time came for her to leave the small Church School which provided an elementary education, he would pay to send her to a High School. Esther walks happily home from school, her head in the air. Carefully folded in her coat pocket lies the certificate from school stating that she has completed successfully all standards and can leave school at the age of thirteen. *"My Dad's going to send me to High School!"* she has boasted for weeks to her schoolmates and even to her teacher, Miss Turner *"where I'll wear a uniform and learn French and Latin and Grammar."* This information had brought varied responses from the sneering to the envious to the well-wishers. Miss Turner had suggested *"Perhaps one day you'll be a teacher"* and Esther, for a moment, had seen herself as the font of all wisdom. Therefore, when she arrives home and hands her leaving certificate to her Father with almost a flourish, she expects him to confide in her his plans for her future. Instead, without comment he takes the piece of paper and puts it high on the shelf in the recess, next to the encyclopaedia. Then he turns away from her to sit in the armchair and bury his head in a newspaper. She hovers for a moment, wanting to ask him

"When am I going to the High School?", but caution, or perhaps fear of his reply, makes her hold her tongue and for the rest of the day she holds onto her dream, making excuses to herself for her father's silence. Later that evening her Mother calls Esther to the kitchen. *"The Father says you've left school. Milly will call for you Monday at half-past seven."* Milly is the sixteen-year-old daughter of a neighbour. Esther is confused. *"With Millie to school?" "School, schmool!"* scoffs her mother, *"you're too old for school. Manny Abelman says you can start at the factory for making cigarettes. It's time you brought some money in instead of head-in-a-book!"*

And so my mother becomes a cigarette-maker for some years, having first been instructed by her mother always to wear demure clothing and never to look the boss, the foreman or any other male in the factory, directly in the face, for tales of seduction, or even rape, are rife, culminating in illegitimate births and utter disgrace for the girl. With regard to education, what little money the family had was spent on Wolfe, Esther's eldest brother.

My father at this time is living with the woman who is to become known as 'the first Mrs. Lahr' and who figures as a harridan in one or two short stories by my father's writer friends, much to my mother's chagrin as she feels that she herself will be mistaken for this character. I know little about this woman except that she ran a lodging house into which my father introduced his anarchist and socialist friends, most of whom were unemployed and down-and-out. Every morning my father awakens them by singing the first two lines of *The Internationale*:

Arise ye starvelings from your slumbers
Arise ye criminals of want.

a practice he is to continue with us throughout our childhood and always badly out of tune, for he is tone deaf.

For my mother, at the age of thirteen, the routine of the factory dulls her spirit, but does not kill it for when her friend Sadie, a tall, buxom, dark-haired girl, in every way a contrast to Esther, says to her *"Let's go to Manchester and try for an audition with Hayley's Juveniles"* Esther is enthusiastic, for all her life she is to love music and move like a dancer. Maybe they'll tell her that she is too short, that her bottom is too near the ground—the words of a Foreman at the factory—but it is well worth a try. Her blue eyes blaze with determination.

In the early hours of the morning, Esther, clutching a paper bag creeps quietly out of the bed which she shares with Becky, and makes her entrance onto the stairs. Becky, whom she had thought to be asleep, unknown to Esther, sits up on her sister's exit and gets out of bed to wait off-stage behind the door while the drama, or farce, is played out. Esther places her feet carefully on each step as if they are leading her into a dance, a simple routine to end in the hallway in a complicated manoeuvre, legs flung into the air, a twist and a twirl, arms flying, head nodding. At last she is in reach of her goal, the front door and freedom, soon to open on a new life which will lead to fame and fortune. Nearly there! As she puts out her hand to unfasten the lock she hears a sharp step behind her and before she can turn a rough hand grabs her shoulder: "*Where do you think you're going!*" She has never heard her father so angry. "*A bad girl you are, want to bring shame on the family, want to be a painted harlot, never come in this house again!*" He gives Esther no opportunity to answer, but propels her into the living-room. "*Sit!*" he commands "*and wait until it's time to go to the factory. I take you there myself.*"

Later, Esther is to hear that the same scene has been enacted in Sadie's house, for Sadie's older sister has discovered the plan, revealed it to her friend Becky, and both of them have informed their parents. Much later, when Gracie Fields becomes famous and it is known that she began her career with Hayley's Juveniles, my mother feels doubly deprived, never watching or listening to Gracie without seeing herself somewhere in the background.

In those days, Becky always seems to be the cause of my mother's downfall. A few years later, my mother remaining intent upon changing her life-style, and interested in the suffragette movement, makes a stand for women's freedom by having her hair bobbed. Her hair is only shoulder length for curly hair never grows too long, but Esther is expected to put it up as best she can and, according to conventional fashion, secure it tightly in hairpins. What nuisance in this procedure every morning and her head always feels as if her hair is being pulled out by the roots. At last the offending hair lies on the floor around the barber's chair, brightening the dull lino, but she feels no regrets, only a sense of liberty as she tosses her head without feeling the pulling of pins against her scalp. She walks, hat in hand, down the Charing Cross Road, turns into Leicester Square, along Coventry Street, to find herself in Piccadilly Circus. The centre of the British Empire! This is surely an appropriate place to strike a blow for women's freedom! She takes a cigarette and a box of matches from the pocket of her long black coat, and lights up. What bliss! She, a woman, daring to smoke in public! One or two passers-by glance at her curiously, and a foxy looking man in a shabby coat and brown hat tries to pick her up, coming alongside to say *"Hello, girlie. I'll see you home."* But she doesn't answer and quickens her pace, so shrugging he goes on his way. Soon Esther decides it is time to go home to the East End and familiar streets, but as the tram nears her stop her courage fails and she jams her hat firmly onto her head before alighting. On arriving home Esther finds her mother in the kitchen while her father sits in his usual armchair and Becky is at the living-room table fitting together pieces of a dress ready for sewing. Becky glances up as Esther, still wearing her hat, passes by and then suddenly, with one movement, Becky pulls the hat from off her sister's head. *"Look! Look!"* she shrieks *"she's had her hair bobbed!"*

And yet it was this same Becky, who, together with the Mother, tended Esther day and night when she was near death with the influenza which swept through Europe and the British Isles at the close of the First World War. This epidemic doubling the war casualties.

No, it was no problem for my mother to forgive her father for unimagined wrongs; it was herself she could not forgive. For she saw herself as a collaborator in her father's early death. This, because when Rachel, after the death of her eldest daughter Flora and two of the grandchildren in the fire, asked Esther and her siblings *"Do you want to go back to London?"* None of them understood that this would be a life and death decision for their father, for there he would not only once more breathe in City smog, he would return to line his lungs with hair from barbering. *"London!"* Esther and her siblings shouted *"Let's go to London!"*

But it was London which gave me life, for my parents met in the Charlotte Street Socialist Club after the First World War, when my father had been released from internment at Alexandra Palace. It should be put on record that my parents were introduced by young Rocker, the son of Rudolf Rocker, appearing in books by William Fishman and spoken about by him on the radio.

New Coteries

My birth coincides with my parents' literary magazine: We move to Fairbridge Road: My Tante fails to take care of me.

As my mother labours to bring forth one insignificant human being, her struggles are mirrored daily by thousands of craftsmen and labourers who, with much dirt, debris, bang and clatter, are acting as midwives to the rebirth of the City, which is to deliver in ten years more than 250,000 new buildings. It is a recreation of the environment referred to in the press as 'an unprecedented building boom' for the new is replacing the old with 'bigger and more modern structures' while remodelled roads are concretising into ever widening channels. But each building as it rises, or falls, casts a shadow of what has gone before and what is yet to come, so that even more 'modern' buildings can be seen waiting impatiently in the wings. Around them the shadow of motorways, the hedgerows and fields of former centuries reflected in the macadam to join with the flora and fauna of the bomb sites when the frenetic dance of urban demolition is given a starring role. Above it all hangs a nuclear mushroom.

Compared to all this the result of my mother's efforts is puny, but I am the first child ever to be born, so my parents convey me home to their flat in Rosebery Avenue, Finsbury, opposite to which with much dust and noise the 16th Century Thomas Sadler's Musick House is exiting to allow Sadler's Wells Theatre to make its appearance—a debut which inspires my mother, as she nurses me in her arms, to dream for me the future denied her: a future as a dancer, a great ballet dancer, a great singer, a great musician, a great actress, a great writer. But, as she muses, the wreckers move in and the disintegrating flat moves off stage.

Thereafter, we take all that we own and make our way to a house in Fairbridge Road, Holloway, for our exodus from the inner city is to be gradual. It should be noted here that while my mother is taking possession of the downstairs flat of the house, assisting my father to lay lino (which he does in a hurry and without proper measurement) arranging furniture in rooms for which it was not bought, wiping down woodwork, hanging curtains and generally making order out of chaos, Vienna is rocked by revolutionary demonstrations and Germany, in which the salutation 'Heil Hitler' is now common, demands the annexation of Austria. In America, Sacco shouts 'Long Live Anarchy' as he and Vanzetti go to the electric chair.

But these events pass my mother by at a distance, for her greatest concern, apart from myself, is the demise of *The New Coterie–A Quarterly Magazine of Art and Literature* published at three-monthly intervals between November 1925 and Summer/Autumn 1927, under her adopted maiden name of Archer. This magazine is a revival of an enormously influential, but short-lived, magazine published by Frank Henderson at his left-wing bookshop and which my parents hope will bring them recognition, for they are to publish such writers as D.H. Lawrence, H.E. Bates, Rhys Davies, Liam O'Flaherty, Aldous Huxley, T.F. Powys, Louis Golding, Geoffrey West, Faith Compton Mackenzie, Michael Joseph, Jean Devanny and more. Therefore, my advent has corresponded with the dashing of their hopes for fame, if not fortune. It is as if my procreation and birth have drained from them all creative energy leaving them squeezed and dry.

At Wilton Road I grow up with the characters of *The New Coterie*, piled in their dwellings around me, as if they are part of our extended family. Now, I have one set only, given to me by my mother as if she were handing on to me my inheritance. And, as I grow older, travelling backwards to meet my parents on the mound, these characters, caught up in their time capsules, remain as they ever were, cocking a snook at their disintegrated progenitors.

The mother-fixated man from No. 6 again and again walks the country lane on his way home after years abroad. His thoughts filled by love for his mother and hate for the girl by whom he was jilted many years before. His anger conjures up the girl and she stands before him invitingly on the path. In a sexual frenzy he carries the now willing woman into the woods where they couple. Of course, the woman is not the 'lost love', but is the man's widowed mother out for what Erica Jong in *Fear of Flying* called "*a zipless fuck*", and the woman knows that we know and lives out her shame until the paper crumbles, but her son, this 20th Century Oedipus again and again leaves home and returns abroad unaware that he has once more violated his mother.[1]

In No. 4 the blonde Mrs. Salgast lies in childbed, dismayed because she has given birth to a Maori baby while her husband is white and supposedly of English heritage. Down the road in this New Zealand mining town her racist husband rages at the local Maori who laughs loud and long before revealing that the outraged husband is half Maori, but adopted by English parents.[2]

The jaded housewife from No. 4 is on holiday in Spain where she flirts with the elements to indulge in a sensual affair with the sun. "*I am another being*" she says to herself as she looks at her red-gold breasts and thighs.[3]

In Deauville, the middle-aged, middle-class spinster from No. 5 sits at the side of a dance floor. She is waiting vainly to be asked to dance. The author, in an estimation of this plain creature, has named her 'Miss Drone': Barren, sex-starved, surplus. Intolerant of her own creation, the author does not see Miss Drone's brave smile as the couples swing past and the music blares out its cheerful tunes. She is blind to Miss Drone's tremulous smile of pretence that she has chosen to be a wallflower. Instead, the author smirks in malicious glee as the plot develops and a young man, a little the worse for drink, asks Miss Drone to see him to his hotel room. In some trepidation she agrees and accepts his invitation to stay the night. Now the author laughs out loud. She has got Miss Drone where she wants her, for the 'young man' is discovered to be a young woman in male clothing. The author, finished with her story, mails it to *The New Coterie*, and remains unaware that Miss Drone has escaped her and set up home with

1. Hexilda Beaufort, *The Path*.
2. Jean Devanny, *Mrs. Salgast's Baby*. Jean Devanny was an Australian and Virago republished her book *Cindy* (first published in 1949) in 1986. Her writings and this book were frowned upon by the Communist Party, of which she was a member, because she deviated from the party line by exposing the racism of the Labour movement.
3. D.H. Lawrence, *Sun*.

her new-found friend, the two of them living happily together as a couple.[4]

At another time and place, two young men from No. 1, Republicans, crouch on a roof somewhere in Ireland, pistols in hand, waiting for death meted out already to their companions by British soldiers. The younger man, an IRA Lieutenant, white-faced, closes his eyes, hoping to shut out the scene and imagine himself some place else. His companion, the Quarter-Master, despises his companion and swears that he will shoot him at the first sign of surrender. At long last a shot rings out and the Quarter-Master falls forward as the British climb over the roof. With a sigh of relief, the Lieutenant pulls himself to his feet, hands over head in surrender. *"Let's give it to the bastard"* says one of the soldiers and they fire point-blank into his head.[5]

Unaware of the Civil War being played out around him, the senile old man in No. 4 opens the canary's cage and urges it to fly away for no more can he bear to hear it sing.[6]

Muriel from No. 6 sits in a cafe opposite a woman friend who talks continually about nothing, her empty voice falling into the space between them. Muriel, only half listening, concentrates her thoughts upon the lampshades: *"Great yellow lampshades, floating... spreading a warm glow... hazy and warm."*[7]

In No. 3 a man lies dying, his thoughts wandering:

> *He imagines a murderer coming out of his cell to take those few steps to the hangman's shed... He thinks of the homeless searching about for shelter, warmth, food... His mind wanders farther afield and he pictures his wife about to give birth... he imagines a man in the throes of torture... boiling oil... the rack... castration... he thinks of a harem with beautiful scented maidens...*[8]

The Editor, whom I suspect was Paul Selver—the translator of the first published *The Good Soldier Schweik* by Jaroslav Hasek—decrees that all these characters must live out their lives, if not conventionally, in conventional forms, within the confines of classical literature. For this deity, fastidious in his selection of material for the magazine, eschews the writers experimental in

4. Helen Todd, *Waiting*.
5. Liam O'Flaherty, *Civil War*.
6. Gerald Bullitt, *The Grasshopper*.
7. Caryl Brahms, *Lampshades*.
8. Andrew Block, *The Man in Bed*.

form, disapproving of Jean Cocteau and dubbing the Imagists
'Our impetuous young friends'. On hearing that James Joyce has
been translated into French, he asks *"But who is going to translate
him into English?"*

And yet, in spite of all the editor's efforts, newspapers which
published reviews of the magazine, complain:

> *The latest exponent of that somewhat curious class of wielders of
> the pen and pencil which the modern age has produced, who, we
> believe, are known (or call themselves) Impressionists, Realists,
> Decadents, or what not; very young men who view life through
> distorted, cracked and muddy spectacles and confusedly imagine
> that 'Literature' should be spelled 'Muckraking'!*

The Editor, taken up by these polemics, his head bent over pen
and paper, does not hear the doctor's experiments with sound in
No. 2.,[9] nor does he see the black and white illustrations or hear
the singing poetry. Sidney Hunt's machine-like *Beauty Chorus*
pass him by as they dance off stage, hidden behind them Liam
O'Flaherty's fratricide from No. 3. Bent over his desk he misses
Coralie Hobson's partying group as they pass by Jean de Boss-
chere's frontispiece to No. 2, laughing uneasily at the two men
(or is one of them a woman?), hanging from gibbets and engaging
each other in sword play. Nor does he hear the priest reading
prayers, while an angel weeps.

This Editor is blind also to Richard Wyndham's lines of washing in No. 2, counterpanes, curtains, sheets and a single dark
dress, blow and billow in the wind, hanging at various levels so as
to almost obscure houses and the potted plants on window-sills.
That black dress must surely belong to Miss Morgan from No. 2
who will wear it at her authoritarian father's funeral. There she
stands, before the open grave, counting out the inherited wealth
which will buy her a husband.[10]

Willy nilly these characters, among others, live out their lives
in the pages of *The New Coterie* (Cover designed by William Roberts).

At Wilton Road, piled up bundles of unsold *New Coteries*, in
the press room, or stacked on bookshelves, form a constant re-
minder to my parents of their lost hopes and a rebuke to me
for my supersedence. Sometimes, I take a copy from a shelf and,

9. T.F. Powys, *A Stubborn Tree*.
10. Rhys Davies, *A Gift of Death*.

having prevailed upon my father to cut the pages to set the characters free, I enter into their lives which become inextricably intertwined with mine. But it is only recently that I have perused each issue intently from cover to cover, reading carefully each Editorial, story, poem, both original and in translation. I have looked at, and fantasised over, the art-work. This is an endeavour to find the key to my parents' and my own lives.

My father bought William Morris' old press, and so the Blue Moon Press had also been launched by my parents—given its name because the intention was to publish occasionally and selectively fine, limited editions. This took up a room in our house and was manipulated by a printer named Herbert Jones. Outside the Progressive Bookshop, 68/69 Red Lion Street, Holborn, a crescent moon painted blue hung upon a chain from a wall bracket. With what pride my father climbs up the ladder, precariously perched against the wall, to hang this symbol, while my mother watches from the street, instructing him to move the angle-iron this way, or that. Henceforth they would be recognised not only as booksellers, but as publishers.

All this at the beginning of a recession which bounded across the Atlantic, to bounce the Rt. Hon. Ramsay MacDonald M.P., tossing his fine mane of white hair, into mixed metaphors by naming an 'economic lifeboat crew' of Government Ministers to save the country as it 'lurches over the precipice'. He rejects the solution of pump priming the economy offered by Maynard Keynes.

On Wall Street the police disperse hysterical crowds howling against the plummeting of their stocks. In Berlin, the Nazis are out on the street, standing on street corners like an invading and avenging army, intent upon beating up Jews and 'reds'. My mother is fearful. Pogroms threaten, Slump and depression. The world is out of kilter. In Palestine, British troops intervene with firepower between fighting Jews and Arabs. In Russia, Stalin declares all farms as Collectives: *"So began the strange Carnival over which despair presided and over which fury filled the fleshpots."*[11]

The bookshop and the Blue Moon press limp on, but the press produces less and less as the years progress, until only the occasional leaflet, or card of poetry, is published 'once in a blue moon'. It is fitting that the blue metal moon, which hung so proudly in

---

11. Isaac Deutscher , *The Prophet Outcast* (1963).

front of the shop—until the day a bomb destroys the bookshop during the Blitz of the Second World War—was decrescent, on the wane: for in this case the moon did not lie.

Most of the first two years of my life are to be spent in Fairbridge Road, to which we had moved from Rosebery Avenue. This road, lying between Hornsey and Holloway Roads, Islington, had been formed in 1878 by a short street of isolated cottages near to Hornsey Road; the type of area seen as ripe for development. By 1882 builders, encouraged by the expansion of the railway network, had quickly erected pristine, red-brick Victorian terrace houses, complete with bay windows or sash windows, which they then decorated with mock Corinthian columns, incorporating, as they built, the former Esher Road. Once the road was laid and all signs of flourishing nature subdued, in moved the Pooters, the Cummings and the Gowings[12] together with their wives, children and maidservants, to live hedged in by heavy furnishings, multiple ornaments of china shepherdesses, rose baskets, and golden-framed reproductions of 'The Stag at Bay' or 'Virtue Rewarded'.

As it happens, at No. 155 for four years from 1904 lived Samuel Lazarby of the Amalgamated Society of Railway Servants. For this was truly 'the age of the train'. How self-importantly he leaves the house each morning dressed in clean white shirt, stiff collar, dark suit, fob watch, high hat and carrying an attache case and rolled black umbrella, his wife and maidservant watching his progress from the front doorway. The self-absorbed Samuel Lazarby, walking tall, fails to look about him. If he had done so, he might have spied the slightly less affluent houses of the 1920s and 1930s, let out as flats. Many of these have open doorways through which children spill onto the street, to shout and laugh as they skip, stringing a rope across the road, or chasing each other back and forth across the road in a game of 'it', or dodging behind garden walls and dustbins in a game of hide-and-seek, or in so many other games known only to children. Does he feel their unseen eyes as he crosses the hop-scotch grids to be chalked on the pavements, or is he instead frightened by the deathly silence descending in the 1940s when the children have been sent out of London to escape the bombing? An unnatural silence bro-

---

12. George and Weedon Grossmith, *The Diary of a Nobody*. First published in 1892 and thereafter by Penguin books.

ken by sirens, bombs whining down and exploding, the fire of anti-aircraft guns. And, at the same time, does he uneasily feel the presence of parked cars which are to eventually de-grade his members?

Nowadays, Fairbridge Road is much as when first built, apart from its environment of motor traffic and stationary vehicles. The net-curtained houses, most of them owner-occupied in recent times, present a quiet front to the world. Only the Hornsey Road end, the original Fairbridge Road, has been obliterated by a wood yard which spills its planks onto the pavement, next to which is a transport firm from which trucks send out noise, fumes and danger to pedestrians: both activities presenting a general air of dirt and disorder. At this end has also been built large blocks of low rise council flats. It is as if the former Esher Road is intent upon obliterating all evidence of its usurpation. Because of these industrial activities and the proximity of the busy Hornsey Road, with its small ethnic shops and cosmopolitan population, it is unlikely that Fairbridge Road will regain its original gentrification, for the professional classes prefer to be cocooned in their classical Georgian Squares away from the hustle and bustle of urban street life.

Perhaps, in 1929, the signs of the inner city throwing out its tentacles to grasp this part of North London, decide my parents to move on to Muswell Hill, but for the short time we live in Fairbridge Road our family becomes extended by my father's sister Tante Maria and Margot, the illegitimate daughter of my mother's friend Dornan. Margot, a child some five years older than me.

"Why don't you bring Maria over to England?" suggests my Aunt Mary (christened Anna Maria) to my father. My Aunt Mary lives and works at a West London hotel and today is her 'day off', so she has visited my father, her brother, at the bookshop. *"She'd be glad to come over to mind the baby while Esther works in the shop."* The expression on my father's face is doubtful, for his sister Maria is barely known to him and when they met briefly, during his visit to the Rhineland in 1927, he found almost nothing to say to her. *"Esther would never agree"* he mutters. *"Esther would prefer to be at the shop"* my Aunt wheedles. *"She'll soon get bored at home, you haven't married a domesticated woman. Maria would take better care of the baby."* My father looks worried, but he doesn't refuse the suggestion outright, and my Aunt comes in for the kill.

"You remember how Maria and the others were worked half to death and half-starved by Fritz, our dear brother! After Mother and Father had died and he took Hof Iben?" This was guaranteed to encourage in my father a feeling of guilt at being so far away when both parents died, one after the other, his mother, Barbara geb. Schlamp in 1909, worn out with bearing fourteen children of whom my father was the eldest, and his father, Philipp in 1911, worn down by sowing and reaping. As my father, his brother Heinrich (called by us 'Henry') and Aunt Mary were in England, only Fritz was adult enough and on the spot to run the farm. My Uncle Fritz, determining to make the farm pay, worked his younger brothers and sisters mercilessly and fed them little. The nearby villages buzzed with the scandal and within a short time a family meeting was called by the Aunts and Uncles, to reach an agreement upon apportioning the children among them. Then, they climbed the steep hill to Hof Iben and descended upon the fields like an avenging army, to wrest this cold and hungry store of cheap labour from the grasp of the sullen, yet frightened, Fritz. *"Fritz was punished, of course"* says my Aunt with satisfaction, as she views Fritz's crushed body beneath the hoofs of the horses. *"But not before he had cheated us out of our share of Hof Iben and left it to that useless wife of his!"*

My father goes home to Fairbridge Road. *"Mary says my sister Maria would be willing to come over here and take care of the baby while you're in the shop"* my father tells my mother, carelessly, as if he is not pushing the matter. My mother's first reaction is to say no, but marooned within the flat with a small baby while my father is experiencing 'true living', has begun to take its toll. She wants to take care of me, her first live child, and yet, and yet, and yet… She has no affection for my Aunt Mary, whom she sees as overbearing and malicious, and suspects that Maria will be a second edition of Mary, and yet, and yet, and yet… My father will not let the matter alone. He cannot manage in the shop. He has to close when he goes round the secondhand bookstalls and the publishers. My mother knows what this means—loss of custom and, therefore, money and loss of passing trade, which also spells money. His sister Maria is a peasant woman, an earth mother, my father tells my mother, she knows about babies, knows more than does my mother. Unlike my mother, Maria wants nothing more out of life than *Kinder und Küche*.

But it is my mother's friend, Dornan, who solves for my mother her dilemma between baby and shop so that she agrees to let my Tante into the house. This comes about because Dornan's fostering arrangements for her child at a private residential nursery have broken down. *"She's not happy there"* says Dornan *"it's all terribly hygienic, but no stimulation. You and Charlie would be good for her and while your sister-in-law's caring for one child, she might as well care for two. We'll fix terms."*

And so my Tante arrives to live with us, an early version of an au pair, trailing in her wake the strawberries which several years later would become her life's work in Odenwald. Strawberries, in German, *'Die Erdbeeren'*—the earth berries: Truly, my Tante is to become an 'earth mother'!

> *A real Truby King baby (is) fed four-hourly from birth, and they do not have any night feeds. A Truby King baby has as much fresh air and sunshine as possible and the right amount of sleep. His education begins from the very first week, good habits being established which remain all his life.*[13]

Truby King, one time superintendent of the Seacliff Lunatic Asylum at Dunedin, New Zealand, was at that time the writer of fashionable baby books. He ordained that baby be 'fed by the clock'. *"Mothers become absurdly distressed by the sound of a mere hour or so of crying. The great value of a trained nurse was that she could override all maternal objections and make sure that the baby was kept on a routine until it despaired of anything better"* said Truby King and he was sure that if only men were able to secrete milk, they would make much better parents than *"sentimental mothers."*

Christine Hardyment writes in *Dream Babies*:

> *The war-time habits of obedience to authority extended into the shaky years of peace that followed. Depression reinforced the need for firm leadership and the build-up to the second world war... left parents as resigned to following bulletins of approved infant-care practice as they were to coping with ration books. In England infant welfare legislation in 1918 set up centres for parents to learn the newest methods of child-care. In America the Sheppard-Towner Act of 1921 played a similar role.*

---

13. Christina Hardyment, *Dream Babies: Child Care From Locke To Spock*, Jonathan Cape 1983.

But even my politicised mother did not understand this manipulation of society and accepted that 'educated' mothers brought up their children according to the latest ideas—for after all, it was 'in the book'. Of course, to my Tante, such a regime for a baby is as much gobbledegook as the noises coming out of the mouths of the persons around her, for she knows no English. As strange to her as the miles of terrace houses lining long hard roads and the thought of being surrounded in London by eight million strangers. Coming from a peasant community where the rhythm of life is geared to work in the fields and the women not given to reading baby books, how could my Tante know that I, together with my contemporaries, am being trained for life in an industrial society, from cradle to grave, for the cold inexorable demands of the machine and the callousness of war. However, she shrugs and says to herself, if this is the English way, she will go along with it.

She is introduced to Margot. *"Whose child is that?"* and listens with scepticism to my mother's explanation. *"Schnell, schnell Margot (with a hard 't') kommt wasch die Hände."* A quick wipe with a flannel. *"Schnell, schnell, schnell, Shul'."* My Tante rushing the pram up the road, me dumped inside it and Margot hanging on to its side.

Or, *"Ba-by hungry"* Margot pointing to her own mouth. *"Baby cry-ing,"* Margot wailing in imitation of my cry. *"Draussen!"* The back door opens and with a sharp thrust Margot is pushed outside. My Tante instinctively in this urban environment carrying out the prescriptive regime of Watson the Behavourist whose baby books were also fashionable and who saw mother love as ruining a child's character:

> Put the child out in the backyard a large part of the time... away from your watchful eye...[14]

I am fed, changed, fed, changed, fed, changed; sometimes the bottle propped up in the pram where I search for it with my mouth. But while the housework and the children pose no problem for my Tante, it is the isolation which she hates.

Sunday is my parents' day for receiving visitors and for the first two Sundays my young Tante dons her best dress and carefully combs out her brown hair from its usual bun. But after one

---

14. *Dream Babies, op. cit.*

or two such Sundays she can see that this company is no good
to her. Mouths opening and shutting in argument, gesticulation,
voices growing louder cutting across one another, "Was ist los?"
asks my Tante in consternation. "Politisch, politisch" explains my
mother, and my Tante sneers. Politicians! The very people who
have sold out the German people and left them to starve! What
care she about the Tory government's Trades Dispute Act, or the
murder of trade unionists and Communists by Chiang Kai-shek,
or the expulsion of Trotsky and Zinoviev from the Soviet Communist Party? Not even street fighting between Nazis and Communists in Berlin interests my Tante for she has never been there:

> Du bist verrückt mein Kind,
> Du musst nach Berlin...[15]

says a popular song. As for my Tante, she has enough to contend
with, coping each day in this foreign City with her equally foreign brother and sister-in-law.

My father introduces her to writers who come to the house—
Rhys Davies, John Arrow, James Hanley, Liam O'Flaherty, Malachi Whitaker, Gay Taylor and the artists William Roberts and
Jacob Kramer. Sarah Roberts comes also for she is the wife of
William and the sister of Jacob. But my Tante reads nothing apart
from romantic magazines which she calls 'books' and Roberts
she regards as a poor painter. His machine-like men don't look
like proper people and even his portrait of my mother makes her
look gaunt and miserable. She likes pictures of pretty country
scenes, landscapes, dream places where it would be pleasant to
stay.

The highlights of my Tante's stay in England are her visits
to my Aunt Mary. Days which to her are a coming home. She
counts up the time between them, hoarding scraps of news from
their sisters' letters, or from my parents' lives. With her sister
Mary, all day she is able to sit in the hotel kitchen eating, drinking coffee and gossiping. Of course, my Aunt Mary relates to my
Tante what she knows of my father's past life and my mother's
antecedents. And what she doesn't know, she assumes.

My mother had been a member of the British Socialist Party,
which following the Russian Revolution, dissolved itself into the
newly formed Communist Party of Great Britain. My father had

15. "You are mad my child, you should go to Berlin!"—a one-time
popular song in Germany.

always considered himself an Anarchist, anarchism originally having been part of the Communist movement. However, both of my parents were distressed at the shooting down of the rebellious sailors at Kronstadt and although they remained at that time within the Communist Party, they became more and more uneasy as Stalinism took hold. This unease bringing in its train cynicism was to lead to my father's expulsion from the Party. It happened like this. He had hung in the bookshop an abstract painting depicting various shapes and colours, which attracted attention from customers who asked: *"What's that supposed to be, Charlie?" "That's the comrades at the barricades—all six of them!"* my father replied.

This was reported to my father's Party branch and he was expelled for 'levity'. My mother resigned from the Party in disgust. Later, a rumour was circulated that my father was a police spy and Henry Sara, who was to later found the Balham Trotskyist Group, told my parents many years later that he had been instructed to stand around in the bookshop and report back to the Party my father's conversations.

Now, my Aunt Mary spoke of my parents as 'reds' and Bloomsburyites, making it all sound a little shabby. My Aunt speaks bitterly also of the man she had met on arrival in England at the age of eighteen. Frederick Eugene Stone, twenty years older than she, had made her pregnant with Edwin (known as 'Ted'). They had married, but he had deserted them shortly after Cecil's birth in 1916, and died of tuberculosis in 1926. *"I'd divorced him by then"* complains my Aunt, *"so there was no pension. No more use to me dead than alive!"*

My Aunt, shortly before I was born, had written a story for a *Daily Express* 1927 St. Valentine's Day competition, under the name of Marion Young, for which she won a prize of £5.00. This, she was sure, had made her my parents' literary equal and she longed for their recognition. She was unaware that my father, proud of any literary success within the family, had saved the newspaper in which the story appeared. Many years later, and shortly before my father's death in 1971, and in spite of the intervening years during which my parents had refused all traffic with my Aunt, my father gave this story to me for safe-keeping. My Aunt writes:

The Spring of 1918 found me living in a third-rate lodging-house in Soho. The entrance to it was in a dismal court, and I rented the attic on the top floor back.

Being a widow with two small boys to support, I could not study my own comfort and although I hated bare boards, the slanting walls, and the view it gave me of half of the chimney-pots in London, I also appreciated its advantages. It enabled me to walk to my work in a West End restaurant and, considering it was harvest-time for greedy landladies, it was cheap.

Reaching home one night, I found a telegram to say my eldest boy, Sonny, was very ill. The tubes were closed and the omnibuses had ceased running, so I walked the eight miles to my baby. The doctor advised me to nurse him myself if I wanted him to get better. But the foster-mother, feeling herself slighted, told me I could take my boy to my own place as soon as I liked.

So, I wrapped him in a blanket and took him to my attic. There I fought for his precious life throughout long days and longer nights. To make things worse, my landlady, the only person I knew in the house refused to help me in any way. She said that I ought to have asked her permission to bring my child there, and how was she to know that Sonny's complaint was not catching?"

This story entitled 'Impossible Love' above a by-line 'Had He Been A White Man I Should Have Been Proud To Become His Wife' goes on to tell of how my Aunt considers suicide *"For one wild moment I thought of taking Sonny and myself to find rest in the dark waters of the Thames. The same instant, the happy face of my little Jim seemed to look at me through the gloom of the attic. I had nearly forgotten him in the stress of the last few days…"* But then my Aunt is befriended by a Chinese lodger in the house who sits with Sonny while she goes out on errands, and provides her with good food for the child:

"At last I got back, and tearing up the stairs two at a time, I could hear my boy laughing merrily…" *"You wait Uncle Chong, till I am well again. You just show me the boy who peppered your face with a pea-shooter; I'll fight him for you…"*

Later, my Aunt having walked along the street with Chong to receive nasty looks and exclamations of *"abominable, disgusting"* decides that she cannot marry him. *"He wanted to know if I would have accepted him had he been a white man, and I answered truthfully that I would have been proud to be his wife."*

Moving

We move to Muswell Hill: Picture Palaces, Hollywood and my mother: The Slump: Fascism: The writer James Hanley stays with us: The Saving Sailor.

Yes, my Aunt had it hard and by the time he is of school age, *"Little Jim's 'happy' face"* is not seen too often. But at that time my Aunt was able to put a gloss on necessities and she boasts to my Tante while they sit together in the hotel kitchen, of the secondary school education her boys are receiving in Paris, secondary education not being general in England at that time unless paid for or won by scholarship limited to a few . And she proudly shows my Tante letters penned neatly by Edwin (called 'Ted'), reading them out loud as my Tante cannot read English:

Dear Mummy,

We are quite well. Everyone is kind to us. Please do not worry about us. We look forward to seeing you in the holidays. We are learning a lot of French and Cecil is well and happy. Please do not worry about us. Do not work too hard for us. Much love from me and Cecil,

your loving son, Ted.

Of course, my cousin lies, as he sits writing in a bleak classroom, Cecil beside him weeping so that his tears mingle with the black ink from Ted's pen. Ted is barely ten months older than his brother, but cannot remain a child for long, instead he must pack three score years and ten into his life-time of twenty-eight years.

336 months, 9856 days, with two or three extra to allow for leap years. Not many revolutions around the sun before Ted is pulled down under the heap.

On these visits of my Tante to my Aunt, both women spend much time in speculating as to whether my father was the progenitor of Dornan's daughter, Margot. Had my mother been daft enough to take in her husband's bastard? Or had she been deceived in the matter? Their opinions varied according to the trials and tribulations of their day and, of course, there was no proof either way.

"Esther" Margot says seriously, on returning home from an outing with her mother. *"My Auntie says she's really my mother!"* Margot looks up into my mother's face, watching her closely as if to determine the truth of the matter. *"That's right"* my mother confirms *"she is your mother. I'm glad you know that now."* Margot, seemingly satisfied, says nothing more, but it is some time before she remembers to call Dornan *"Mummy"* without first having called her *"Auntie."*

My mother might have hoped that the revelation to the child of her true parentage would effect a psychological change, so curing Margot of an annoying habit of helping herself from the well-stocked fruit bowl, sinking her teeth once only into each fruit and leaving the rest of the apple to moulder on any conveniently placed piece of furniture. My mother, collecting up the damaged fruit from chairs, tables, sideboard, bookshelf, remonstrates with my Tante:

"Can't you stop her? It's so expensive—ist so teuer!" *"Margot! Die Äpfeln!"* my Tante exclaims, throwing up her hands in horror, shrugging and rolling her eyes. And that is as far as the matter goes. This one bite and the decorating of the room with decaying fruits becomes Margot's trademark, determining her identity and allowing her to control her environment.

Alone all day, without adult company, my Tante hopes to find a friend from among the neighbours, but they are suspicious of our family who appear to be of no recognizable social class and, what is more, are foreigners, bohemians and probably Jews. In those days, to the English, every foreigner was a Jew.

"Jerry, Germy Germans, dirty filthy Jerries, Jew boys, Yids, Jewesses, bang, bang, bang, we'll shoot ya—*stick ya bellies, go back where you come from"* shout the children. Bored of an evening they gather outside my Uncle Henry's bakers shop in St. James' Road, Islington (now

Mackenzie Road). The children ready to run should my Uncle, a well set up man of medium height, come to the door. One of the children was Rose Howe whom I met years later when she had become Rose Blake and both she and her husband Ron were Trotskyists. She had been at school with my cousin Dora Lahr and had nothing against her, but this baiting of a supposed enemy provided a heady excitement; an excitement, which could be obtained from nowhere else in the dull deprived lives of these children. Some of the bolder boys pick up a stone, the shop door is flung open and my Uncle appears. He is angry, shouting out that he has called the police. With screams of delight the children scarper. At the back of the shop, Dora, her sister Joan and my Aunt Emma (an Englishwoman) cling together. Joan white-faced, Dora crying and my Aunt regretting once again that she has married a German—a hard worker, a good provider, a good man, member of the Lutheran Church and a sharp businessman (these latter two virtues alienating him from my father) but nevertheless, a German.

As for my two cousins, it was memory of these very events which made them both determine to leave for America, by marrying during the Second World War GIs of German descent and, at the same time, decide to have no further truck with the extended family Lahr.

Certainly, this antagonism of the local populace was a form of war memorial more potent than the stone crosses placed in Cities and villages and decorated with poppies every November.

Under these circumstances, it is unlikely that my Tante will find friends among neighbours, even without the problem of language. And so my isolated Tante continues to carry out her day to day routine, each day like the one that went before, so that time passes hardly at all and my Tante fails to notice that I am growing from a baby into a child. Therefore, I suck at bottle after bottle after bottle long after the age when I should have been given solid food.

My mother is not insensible to my lack of progress, for in spite of the daily dose of fresh air I am a pale, wan child. At times I attempt to pull myself up in my cot, or hold onto the sides of furniture, but my legs refuse to support me and I fall plop, onto my bottom. *"She is not doing well"* my mother says, her blue eyes clouded, her mouth drooping.

"Leave her to Maria" mutters my father *" domestic work is what she does"* and he repeats his estimation of my Tante as an earth mother. *"The child will grow up to be an intellectual, not a farm labourer"* he adds, falsely equating rude health with manual occupation—brawn not brain. My mother says to herself *"perhaps it is true, my daughter is a carriage horse, not a cart horse"* making a distinction which she is to use throughout her life. But she is not happy and watches me daily, her eyes constantly seeking out the swallowing heap of dead history into which she fears I might fall. And so it continues, until the arrival of my Aunt Becky at our house acts as a catalyst.

Together with her three children, Florrie, Woolfie and Helen, she descends upon my parents one Sunday without warning. My Tante is out visiting my Aunt Mary and Margot has been taken out for the day by her mother. My mother, uneasy, as always in the presence of her sister. Sibling jealousy might have been the cause of the original breach, but this could have been resolved if their interests, attitudes and life-styles had not diverged. Certainly my mother has never forgiven Becky for her behaviour at my grandfather's death bed, but she is not a person to harbour a grudge if it is not nourished. As it is, my mother sees my Aunt Becky as representing a confining life with a rigid code of behaviour sustained by superstitious beliefs. An environment from which she herself has escaped. My Aunt Becky, on the other hand, considers that my mother has discarded her Jewish roots in favour of arty-farty pretentiousness, literary poseurs and wild revolutionaries. If my parents had opened a grocery shop she would have applauded and boasted of the venture, but a bookshop! Who's going to buy books! Only people with nothing better to do and more money than sense!

However, my mother is fond of Florrie, named for her dead half-sister, Flora. Florrie is now about twelve years old and before my mother had become so involved with the shop and her own child, she had taken Florrie on outings regularly. *"Auntie"* demands Florrie *"Where's the baby?"* *"In her cot. She's sleeping"* says my mother. *"Let's see her then"* hectors my Aunt. Florrie runs into the bedroom behind my mother and the child returns holding me carefully in her arms. Woolfie is down on the floor under the table acting out a game, Helen is struggling to climb down from her mother's lap. As Florrie brings me into the room, lying supinely against her shoulder, my Aunt Becky lets Helen down to the floor and puts out her arms to me: *"Come to your Auntie, then"* she purrs. I give a feeble cry as she takes hold of me. She looks me, over long and hard. *"What's the matter with her?"* she asks bluntly. *"Nothing"* my mother says doubtfully. *"She's always quiet."* My Aunt snorts derisively. Helen is at the sideboard, door open and to my mother's consternation china and glass are being lifted from the cupboard by small hands, and deposited on the floor. My mother stirs uncomfortably and my Aunt follows her gaze. *"Come away"* she shouts *"Florrie, put the glass and china back and take your sister in the garden. You go as well,"* she instructs Woolfie. *"What are you feeding her on?"* *"She has her bottle"* my mother falters. *"Bottle, schmottle! How old is she? Don't tell me, sixteen, eighteen months. Isn't she weaned?"* *"Doesn't she have proper food?"* *"Maria sees to her"* admits my mother. *"I have tried her with a little cereal or a rusk, but she spits them out."*

My Aunt holds me up and looks me over critically. *"She needs a good meal inside of her"* she decides *"she's what they call 'malnourished'. Starved."* She proceeds then to tell my mother how she, herself, had weaned her children at nine months and continues by enumerating all that they eat within the waking day, emphasizing the vegetables, fruit, cereals, meats and bread, understating the sweets, biscuits and cakes.

"What time does Maria get home?" *"Not until six"* replies my mother. She is now seriously worried and for the first time welcomes her sister's intervention. While this is happening, my father is in the bedroom sorting through books and papers. Having greeted my Aunt and made funny faces at the children, he is pleased to creep out of the way and shut the door against intruders.

"I'll stay until Maria gets home" promises my Aunt and as good as her word there she stays, sitting in a chair and calling out to my mother with the latest family gossip, while my mother butters and jams bread for the children and makes a quick salad for the adults. My Aunt even tries to get me to take a little bread and milk, my mother hovering guiltily, but determinedly I clench my mouth shut and push away the spoon.

At last my Tante returns home. She is happy. The bus conductor, a clean looking man of about her own age, has smiled at her and said a few words. She could not understand him, but is sure that he has asked her for a date. She had smiled in return and shaken her head, but she could not deny that things were looking up. Who knew what the future might hold? My mother and Aunt hear my Tante's key in the door and mark her footsteps coming down the hallway, their eyes watching for the living-room door to open.

My Aunt Becky pounces. *"What are you feeding the baby on?"* she shouts in Yiddish, for she is sure that Yiddish is close enough to German for my Tante to understand. My Tante is confused. She remembers that this is my mother's sister, for she has met her once before, but she cannot understand why she should be shouting at her. "Was, was?" she asks in German and my mother translates Becky into German, Hof Deutsch. *"Speak more slowly"* my mother instructs my Aunt. *"She can't understand."* Aunt Becky continues with her interrogation, watched wide-eyed by Florrie and Woolfie who have come in from the garden, Helen taking the opportunity to once again attack the crockery in the sideboard.

Finally, my triumphant Aunt determines from my defensive Tante that I am being fed nothing but bottled cows' milk. *"I do what I am told"* insists my Tante. *"A bottle at six, at ten, at two and at six again. Sometimes I give her two bottles at one time"* she adds proudly and in exculpation. Once or twice my father has ventured out of the bedroom, but on hearing my Aunt Becky's shrill voice, my mother's interpolations and my Tante's shouts of innocence, he has retreated. This is women's business.

Now, my mother appears at the bedroom door. Her eyes wild, her face red. *"That woman—Maria—she's got to go. My child is starving to death."* The terrible look on my mother's face forbids my father to argue. Instead, he crawls out of the room to take Becky and her children home by bus and tram, receiving on the way my Aunt's views on childcare and a retailing of my mother's lack of common sense. *"She's always been the same"* declares my Aunt, vindicated *"head -in -a-book and airy-fairy."*

After that, my mother stays home with me, refusing to speak to the puzzled Maria, or to allow her anywhere near me. My Tante, for most of the time, continues to take and collect Margot to and from school, but with little demands made upon her she stays in her room writing letters to her sisters or goes for walks, wandering the streets, sometimes appearing at inconvenient times at the hotel in which my Aunt Mary works. Every evening, when my father returns home, my mother hisses at him *"Tell her she must go. Tell her! Tell her!"*

My mother spends her days in holding me in her arms and trying to coax me into eating the diet set out in the long neglected baby book. I, unappreciative of her efforts to fill me with earthy substances, refuse to allow a morsel past my lips, which I clench, pushing the spoon away with my hands or moving my head about to avoid it. Only when I open my mouth to cry is my mother able to push in a spoonful of food, but it does her no good for promptly I spit it out again or cough and am sick. My father begins to dread his arrivals home to a distraught and exhausted wife and a sulking and confused sister. At last he speaks to my Tante. He hums and ha's and hardly meets her eyes.

"The doctor says Esther should stay at home with the child" he mumbles. *"She gets very upset. She worries. She's not very strong. We're starting another child and she miscarried several times when working at the shop. It was too much for her." "Ja, ja"* says my Tante, nodding and waiting for the crunch line. *"Margot's going to boarding-school"* my father says *"and so her mother won't be paying us any more."* He offers to buy my Tante a ticket home, unless their sister Mary could find her a job in the hotel. But my Tante is homesick. She wants to return to a community in which she feels at ease and whose language and interests she understands. She would have a great deal to tell them about our strange ways and she welcomes the prospect. *"Ich habe Heimweh"* she says pathetically *"Ich fahre nach Deutschland züruck."*

My mother takes me to the hospital where I am diagnosed as suffering from rickets, my legs bowed, my knees knocked. A diet is prescribed, but I steadfastly refuse to eat, so there follows for me forcible feeding, as if I am a small and late suffragette. My mother weeping and wailing stands outside the room in which nourishment is forced down my gullet by a strange hand. I scream my protest for I take no pleasure in such sustenance and am willing to turn my back on this cruel world. But the treatment continues until I within, exhausted, capitulate, and my mother, without, collapses from anxiety.

Far away, in China, famine forces the Chinese peasants to sell their children, the girls to brothels, the boys to childless couples.

My hunger strike is over, but it should be recorded that although I have been scooped out of the overtaking mound of death by my agreement to pass through my corporeal self plant and animal life, almost immediately I attempt to crawl back beyond my origins. Once again to be thwarted by my mother's family, in the person of my Uncle Gussy's cousin, Annie.

My mother has taken me to visit my grandmother, Rachel. Once again I am fretful and lethargic, but I agree to sip my grandmother's lokshen soup from a spoon. My mother sighs in relief. I am eating. I must be well. Perhaps the journey has tired me, or I am teething. My grandmother pets me, talking softly in Yiddish and lies me down on her big high bed with the bed-ends of shining brass. I slide into the concave middle to dream of the time, a few years later, when I will be alone in this room and let myself fall into the depth of the bed, while in the other room the adults sit shiva for my grandmother, the thick candles throwing pale light and shadows onto the wall.

Annie, a well built, sturdy young immigrant woman from Poland calls. Dragging with her the shadow that I remember of a large, bowed old woman, leaning always on a pushchair, for her breaths are short. For the present, she moves rapidly into my grandmother's house and my grandmother says to her in Yiddish: *"Esther's baby is not well. Take a look at her."* Annie comes into the bedroom and peers at me. *"I take her to London Hospital"* she says and sweeping me up into her arms, runs from the house quickly, leaving my mother frightened and confused, to be comforted by my grandmother.

They wait and they wait, my mother unable to keep still, my grandmother telling her *"Annie knows—she has so many children. The baby will be all right."* At last Annie returns. I am in her arms and sleeping. I have received treatment on an electric belt and the doctor has said to Annie *"Mother, you are only just in time—another day and this child could have died from pneumonia."* Pneumonia, pleurisy—diseases which dog my growing-up years.

Margot by now is at boarding-school in Muswell Hill, for her stories to Dornan of my Tante's shouting and slapping have for some time made her mother uneasy. But it is the situation she has found in the house on her Sunday visits, my mother's obsession with my food, a sulking Tante who stumps about banging doors, my father greeting Dornan with a goat-like laugh and then creeping away to hide in the bedroom, which has convinced her that this is no place for Margot.

Margot's boarding-school was situated off Muswell Hill Broadway and later, when we move to Wilton Road, we often pass the two old houses made into one, set back a little from the road. At those times my mother remarks *"That's Margot's school."* But by then Margot is only a name to me and I now have but one memory of the girl who for a time was an older sister. For when I was about seven years old, my sister and I return home with my mother to Wilton Road, to find in the garden two strange girls, dressed in school uniform, one of them leaning over a flower-bed indicating a plant. Wide-eyed, I rush indoors to blurt out this surprising and somehow, alarming news. My mother hurries outside to bring both girls back with her. *"Don't you remember Margot?"* she asks me, pointing to one of the girls. I stand on an old settee, confused by this invasion of big girls whom I do not know, and yet am expected to remember. I shake my head and refuse to speak.

This was not a happy visit for by now we are poor, living in the lower part of the house, the top half let to tenants, and my mother once again feels at a disadvantage. These are only twelve year old girls, but their middle-class accents and airs of confidence have the effect of returning my mother to her roots from which she suspects she will never escape.

Margot must have retained some memories of my Tante, but I know her only by reputation until I meet her again in 1954 at a Confirmation Party in Steinbockenheim: We sit on a wooden bench before a wooden table, among salad, cheeses, fruits piled high and bottles of wine. Around me in this large back room of a stone-built peasant house, a hundred or more men, women and children eat, drink and be merry. My cousin Christel, dressed in black, has that day been confirmed in her faith, a faith which will lead her to marry, produce three daughters and work long hours in a launderette. Tante Maria, a middle-aged obese woman, sits opposite me, alongside her husband Georg, a small man who smiles continually.

"How is Margot? Dornan?" she asks me in German and is obviously astonished at my reply that I know nothing of them. Her amazement opens to me another life in which my parents have brought up Margot as a daughter and my older sister and in which my parents have remained close to Dornan. I am able to partly satisfy my Tante's curiosity by telling her that Dornan had married a wealthy man, but I do not tell her that on at least two occasions when my mother had been desperate for money, she had written to her former friend and received in reply a few pounds.

If it had not been for a sudden stroke of luck, my parents might have continued to rent a flat in Fairbridge road, but suddenly, out of the blue, £500 is thrust into my father's hands. It happens like this. A booklet entitled *Echoes* by Rudyard Kipling had been put up for auction and sold for £500. My father produces a second copy which puts the auctioneers in a quandary. If this copy goes for less, the first will lose its value. So £500 is paid to my father—a fortune in those days. And this decides my parents to buy a house.

What pleasure to view houses up for sale, old houses, new houses, houses under construction, all offering prospects of a variety of lives. My mother views each dwelling as a stage set for herself and her family. A long hallway, a flight of stairs, exit to room right, to room left... This search for the perfect abode becomes so interesting to my mother that even when settled, and later mired, in Wilton Road, accompanied by her children she continues her peregrinations around every empty house, or house in the process of being built

Before Wilton Road is decided upon, several houses are turned down and in later years my mother is to point out to me, almost regretfully, streets in which we might have lived, as if she thought that a different address would have provided a different sequence of events in our lives.

But, as it happens, my mother has fallen in love with Wilton Road at first sight, for it makes her think of a doll's house. Had she been a devotee of Ibsen this might have persuaded her against it, but at the time it symbolized for her happiness, tranquillity, security. Within a doll's house all is controllable and manageable. Here she will find shelter with her two children, for by now my sister has been born and is three months old. My mother maintains this illusion of a doll's house over the years, even when it is clear that events both inside and outside the house are beyond her control, by periodically changing around the furniture, as if by providing different aspects within the rooms she will be making fundamental changes to our lives.

The house is to be named 'Echoes' in honour of our good fortune, and my father takes the first steps by washing out the name 'Suffolk House' written in gold lettering over the front door. Perched on a step-ladder he rubs hard with cloth, scraper and turps, until the last gold letter is gone. But he never gets around to substituting 'Echoes' in its place and so the glass frame remains blank, the gold enclosing only space. Name, unnamed.

Wilton Road was built on part of the Halliwick Manor Estate, dating back to 1066, when it was owned by Robert de Moreton. In 1226 it passed to Henry III, who granted it to Henry de Aldehele—and so on down the generations, being rebuilt in the 16th Century. However, in 1832 the St. Pancras and Islington Council bought 87 acres of the grounds to form a cemetery and by 1918 the Manor House had become a furniture store used by Jelks, the second-hand furniture dealers. Apparently, it continued to be used in this fashion until 1932 when the Urban District Council demanded rates, which resulted in the Manor House being demolished. And so the mighty are fallen.

I knew nothing of this history during my childhood in Wilton Road, the road itself sloping down from Colney Hatch Lane before it rises again to meet with Coppetts Road, an incline which I learn to treat with care for one winter throwing myself forward to slide down its icy surface and enjoy the sensation of flying, my legs escape from under me and I fall heavily on my back. I look up the road and see in my mind's eye on the same side as Wilton Road, the Friern Manor Dairy Farm, fronted by white palings, the leftover of a rural past soon to be buried in concrete and crowded flats which cover old cowsheds.[1] It is while cycling past these flats on his way home from the bookshop that my father is to see a small girl in flames. Desperately, she rushes out of the front door into the forecourt where the evening breeze whips the flames into a frenzy. A human torch, she turns and runs back into the building, the whole scene passing before my father's eyes in a fiery blur. Before these flats were built, I remember looking through broken fencing and espying down a slope old and disused tennis courts. I always wished that I had courage enough to climb down and explore the terrain. But I never did.

In front of our house stands an Ash tree, its pinnate leaves stretching like many fingered hands to protect us from storm and, during the Second-World War, from blast. In Autumn its winged brown fruit dances in the breeze, to settle in the earth and push up shoots—shoots soon removed by my father. Directly outside the house the Council has laid a drain, a conduit which overflows in response to a heavy rainstorm, sending into our front and back gardens a flood of sewage. For a time my father regarded the outpourings of his children's bowels and urinary

_____

1. This Dairy was absorbed into the United Dairies during the 1930s.

tracts as rich manure, but the waste of strangers is not welcome and my mother spends many fruitless years in arguments with the Council.

While my mother argues with authority, I sit in the conservatory, or lean-to, on the saddle of my blue Raleigh bicycle which is set up on its stand, turning the handlebars this way and that. Around me the storm rages and I can see the waters swirling down the garden path, over the vegetable plots, covering the patch of grass. Lost in the sound of rushing waters, I guide my craft across turbulent seas and at last to safety.

Some time in 1955, the Council at last examines my mother's complaints against their drain and, triumphantly, state that the Ash Tree is the cause of flooding for, it is claimed, the tree is sending its roots into the drain and so interfering with its proper function. The tree is ordered to be felled at my mother's expense and falls with a groan at the ingratitude of human kind.

Now, when I look down Wilton Road from Colney Hatch Lane, I note the high grey pointed roofs which form two lines of grey triangles, the terrace effect broken only on the odd side by number 9 which is detached, smaller, plainer and squarer. Should I walk, or drive, through the road I see the bay, or sash, windows with their suggestion of Corinthian columns and I notice the 'new' houses built in a different style, on both sides of the road to replace those destroyed by bombing. For Wilton Road had the distinction of being the only road in the area to be hit by two bombs in two succeeding weeks.

In those days we shopped locally and although the shops might well have been part of a chain, service was personal and over a counter. Stevens and Steeds—where a light to determine goodness is shone through every egg sold—is where we can buy broken biscuits cheaply, served from large square tin boxes with glass lids, these lining the outside front of the counter. A wonderful mixture of biscuits of every kind. Grocers in those days paid one farthing for every jam jar returned, so we often begged, borrowed, or stole jam jars and used the proceeds to buy sweets, or broken biscuits. Coopers—also a grocery store, but containing a sub-post office—behind the grille of which an unaging woman, carefully dressed and coiffeured, sits throughout my childhood and into my adulthood: austere and sharp-tongued, quick to remind children to say 'please' and 'thank-you' so that even when I have children of my own, a purchase from this sub-post-office reduces me to infancy. On this parade also was a fish and chip shop, a butchers and the Off Licence where my father sent me on a Sunday to buy for him a bottle of beer to take with his dinner. Then there was Torrys, newspapers and confectionery, where I spend on sweets the ha'penny a day allowed me by my mother; a packet of sweet, brown, coconut 'tobacco'; a packet of sherbet with lollipop or liquorice stick; packets of chewing gum; bubble gum; large gobstoppers, and from big glass jars; a variety of sweets; bulls eyes; aniseed balls; pear drops with their smell of nail varnish; peppermints and many other flavours of boiled sweets. Torrys, a shop in which my father was to refuse to set foot for many years. There was another sweet shop on the parade at the top of Wilton Road, but we used it only rarely, and then only to buy phallic shaped ice lollies wrapped in paper. Dettmers, the greengrocers; Mrs. Dettmer so admiring my mother's curly hair that as soon as permanent waving becomes available she suffers regularly and willingly the then seven or eight hours necessary torture. Mr. Dettmer, like my father, is German and his daughter Joyce, a little older than myself, at one time tells me solemnly that being of German and English blood, she is a 'half-caste'!

There is also what is known as an 'oil shop' run by Mr. Carver, a small wizened man who wears thick lenses glasses with tortoise-shell frames, and whose daughter, older than me, is a pupil at the Convent. From the 'oil-shop we buy vinegar, loose, taking with us a bottle, cereals—'Force' is the brand of cornflakes sold in those days, a picture of 'Mr. Force', a cartoon type character on every packet, and maybe we bought oil. There are two laundries on the parade at opposite ends, Wilton Road in between. Boring shops to a child for there is nothing at which to look, apart from the counter over which the washing is passed. However, a notice on the counter of both laundries fascinates me, for it says that the shop is not responsible for washing lost as a result of revolution, war or Civil war. Is it safe to leave our washing here? What if we step outside to find revolution, or war raging, soldiers fighting in the streets or revolutionaries behind barricades of ripped up paving stones or discarded furniture. Could we step back inside and reclaim our laundry, or would we be refused? Shades of Genet's 'Balcony' outside a laundry instead of a brothel!

Later, and shortly before WW2, a further line of shops is erected farther down Colney Hatch Lane. but we use them only occasionally, perhaps when the grocers Buyansave has a special offer.

For items of clothing or drapery, we go to Muswell Hill Broadway, described by Bruce Stevenson in *Middlesex* (pubd. Batsford):

> *The late-Victorian shopping centre has one merit: it is all of a piece and has a beginning and an ending 'a period piece of unruffled cheerfulness' says Ian Nairn. The views down the side streets, though Urban, are fascinating.*

At least once a week we take the 1d bus ride up the hill and just as I have learned to remember the number of the red double-decker bus, 135, the number is changed to 134! It was a high day when I was judged old enough to catch the bus up the hill on my own! At other times we trudge up the hill past the big old houses with their large landscaped gardens and driveways, sweeping up to their front doors. Houses, in the midst of which, flats were to grow to occupy their space. Flats which, while under construction were illustrated on upright wooden boards to demonstrate their final glory, each flat with its small windows forced onto or against its replica. My sister and I named them 'elf prisons' and made up stories about their miscreant occupants.

On the other side of the road the tall houses of some three or four floors, now divided into flats, remain much the same. Grimly they remind me of when I was locked into a top room, possibly for no more than a few minutes, but in my panic it seemed like forever. I had been invited to tea by Mary Sinclair whose father had died before she was born. Her mother acts as caretaker to one of these tall houses, occupying, with Mary, the ground floor. The rest of the house untenanted. Mary and I play hide-and-seek and I am fascinated by so much space and the bare boards of empty rooms, that is, until Mary decides to lock me in!

At the Broadway, I walk with my mother past Monnickendams, the Jewish bakery. Members of the British Union of Fascists stand outside, displaying their newspaper and disseminating anti-Semitic literature. Blackshirted, white-faced young men. A little up the road, the Communist Party shows its opposition by selling the *Daily Worker*. My mother stiffens as she nears the fascists and I too feel under their threat. We buy rye bread at Monnickendams and then deliberately and defiantly, my mother approaches the Communist Party sellers and buys the *Daily Worker*. Stalinism, she decides, being the better of two evils.

For school clothes we shop at Arthur Humphreys in which there is a full-sized rocking-horse covered in soft short brown hair. I climb upon its back, take the reins and rock gently backwards and forwards. Thudding hoofs, warm sunshine, I gallop over aromatic bright green grass. I jump streams and fences, my legs tightly gripping the living body of the horse.

At other times we go to the North London Drapery Stores at which I am fascinated by the network of cables above my head, along which shoot cup-shaped vessels in which change, or receipts, are sent from office to counter.

Woolworths is a treasure trove—a 3d and 6d treasure store. Anything can be bought, wonderful mechanical toys, soft toys, notebooks, crockery, buttons, elastic, underclothing. *"Do you go to Woolworths"* sneers Dorothy Tibbs, a girl in my class at school. I wish that I had the confidence to reply, *"Yes, don't you?"* but instead I say weakly *"my friend wanted to go in there."* Years later I am to discover that girls from Ladies' Cheltenham College were not allowed to be seen in Woolworths, because from their point of view it was for the working-classes only—not people like them.

My sister and I often buy my mother a present at Woolworths. On one occasion a vest for 6d because she had complained of feeling cold and had no money for clothes. We are always guilty with the thought that she deprives herself for us.

Quite often we go to the Broadway to the cinema, called 'the picture palace' in those days. There we become lost in larger than life celluloid, characters appearing before us instead of being confined to black print. In front of the silver screen my mother escapes for a short time the hardships of reality—lack of money aggravated by bills dropping on the mat, the letterbox clanking shut as if a trap. A shortage of money which makes each day a struggle to feed us, clothe us and keep us warm; films are also an escape from my poor health and my sister's bedwetting; my lack of achievement at school; my father's secret life, for unless he were at home my mother could never be sure as to his whereabouts; and a growing anti-semitism which she fears will cross from Germany to meet with British hatred of Jews, to produce a British Führer. At the pictures, wrapped in bathos or comedy, my mother becomes at one with this romantic world where the bad are punished and the good rewarded, where true love triumphs and everyone is well-fed, well-clothed and lives in beautiful apartments. As has been said before, human kind cannot take too much reality.

The picture palaces for the first few years were the Athenaeum which in September 1936 is to be usurped by the Odeon which was built opposite, demolishing several late Victorian houses, and the Summerland, or Electric Theatre, at the bottom of the hill called Summerland Gardens, off Colney Hatch Lane. The Summerland closed in 1938, having fallen into dereliction once the Ritz, built on Muswell Hill, opened three months after the Odeon; the Ritz to be superseded in its turn by a pub and restaurant above which are offices. For everything is in a state of flux, as Heraclitus remarked five hundred years before Christ. The only certainty is uncertainty.

The Athenaeum had been built in 1900 as a dance-hall and was used at different times as a conservatoire of music, a girls' school, a cinema, by the Muswell Hill Parliament (a debating society), a spiritualist church and a synagogue. An impressive building, its name demanding neo-classical columns to the front of its second and third floors.

Of the Summerland, I seem to have a clear picture of a plain, square building, the exterior cement-washed yellow or beige. In front of the screen and on the floor are tubs of plants and flowers, probably artificial. Jack Whitehead in *The Growth of Muswell Hill* (pubd. 1995) remarks that the Summerland was *"like a theatre at the end of a seaside pier."* I am almost sure that it was at the Summerland that I watched a Laurel and Hardy film in which a piano falls down a flight of steps, taking one of the actors with it. I see no humour in this episode, for to me it is a terrible and painful accident, and I scream so loudly that the Manager asks my mother to leave and take me with her.

While in the toilet at the Summerland, together with my mother and sister, Sheila Leckie, a freckled girl at my school, peers through the small open window, much to my mother's annoyance. *"rude child!"* she snaps *"no manners!."* Uncertainty or not, she had a fixed idea of propriety!

My mother goes so often to the cinema that she is known to the cashiers at both picture palaces and so these young women never charge for us children, the three of us going in for 6d. My mother is much put out when the Odeon and the Ritz are built and operate on a much more impersonal basis. However, she continues to go to one cinema or the other weekly and it is films, together with the reading of books, which make her view life as a continuing drama of people's relationships. Life stories, motivations, the hand dealt out by fate, emotions, strengths and weaknesses, response to adversity, so that she takes this interest into the lives of friends and neighbours, making them all into characters in stories.

As for the architecture of the cinemas themselves, at that time the Athenaeum and the Summerland were mere walls and seats enclosing us as we immersed ourselves in the more than life-sized adventures on the big screen. The Ritz, and especially the Odeon are another matter, for their architecture and interior decoration aim at separating us from the poverty, hardships and anxieties of our lives outside their walls. Within their magnificence we can truly believe that there is always a happy ending, and that 'good' and 'bad' are immutable individual human characteristics resulting in persons making their own decisions without reference to circumstance or the economic and political superstructure. The message: Life is Hollywood, glitzy and what we ourselves make it.

"Can anyone go in there?" asks a middle-aged woman in a 1930s cartoon reproduced in a 1992 calendar issued by Sound Associates. The woman dressed in a long coat, wearing a hat and carrying an umbrella, is addressing a policeman. They are standing in front of the 'Superbia Cinema'. Through an open door can be seen a wide carpeted flight of stairs flanked by a uniformed doorman and a bell-boy on each side. A board announces 'Continuous Performance'. Those 'continuous performances'! We often come into a cinema after the film has started, and so stay on when it has finished to watch the beginning, joining the two parts up in our minds. A skill lost to succeeding generations, for when I took my youngest daughter, Esther, to a Walt Disney film, arriving late and so sitting on to see how it began, she complained bitterly that she had seen *"a happy ending and a sad beginning"*!

The Sound Associates Calendar contains also a black and white photo of the interior of The Odeon, Muswell Hill, opened September 1936. Designed by George Coles, FRIBA *"adapting his style to suit the simple modernism preferred by the Odeon circuit."* The picture shows columns, potted palms, an octagon cashiers' box and an intimation of a similar shape for the ceiling. A smaller picture of the exterior shows the wide glass doors, covered by a portico on which the squared letters of 'Odeon' are balanced.

"*Now tripled but retaining most of the original features*" declares the calendar.

The cinema is part of my life, and when my sister and I are older, on returning home from school before my mother has arrived home from her weekly film trip, we further her escapism by pretending that our living-room is a cafe. I write out in crayon on a piece of paper 'Cafe Wilton', or 'Cafe Lahr', or a conglomeration of both our names 'Cafe Ooshe' and prop the written name on the high mantelpiece above the Ideal Boiler. We lay the table carefully, first putting upon it a clean tablecloth. My sister takes slices of bread and cuts them into shapes, making designs with an apple corer so that sometimes there are more holes than bread. I put onto the table whatever is available, jam, a savoury spread, cream cheese, and then write out a menu decorated by crayoned drawings. In anticipation we wait for my mother's return so that we can once more wrap her in the land of make-believe, and at last she arrives and we call her Madam and present the menu, my sister and I acting as waitresses. Until the game is exhausted and we all sit down to tea and my mother tells us the story of at least one of the two films.

These are my early memories of Muswell Hill, which the guide books tell us was originally Mus Well, meaning a mossy well. This well in the Middle Ages was reputed to possess curative powers, so attracting many thousands of pilgrims and I can see them now, the lame, the halt, the blind, the distressed, feeling their way, stumbling and dragging their feet, quietly weeping, the intact bearing the bed-sick on litters, from north, south, east and west, to impinge upon the mossy well where all ills will be cured.

This evidence of Muswell Hill's religious past causes much excitement in my childhood, for during the building of the new Catholic Church, Our Lady of Muswell, in Colney Hatch Lane, near to the Broadway (the previous church at the back of the site having been relegated to a hall) a relic is found. This is a broken statue of the Virgin Mary, plain, clean lines, plaster coloured, resembling in its simplicity modern art. A relic, which as a child, I find disappointing, for I prefer the ornate gold and blue painted statues.

Once the foundations of the new church have been laid, several hundred of us, men, women and children, stand in the open air within their confines, surrounded by building materials, for the blessing, followed by the priest preaching the good news that replicas of this excavated Virgin Mary were to be made for sale, to raise money for the church, and that pictures of the Virgin would appear on an informative leaflet. The well itself, he tells us, is in a garden of a house in Muswell Avenue, but the spring which feeds it had been uncovered on the church site and a small pond would be included in the landscaping around the church. Before the building of the new church, my sister and I have been baptized into the Catholic Church.

My parents on moving to Muswell Hill would have been uninterested in its religious past, but proud of the area's literary connections, for Wilkie Collins, Coventry Patmore and W.E. Henley all at one time lived within the district:

Out of the night that covers me,
Black as the pit from pole to pole
I thank whatever god's may be
For my unconquerable soul.
My head is bloody, but unbowed.
I am the master of my fate:
I am the captain of my soul.

Declaims my father, not entirely seriously, at odd moments. The poem by W.E. Henley appearing in a book called *London Voluntaries* and dated in its preface 1897 Muswell Hill. Coincidentally, it comes within a group of poems called 'Echoes'.

Thomas Moore, the Irish poet, lived also in Muswell Hill and while residing at its foot wrote *Lalla Rookh* (published 1817)—that strange Eastern romance which takes up 104 pages of small print in my old book of his collected works. Moore sits in a small stone cottage behind which rises the green hill set in fields of waving corn. In the distance a dairy herd grazes. But Moore sees none of this for his eyes behold *"bazaars and baths covered by rich tapestry, hundreds of gilded barges upon the river Jumna, banners shining in the water, while through the streets beautiful children go, strewing the most delicious flowers around."* Dipping his pen into the black Indian ink, Moore writes:

Before the porphyry pillars, that uphold
the rich moresque-work of the roof of gold,
Aloft the Harem's curtained galleries rise,
Where through the silken network, glancing eyes,

From time to time, like sudden gleans that glow
Through Autumn clouds, shine o'er the pomp below

My own connection with Thomas Moore came through one of his songs 'The Minstrel Boy' as androgynously I identified with the youth, fearless *"in the ranks of death"*:

Land of song! said the warrior bard,
Though all the world betray thee,
One sword at least thy rights shall guard,
One, faithful harp shall praise thee.

I sing, standing straight, chin up, determined to meet with valour the surrounding enemy.

The pub in Colney Hatch Lane, opposite Wilton Road, was until recently named 'The Minstrel Boy', and was not built until after the Second World War. During my childhood its site was a wasteland flanked by advertising boards (as was the site which is now the public library). Previously, and from the time we first moved into Wilton Road, the respectable working-class and lower middle-class—busmen, post office workers, clerks, railwaymen, small shopkeepers—disturbed by the building of a Council estate off Coppetts Road, sent round a petition against it every time a pub was proposed for this site. For they were convinced that its erection would result in sober, respectable, industrious, thrifty Wilton Road being invaded night after night by disreputable, disrespectabale, drunk, lazy, spendthrift Council tenants disturbing the peace as they sing their way to their estate. I am an adult before the pub sign 'The Minstrel Boy' declares a victory for song.

And so, in 1929 we settle in Wilton Road. The year of the Wall Street Crash, bringing with it world slump, unemployment, depression. For a time we live on what is left of the £500 received for the Kipling booklet 'Echoes' and on what my father can earn from the shop. We are even able to employ a succession of live-in maids, country girls who come from large families to look for work in the city and can settle into the only type of job for which they have any training. In those days, nearly every suburban home employed a live-in maid who received her keep and a few shillings each week. Most of them dressed in frilly aprons and frilly hats to announce not only their own status, but that of their employers.

I cannot remember whether our maids wore uniform, but my mother, with her constant interest in human stories, spent much time in listening to their tales of romance and, in some cases, in talking a reluctant father-to-be into marrying a distraught maid who dare not return to her parents' home in 'trouble'. *"I knew you were a lady"* one such young man tells my mother solemnly, my mother having come to the door bare-foot *"because your feet are so well-kept."*

A snapshot of this period stares up at me. I am at the seaside and I am running out of the sea, my dress tucked into my knickers, my arms outstretched, my mouth wide open to form an 'O'. Behind me the waves are high. I have been taken to the seaside by one of our maids and her boy-friend and she assures my mother that I am shouting *"Oh, my bummy!"* A mortgage and a maid told my mother that she had arrived. She had bettered herself and her lowly roots were shrivelled. As it happens, ours was one of the few owner-occupied houses in Wilton Road, for almost all were let out as two self-contained flats, tenants gaining their status from the type and size of property which they could afford to rent. In fact, to this day the end house of Sutton Road, which runs parallel to Wilton Road, continues to bear the legend on its brickwork:

To Let–Self-Contained Flat With Gardens

With regard to Wilton Road, the *Hornsey Journal* for 1905 had advertised:

Superior and Substantially Well-built
7 ROOMED HOUSES.
Side entrance, long gardens—price £425.
Ground Rent £7:7s. Rent £40.

But my mother has risen above this, she is a property owner. And yet she is a socialist and sincerely believes in the reconstruction of the world into one in which all are equal. In the meantime she has to live within the confines of what is and make her mark within its boundaries. Life splits us all into a million fragments which impinge upon one another as if they were parts of a jigsaw made up of different and differing pictures placed together haphazardly. Therefore, our perception is inconstant, vacillating, variable, unsteady, unstable, erratic, mutable, mercurial, volatile, unsettled, capricious, fickle, uncertain. From infancy we are moulded and twisted to conform to what is expedient, to divide our wants from our needs, knowledge from understanding, intelligence from rote learning, sex from caring, fecundity from respectability, thought from action, theory from practice.

In fact, Werner Heisenberg published his 'Uncertainty Principle' in the year of my birth, 1927. A theory which the newspapers declared undermined the whole idea of exact measurement, stating as it did that the more precisely one tried to fix the position of a body, the more uncertain was its momentum, and vice versa. A dialectical approach stated by Heraclitus and developed by Marx and Engels into a scientific theory applied to the development of societies; they saw economic systems as nurturing within themselves the seeds of their own destruction and re-creation. The twins subversion and creation form a unity of opposites, incessantly reacting one against the other in a continual friction. Until, at long last, a vast explosion of revolutionary energy scatters the heap of history far and wide, transforming and levelling the prospect—as said by Walter Benjamin who saw revolution as interrupting the course of history. When the dust, the ashes and the detritus settle once more and the coughing and spluttering comes to an end, the mountain is seen to be reconstituted into a manageable pile. The wreckage of capitalism upon which it is possible to build a harmonious socialist society.

However, until this happy state of affairs is achieved, it is unreasonable to expect me, or the persons presented by me, to behave consistently, or consistently inconsistently. My own perception cannot be other than flawed and I can do no more than interpret the facts as they appear to me.

Since moving to Wilton Road, my mother has stayed home with her children for my Tante's inadequate care of myself has convinced her that she must personally care for us. She has taken her second full-time pregnancy very seriously by giving up smoking cigarettes for the time being and eating a well-balanced diet. Once my sister is born she concentrates on her feeding, much to the disgust of the baby clinic which, on hearing that the baby is being fed on solids at six months old, insists *"Mother! You'll kill that child!"* But my mother is unrepentant. She is compensating my sister and herself for all the nourishment owed to me in my early days, and my sister is a bonny, bouncing baby. *"What a beautiful baby!"* the old ladies compliment my mother as she pushes the pram up the street and my mother glows with pride. She has proved her worth as a mother and as a woman.

For a time, the writer James Hanley lodges with us and my mother compares him favourably to my father who has little ambition and treats each day as if it were separate from the one that went before, or after. Added to which, my father is away from home for long hours and returns to the house tired and unwilling for social intercourse. To my mother, James Hanley is a life-line and in the summer of 1992 he re-entered my life in the person of a Mr. Fordham who in the midst of writing a doctoral thesis on James Hanley contacted me for any information I might possess. This directed me towards obtaining through my youngest daughter, Esther, from the University of London Library, copies of letters sent from Hanley to my parents and deposited at the Library.

Although the letters do not bear it out, I was told by my mother, that Hanley preferred my sister to myself and I like to think that this was because she was at the cute baby stage. I, on the other hand, was demanding of attention, pulling at my mother's skirts, pushing myself between them, sulking when ignored, slinging myself down to scream in a tantrum, my heels drumming the floor.

"The children are great" writes Hanley to my mother. He is baby-sitting us while my mother is in hospital for an operation during which her appendix is removed:

> *Mr. Lahr washes the children and they have their breakfast before he goes out… I feed Sheila with the right hand and Oonagh with the left… from a communal pool… Sheila is getting to like me better every day so the competition is rather fierce and at mealtimes it's quite a fight for first place.*

> *Sheila has gone up to the Dawsons and goes every day.[2]*

> *Your mother departed this morning and I'm not sorry either… I wrote my cousin in the South of Ireland and if she doesn't come another girl will. But you'll have to pay a good Irish girl fifteen*

2. Mr. Arthur Dawson was a customer in my father's shop. At that time he lived with his wife and adopted son John, in Coldfall Avenue, near to Wilton Road.

> *shillings per week... Charlotte (our maid) is managing all right, but I really think it takes Irishmen and Frenchmen to look after children... Mrs. Pierce (our charlady) is alright, just the same old way, pottering to and fro as if she was carrying the Southern hemisphere on her back...*

Some time later:

> *I don't know how many more rumours will be flying about, but it seems to me that there must be some people who know of the row we had trying to make things a bloody sight blacker for me. Of course, considering that nothing else would make it appear even worse... Fact is I said all along weeks and weeks ago that Sterling[3] had to get a 'Boy'[4]... I'm glad this damned business is over. We are all apt to say mad things when angry. I personally am willing to forget... For Christ's sake don't believe everything you hear about me. How you can like Sterling is a bloody mystery to me.*

"Of course, Hanley had been a sailor" my mother says, admiration in her voice.

> *The steward now placed his hand behind the boy's head to support him. Again he gave the boy a drink from the bottle. Then he leaned back as though to get a better focus upon this boy, who had dared a horrible death in order to get away to sea... 'No boy', he told himself 'would do such a thing unless quite desperate...'*

writes Hanley in *Boy*, a novel which tells of a boy who at the age of thirteen runs away to sea to escape poverty, a domineering father and noxious work on the docks—only to be raped by his shipmates, to contract syphilis, to be put down by the Captain and thrown overboard. Of course, the members of the establishment reared on glorious tales of Britain's Imperial might, Drake, Nelson, the *Boys' Own Paper*, Hearts of Oak are our ships, Hearts of Oak are our men, 'Rule Britannia, Britannia Rules the Waves', shocked and horrified by this unromantic story of the sea, ensure that it is banned on its first publication in 1931.

---

3. Sir Louis Sterling. He bought fine editions from my father and took an interest in our family. In his Will he left money for the establishment of a Sterling Library at University College, London.
4. James Hanley, *Boy*, first published in 1931 and banned three years later on grounds of obscene libel. First unexpurgated edition published in 1990 by Andre Deutsch, with an introduction by Anthony Burgess.

"Hanley climbed up that drainpipe" my mother says to me for the umpteenth time, indicating the pipe which runs past the bathroom window. We are standing in the garden of Wilton Road, at the side of the house. I narrow my eyes to see a blue-clad figure lightly making his way up the pipe. Grasping it between his knees and moving his hands one over the other, hornpipe fashion.

"She had an affair with Hanley" says my father, his voice changing timbre as he thinks back over the years. As had been usual since the shock of my mother's death on 12th January 1970, my father sits on a wooden chair, close to middle of the three windows, peering out into Wilton Road, intent upon devouring the life going on outside. Around him is tumbled his life—stacks of books and newspapers, pamphlets and booklets. The large double-bed, a survivor of the marriage, is littered with letters in and out of envelopes. Almost every letter received in his eighty-six years. At the side of the room stands a small table and on this is placed a bottle of orange juice and glasses. It is the quiet part of the day, early afternoon when the children are at school, the babies at rest, the adults at work. There is nothing and no one of interest in the street below and the doors of the houses remain tightly closed. As I enter the room alone he turns from the window to stagger to the bed and sit down heavily on its side. I cross to sit on the chair which he has vacated, turning it to face into the room. For some while we have said little to one another, the gulf of my mother's death between us.

"She had an affair with Hanley. I found her in bed with him. I punched him on the jaw" he adds in pain and pleasure. Later, and nearer to the end of his life, my father becomes convinced that Hanley will visit him. *"He'll come today; or perhaps tomorrow."* As if he had come to believe that this sight of Hanley, who in my father's mind's eyes was yet a young man, would expunge the intervening years and my mother would be restored with her tight curly hair, bright blue eyes, quick movement and laughter. And he, once again, would be in his prime. But this transmogrification did not take place for Hanley did not come and my father, like my mother, passed into the dust pile of history.

"Hanley was a sailor" says my mother *"The sailors would have saved my sister Flora and her children from the fire in Portsmouth. If only they had known that they were still in the house."* To my mother, Hanley was the saving sailor.

Fire

How in 1912 my Half-Aunt Flora and her children died in a Portsmouth fire.

The fourteen year old Esther wakes in the early hours of the morning with a premonition of disaster. She lies still for a moment, straining her eyes against the greyness of the room which presses in heavily upon her. She feels hot. She sits up. She sits up to push away the darkness and climbs out of bed quietly so as not to wake Becky.

Creeping out of the room dressed only in her long white cotton nightgown, she makes her way down the stairs. In the kitchen, she feels about the dresser for matches to light the gas mantel, the faint light of which darkens for Esther each corner of the room so that she imagines things unseen waiting, and fears to move away from the room's centre. What's the time? she wonders and looks towards the bracket-type clock with its round face, ticking away on the dresser, the very same clock which is to stop its ticking at the moment of her father's death. It is a little after 1 a.m. and she shivers. Cold. She feels the stove. Cold. Too cold for a kettle. She walks this way and that. Agitatedly. Touching household implements until she knocks over an enamel jug which falls with a crash to the floor. Nearby, outside 94 Queen Street, the home of Esther's half-sister Flora, her husband Harry and four children, able seaman Edward Morgan, serving on HMS Revenge serving on HMS Revenge, shouts *"FIRE!"* and bangs with both fists on the front door.

Esther hears a sound behind her and turns round quickly to find her 15-year old brother Mark. She is not surprised for sometimes he and she at night share the same dreams. *"Cold?"* asks Mark and when she nods, he goes out of the room to return with her coat which she wraps around herself. They sit on the hard kitchen chairs without speaking, as if keeping a vigil. But Esther must have dozed for when the knocking sounds on the front door she starts up as if out of sleep.

Bang. Bang. Bang. The sound is ominous. Loud enough to wake the dead. She shivers. She stands up, but can move no farther. Helplessly, she looks at Mark. *"You go!"* she whispers and waits passively for Mark's return without so much as straining to hear the conversation taking place in the hallway. Mark returns. *"It's Harry"* he says. *"He says there's been a fire, but Flora and the children are all right, but he doesn't know where they've gone. He thinks they might be at the Sailors' Home, but he's not sure. I'd better wake up Mum and Dad."* But they are already awake.

After that time and occurrences run into one another to form a jumble of events which cannot be untwisted or put in order. Her father and Wolfe dressing hurriedly and running out of the house. She, Becky and Mark huddling together in the kitchen, near to their mother who goes automatically about her morning chores as if this day is like all others. The policeman arriving at their door carrying in his arms the white-facade, shocked, six-year-old Celia; the child unable to reply to her grandmother's urgent questions. Esther taking the small, shaking body into her own arms. The Father and Wolfe returning, anxious and ill at ease. The question in her mother's eyes and her father avoiding their look. *"Won't let us in"* he mumbles *"the fire brigade's there."* *"Didn't you ask? the mother screams, throwing her arms wide. Keening, sitting in a chair, her legs unable to support her body, she rocks herself backwards and forwards."* *"Where's my Flora. My grandchildren!"* *"Reminding the Father that he is only their step-parent."* *"Ask! Ask! Ask!"* shouts the Father in an explosion of energy.

Esther takes Celia into the living-room where they sit with their arms about each other. Celia's head resting against her chest. Another policeman at the door. Her parents talking urgently. Her mother's howl of anguish. Her weeping. The Father looking on helplessly.

In 1993 I obtain from the Newspaper Library at Colindale a copy of the *Portsmouth Times* for Saturday 20th April 1912 in which is set out the report of the Coroner's Inquest. As I read, I span the years and I am there at 94 Queen Street, a one-time public house converted by Harry Brentman into three shops, by the use of matchboard, lath and plaster. Harry trading as a seaman's outfitter in one of the shops and the family, with the addition of a nursemaid, a girl of 16 (referred to in the Coroner's Report as 'the servant') living on the two upper floors.

I stand in the dull room, lit by a candle, for only the shop, the cutting-room and the upstairs sitting-room are wired for electricity. Harry and Flora are preparing for bed. Dressed in a nightshirt, Harry extinguishes the candle, taking the wick between thumb and index finger, and climbs into bed alongside Flora, the four-month-old baby, Cecil, between them.

Flora starts out of sleep. *"Harry, Harry! someone's knocking at the door! Go and see!"* He climbs slowly out of bed, pulls on his trousers and in the dark runs down the stairs to the first floor where he opens a window and looks out into Queen Street, to see in the shop windows opposite the pale reflection of red and orange flames, leaping and swaying in a death defying dance. *"Fire! Fire!"* he calls hoarsely, so that able seaman Morgan stops his knocking and moves away to look up at the window.

Now, this is where Harry's story differs from that told me by my mother and told by Becky to her children and my grandmother's sisters to their children. For Harry informs the Court that on running back up the stairs to the bedroom he found no-one there except the baby lying on the bed. *"I picked the child up in my arms and returning to the first floor went to a window and eventually dropped the child into an overcoat which people held up."* My mother always said that Flora sent the baby to safety out of the window, but then neither she, nor her siblings, nor parents would give Harry credit for one good action. And in the light of what follows, who can blame them? The only evidence on the saviour of the baby is given as follows by able seaman Morgan who says:

> *A person came to the first floor with a baby, and I took an overcoat from a gentleman and both of us held it out and caught the child. A quilt was also obtained and the person was asked to jump, but would not do so.*

Note that, not 'a man' not 'a woman', 'a person'—so Able Seaman Morgan's evidence cannot decide us one way or the other as to which of the parents saved the baby. *"Flora refused to jump"* my cousin Florrie said to me only recently.

"Flames were coming up the staircase" Harry Brentman tells the Court. He is a little man not much taller than the five foot Flora, a man with round immature face which sports a small moustache. *"So I walked along the fascia outside to a neighbour's, McCarthy's, where he took me in."* On first going downstairs he had heard his wife calling out to the servant *"Nellie! Nellie! Nellie! It's a fire!"* but he did not see her again, and if the body was found in the other bedroom he supposed she went there to endeavour to rescue the other children. He was very dazed and exhausted when he went to McCarthys and thought his wife and children were safe, being told that they were at the Sailor's Home.

Henry John Williams, labourer at Brickwoods Brewery, trudging home just after 1 a.m. turns into Queen Street to be met by fire and smoke. *"Fire! Fire! Fire!"* he shouts, running the length of the street to the accompaniment of Police Constable Hancock's whistle. Harry Reed, licensee of the 'Camden' public house is awakened by his wife, dresses and goes out and, as he crosses the road, sees the 28-year-old Flora and 16-year-old Nellie Mason at an upstairs window, screaming for help. Breaking a window in Admiralty Row he makes desperate attempts to enter the house, only to be driven back by smoke. He races back to the Camden and phones the Fire Brigade, to be told that they were already on their way. Rushing back to the burning shop he asks the gathering crowd if all the people were out. *"They're all at the Sailors Home"* someone says and this information is repeated in a murmur throughout the crowd, the words spreading their way from one to another. Like fire.

Police-Sergeant John Patterson of the Water Police arrives at the Landing Stage of the Dockyard, hears the police whistle and in search of its origin comes upon the glaring reflection of flames and smoke in a shop window. Taking two Police Constables to the burning building he is told that there is a child inside still alive. He sends to the dockyard for a fire ladder which he rears against the Admiralty-row side of the building and endeavours to enter a room on the second floor, from which he thinks he has heard a scream. But he is driven back by smoke. Breathing heavily, he climbs down the ladder for a breather, but then climbs up again and lights matches to look into the room. He can see nothing. Then Fireman White mounts the ladder, carrying a lamp which lifted to the window reveals the 6-year-old Celia lying on a bed. Smashing the window, Fireman White jumps down into the room, picks up the child and hands her to the Police Sergeant.

"A sailor saves Celia" says my mother. *"Flora had dragged her to a window and a sailor saw her arm over the sill and climbed up the drain-pipe."*

But Fireman White can go no farther into the building for the smoke is too dense. Coughing, he and Police-Sergeant Patterson make their way down to ground level.

Outside the shop, Harry Brentman screams and shouts, he behaves like a madman. Police Constables Hancock and Puchini, one on each side of him, shout at him *"Is anyone else in there?"* Constable Hancock comes round to face Harry, to impede his agitated movement for a moment. *"Is anyone else in there?"* he shouts once again, attempting to get Harry to meet his eyes. But the policemen can get no coherent answer from Harry. *"They're all out, they're all out, at the Sailors' Welcome"* people in the crowd call out and the Police Constables are satisfied. It is only later that a woman informs Acting Sergeant Lock of the Fire Brigade that two women have been seen at a window.

The fire extinguished, the sizzling embers and charred wood cooling so that by morning they are cold and only a noxious smell remains, Acting Sergeant Lock goes into the building to find Flora in death lying on a bed, her nightdress pulled up to shelter the small body of two-year-old Sarah. Sixteen-year-old Nellie Mason lies dead on the floor. The body of four-year-old Philip is found crouching on hands and knees in a corner of the room.

Dr. Francis Stokes, *locum tenens* to Dr. Lysander Maybury, after a post mortem states that the cause of death in each case is suffocation. *"Burns on the bodies were sustained after death."*

"He set the fire for the insurance" says my mother, hating Harry as she remembers her sister, the slim, curly-haired blue-eyed girl so like herself, and yet unlike. For Flora almost from the first had been made aware of the transience of life. She had seen her father and full siblings die, one by one, until only she and her mother remained to comfort and care for each other. Following these deaths, when she was little more than a baby, she had made, together with her mother, the long arduous journey over sea and land back to Poland. Travelling steerage; sitting on hard wooden train seats; walking miles and miles and sleeping where they fell in tiredness. And then, when it was arranged that her mother, my

grandmother, marry Samuel Argeband in Rogowa, once more mother and daughter set out on the long, uncomfortable, trek back to England. But this time Sam, my grandfather, was there to help, to carry Flora when she tired, to take their bundles and share their burdens. When her half-siblings were born, Flora became her mother's help-meet, kind, hard-working, asking little for herself, the family's angel, and this role she had taken into marriage and motherhood.

In summing up, the Coroner states that all sorts of sinister rumours and suggestions had been thrown out, reflecting on different persons. He would make no comment, but would call attention to them so that they could be thoroughly dealt with and thrashed out. He, himself, could see nothing in the evidence to bear out these rumours as to the cause of the fire, or the alleged delay in the arrival of the Fire Brigade. The fire was due to accidental causes. The Jury returned a verdict to the effect that the women and children had been accidentally suffocated and there was no evidence to show the cause of the fire. The Fire Brigade had arrived promptly. The Water police and everyone concerned had behaved extremely well.

The Father, Wolfe and Mark dress for the funeral. Three coffins. Two of them such small boxes. *"They look like they're sleeping"* the Father says to reassure his wife. In his mind's eye he cannot shut out the sight of charred bodies. *"Peacefully sleeping." "Where's the baby?"* the Mother asks, as if it were only now she could total her loss. The Father looks at his wife blankly. For a moment they both imagine that they had misunderstood the evidence. Perhaps that was some other baby dropped from a window and Flora's child had been lost in the fire. Who knows what could happen to so small a baby in a fire. He could be consumed entirely by smoke and flames. *"The evidence given must be right"* says Wolfe firmly *"someone's taken the baby in."*

But they continue to fret over the missing baby during the seven days of shiva.[1] The Mother crumpled in a low chair where she receives visitors—Uncles, Aunts, cousins, friends, neighbours. A

1. Shiva, the First Seven Days of Mourning. Shiva is observed in the home as an intensive mourning period for close relatives. After the burial, mourners return home (or, ideally, to the home of the deceased) to sit shiva for seven days. Shiva is simply the Hebrew word for seven. During the shiva week, mourners are expected to remain at home and sit on low stools.

continual tread of feet. The men unshaven. The mirrors covered over. Harry creeping in and out, his head bowed. Three days of weeping and four days of eulogy. What was there to say about children who had lived such a short space of time, except to remember their sweet ways and clever sayings. *"Philip used to stand behind his father and copy the way he stood, feet apart, hands on hips—it used to make Harry laugh,"* says my mother. *"The little boy was such a comic. Harry was paid out for what he did. He lost his favourite child."*

Before the end of the thirty days lesser mourning and the eleven months during which the mourner recites the Kaddish— a prayer for the dead—twice daily, the family had moved away from the sailors' town of Portsmouth and back to London.

First, of course, the baby Cecil had to be found and my mother tells me how she and Mark searched for him by questioning neighbours, shopkeepers and others and at last found a witness who had seen the infant dropped from the window and passed from one pair of arms to another, until he had reached the arms of a childless publican who had taken the child home to his wife. *"They bought him a real live monkey!"* says my mother. *"A real live monkey!."* Her eyes wide with astonishment. *"They really loved him and were heartbroken when we took the baby away, but they were gentiles and your Bubba said he had to go to Jewish foster-parents. Until Harry remarried and took both children to live with him. He came to the house and asked Bubba to marry him—in good Biblical tradition—but she told him in no uncertain language where to go!"* my mother says, in an unusual admiration of her sister.

Celia, until her father's remarriage, lived with my grandmother and shared my mother's bed. *"She was terrified of the dark after the fire"* says my mother *"and I had to argue with your Bubba to allow her a night-light. But once I was reading by candle-light and the candle fell over and set fire to some papers. Celia was asleep and I put the fire out quickly and hid the evidence, but in the morning she said 'I dreamt of the fire last night' and I felt so guilty!"*

The baby Cecil carried the scars of the night of the fire with him into old age, so that even a wife, family and successful real estate business could not compensate for his early loss. At long last, and nearing old age, he found his mother's family and thereafter was seen at weddings and funerals. This story of his loss he told to his children again and again, throughout their growing up years, which led to his daughter, Cynthia, in middle-age compiling a family history which has been most helpful to myself.

"*The sailors would have saved them all*" my mother continues to lament.

.

.

Crisis

A Herne Bay Residential Nursery: The Red Lion Street bookshop: Political Action: The might of the Catholic Church.

My parents, settled now for the rest of their lives into Wilton Road, are by 1930 in deep financial trouble. The depression is biting, devouring all in its path and while the minority MacDonald Labour government is under pressure to boost the economy, the economic lifeboat crew of government Ministers named by Macdonald are unsure as to the direction in which they should set sail.

Our savings all but spent and my father earning little in the shop, the streetwise logic of my Aunt Becky comes into its own— a grocer's shop is a necessity, who wants books? My mother must return to work in the shop so that it can remain open for maximum hours. Her presence is also necessary to remind my father that first and foremost the bookshop is a source of income, for he is apt to refuse to sell a book of which he is particularly fond. Rhys Davies writes in his obituary for my father in *The Times* in August 1971: "*Charles Lahr who has died aged 86, was a wayward London bookseller who disliked selling a good book to the wrong customer, his knowledge of the former as instinctive as it was of the latter... sized up instantly and admitted (or not) to a free run of the stock, and pay what you could afford or else borrow a book for a week or two.*"

Apart from her need to be the business-like end of the partnership, my mother misses the book trade and can no longer ignore its siren call. Muswell Hill and Wilton Road have become a straitjacket imprisoning her intellectual curiosity and energy.

She is shut away in mundane household tasks and dull exchanges with neighbours. Her conditions of life made worse by the ending of her love affair with James Hanley. She is bereft even though she knows that the affair was doomed from its beginning. The return to work at the bookshop in Red Lion Street will throw her once more into the turmoil of living. She will take up old interests and contacts, develop her mind and knowledge, be someone in her own right.

Kenneth Hopkins who lodged for a time in a room above the bookshop, let to him by my father, writes in *The Corruption of the Poet*[1]:

> *Red Lion Street is ancient, it runs as it did perhaps four hundred years ago, straight down towards the old Foundling Hospital. Most of the grime of those centuries seems to have stuck to its old houses and shops... Here and there one of the shops has its old eighteenth-century front window, behind whose misty panes can be seen broken china, tarnished brass, and all the accumulated rubbish of years in the old junk trade. It is a busy little street and at the bottom the clanging of the trams in Theobalds Road joins with the roar of the buses at the top end, in High Holborn.*

To my mother, the very noise and pressure of people promised excitement. She loved the journey by bus and tram through so many districts—shops, street markets, buildings of all shapes and sizes. To look out upon people going about their daily business and wonder about their lives and purpose. The walk down Red Lion Street for she knows every brick and stone of this street. Past the small shops. She gazes into their windows, sometimes receiving a nod and a smile from the shopkeeper who recognizes her as part of the fraternity. The unlocking of the bookshop door to be surrounded by histories, philosophies, political economies, novels, poetry, lives, all in their different colours, red, black, blue, some gold edged, all of them reaching out to her as if they were living entities.

Overshadowing the shop, and unseen by her, is the pile of rubble it will become during the Blitz of 1941, but she refuses to notice my father clambering over the ruins in open sandals, intent upon salvaging something whole, and pays no attention to his cry

---

1. Kenneth Hopkins, *The Corruption of the Poet*, London: James Barrie, 1954.

of pain as a splinter pierces his foot. Nor does she see, or enter, the Income Tax office, solid and squat, which rises on the ruins of the fragile bookshop.

But first my mother must place her children in a place of safety. I have recovered from the setbacks of my first eighteen months and my sister is a bonny, bouncing baby. A childminder might prove to be no better at child rearing than my Tante Maria. If my mother were to return to work my sister and I must be cared for adequately, confined within a hygienic environment, fed a balanced diet and provided with fresh air and exercise. After much thought, and heart searching and consultation with friends, she decides that the answer is a private residential Home and Nursery at Herne Bay, to which I am despatched first to prepare the way, my sister to arrive later.

"I am sure they will both do well at Herne Bay," writes James Hanley in a letter to my mother.

I am standing in a room leaning over a low table to crayon in a picture. About me I can feel the presence of others, but they are not my concern. I press down hard on the crayon to concentrate upon filling in the confines of the outline in this book of outlines. I feel the door open behind me and a voice says cheerfully *"Here's your little sister. Isn't that nice!"* I turn to glance shortly at the nurse and a young child in woollen leggings and hat in the nurse's arms and, in confusion, turn back to my picture to once more press down hard upon the crayon. If my sister is here, where is my mother?

I am sitting on a potty in a white room, on either side of me are other children likewise engaged. We sit there for ever.

I am walking down a street in a crocodile of children. I am dragging along, children in front of me and behind. The nurse calls upon us to stand still and points towards a high window where two boys, dressed in smart navy blue overcoats, stand. We wave at them and they wave back at us. I understand vaguely that until recently they were inmates of the nursery, but now they are in this tall and seemingly grim building. Why?

I am in the grounds of the Home pedalling my kiddy car up and down the path. I feel the car turning over and my body twisting with it. There is nothing I can do. It is without my volition. I am lying on the ground, my head against a sharp rock. Screaming, crying, shouting around me and within me. I am lifted up, to find myself in a bathroom and I catch sight of myself in a mirror. *"I've got red hair!"* I say in surprise.

The room is dark. I am lying in a cot. I can see the outline of other cots in the room. My sister is in one of them. We have chickenpox. The other children have a magazine tied round each arm. I have none. My arms are free, but I wish that I, like them, had my arms constricted by magazines.

I am in the grounds walking along a path with other girls. Bigger boys come from the opposite direction. *"He'll get you!"* they jeer. Others take up the cry. *"Watch out! He'll get you!"*

We have been promised that 'He' will come down the chimney. 'He' will reward the good. 'He' will be cross with the bad. We are anxious for the divide between 'good' and 'bad' is outside our control and variable. When 'He' comes we are sitting cross-legged on the floor, in front of a Christmas tree, waiting. *"Children! Here he comes!"* a nurse calls out happily. We scream and clutch at one another. The red-clad figure pulls off hat and gown to reveal Matron. She is angry and we hang our heads in shame. Next day the big boys waylay us and sneer *"Who's afraid of Father Christmas then?"*

I am in a car with Matron and one other. *"We mustn't cross the white line"* says Matron. Why? What could happen once we cross this line? I tingle with premonition and hug this bit of knowledge to myself. I am sitting on a table, a nurse cutting my hair. She runs a blunt razor up the nape of my neck and I wriggle and cry. She is angry with me.

This time for me is frozen in photos—a nurse in traditional head-dress and long white dress holds my sister in her arms while I perch on a window-sill. My mother poses with my sister and me. My mother's dark hair in this monochrome. Me and my mother with the writer John Arrow, a dark-haired handsome man. The adults smile at me. My father is in none of the photos. Perhaps it was he who took them? *"Keep still, look at me, smile."* And in all these remembered instances, there is something else just out of reach.

In the meantime, my mother busies herself in the Holborn bookshop, each morning walking the route said to be taken by the shades of Oliver Cromwell, Henry Ireton and John Bradshaw who are said to 'walk' this district. For it is in the Red Lion Tavern that on the night of 29th January 1661 that their embalmed bodies lie overnight on their way to be drawn by sled to Tyburn for ritual beheading and execution. Now, lost in deep conversation, they traverse a path now lost, so walking the old and the new, the old in the new and the new in the old of Holborn—the bourne, or river, in the hollow which runs its way into the lost river Fleet on its way to the Thames. The three wraiths stand to watch others—the condemned tied to hurdles and dragged down the steep river banks, on their way to execution at Tyburn. Aware at the same time of the Victorian Holborn Viaduct and the busy traffic-ridden, dry streets. On a day in 1698 they stand bemused to watch the foundations of Red Lion Square being laid by workmen employed by the speculator-developer jerry-builder Nicholas Barbon. All at once the noise of the workmen's clanging and banging are drowned out by the sound of running footsteps and shouting. A crowd, mainly of men, but with a sprinkling of women, armed with sticks and stones, run fast into the Square. The workmen watch open-mouthed, hesitant, for they cannot be sure that they are the quarry—and the crowd is upon them.

The three shades move through High Holborn's imposing Victorian tower blocks and the massive post-war blocks. Simultaneously watching Kings and Queens on their way down the country lane Theobalds Road, to their Palace in Theobalds in Hertfordshire.

My parents would have been happy to entertain three such guests, my father would lend them books—*A Guide to the British Constitution, The Levellers, The Rights of Man, A Short History of the World, A Textbook on Common Law, Socialism-Scientific and Utopian, The Poverty of Philosophy, Capital.* And, as she had hoped, my mother flourishes now that her exile is at an end and once again she has a place in the world. Later she is to confide in us as if we were adults, but at this time we are too young to absorb her mental energy.

Now that my sister and I are cared for elsewhere, my mother is free once more to throw herself into political action. For at a conservative estimate, there are 2,000,000 unemployed and all over the country protest marches are being dispersed by police baton charges. On 30th October 1932 police attack a mass meeting called by the National Unemployed Workers' Movement in Trafalgar Square, to which the unemployed have marched from all over the country.

Esther sits on a high wall waiting for the march against unemployment to pass. Others sit alongside her talking and laughing.

The pavement lined with the waiting crowd. The very air bristles with excitement as if this were a Bank Holiday celebration. At last she hears the sound of a pipe band followed by the vibrancy of marching feet and the demonstration comes into view. Others jump down to pavement level, but Esther is happy perched up there. Police line the streets, their dark uniforms dominating the scene. The tramping of thousands of feet makes the very roadway tremble and the roar of shouted slogans crash against the walls of surrounding buildings and thunder against the Autumn sky.

WORK OR FULL MAINTENANCE!
DOWN WITH THE MEANS TEST!
WE WANT BREAD!
WE REFUSE TO STARVE IN SILENCE!

Many hold banners and posters. The waiting crowd on the pavement wave to friends or run to join in the march, but Esther stays put. Suddenly there is a shouting and the march scatters. Mounted police are riding into the crowd. Banners are trampled underfoot as both marchers and spectators struggle to escape the horses' hoofs and the staves of the policemen on foot. In line with Esther is a one-legged man, moving ponderously on crutches. He has been struggling to keep up with his comrades by planting the crutches down firmly and hopping his one leg forward. In the melee the crutches are knocked from under his arms, to be kicked along the ground and the man stands in terror trying to keep his balance, hopping on his one leg. And then Esther sees a policeman, stave raised above the amputee's head while he, futilely, tries to move away. Galvanized, Esther jumps down from the wall to run into the line and grab the policeman's arm. *"He's only got one leg!"* she shouts *"Can't you see?"* The policeman lowers his arm and looks at her confusedly, his eyes glazed. She smells alcohol on his breath. *"He shouldn't be here"* he mumbles and walks away.[2]

At the time, the *New Statesman and Nation* reported:

> *Suddenly, for no apparent reason, the mounted police, accompanied by foot police, began to charge the crowd right and left…*

---

2. Olive Moore included this incident, related to her by my mother in one of her books.

both unemployed and innocent spectators and passers-by. People were forced to run for their lives in order to escape being trampled upon by the police horses or beaten by staves. There was no kind of disorder at any of these meetings, and no reason at all for the police to charge into them in the wanton way they did.

The newspapers report fifty injured and fourteen arrested.

In desperation, the government has appointed J.H. Thomas, the railway union's former leader, as Minister of Unemployment. *"I broke all records in the number of unemployed"* he jokes. Strikes and lockouts take place as employers cut wages. John Beard addressing the TUC says *"Expediency must be our guide. 2,000,000 does not appal me."* On August 23rd 1931 the Cabinet splits and the next day MacDonald, Snowden, Thomas and Lord Sankey combine in a coalition with the Tories and Liberals. A General Election in October confirming this coalition in office when it is elected as a National Government with 554 seats and 56 for Labour. Of the former Labour Ministers, only honest George Lansbury is elected. Now follows cuts in both social services and local government expenditure. The numbers on poor relief rise rapidly and the Socialist Medical Association reports:

"Unemployment benefit and poor relief are entirely insufficient to keep their recipients in physiological health." While the Public Health Committee of Deptford states *"It is clear that families in receipt of public assistance… cannot obtain the minimum varied diet recommended by the Ministry of Health."*

In *I Was One Of The Unemployed*[3] Max Cohen writes:

I discovered that the symptoms of hunger are not quite so easy to ignore as is imagined by those who have not experienced that enervating sensation. The hunger itself appears to be a hungry, voracious animal, a beast of prey, steadfastly pursuing its course of swallowing its victim whole. I lived in dread of those empty, boring monotonous days of walking about searching for a job that was never there, and returning to a lodging bereft of warmth and stimulating food. The emptiness of the belly, and the accompanying tension and worry, produced an emptiness of the brain and of the spirit.

---

3. Max Cohen, *I Was One Of The Unemployed*, Left Book Club, Victor Gollancz, 1945.

My father-in-law, George Tiley, who at this time was working for the Producers and Consumers Dairies as a driver, writes:

> The working hours were just over sixty per week and the wage was £2:10s. And you earned your wages.[4]

Cuts in the salaries of Civil Servants and public employees lead to demonstrations. Representatives of the police assemble in a special meeting of their Federation at Scotland Yard to protest strongly at the cuts imposed upon them. Unemployment benefit is cut by one-tenth and a Means Test introduced to determine how much benefit should be given to those who have been out of work for more than six months.

On 12th September, 1932 the First Lord of the Admiralty announces cuts which are to apply to Officers and Ratings of 1s. per day, leaving the ratings with 3s. per day only. Three days after the announcement, the Atlantic Fleet, preparing to leave from Invergordon for Autumn exercises, refuse to sail. The rest of the Fleet following suit. By the end of the week a frightened Admiralty capitulates and revises the pay cuts on a percentage basis. A month later twenty-four ratings considered to be leading spirits are discharged: 'services no longer required'.

In Germany, on 31st July 1932 the Nazis double their seats in the Reichstag, in time to take the credit for an agreement by the allies to suspend the payment of reparations, in order to ease Germany's economic crisis. In England Oswald Mosley forms the British Union of Fascists. As Sean O'Casey says in *Juno and the Paycock*, the world is in *"a terrible state o' chassis"*!

Is it any wonder that my mother wants to leave my sister and me at Herne Bay until we are young adults, for she cannot bear for her children to be caught up helplessly in this political and economic maelstrom. She sees the Home at Herne Bay as a no-mans land in which we are cocooned from economic, political and marital trauma. Instead, my father insists that we return home to Wilton Road and miserably my mother concurs, for by now they are having difficulty in meeting the fees charged by the Home. And my mother's work at the shop is not compensating for outgoings. Therefore, with heavy heart my mother collects

---

4. The Journal of George Leslie Tiley, published as a serial by the Islington Local History Education Trust in its *Quarterly Journal*, 1987-8.

us from Herne Bay and we make the return journey to Wilton Road. Where next can my mother hide us?

I am of school age and Coldfall Council School is only a few minutes walk away, but my mother hesitates. She remembers her own frustration at receiving the minimum education to allow her to leave school and go to work. She fears also that we will be bullied by rough children, the types by whom she herself was waylaid as a child and who responded with vicious malice to any child different to themselves.

"They'll learn to drop their aitches and say ain't at a Council school" says my mother *"they'll say 'me' instead of 'my'."* Her love of language was such that it was almost a physical hurt for her to hear a mispronunciation and an ignorance of the glottal stop made her wince.

While at that time there was a scholarship at the Council schools, sat at the age of eleven years, a few being chosen to go on to Grammar School, this was a lottery and she would not gamble on her children's education. Somehow, she and my father must find the fees for a private school, for apart from all other considerations, my mother wanted us to continue her own ascent up the social ladder. An ascent which would provide for us some element of choice in and control over our own lives.

My mother and I spend some weeks in traipsing around numerous small private educational establishments, for in the 1920s and 30s these were legion. The most important product of the education they provided appeared to be a smart school uniform, for their staff were uncertificated and their curriculum unorganized, if not disorganized. These schools were successors to the much earlier Dame Schools and attracted parents from a similar milieu. About these William Blake wrote:

> But to go to school in a summer morn
> O! it drives all joy away;
> Under a cruel eye outworn,
> The little ones spend their day,
> In sighing and dismay.[5]

The premises used were large, or largish, old houses adapted to a greater, or lesser, extent. I have a vague recollection of a cloakroom in a house, the walls filled on all sides by pegs from

---

5. William Blake, 'The Schoolboy', from *Songs of Experience*.

which hang coats and shoe-bags. The room smells damp and I find something frightening about these deserted clothes hanging silently from their hooks as if they have no real connection with human kind. Staying close to my mother I follow a strange woman as she opens and closes doors and speaks words which make no connection with myself. At last the front door shuts behind us, and with relief I find myself with my mother on the more familiar street.

And so we search both high and low, and at last my mother finds the ideal school in which to immure her daughters—St. Martin's Convent, Pages Lane, Muswell Hill.[6] A school which has the added advantage of not being balanced precariously on the edge of bankruptcy, as was the case with many a private school. Perhaps she foresees the difficulties which will occur at times in meeting the school fees promptly and prefers a school which can afford some tolerance in this respect. A school which takes children from the age of three years so that my sister is included. However, these are not the only considerations, for more importantly my mother sees herself as hiding her children among the praying nuns garbed in their black and white habits, and the uniformed children dressed in navy and white sitting in neat rows, or walking in tidy lines. Nuns and children alike surrounded and protected by the might of the Catholic Church.

Ora pro nobis

---

6. Now a State Primary school and re-named Our Lady's Convent.

Convent Games

St. Martin's Convent: Play and rhymes: The Nazis take power in Germany: I am baptised and learn the catechism and also to dissimulate.

The Convent School is entered by a narrow gate set into the railings and this opens onto a wide triangle of gravelled ground[1]—ground which hides the marks of shoes within which feet have planted themselves solidly, refusing to move forward to the narrow entrance guarded by Sister St. Clare, the Kindergarten teacher, a plump, white moon-faced nun who opens the gate four times a day, two of these at least being happy occasions for she lets the children out. Behind the footprints are drag marks which move inexorably towards the door, leaving behind them a mist of misery. Marks made by generations of children, but those which most draw my attention are made by Gracie James, a small dark girl brought into school each morning by an adult sister whose fate even then was sealed. For she was to die of tuberculosis and Gracie, perhaps in an act of premature, yet genuine, mourning, weeps bitterly each day on being left at the Hall in which we gather for Assembly. Until, one morning, Sister St. Clare and Sister St. Francois—the latter an elderly red-faced nun with pockmarked skin—pounce, lift Gracie between them and thrust her into a dark cupboard, to teach Gracie that children must come willingly and happily to school. Not long afterwards, the Sisters set free that part seen by them as the Infant Gracie James, but unseen something of Gracie is left behind to hide in dark corners and throw itself against locked doors. And

---

1. Now largely built over by extensions to the school.

so, in later years, when Gracie has escaped the Convent and left it far behind, her husband and children suspect often that part of Gracie is shut away beyond their reach.

On the triangle grow several large lime trees and these at least give us some pleasure, for we are able to pick a leaf from a low-lying branch and pull out the green between the veins to produce a 'fishbone'. Should a vein be broken in the process, we pick a second leaf and so on until the skeleton is perfect.

These trees bear also the mark of children's hands, feet, arms and tears, many hiding behind or clinging to their thick trunks, or longing to climb and hide themselves in their lush foliage. One of them is especially stained and the branches sing out to me the screams and cries of Mona who, eager to escape school at the end of the day, fails to operate the brakes of her bicycle and goes slap-bang into a trunk of a tree. I stand amidst the gaping crowd of children and mothers and, being of an age to experiment with language, for several years am confused as to the connection between Mona's name and her lamentations.

If entering the official, approved, narrow door into school is a trial for us children, woe betide those who arrive late after Sister St. Clare has locked and bolted the door, for then we must knock at the front door leading into the nuns' quarters, an old house onto which the school has been grafted. Many are the times when on my way to school I hear the bell tolling high in the tower and envisage Sister St. John, a young, fresh-faced nun, pulling on the red and yellow bell-rope, the strenuous exercise disturbing the top half of her black habit to reveal an edge of pink corset. An item of lingerie never failing to surprise me for it labelled the sexless nun as a woman. Before the bell ceases, I know I must be at school, if I am not to be forced to knock on the nuns' door.

If I do arrive after the school door is closed, I must walk at the side of the triangle to the solid front door, which in response to my ring is opened by a kitchen nun who is distinguished by her head-dress, foreshortened, without white ruff around the neck and over the shoulders to be softened by the steam of cooking. She looks at me angrily, for her duties have been interrupted by my tardiness. I apologize, hanging my head, and creep past her quietly, to turn into the passage with its brown patterned lino and shiny varnished, forbidden doors. The smell of floor polish and incense hanging about me like a pall. Hung on the wall is a large, framed, dark-tinted print of St. Martin, a Patron Saint of France. His noble countenance ablaze with love as he leans sideways from his horse, sword drawn to rend in two his more than ample cloak, so that the almost naked beggar kneeling in supplication at the City gates can be clothed. It does not occur to me to ask myself why St. Martin should possess such a fine garment while the beggar shivers in his nakedness, for did not Christ himself say "*for the poor always ye have with you*"? Nor do I question St. Martin's motives, and wonder whether he is intent upon providing the beggar with warmth, or is offended by his show of flesh.

Then I turn away from St. Martin and his charity to follow the brown patterned lino past the WC in an alcove to the side of the nuns' stairs. This is properly part of the Sisters' house, but near enough to the school to be made use of occasionally by the pupils. It is here that Sister St. Francois, having left the WC, automatically slips the outside bolt on me within. I hear its movement, but cannot believe that like Gracie James I am imprisoned, until on turning the handle and on pushing at the door, it refused to give. I scream and cry out in panic, banging on the door, until the nun returns to let me out, indicating as she does so her disapproval at my protestations.

I cross from the lino to the grey stone floor and brownish distempered walls of the school building and make for the stone stairs which will lead me to my classroom on the first floor. Now I must face up to the worst of my ordeals—entering the classroom after the lesson has begun. I peer through the square glass window set into the door, to see the Sister, or one of the lay teachers, squatting at her desk in front of the class, maintaining a close watch while the heads of the children are bent over their books. Always there are one or two who glance towards the door and while no obvious signal is given, surreptitious sideways glances at each other and at the closed door reveal that my classmates are aware of my plight. I summon up the courage to knock timidly, but the teacher may not at first hear my tapping. However, one or two hands are raised eagerly, "*please Sister (or Miss) someone's at the door.*" The teacher looks sharply in my direction. Then, I might be ordered to stand in the corridor until the lesson is over; or I am called into the classroom to stand in a corner with my face against the wall; or, if the teacher has woken that morning in a happy, hopeful, frame of mind—a good temper which will last until mid-morning at least—I am told to go quickly to my place and take out my books.

But, at the beginning, before I am old enough to walk alone, or with my sister, to school, my mother takes both of us there and leaves us to be drawn in by Sister St. Clare.

While the grounds at the front of the Convent stretch away from us, those at the back are sweeping. At each recreation period we walk in a long file past kitchen gardens circled by a curving path. Past the shrine occupied by a plaster saint and ignored on our outward journey, but to whom we must genuflect when met with face to face on our return. Our goal is the playground which is surrounded by a high wire fence, and doubles as a hard tennis court. On one side of this playground is a grassy bank on which we can sit when watching a tennis match, but at playtime it becomes the terrain of our games. Behind this grassy bank is a fence and behind that the gardens of houses in King's Avenue. The proximity of the houses made no impression on me, for my sister and I were now boarding and I was confined within the Convent precincts. Until a day girl, for domestic reasons, must spend a Saturday at the Convent, climbs the bank and calls over a fence *"Dad, can I have my doll's pram,"* the pram to appear promptly over the top of the fence. If I but lived there I would scale this barrier and stay in my own home forever.

At one time it was a fashion for the boarders to make small, pretend gardens, on the bank, decorated with berries, pieces of glass, leaves, twigs and whatever we could find, but they were soon trampled down by the day pupils in their games, leaving in me a sense of loss.

We play all manner of games on that playground, milling around in our separate groups, but on wet days we play in the Assembly Hall and it is a great surprise to me in the 1970s, when teaching in inner city schools, to find that on rainy days the children were made to sit quietly in their classrooms or in the hall, allowed to look at comics, but forbidden to move. For in our hall we were able to play exactly the same type of game as on the playground.

Sociologists and psychologists who have made a study of play, see it as a catharsis for children who, in appropriating to themselves the power of adults, or in acting out the role of the child as seen by adults, integrate themselves into the world around them. And certainly our games of 'mothers and fathers', on first going to school, reflect 'family values'. Mother is the main player, bustling about 'doing the work' and nagging at the children. The children take delight in disobeying her and in being 'naughty'. Father's is a minor role, he goes to work each morning and comes home in the evening for his dinner.

Or 'schools' in which the 'children' are lined up in front of 'teacher' who asks them a number of questions "*say your two times table*" or "*how do you spell 'school'*," one child at least taking delight in getting all the answers wrong, until she is sent 'outside'. A spin-off from the cinema are our games of cowboys and Indians (I always choosing to be an Indian because that was where my family's sympathies lie), or 'cops and robbers'. Both of these games requiring much rushing about in an attempt to catch, or capture, each other and cries of 'bang-bang'.

Adults, of course, see play as time-wasting, or as a short break between work tasks. Certainly, Fröbel's[2] and other educationalists' theories that children learn by play remain controversial and are an emotive subject to governments which distrust the free rein of the imagination, or energies, of the people. Obedience, lack of self-respect, lack of self-confidence, greed, competitiveness, dullness, are the virtues governments and industry are keen to inculcate. If learning by play has gained a certain credence during times of economic boom (now called upswing) when the populace are allowed some leeway, it soon finds itself under attack when slump (now called recession) bites and social control is the order of the day.

However, unaware of theories and attitudes towards our play, we engage ourselves also in games to an age old routine: 'In and out the dusty bluebells' (or windows), 'The farmer's in his dell', 'Poor Jenny is a-weeping', 'I sent a letter to my love'—games which to me are often an ordeal, for they require each participant to be chosen by the one who went before, I fear always that I will never be called, until at last I feel a soft touch on my shoulder and throw myself wholeheartedly into the game.

During at least one period of the year, usually in the Spring, we rush home to demand of our mothers a skipping rope and on the following day skip to school, more intent upon our journeying than destination. "*Has yours got ball-bearings? Let's see.*" The

2. Friedrich Fröbel, German educationalist, best known as the originator of the kindergarten system.

playground has become a seething mass of swinging ropes and chanting and springing girls as one after another we run in to jump over the turning rope held on each side by an 'ender'. The mathematical calculation required to decide when to run in and jump being certainly more skilled than that required to add or subtract numbers on a page:

> *I am a Girl Guide dressed in blue*
> *These are the things we have to do*
> *Salute to the Captain*
> *Bow to the Queen*
> *Turn right round and face the King*

The patriotic sentiments of this skipping rhyme not preventing us from singing on the way home:

> *God save our old tom cat*
> *Feed him on bread and fat*
> *God save our cat*

or the equally irreverent:

> *Land of soap and water,*
> *Mother wash my feet*
> *Father cut my toe-nails*
> *Give them to baby to eat*

Imprisoned within our child's world we cock a snook at the world of dominating adults. Often we play 'He', called by Council-school children 'It', just as they say 'faynites' while we say 'pax' for a temporary cessation of the game:

> *Dip, dip sky blue*
> *Who's it, not you*
> *O U T spells out*
> *So out of this game you must go*
> *Because my mother told me so*

In this way we choose the first person to be 'He' and chase after those in the game until another is caught and she becomes 'He'. And, of course, we use most of the dips and skipping rhymes, perhaps with minor variations, recorded so meticulously, if joylessly, by the Opies. One of our rhymes indicates that the attitudes of imperialism had seeped into our souls:

> *Chinkee chinkee Chinaman*

Muchee muchee glad
Chinkee chinkee Chinaman
Muchee muchee sad

But this Chinaman is a cartoon figure wearing a pigtail, mandarin moustache, round cloth cap, loose blouse and wide trousers. How can we connect him with the struggle of the Chinese people against Colonialism? The myriad politics and tactics of what is now called the 'First World', the opportunism of Stalinism and the policies of Chiang Kai-shek were not subjects covered in our school curriculum! Instead, unknowingly, we imbibe the fear dispensed by a tabloid press against 'the yellow peril'—'they were breeding too fast and would soon overrun 'us'. A press which itself comes to be called 'yellow'. The tabloid press speaks of opium dens in Limehouse in which Chinamen seduce young and, of course, beautiful, white girls. What do we know of the 19th Century Opium Wars (1839-42) in which Britain went to war against China to force the import of opium?

Coming from a political family, I do know during the Sino-Japanese war that the Chinese are 'good' and the Japanese 'bad'. and, in fact, I can remember sitting on a seat on a platform at Muswell Hill railway station and telling a young woman sitting alongside that my father said that we should not buy Japanese goods; a difficult task for in those days Japanese goods fulfilled the role taken later in the century by goods from Hong Kong and Taiwan. Woolworths consisted almost entirely of Japanese goods.

But, of course, our school history told us none of this. Instead, we learned lists of Kings and Queens of England and the dates they reigned, out of context and like a shopping list. These 'facts' interspersed with such tales as King Alfred burning the cakes. This, of course, was general to all schools and while the French and a few Irish nuns may not themselves have been infected by British imperialism, they aimed at pleasing English fee-paying parents, the larger of whom came from non-Catholic homes. These pupils were the children of small shop-keepers, artisans, white-collar workers and others with a regular income and no more than one or two children. The common denominator for these parents being a determination to save their children from the 'common' Council school where they would mix with 'rough' children.

A second group of pupils are those who require the Convent's boarding facilities, such as the children of Civil Servants who have been posted to the far-flung outposts of the Empire. Places about which we learn in geography as wild, uncivilized and heathen. Places which are in urgent need of Catholic missionaries. Hanging on the wall is an illustration of rising steps going up and up and up, at the top clouds denote Heaven. For 1d each child can choose a small cut-out figure of a child of the Empire—Chinese, African, Indian. Children in need of salvation. A 1d pins the figure to the first step and each subsequent 1d takes the child a step nearer heaven. When, at last, the cut-out child arrives with her head in the clouds—and pennies being in short supply in those days many never made it—the sponsoring child gives her convert a name and in return is given a holy picture stating that she is godmother. To be a godmother! That sounds important to me and so I go without my daily cocoa, which costs a 1d per day, and quickly send my child, whom I name Maria, up those steps to paradise. After such an effort, I tire and a future cut-out child remains with most of the others, about a quarter of the way to salvation.

The Convent of St. Martins had been brought to Muswell Hill to continue the charitable work of its patron saint in providing a Catholic education and to ensure that Catholics in the vicinity should not be corrupted by Protestantism. Therefore, while the Convent was intent upon receiving fees from non-Catholic parents, the Reverend Mother was always ready to offer a reduction in fees, or even to provide free schooling, so as to ensure that a Catholic child remain within the community. In fact, when following the baptism of myself and my sister, my parents find themselves with no money for fees, my mother makes over to the Convent an endowment policy payable when I am fifteen years of age. By that time I have long left that Convent, but my mother's sense of probity ensures that the payment is made in full.

The Mother House of the Order of St. Martin is situated in Tours in the Loire Valley. Tours, named for a Celtic tribe, the Turanes, and the district first became prosperous in the days of the Pax Romano under the name of Caesarodunum (Caesar's Hill). It was in 360 AD that St. Martin founded a monastery for it appears that his experience with the beggar had decided him upon a religious path. Convinced that the whole episode had been a direct test from God, and it was Christ himself who had appeared to him in the guise of a mendicant, he ended the military service for which he had come to Northern Gaul and gave himself to good works.

St. Martin's remains lie in Tours, and three Basilica, two of them in ruins, ensure that he is not forgotten, especially by tourists. Three basilicas, because while in life St. Martin abandoned military action, in death he was bedevilled by its violence. The first basilica was destroyed by the Normans in the 14th Century and the second by the Hugenots during the religious wars of 1562. The third basilica was not built until 1924:

The *Penguin Guide to France 1989* writes:

> *Today the 15th Century half-timbered houses and gabled facades of the Old City shelter seductive sidewalk cafes and restaurants. Various styles of town houses cluster on rue Briconnet near the Musee de Gemmail. The relatively modern art of Gemmail, colourful glass pieces assembled and artificially lighted from the back, or inside, to create a contemporary version of stained glass, was invented by the painter John Crotti (1878-1958).*

And, I daresay, there's a McDonalds somewhere.

Looking back over the years, I cannot now remember my first reaction to the appearance of the nuns in their long, dark black dresses and stiff white bonnets, ending on chest and shoulders, covering every vestige of possible heads of hair. A black veil hangs from the back of the bonnet and ends in a point. A large crucifix strung on a black cord hangs around the neck, and to the side of the full long black skirt hangs a black rosary. Beatrice Hastings, ex-artists' model, ex-mistress of Modigliani, ex-suffragette and democratic anarchist, refers to them as 'penguins' when she comes with my mother to meet us from school. But apart from their similar black and white colouring, I could not see this resemblance, for even the Kings, seen at the London Zoo, were much smaller than the overpowering nuns and posed no threat.

On first going to school and in the kindergarten, I sit at a table at the back of the large classroom. If I turn my head I can see a picture of the Sacred Heart, his red heart exposed to my gaze as he fingers it gently. He is dressed in a white gown and red cloak. His hair is long and a crown of thorns surrounds his head. Today, this picture joins with the Sacred Heart at the very top of an over-mantel over-seeing my cousin Cecil's ruined room. On the bed, my Aunt Mary lies dying. Tumbled among the old newspapers, trampled clothing, plates of dried food and cat shit are my Aunt's prescribed heart pills, red, green and yellow.

In the classroom, and on the other side of the room, the Virgin Mary stands high on a small shelf, her blue-painted gown faded and dusty. My sister is at the other end of the room with the under fives and over us all hangs the moon face of Sister St. Clare, surrounded by her dark habit. I sit writing at a table, carefully tracing over with my pencil the light blue lines of the alphabet presented in an exercise book. I do not know what the letters mean for I cannot read, but there is some amusement in trying to keep the pencil on the narrow lines. My neighbour, Betty Scott, whispers to me. I cannot hear what she says, but Sister St. Clare's whipcrack of a voice breaks the quietness of the classroom. *"No talking!"* I cower in my seat in resentment against Betty for including me in her shame.

At the side of the classroom, under a window, stands a wooden sand-tray painted green and raised on legs to child height. Sometimes, I gaze at the loose, yellowish sand and vaguely wonder what it is doing there. I know its purpose, for my mother, as a concession, has made my sister and me a sandpit in our garden— a place where we bury my mother's cutlery. Here it appears to be out of place for we are forbidden to use it. I have no doubt that Sister St. Clare herself must have been equally puzzled at its inclusion within her classroom for the teachings of Montessori and Fröbel are outside the experience of the nuns who believe in obedience and penance.

At times, Sister St. Clare leaves the classroom for a short space of time, first announcing her intended departure: *"I am going just outside the door and will be able to hear you. You must count 1, 2, 3, 4 and so on until I come back."* At other times the instruction is to recite the alphabet, or the two times table. And so we set up a drone *"twice one are two twice two are four twice three are six..."* not daring to break for a second, for we know that God is everywhere and attribute a similar ubiquity to Sister St. Clare.

My sister and I had, of course, entered the Convent as non-Catholics, a category covering all branches of religion and none, but by the time my sister is six and I am eight years, my mother decides that her two children should be baptized as Catholics, my father putting up no argument against it. Instead, he rationalizes *"If they've got any intelligence, they'll come away from religion when they're old enough to think for themselves."* I see my mother's decision as partly due to her own childhood experience at a Portsmouth Church of England school. The Head Teacher had been instructed by my grandfather that his daughter must in no circumstances sit in on lessons about the New Testament, nor must she attend at Christian prayers. This meant that my mother must wait together with two or three other Jewish girls until morning Assembly was over, and when the New Testament was the subject of a lesson, she must walk out of the classroom under all watching eyes, separating herself from her peers, and from the host culture. Undeniably, the insecurity of the immigrant had been transmitted to my mother from her parents and this coalesced with the anti-Semitism she had herself experienced as a child and the growth in the 1930s of fascist and Nazi organisations. My mother wanted my sister and me to feel as if we belonged, to be at one with our peer group, and to escape persecution, by being presented as Catholics.

Of course, the news from Germany added to my mother's paranoia and possibly was the deciding factor in my sister's and my own conversion. For in January 1933, with the connivance of President von Hindenburg, Chancellor von Papen and the Cologne Banker Kurt von Schroeder, Hitler had been appointed Chancellor. A month later the Reichstag went up in flames and von Hindenburg signed a decree suspending all legal guarantees for personal liberty, freedom of speech and the press, and the right of Assembly. At a meeting held at Berlin's Kroll Opera House, in sight of the burned out Reichstag, an Enabling Bill had been carried out with the support of the Nationalists and the Centre Party which allowed Hitler to rule by Decree.

Dr. Goebbels denounces the 'Jewish vampires'. Storm troopers roam the streets looking for Jews to beat up, their victims being left lying on the pavement, avoided by passers-by. Nazi thugs burst into the Dresden Opera House and eject the musical director Fritz Busch. The Berlin home of Leon Feuchtwanger, author of *Jew Süß*, is broken into by Nazis who tear up papers and steal the manuscript of his new novel, *Josephine*.[3] In April, a boycott of Jewish businesses is ordered by the Nazi government. Windows of Jewish shops are smashed and posters pasted up which

3. *Jew Süß*—a 1940 Nazi propaganda film produced at the behest of Joseph Goebbels, considered one of the most antisemitic films of all time.

read *"Germans defend yourselves against Jewish atrocity propaganda. Buy only at German shops."* This boycott is enforced by beefy, uniformed SA Guards who stand threateningly outside Jewish shops. Jewish professors are prevented from entering the University of Münster, lawyers and bankers barred from their offices. Insurance Companies complain that they are out of pocket from the damage to Jewish property and that national property is being destroyed.

A huge bonfire of books burn in the square in front of Berlin University and a similar pile burns in Munich, watched by thousands of school-children: the works of Heinrich Mann, Upton Sinclair, Erich Maria Remarque. The bookshops stock Hitler's *Mein Kampf*. This alone must have terrified my parents who could envisage their own precious stock of books piled in the street to form a bonfire-night pyre. And yet a few years later their books are to be burned.

In Germany, the trade union movement is purged and Storm Troopers sweeping through their offices seize files and arrest labour leaders. Dr. Robert Ley, an alcoholic chemist from Cologne, becomes the head of the new German Work Front.

By June, Germany has become a one-party State and school text-books are being rewritten to include such subjects as 'racial science'. In July the Nazis announce a programme of sterilization of 'imperfect' Germans. By August, the Jews are herded into concentration camps. The outlawed Socialist Party reporting that 45,000 socialists were also being held in 65 camps, the largest at Dachau.

> *The space between the double fence is patrolled by armed sentries who shoot anyone attempting to escape without challenge. Herr Wekerle, the Prison Commandant, said 'four men made a dash for it last week. They got a hundred yards before the bullets hit them.'*

In January 1934, Oswald Mosley, speaking in Birmingham calls for a modern dictatorship. Many of the British Union of Fascist members present wear black shirts and leather belts, a uniform copied from Mussolini.

Around us, conveyer-belt death trains feed human cargoes to the camps to be piled onto the mountains of living skeletons. My mother is able to bravely face the threat to herself, but she cannot accept it for her children. We are to be concealed behind the facade of the Catholic Church.

Shortly after my birth, my mother, intent upon pleasing her family, had taken me to the synagogue to be named 'Simcha', which means joy, a name translated by my Aunt Becky into 'Seema' for one of her daughters. Simcha in honour of my grandfather, Samuel. As it happens, while my parents' first wedding had been in a Registrar's office near to Farringdon Road—my mother arriving late for the ceremony due to becoming immersed in the wares of the book market—later they had agreed to go through a Shul ceremony for which my mother wore a light grey beaded dress. My father agreed also to become Jewish and be circumcised, an uncomfortable operation for a man nearing 40 years, who could take no time out from work and must cycle about his business. Of course, as an atheist, he did not take this conversion too seriously, and yet regarded it as a gesture.

Now, I am to become a Catholic. The baptism takes place at Our Lady of Muswell, the old church at the back of the grounds soon to be relegated to Church Hall. As I wait at the fount, dressed in the white satin gown, made from material, sacrificed by my mother from a time closed to me, a future self lurks in the shadows to walk across the altar replaced by a stage, to dance at Church socials, to take part in a nativity play as a Roman soldier while the mob shouts *"rhubarb, rhubarb, rhubarb."*

I finger the white transparent beads adorning the collar of my Christening Robe while the ceremony drones on with questions from the priest and responses from the godparents. Godfather to both of us is the writer John Brophy (father of Brigid). He is not a Catholic but has a Catholic wife. We have been given separate godmothers, mine Ann Aldred, daughter-in-law of Guy and my sisters' godmother is Maireen Mitchell, a character actress seen in long gown and beaded skull cap as the nurse in the film of *Romeo and Juliet*. Ann Aldred is unable to attend, and so an old lady stands in as proxy. Maireen is to take her role seriously, for once or twice a year, she takes my sister out for the day, and at these times I am a little jealous. At last the ceremony is over and we both have now the Christian name of 'Maria'.

While these preparations for integration are under way, my mother pushes to the back of her mind the nagging worry which gnaws away like a toothache—what will her family say? She takes comfort in the thought that the East End is a long way away, almost in another time zone. Little does she know that events are in train which will bring her sister Becky and her family to Barnet, within the environs of Muswell Hill. In the meantime, I am to reconcile the religious doubts of atheism and libertarian socialism with the certainties of Catholicism, for the catechism asks and answers:

Q. Who made you?
A. God made me.
Q. Why did God make you?
A. He made me to know him and love him and serve him in this world and to be happy with him forever in the next.
Q. In whose image and likeness did God make you?
A. God made me in his own image and likeness.
Q. Is this image to God in your body or in your soul?
A. This likeness to God is chiefly in my soul.

and so on.

From now on I am to be indoctrinated into religious belief which allows no opportunity for argument or discussion. I either know the answer or I don't. For, as Dr. R.L. Worrall writes in *Time and Lifetime*, *"Religious belief demands a surrendering of past, present and future to the dictates of dogma and the capriciousness of an unseen deity. In this way, the marrying of knowledge and memory/experience becomes a misalliance. And we are unable to master the march of time."*[4] Such religious belief surrounds our days; the Catechism, prayers, the Lives of the Saints, the Old and New Testaments, attendance at the small Convent Chapel, Mass on Sundays, preparation classes for making a First Confession, First Communion, Confirmation.

The non-Catholic girls withdraw for these lessons, staying only for those on the Bible, but for us Catholics faith invades even our lay lessons, classed as endeavors which we virtuously offer up to God. Original Sin, Mortal Sin, Venial Sin—daily these are in danger of staining our soul and we will be saved only by faith, confession and penance.

Father Clayton visits the infant classes. He is the parish priest and to us children an ancient—white hair, fat double chin, ruddy face, rounded shoulders. He carries with him always a bag of

---

4. Dr. R.L. Worrall, *Time and Lifetime*, 1989.

boiled sweets. As he walks the district, paper bag in hand, he offers the unwrapped sticky confection to any young child crossing his path. My mother, in whom the hygiene laws of her youth persist, makes sure to hurry us away as soon as she spies in the distance his rounded figure and black broad-brimmed hat.

Father Clayton knows better than to offer sweets while in the Convent and under supervision of the nuns. Instead, with a captive audience of infants, he enlarges upon the Blessed Sacraments. He sits on a chair in front of the class, facing the wide-eyed infants who wait and watch. On and on his voice drones. He is speaking of Holy Communion, but we understand little of what he says. Except for one small, bright, blond boy named Timothy Smiley. He puts up his hand. "*What is it Timothy?*" Sister St. Clare asks, sharply. She is hovering behind Father Clayton's chair, her very presence daring the children to misbehave. "*Please Sister St. Clare, please Father Clayton*" blurts out the earnest Timothy "*if we eat the body and blood of Jesus Christ we must be cannibals!*" Sister St. Clare frowns in consternation, but Father Clayton, who is very deaf, cups his hand to his ear and leans forward to catch Timothy's words: "*What's that boy? Cannonballs?*" It is incidents such as these which I take home to delight my parents.

At that time I live in two worlds. Home, where feelings can be expressed and all is open to criticism, explanation and discussion, and school where precepts are set fast. There I must be ever watchful not to betray that part of me which comes into being at Wilton Road and this schizophrenic development of the psyche is known as socialization. However, in spite of my developing ability to divide my world and myself into two separate spheres and my growing cleverness of dissimulation, there remain times when I am shocked at the clashing of my two cultures.

One overcast afternoon, Annette Giddon, a plump infant, and I put up our hands so as to be allowed to go to the WC. As it happens, in the case of two infants needing to relieve themselves simultaneously one is supposed to wait outside the classroom door until the other returns. Today, as I stand by the door, I see Annette hovering. The day is stormy and almost as dark as night. Annette gazes fearfully at the shadowy passage which leads to the WC, near to Reverend Mother's room. "*Let's go together*" she pleads and takes me by the hand. As we come out of the WC together, Reverend Mother passes by. She is an elderly, bent nun, face wrinkled, eyes sharp behind wire-framed spectacles. Lips pursed, she waits as the door closes behind us and then demands in her French accented voice *"What were you doing in there together?"* We know that she means the WC, but cannot understand the import of the question and so look at her in confusion. At last Annette stammers *"Sister St. Clare said we could go."* *"Why two together?"* the nun persists. We do not know how to answer. *"Come to my room"* she instructs and we follow her bent, yet stiff, figure in its long black gown into a room to stand in front of the large desk on which lie neat piles of correspondence. Reverend Mother sits herself behind it in the carved chair and I watch the dull light filtering through the open slats of the venetian blinds. *"What were you doing in that place together?"* she persists, catechizing us, but unlike the catechism there are no set answers. *"Why two together?"* At last I find words. *"Annette doesn't like the dark"* I say timidly *"she was frightened at going in there on her own."* The Reverend Mother's face brightens. Our sin is not of the flesh, but of a lack of faith.

"There is no harm in God's darkness" she informs us. *"You must pray for faith. Always go to that place alone. Never with anyone else."* Sister St. Clare must also have been reprimanded for both Annette and I receive sour looks from that direction for the rest of the week.

But I am left puzzled. I have been found guilty, but of what? At home, my sister and I often go into the bathroom together, or with our mother. Is this a further example of Lahr depravity which must at all cost be kept hidden from the nuns?

For the most part, however, so swiftly am I able to change my persona at the first step into Wilton Road, that my parents fail to recognize my double identity.

Crime and Punishment

We let to tenants—the Dawsons: Ballet and piano lessons: H.E. Bates bases a short story on a court case against my father: My father is sent to prison: My mother takes over the bookshop: Mrs. Wheatley, the caretaker of Alexandra Palace does her best to care for us.

My parents are immersed in their financial problems. Bills are pushed through the letter-box to lie uneasily on the mat; summonses, threats of disconnection... to pile up and up into a nightmare of demands. My father refuses to discuss the matter. There is nothing he can do. My mother robs Peter to pay Paul, borrows money from friends, runs to Court to plead tearfully for time to pay. But as my father's meagre earnings from the shop fluctuate from week to week, my mother never knows how much there is to spend. My father has never discovered his average earnings for he keeps no account books, which at times brings him into conflict with the Inland Revenue. My mother remarks plaintively to an old friend, Mr. Grainger, following a brush by my father with the Income Tax Inspector, *"Charles does keep books spasmodically."* "Oh, well," Grainger replies *"why don't you claim you're following a new system—spasmodic book-keeping!"* It is ironic that a tax office is to replace the shop at 68/69 Red Lion Street; premises which maybe my father now haunts, waving before the frightened faces of the Inspectors and Clerks empty account books and theories of spasmodic book-keeping.

Micawberishly, my father goes from day to day convinced that something will turn up. My mother calls in the Relieving Officer. *"Sell everything"* he demands. The only furniture allowed is a table and a chair and bed each. My father shrugs. He does not need more than the minimum of furniture provided he is allowed to keep his books. My distraught mother looks about her house and sees it denuded of all that she has built up over the years and which exhibit her rise from a poor immigrant family. In her valued home all that would be left to denote her improved status is the Ideal Boiler. A boiler which she polishes as if it were Aladdin's Lamp, rubbing it down with emery paper until it shines, for to her it is magic, providing a warmth unknown to the cold rooms of her childhood, and the glory of running hot water. Deep in thought as to the future, she lifts the coal scuttle and feeds the boiler with shiny black coke; coke which is delivered several hundredweight at a time and tipped out with a shush and a bang into the coal-shed outside the kitchen window, my mother watching and counting in the bags.

At last my mother makes a decision. No, she will not sell up her precious home, furniture over which when especially depressed she sings a hymn learned long ago at her Portsmouth Church School:-

> *When upon life's billows you are tempest toss'd*
> *When you are discouraged thinking all is lost,*
> *Count your many blessings, name them one by one*
> *And it will surprise you what the Lord hath done.*
> *Count your blessings, name them one by one,*
> *Count your blessing see what God hath done,*
> *Count your blessings, name them one by one,*
> *And it will surprise you what the Lord hath done.*

As she sings, she counts out all that she values in the home, beginning, of course , with my sister and me, after which comes first the cherrywood Stromenger piano and after that the rest of the furniture.

My mother decides that because a regular income is necessary the top flat of our small house must be let out. And so my mother relinquishes her dream house to two over-crowded flats. We occupying the downstairs flat into which all our furniture is pushed.

The Dawsons move in, father, mother and two boys. My sister and I station ourselves behind the living-room door and gaze through the glass panel, into the hall to watch the arrival of the unknown. The boys dressed in short trousers and trailing behind their luggage laden parents until they mount the stairs and are lost to view. We listen for their footsteps above our heads in the three rooms lost to us. Now we must settle into the front room which becomes our bedroom, the living-room and a scullery. Later, my father is to add a conservatory, or lean-to, a playground for us children and a place to store bikes and garden tools. However, badly constructed by my father, it always leaks water and is too flimsy to be counted as an extra room.

There is, of course, the press room, empty by now of the press, but filled by books arranged on roughly built shelves on each wall and on and over the marble-type mantelpiece which eventually collapses under the weight, sending shock waves throughout the house. An overspill of books is set up in piles on the floor. This room is a dark place, the natural light coming only from French windows which open out to half a dozen concrete steps and overlook uneven asphalt, a drain and the old coke shed. For most of my childhood this room is kept locked and is, therefore, unfamiliar territory, so that even when quite big, I fear that some dark presence lurks behind the locked door. I stay close to my mother, or if I am alone in the house, I will not stay there, but go out and visit a friend.

Now that the top half of the house is let, all four of us pile into the front room to sleep and every morning my father awakens us with the first lines of *The Internationale*—"*Arise ye starvelings from your slumbers*"—in memory of his carefree earlier days in the lodging house run by the first 'Mrs.' Lahr. Soon the books from the press room next door are to spill over to usurp our living space between a double and two single beds, a tallboy and a wardrobe.

Upstairs, the Dawsons settle into their new-found home. Two of their three rooms are used for sleeping, but intent upon maintaining a 'parlour', the boys sleep in extending chairs in the large front room, these 'beds' being closed away each morning. Our toilet is outside, but it it necessary for us to share with the Dawsons the upstairs bath and wash-basin.

Boys are an unknown quantity to my sister and me—for while the Convent takes boys up to the age of eight years, they sit separately from the girls and play together, our eyes following them admiringly from a distance. We see them as free spirits, fearless, athletic, able to climb trees, to kick a ball and rush after it madly, play at fighting, get together in a scrum, form a unified lively and noisy group. All this acceptable because they are boys: "*Boys will be boys."* Certainly, they risk the cane, a punishment forbidden to us girls, but this makes them the more special in our eyes for they take it with a swagger and without a sound escaping through their clenched lips. Julian, an active force who whirls past us in the playground, and is known to us girls as 'the leader of the boys' is the most often caned by an irate nun, and we admire him totally. The sisters, shutting themselves away from close contact with the male sex, must have seen the punishment of these small boys as self-immolation.

Now, two of these magnificent creatures are to live close by us, but Alf and Fred attend the Council school and much to my mother's chagrin say 'me' instead of 'my' and drop their aitches. My mother is drawn three ways, between her financial need, her nurture of the Dawsons as good tenants, considerate and never behind with the rent, and her fear that my sister and I will pick up the boys' speaking habits. She retaliates by taking extra pains to maintain and raise our cultural standards. *"Where's me 'at"* she mimics them to us, so as to point out the missing aspirates. At this I lead my sister into a search for fallen aitches, all through our part of the house. *"I've found a dropped aitch!"* I call out, pretending to pick up something from the floor. *"So have I!"* says my sister gamely.

At that time standard English only is acceptable in 'educated' circles and cockney is the most frowned upon of dialects. As can be noted from old black and white English films shown on TV, in those days they presented all their characters, whether from villages or towns both north and south, as speaking RADA standard English. In my mother, alongside the normal aspirations of the intelligentsia there operated the craving of the immigrant to make 'good' in a new land, this spiced with a love of learning. She had no wish for my sister and me to be identified by our speech as working-class. She wanted her children to be accomplished and achieve and she longed for us to enter the professions or the arts. She saw the Convent curriculum, which included French, algebra and geometry, as offering so much more than her own schooling. Our opportunities and choices appeared to be wide open. It did not occur to my mother to question the calibre, or methods, of the teaching, or the rigours of the curriculum.

My mother determined to offer us an opportunity to excel in the arts, observes me with a gleam in her eye. She had read that Pavlova, a sickly child, had first been sent to ballet lessons to improve her health. I am knock-kneed from rickets, one foot turns inwards, I am round-shouldered and small for my age:

"Oonagh looks three times bigger in that photo" writes James Hanley to my mother *"Oonagh seems to swamp Sheila."* In compensation, he dedicates his book *"Sheila Moynihan"* to me.

Therefore, I am enrolled to attend at Gabrielle Rowley's Ballet School. My sister is enrolled to learn tap dancing. My mother does not view tap dancing as on the same cultural level as ballet, but perhaps she sees my prettier and sturdier sister as a future Ginger Rogers. And so she dreams Hollywood dreams.

At school we take piano lessons which are an extra and taught by an ice-maiden, Miss Batchelor. My sister is to continue with piano lessons into her teens, often perching a book on the music stand while practicing. *"How's your younger daughter?"* asks a neighbour. *"Playing Edgar Allen Poe on the piano!"* quips my mother. By that time I have long dropped out of piano lessons, the teacher's cold manner providing no encouragement. Every Good Boy Deserves Favour, **F A C E**: I saw no sense in such mouthings. Later, I am to learn the violin, progressing further than with the piano, but never very far.

However, in spite of these cultural advantages, Fred Dawson, three months younger than me, learns to read before I do so. My mother is mortified. Fred is a quiet, serious boy disciplined into quietness by home circumstances. He reads comics to me while we sit together on our kitchen floor; my mother fuming because, on the one hand I am unable to read them for myself, and on the other hand because she despises comics. Paradoxically, she frequently speaks to us with affection for the popular children's magazines of her youth, *The Gem*, *The Magnet*, *Greyfriars*, Bob Cherry, Billy Bunter. These, of course, were presented in written language without pictures, except by way of illustration. In time, with Fred's help, I learn to decipher the words bubbling out of the characters' mouths and this is how I learn to read. The school method of a large calendar-type book hoisted over the blackboard, each page showing a colour picture and a sentence such as 'Nat has a bat' or 'Dan has a pan' failing to interest me into literacy.

My mother is never to overcome her prejudice against comics, although when she finds that my sister and I are buying them anyway with our daily halfpennies—my sister *The Butterfly* and me *Jingles*, hiding ourselves in the upstairs bathroom to read them, she agrees to my father buying them for us at trade prices. To these comics my father adds the *Mickey Mouse Weekly*.

Mr. Dawson works as a night telephonist for the Post Office (nowadays British Telecom) earning some £3.00 per week, a good wage in those days, but while in the house the boys' lives are circumscribed by their father's need to sleep during the day, as are our own lives once the Dawsons move into Wilton Road. As there is more room to move about downstairs, which includes the garden, if we pass the boys in the hall, or they see my sister and I playing outside, they whisper, or signal *"ask us down to play!"* Once I have learned to read, the boys let down a message on a string from the bathroom window *"Ask my mum if we can come out to play,"* to which I write a short reply *"yes"* and watch the string being pulled up into Alf's hands. Then I climb the stairs to knock on the door of Mrs. Dawson's small kitchen. Sometimes Mrs. Dawson regards my intrusion with discomfiture, but pulling herself together she usually agrees to my request. This gives Alf, four years older than myself, an excuse to escape from parental supervision and creep out of the house to play with friends. But Fred is happy to be our companion, even though because of Mr. Dawson's work we must play quietly. Years later my mother is to remark how stressful she had found this situation, for she worried continually about the noise level, or if we were quiet, how long this comparative silence would last.

The Dawsons pay my mother fifteen shillings per week rent and, to supplement the family income, Mrs. Dawson works as a cleaner for private households. At home, she bustles about endlessly pursuing household tasks and my mental picture of her is of a sturdy woman, brown hair pulled back neatly, dressed in overalls and sweeping down the stair carpet with a hard brush. When my sister and I pass through the hallway, dressed-up in our mother's clothes with perhaps a net curtain over our heads, she turns to ask jokingly *"Who are you, then? The Queen of Sheba?"* It may well be that my sister still walks up those stairs carefully, flattening herself against the wall so as to avoid stepping on the kneeling, hard at work, Mrs. Dawson. At the top of the stairs my sister turns to answer the ever present question. *"The Queen of Sheba? No. I don't know who I am. I'm just dressed up."*

For the next few years, we are to live in close proximity to this English working-class family, but while our families are on friendly terms, we are never close and the relationship lasts only while we share a house. My father plays darts each Sunday with Mr. Dawson, a board set up in the conservatory, hung on a nail hammered into the outside wall of the house. My mother chats to Mrs. Dawson and takes an interest in her relatives. We play with Fred and welcome Alf, but too much militates against a close friendship.

Neither of my parents' cultural roots are with the English working-class, added to which we are landlords, they are tenants; we are 'in business', they are employees; we are at a private school, the boys are at a Council school. These attitudes are enforced by attendance at a fee-paying school, for all such establishments are blanketed by an aura of snobbery which hangs like a pall to blinker parents and children alike.

My mother, despite her socialist convictions, grasps at these evidences of our superiority for she needs to maintain faith in our family's cultural advancement so as to nourish her self-esteem. This because of our lack of material success declares us to the world to be of little worth—if you're so smart, why ain't you rich? And so, in this manner our house is divided, my sister and I are undergoing religious and social indoctrination and I am called to the barre. But there is worse to come.

The catastrophe comes about because my father cannot refuse to buy second-hand books offered him by customers, or visitors, to the shop. Books produced from battered suitcases, Gladstone bags, cardboard boxes, orange boxes or coat pockets. My father, who shed blood whenever he sold a book, could not envisage anyone voluntarily selling their library unless at starvation's door, or on the point of eviction from hearth and home. Therefore, whether he wanted the books or not—and some weeks he must have bought more books than he sold—he made a fair offer.

At the same time, while my father dealt mainly in secondhand books, he obtained new books to order and somehow it came to the attention of publishers, and the larger booksellers, that he was selling these below the Net Book Agreement price. In fact, it was not until 1989 that the Net Book Agreement was challenged by the larger booksellers and suggestion made that it should come under scrutiny from proposed restrictive practices legislation. In the 30s it was the order of the day and rumblings against my father and his undercutting in his small bookshop were gaining momentum. And then suddenly it comes to the attention of Foyles that some of their books had been stolen by 'customers' and sold to my father. At confirmation of this they pounce, intent upon killing two birds with one stone. My father is arrested and charged with receiving.

In a short story from *Something Short and Sweet*, titled 'No Country', H.E. Bates describes the Court case.[1] He calls my father 'Oscar' and begins:

> *Oscar's wife was Jewish. She was crying hard when I got to the Court. Oscar's face was strange, very yellow. It was as though he knew he were doomed himself.* "They'll deport me" *he said. He was tied up in knots of fear, almost beside himself.* "They'll turn me over to the Nazis. I know they'll deport me."
>
> "Have you said anything?" *I said.* "Have you signed anything?"
> "I made a statement." *He was done. I knew it.* "Did they make you do that?" *I said. No. He went down voluntarily. He dictated it. He had to. He knew if he didn't they'd send him back to Germany. To the Nazis. Now he'd put the statement in they'd give him a month and it would all be over.*
>
> "But you didn't do it… you haven't done anything. Just because somebody steals books and then brings them to you to sell doesn't mean you're a criminal. You didn't do anything."

Bates continues that my father stood in the dock: *"not only doomed, but already dead. His face had gone beyond yellow to dead whiteness, beyond fear of not knowing into the terror of knowledge."*

He describes the Magistrate as resembling *"a polished bladder of pink lard"* who insists on calling my father *"Obermann"* and after several irrelevant and taunting remarks, this personage hands down to my father a sentence of six months.

There is no doubt that Bates reports sympathetically the shocked reaction of my parents to this shattering of their lives, but he seems skeptical in the story of my parents' claims that my father is being persecuted for his politics. In private letters, though, he affirms it and rallies other for help. My parents insisted then, and always, that the detectives assigned to the case had threatened my father that if he did not plead guilty they would ask for his deportation to Germany. They would present him before the Court as a former member of the Communist Party and an associate of undesirables, such as socialists and an-

---

1. H.E. Bates, 'No Country', in *Something Short and Sweet*, 1937.

archists. My father, terrified of a Nazi concentration camp, was prepared to make a deal with the devil himself.

As it happens, in spite of my father's co-operation, the two detectives involved did apply for my father's deportation to Germany, but here my father was saved by his principles of internationalism, his refusal to belong to any country. He was found to be stateless and, therefore, without a country to which he could be deported. If only he had understood this point before pleading Guilty!

In prison, my father's humiliation, frustration and incarceration break out as a fierce, red rash which covers the whole of his body, itching and chafing against his rough clothing. Throwing them off he sits naked in his cell, covered in ointment provided as a balm. Born in him at this time are the anxieties which control him many years later when, at the age of eighty, and in a General Hospital, suffering from bronchial pneumonia, under the jurisdiction of others he is in panic. He will never get out, he will die here. He watches the door for my mother to come and take him by the hand. To lead him home. He knows she will never come. His eyes stare at the walls in fear, his shoulders erect, body stiff, face rigid. The lines ironed out by tension. He neither sees nor hears any of those around him.

Whether or not my mother visited my father in prison, I do not know. She did send him a bitter and accusing letter, although it was not only the events leading to his prison sentence which made her do this, but also details of his life which came to light once she had taken over management of the bookshop. In desperation she dips her pen in vitriol and watches as the marks she makes seep through the record of her anger and despair, searing past, present and future. The prison censor, opening her missive, finds his hands on fire and his eyes turned to water. Quickly pushing the letter away, he returns it to my mother as unfit for human consumption.

During my father's absence, it is at first agreed that while my mother takes over the management of the bookshop, my sister and I will be cared for daily at Wilton Road by a Mrs. Wheatley. Mrs. Wheatley is the caretaker of Alexandra Palace and an old friend of my father, for he had met her while he was interned there during the First World War. And, for some years, it was usual for my father to take me and my sister to visit her once a week on a Sunday morning. Up Colney Hatch Lane to Muswell

Hill Broadway, a little way down the hill and left and left again into the Grove. Run quickly along the pathway, past all the trees, to find the one that is hollow. Climb in through its rotted doorway to become part of the bark, leaves and birds nesting above. Although, more usually we walk up Goodwyns Vale, into Grosvenor Road, across Alexandra Park Road and down Grove Avenue. In a garden stands the statue of an Indian lady dressed in painted sari and holding with one hand a dish above her head. Her smile, enigmatic. My sister and I rush up the driveway, take her free hand and then relinquishing it, run down again out into the street, before the householder can raise a hue and cry. This statue which is taller than me, but shrinks as I grow.

Next we walk through the solid archway into the Palace, calling out 'hall-oo' and listening for the echo; across the tramlines and up the steps to the terrace to pat the stone lions. A long walk. *"carry me Dad"* and he gives us piggybacks, one at a time.

Mrs. Wheatley's sitting-room in the Palace is nothing extraordinary, except for the enormous circular window which dominates the cheap sticks of furniture, dull mats and lumpy sofa. Sometimes, Mrs. Wheatley takes us up through the trapdoor and onto the glass roof. I look down under my feet and I am walking on air. In the distance the whole world lies about me and I know that I am the only girl at the Convent to reach these strange heights. But I must hug the knowledge to myself for I am low in the pecking-order and any experience outside those of my class-mates will be regarded with disbelief.

Treading carefully on the cool glass, I fail to see myself far away in the then distant July 1980 when watching from a kitchen window, across the housetops, I see the orange and scarlet flames leaping fifteen foot and more into the air. I can almost hear the roar and crackle and cracking and spitting and crashing of falling panes of glass. A blaze warms my childish feet and I am obscured in black, thick smoke. Then we climb down again, through the trapdoor into Mrs. Wheatley's drab living-room.

In the story by H.E. Bates called *The Palace*[2], Mrs. Wheatley is named 'Mrs. Lemon' and presented as a woman well into middle-age, desperate in her isolated situation during the war, for she is as much a prisoner as the internees: *"Cut-off by the 153 steps, half forgotten by the authorities."* In her loneliness she becomes infatu-

---

2., Also in the book of short stories *Something Short and Sweet*, op. cit.

ated with my father, whom Bates has made an Austrian. She offers herself, but is refused.

That is not how my mother told it!

My father's relationship had begun with Mrs. Wheatley at a time when he was locked away into all male company, a hardship for my father who appreciated the presence of woman-kind. Mrs. Wheatley offered friendship and companionship, making him part of her family, for when all is said and done, he was a family man. Soon he had become the man of the house, putting up shelves, or taking them down, banging in nails or pulling them out, shifting furniture, repairing the broken, restoring the faltering and perfecting the imperfect. He took also an interest in Mrs. Wheatley's two young children, a boy and a girl, for she was some years younger than the 48 years given her by Bates. Soon my father becomes a substitute father to these children. At this time Mr. Wheatley, whom Bates describes as *"in uniform more rabbity than ever"* was away in the army. And so my father spent whatever time he could afford away from his duties, in the flat under the glass domes, the light shining down upon his naked head, for claustrophobia had caused him to temporarily lose his hair.

The duties upon which my father was engaged took place in the office where he typed out lists of internees, many of whom were to be sent on to the Isle of Man. This gave my father considerable power: to send only those internees willing to go, or to ruthlessly decide who was to be exiled. Perhaps this dire responsibility raised my father's stature in Mrs. Wheatley's eyes, but it caused my father many a heartache and headache for the Isle of Man camps were feared by all internees.

Peter and Leni Gillman in *Collar the Lot: How Britain Interned and Expelled its War-time Refugees*[3] write that the camp, to be built at a hoped-for profit by the Isle of Man Government, promised to take 5,000 internees. Therefore, the War Office began to ship internees to the island, but by the target date huts were ready for only 750 men. Over 1,300 were squeezed into this camp, while

3. Peter and Leni Gillman, *Collar the Lot: How Britain Interned and Expelled its War-time Refugees*, Quartet Books, 1980.

a further 900 were passed to Cunningham's Camp[4] which had a theoretical capacity of 2,400 and now held 3,300. Internees at Cunningham's Camp staged a protest demonstration against overcrowded conditions and the military guard—reservists from Lancashire and local volunteers—opened fire, killing five internees.

The Alexandra Palace internees sing:

Jesus loves me yes I know
So does the ragtime cowboy Joe,
He will save me if he can,
From going to the Isle of Man!

At that time my father was the ragtime cowboy and I have a photograph of him before he temporarily lost his hair, sitting on the second of four long steps in front of three glass-panelled wooden doors leading into the Palace. He is dressed smartly in a dark suit and tie, his feet well shod, his shoes shined. His dark hair combed to the side, a white parting severing the planes of his head. On his left arm at the cuff he wears a wide band, no doubt denoting his rank. He sports a neat moustache and is frowning. Sitting on his left are two more internees and seated on the fourth seat four more, all similarly dressed. The internees are flanked by khaki-clad soldiers, their legs wound around by puttees. Behind the seated group stand the Officers, NCO's and two civilians, one of the latter wearing a trilby hat and watch-chain.

On my father's release, the love affair with Mrs. Wheatley ended, but either from gratitude, or guilt, my father continues to visit the family. He must atone for she is now alone since Mr. Wheatley, getting wind of the affair, had abandoned his wife and children. The Wheatley son blames my father for the loss of his father; an attitude my father finds hard to take, for hadn't he taught the boy to read? To my father books were the reality. When I was a year or two old, he took me along as a chaperone on these visits. But some fear of hurting Mrs. Wheatley prevented him from telling her of his marriage, and so I am presented as his niece, until I begin to talk and call him Daddy. Then, my father,

---

4. A freelance enterprise owned by a farmer named Cunningham who did his best to make a profit from the ten shillings per week which the government paid to him to house and feed each internee. The internees slept in tents, but with the approach of winter such conditions were untenable.

shame-faced, admits his masquerade. However, Mrs. Wheatley must have forgiven my father, or perhaps she was one of life's natural victims and expected little for herself. Whatever—when the catastrophe struck she agreed to help out.

I remember Mrs. Wheatley as a nervous, plain, dumpy figure, hair pulled back severely, clothes drab. Although she had two grown-up children of her own and was grandmother to a small blond boy, she was always at a loss as to how to talk to both my sister and me. When we visited her at the Palace we were expected to sit quietly on the sofa while she and my father conversed, about what I do not know. Should we show signs of wanting to move about, or explore other rooms, usually the kitchen as the door was left open, she ceased her conversation, or listening, and hovered behind us anxiously and uselessly, until my father, at last noticing her distress, called us to come and sit down again.

On the face of it, the task of caring for my sister and me daily in our own home was not too onerous, for except for Saturday we would be at school all day and, of course, my mother took care of us on Sunday. But, my sister and I were not our normal selves—we were in shock. My father had spent long hours at the shop, but I had always felt that he was on the point of arriving home. Now this comfort was lost. No more Friday evenings, the one day when he made an effort to be home before we went to bed. Sitting in our nightclothes we wait in anticipation for him to come down the side entrance, wheeling his bicycle. He peers at us through the kitchen window and we scream in pleasure. We know that he will have for each of us a Woolworths 3d or 6d toy—a clockwork bird, animal, car, a top or a celluloid doll. Millions, billions, trillions of toys lying on the heap: broken springs, legless dolls, empty teddy bears, torn crayon books and broken crayons. Playthings for dead people. Nor is my father there to rock us one at a time on his knee to recite:

Hoppe, hoppe Reiter,
Wenn er fällt, dann schreit er.
Fällt er in die Hecken,
Pressen ihn die Schnecken,
fällt er in den Klee,
schreit er gleich: O weh!...

At the words '*fällt er in den Klee*' (should he fall in the clover) my father pretended to let us fall, and we squealed in appreciation.

We had known that it was all pretence and that he would never let us down. Now we were not so sure.

Mrs. Wheatley waits upon my sister and me like a timorous ghost and each evening I watch for my mother in an agony of suspense, half believing that she too will be lost to us. I am fretful and uncommunicative and can set my mind to nothing until I hear her key in the door and see her enter.

One week of Mrs. Wheatley doing all she can for us and both my sister and I are in bed with vomiting and diarrhea. Mrs. Wheatley hovering over us and murmuring distractedly that the stew she had served us was good, there was nothing in it which could have made us so sick. The responsibility weighed down upon her. She shrunk in upon herself, her head drooping into her neck, her shoulders bowing, her face fading into the bones of her skull, the bones still and brittle. It is all too much.

I am lying in a room darkened by curtains drawn-to. My sister in her bed, I in mine. At the open doorway my mother and Mrs. Wheatley stand like sullen statues. We are submerged under my mother's frustration and despair and Mrs. Wheatley's impotence. As we watch, my mother looms larger and Mrs. Wheatley shrinks away into the distance until she dwindles away out of our lives. It is at this point it is decided that we board weekly at the Convent.

There is no doubt that a child has much in common with a prisoner, for the infant is subject to the dictates and whims of others. And this lack of authority affects the manner in which time passes, the hours becoming days, the days weeks, the weeks months and the months years. Therefore, I do not know how long I was confined to the Convent, probably for no more than a year, but it was a year which affected all that went before, and after.

Detained

I board at the Convent: My defender Marguerite Poisson: I am visited by my Aunt Mary and Cecil: Poems from hymn titles.

One of the worst aspects of boarding school for me was to watch the day-pupils walk out of the open school door, past the lime trees in the triangular driveway and through the strait iron gateway onto the pavements outside. I follow their progress with my eyes, grieving for my lost freedom.

On Sunday mornings our mother hurries to the Convent to take us home with her until Monday morning, the time passing all too quickly and instead of enjoying my temporary liberty, I fret that I must soon return to the confines of the Convent. Sometimes, on a Monday morning I stretch out on my bed crying that I feel ill and cannot return. My mother, gathering up our clothes, or performing last minute chores, turns away her face, her expression stiff as she is forced by circumstances to close her ears against my entreaties. So once again I return to the Convent with my sister, to sleep in a long white dormitory, the two rows of iron bedsteads covered by dead white counterpanes. Along both side walls stand cubicles from which hang blanched white curtaining. Between these cubicles on both sides of the room, long windows give a glimpse of gardens on the one side and the triangular drive-way on the other.

The cubicles are allocated to the older girls and enviously I wish that I too could hide behind these hangings. Instead, my sister and I sleep on beds alongside one another, she cuddling a brown woolly toy dog, which she tells me she pretends is our mother, me hugging a soft toy cat with light blue-white fur. A larger cubicle at each end of the room is occupied by the two nuns set to guard over us, Sister St. Wilfrid and Sister St. Francois.

To us children, Sister St. Wilfrid dressed in her long black habit, white bonnet and black veil, appears ancient, but my mother surprises me by referring to her as 'a young girl'. She is one of the few Irish nuns at the Convent, tall and thin, the skin of her face pale and freckled, her eyes green, the colours that announce auburn hair. I imagine it as long and luxuriant, pulling on the Sister's tall, narrow frame. But imagination has to suffice, for there is no way in which I am going to see the nun's head without a cover and, anyway, it may well be that her head was shaven.

Sister St. Wilfrid has some sympathy for the children in her charge. Perhaps she is not so many years older than the girls in the cubicles, and finds the elderly French nuns hopelessly old-fashioned, for at night she reads to us not from the slim, green-covered *Children's Realm*, but from what I know later to be *More William* by Richmal Crompton. We lie in our regimented lines on our iron bedsteads while at the further end of the half-lit dormitory Sister St. Wilfrid sits on a chair, her black gown shading into the gloom. If I peep over the blankets I can see the white of her bonnet as she bends her head over the book:

> *William was frankly bored. He disliked facts, and he disliked being tied down to detail, and he disliked answering questions. As a politician a great future would have lain before him.*

Of course, the levity of such as the William books was absolutely forbidden and especially at bedtime, for did not the catechism itself adjure us to lie ourselves down with thoughts of death? This stricture making it necessary for Sister St. Wilfrid to keep handy *The Children's Realm* and should Sister St. Francois appear before her appointed time, slap, bang, wallop, the William book was hidden away and stories of sinning, punishment, repentance and forgiveness, or a story from *The Lives of the Saints* (simplified and expurgated) were substituted.

I liked Sister St. Wilfrid because her disregard for the rules meant that she was on our side. But nothing is consistent in this world for Sister St. Wilfrid's attitude to coughing at night caused me much worry. Coughing seemed to drive her crazy and on the first cough she appeared in a long white nightdress, her head covered by a shawl. *"Stop that coughing!"* she'd hiss, her face looming angrily over the head of the bed. I try to stifle the sound, hand pressed over mouth, throat held still, breath imprisoned, but at last the strangled cough explodes into the night. Sister St. Wilfrid stalks away to leave me to wait in trepidation. Soon she returns with an enamel mug filled by a thick brownish not unpleasant liquid tasting like licorice. A liquid which I would have been glad to receive if I had not first been imbued with a feeling of guilt.

A few years later Sister St. Wilfrid renounces her vows and returns to lay life. When I hear of this defection from my mother, for I am no longer a pupil at that Convent, I find it difficult to understand for in those days to me a nun was a nun was a nun.

Perhaps it is apt that in an environment in which spiritual beings and unseen deities are presented as more real and desirable than human kind, I see visions. Mine, however, are of a different calibre to those seen by St. Bernadette or others of the saints. I lie awake at night, sheet pulled up to my eyes, and watch small, misshapen elfin creatures playing leap-frog across the dormitory. Silently back and forth in a mute dance which I follow with my eyes. Or am I dreaming? Or between waking and sleeping? Or seeing pictures on my inner eye-lid? It seems very real at the time and the memory is unlocked for me by a book by Doris Lessing in *The Children of Violence* series. Whatever—I hugged these visions to myself, for these extra-terrestrials had no place in Catholic doctrine and at home my parents professed to be rationalists. A conviction on which my mother with her love for films, novels and a belief in telepathy, held narrow tenure. But, for their children a belief in fairies or Father Christmas was definitely out. And yet, I am frightened of being alone in that dormitory, not because of anything I can see, but of the unseen lurking behind the icy white cubicle curtains, or just outside the long, second-floor windows, seemingly isolated from the ground: or behind the swing doors at each end of the room: or behind the washroom door: or lying under the cold white counterpanes.

My sister must have had similar fears for on the one occasion when she is ill and left alone, the sole occupant of this seemingly never ending blanched room, she screams so loundly that even in the school hall and dining room her cries can be heard. Hurriedly the nuns confer, talking in French, running this way and that. At last a decision is made. *"Go to your sister"* and I am hauled up two flights of stairs and deposited by her bedside. However, when it is my turn to be ill, I am considered old enough to bear the punishment alone. I lie in bed and watch the dead still cubicle curtains hanging in their stiff folds. I listen to the creaking of the building and await the presence of the maker of creeping footsteps. I watch the swing doors which seem about to open. I wonder who is hiding behind the washroom door. Outside the windows the tops of trees move as if stirred by an unseen hand. I lie and listen to the stillness in which I am wrapped. At last, in panic, I grab my neatly folded clothes from out of the white bedside locker and hurriedly dress myself to run in terror down the long back staircase—straight into the stolid large kitchen nun whose job it is to bring me food. She grabs hold of me and shouts angrily in French, for she knows no English. I watch her large angry face, the eyes glaring, the mouth moving and I shake with fright. She half carries me back to the dormitory, strips me, shoves my nightdress over my head, throws me on to the bed and beats my bare backside, her heavy hands coming down again and again. It is in this manner I discover that human kind with power over the defenceless is more terrible than the supernatural.

My nights and days are filled by arbitrary decisions against which I can make no verbal complaint or explanation, for a child is not allowed to speak to a nun or teacher, except in answer to a direct question. And, of course, in those days absolute silence reigned in the classroom, this was so in all schools, but to the nuns with their admiration for closed and silent orders, such silence must have been doubly valued. The sacrifice of communication being seen as a saviour of souls. It is not for many years that the teachings of Piaget and other educationalists are to perssuade schools that by speech young children, and perhaps all of us, develop thought, for as Mandelstam writes in a poem:

> I have forgotten the word that I wanted to say,
> So my thought, unembodied,
> Returns once more
> To the shadows

An understanding of child development, undermined in the 1990s by Tory and New Labour governments, intent upon returning education to the 1930s.

At that time, in the absence of speech, but overcome by a need for communication, a girl would sometimes post a note to a friend on the other side of the class. This voluntary writing and grammatical phrasing not being valued by the authorities, for if the culprit was caught punishment followed. The note which stands out most clearly in my memory is that seized in passing by Pamela George, a tense, dark-blonde, eight-year-old. The note, intended for the girl sitting by Pamela's side, said no more than *"see you at playtime,"* this message travelling joyfully from one end of the classroom to the other, assisted on its way by classmates until it arrives at Pamela's desk. Seizing it she springs from her seat and triumphantly presents the note to the nun sitting at her desk in front of the class.

Pamela George dies that summer during the holidays and the nuns describe to us children her last agony, how unable to breathe, Pamela had begged to be taken to Mass. They tell us of her goodness, thoughtfulness, obedience... and all I can think of is *"she was a sneak"* and I wish that I had liked her better. However, I ring round in black ink Pamela George's name in my autograph book and take to myself some of the glory of having known someone who had died.

Of course, when it comes to speech, in the dead regime of the Convent where all is ordered from rising to sleeping, words are superfluous. We rise at first bell to be shepherded into the washroom, a line of white pedestal basins, where we dip our hands and faces hurriedly in cold water. In the dormitory we pull on vest, liberty bodice, navy blue knickers, black stockings, a navy blue jumper edged with white, a striped tie. Our shoes are black. In early summer the jumper is replaced by a white blouse and in the midst of summer by a navy blue and white school dress. Dressed and passed as neat and tidy, before breakfast we walk in a line down the stairs to the Chapel, which I see always dressed in Lenten mauve, the statues hidden behind their shrouds. The red glass lamp hangs from the ceiling on a golden chain, a faint glow of light within it announcing the presence of God the Father, the Son and the Holy Ghost. Three persons in one. One morning I disgrace myself in this Chapel for in its quiet cloisters wind blows around my intestines and exits from the only place open to it. Out it comes with a crack, to crash against the walls and tip up the altar, toppling the priest in his long robes arse over head. The light in the red holder flickers, in shock the praying nuns are torn from their seats, their pews cast asunder. I am seized and thrust out of the Chapel, to creep with shame into the Assembly Hall where I sit in a corner, dreading the appearance which I must put in at breakfast:

Bless us O Lord
and these Thy gifts
Which we are about to receive
through Thy bounty
From Christ Our Lord. Amen.

Breakfast begins every morning with a bowl of gruel-like porridge in the centre of which has been placed a desert spoonful of white granulated sugar, wet and brown at the edges, making a raised oval pattern. This uniform shape decorating all the bowls lined up on the long table. And each bowl of porridge which I have eaten since bears this same mark, whether it be stodgy, unsweetened or salty. Just as all custard to me is lumpy, even now when I cook it for myself, smoothing out the lumps before they form. I eat it carefully, feeling each particle with my tongue and I am back in the Convent dining-room, sitting at the table in isolation, for dinner is over for all but me. I must eat my custard. I gag on it. I cry. The salty tears joining the yellow mess on my plate. At last I have eaten enough to satisfy the watching nun and am allowed to go. Or I am weeping in front of a plate of white blancmange covered in a red sauce. Years later, in a restaurant, I try once again to eat this thick glutinous mass and spoon up the red liquid, but cannot do so and sick and shaking at last push it away.

These are the foods I remember, for they made eating a misery. I recall also the clear soup served up every day. A soup, which even the French nuns fail to call *consomme*. Too clear for us, and so we rectify this by breaking bread and dropping the pieces into it, to soak up the colour and texture and lie like dead swimmers in the pale liquid. It is certain that nature, if left to itself, would have us eat only when hungry, but modern civilisation demands set times for everything, so that from childhood we are programmed to respond automatically. Food piled onto a plate and placed before a child at a certain hour demands 'eat or be found guilty'. Therefore, to relieve the tedium of such meals I form the food on my plate into a model world. I demolish mountains, swim seas, land on foreign shores, fall into craters and meet giants.

But the food at meal-times is not the worst of my worries. For as it happens, my sister and I are the youngest boarders and all those older than us, if only by a year or two, are entitled to govern our behaviour. "*Don't hold your knife like a pencil... don't twist round in your chair... keep your elbows off the table... don't eat so quickly... slowly... don't put so much in your mouth... don't... don't... don't... don't your mother and father teach your anything? Do they eat like you... I expect they do!*" I hear the sneer and in frustration my chest becomes taut, my limbs stiffen, my neck rigid, my hands clench and unclench and then the temper welling within me arrives at my face to twist it into the ugliest of grimaces. My tormentors are taken aback. "*Look at her face!*" they gasp. I am odd, beyond their comprehension. A madness. They are uneasy and retreat.

We give Thee thanks O Mighty God
For all Thy benefits
Which we have received through Thy bounty
From Christ Our Lord. Amen.

These bullies can be no more than twelve years old, but to my sister and I they are 'big girls'. The oldest boarders at the Convent at this time are about fourteen or fifteen years of age and the two of them are named Joan: Joan Batchelor and Joan Hastings, and I don't remember either of them ever talking to me. Joan Batchelor's parents are in India and she has been boarding at the Convent since the age of five. A tall, well-built girl, well groomed, face pale and closed in upon itself. She is not a Catholic, nor is Joan Hastings, and I cannot remember whether or not they attended at Chapel. Joan Hastings has short brown hair, ruddy complexion and is livelier than her friend. Once a year Joan Batchelor's parents come to England and visit her at the Convent. They walk around the school premises and Mrs. Batchelor, a beautifully dressed grey-haired lady, bends towards me in the manner usual to an adult towards a small child with whom they have no connection, and says kindly "*you're Sheila.*" I can't deny it, but am embarrassed. Soon both parents, the father tall and grey-haired, move away in stately fashion.

Joan Batchelor is to stay at the Convent until the age of eighteen, when a few months prior to the outbreak of the Second World War, she is to join her parents and return home with them to England after a short holiday. How does she feel? After a gap of thirteen years to live with these stranger parents" For so many years she has been surrounded by women only, now she will learn to know the presence of a man, her father. But this is denied her, for the very day before Joan is to fly out to India, her father is killed in an air crash. She flies out to comfort a mother she barely knows.

The two Joans to me are on a par with the nuns and I have little or no contact with them. It is the younger girls, older than me, who are the bane of my life. For instance, two of the nuns have taken the boarders for a walk for which we form a crocodile and I am walking beside my sister. With mounting excitement I follow the route down Colney Hatch Lane and my heart almost bursts as we turn into Wilton Road. I look across the road to find my house. Yes, it is there, there looking across at me! Is my mother inside, will she open the front door and call me in? I falter. I am a captive in another world, but I can gain some comfort from knowing that the promise of the house is there. *"Hurry up!"* says a girl behind me. *"I'm looking at my house"* I say and all the girls look across at the red brick and brown paint-work of the small semi-detached house at Wilton Road. *"Look at that awful paint-work!"* Ursula says scathingly. *"Can you wonder the two of them are like they are, coming from such a slum!"* The other girls agree and as now miserably I watch my house, the dull brown paint flakes off to leave dirty white scars. The whole house sags.

In my defencelessness, I need to find a protector and I discover this in Marguerite Poisson, a good surname, for I am pisces and my symbol is a fish. She is the daughter of an English mother and French father and while her name has embossed itself in gold letters in my memory, I cannot recall her appearance. I think that she wore her brown hair short, was slightly built and aged about twelve or thirteen. Why she chose to be my guardian I do not know. Perhaps at first it was merely that she was kinder to me than were the others, I showed my liking for her which, in its turn had a knock-on effect. I know that I want to please her and show my gratitude, so that when on one Empire Day 23rd April, for which we are given a half-day holiday from lessons, she explains to me that the British Empire is the biggest in the world, I reply, without any true knowledge, *"but the French Empire is the next biggest"*! It is not that she would intervene with the other girls on my behalf, but she would whisper afterwards *"don't take any notice. They don't mean it."* Or she would listen to me when I spoke to her and answer me pleasantly and seriously.

If I knew more about this girl I could explain a terrible happening when in the middle of supper she runs from the dining-room table and into the Assembly Hall, under the looped climbing ropes hanging from the ceiling, past the wall-bars, the horse and the stacked balancing forms. Marguerite is pursued by Sister St. Francois, the nun's black garments rustling with anger as she treads after the terrified girl, her quarry. The air bristles around us, working itself into a frenzy of electric sparks so that flashes crackle against the walls and hit the ceilings over our heads, paralysing the girls at the table. Marguerite screams and the girls who are placed near to the open connecting door, whisper that Sister St. Francois has hold of her and is banging her head against the wall. Screams, cries, the sound of running footsteps, terror, are all that remain to me now.

My sister and I learn to make the best of it. What else can we do? And we find diversions. For instance, immediately after school on a Wednesday the Catholic children must attend at the chapel for Benediction. When a day girl, I longed to join the non-Catholics and go out of the school door onto the gravelled triangle, past the large lime trees and through the strait gate onto the pavement outside. But the vigilant Sister St. Clare, the keeper of the gate, kept a sharp look out for defaulters so that even on one occasion when I genuinely forgot that it was a Wednesday, she pulled me back inside. Now I am a boarder and dreams of escape impossible. I am done for. Kneeling side by side my sister and I each take a hymn-book from the pew behind. *Tantum ergo* and *O Salutaris Hostia* are our favourites, for they all have the mystery of abracadabra: *"Tantum ergo sacramentum, veneremur cernui"* we sing, rolling our tongues around the unfamiliar words and guessing at the pronunciation. *"Et antiquum documentum, novo cedat ritui."* Our part in the ceremony over and the priest dressed in his long white cassock and gold-threaded stole at the altar, we amuse ourselves by pointing out to each other the title page in the hymn-book, making poems by reading the titles one after another; stifling giggles and bending our heads to hide from authority our enjoymebt:

All creatures of our God and King
Alleluia
Alleluia, sing to Jesue
All God's people come together
All people that on earth do dwell
All the earth proclaim the Lord

Come and bless, come and praise
Come and Worship
Come, my brothers, praise the Lord
Fear not, rejoice and be glad
Glorious God
God is Love
How good it is to know your name
Immortal, invisible, God only wise
It's me, O Lord

We rejoice especially at those titles which seem to fit together snugly:

Ding dong! Merrily on High
Go Tell it on the Mountain

In this manner, and very much a captive audience, we alleviate the boredom of religious practice. **Amen**.

In Trouble

My mother makes unpleasant discoveries: Problems in the extended family: My cousin Florrie needs help: Cecil is incarcerated in Colney Hatch.

Meanwhile, back at Wilton Road my mother hurries each day to the bookshop in Red Lion Street. No longer do Oliver Cromwell, Henry Ireton and John Bradshaw follow at a distance, conversing and traversing a path now lost. Instead their decapitated bodies hang from a gibbet in the Square while my mother walks quickly by, her face averted. And as she half runs, she feels the presence of the condemned on their way to Tyburn struggling vainly to free limbs bound to hurdles which take them inexorably down the concreted-over banks of the lost river Bourne.

I know nothing of how my mother coped from day to day to earn our keep. Her knowledge of the book business was almost as good as my father's and her business sense rather better, but on opening the shop door on that first morning she feels as if this task is insuperable. In *Corruption of a Poet*, Kenneth Hopkins writes:

The shop was about ten feet by twelve, and the front wall was all window... As the window was lined floor to ceiling with books, and had also a screen at the back, practically no light penetrated... The walls were lined with books, and in the middle was a gas radiator over which a rickety arrangement of shelves supported, precariously, a great pile of periodicals, books, pamphlets, a typewriter, string, about two thirds of a loaf, several pipes and various oddments of India rubber, cheese, carbon paper.

That morning there are no customers, but she shrugs off her misery by tidying the heaps, moving them from one pile to another. She then sets about examining the shelves, endeavouring to memorise the whereabouts of the stock. A difficult task, for if my father had any system of classification he kept it to himself. *"Hello!"* says a man's voice behind her. *"I didn't expect to see you open."* She stiffens. Here is someone who knows the dreadful family secret. She returns to confront a respectably dressed man in dark suit and hat. *"Where's Charlie?"* *"He's ill"* my mother mumbles. *"Sorry about that. So you've taken charge. No wonder you're open so early, he's never here before eleven thirty and quite often not until the afternoon."*

This puzzles my mother, for my father has left the house before eight o'clock each morning, having first brought my sister and me the juice of a squeezed out orange. Here is a mystery and she worries over it all day and the next and the next, for the remarks concerning my father's short business hours continue throughout the succeeding days. Of course, she knows it was necessary for my father to shut the shop while he searched for books ordered, cycling round other secondhand bookshops, or the Farringdon Road Book Market, but surely this had not taken up every morning of the working week? She determines upon finding an answer and at last she drags out of friends, acquaintances and customers the reluctant admission that my father spent much time in the pub, both morning and evening, and she also finds out about Phyllis Marshall, who is ever after called 'the fat woman' by my mother. With regard to 'the fat woman', in 1990 my sister tells me a story which I must have heard previously and then put away in the folded recesses of my memory. My sister says:

> My mother is home alone with a small child and a baby, the time dragging by, almost standing still, as she wipes over the scullery floor, sweeps the kitchen and undertakes the hundred and one tasks necessary for the care of a family. If Sheila and the baby sleep for an hour or two this afternoon she can live vicariously in a book, a few pages of which she snatches at each day. Suddenly, she hears a key in the door. My father? She glances at the clock. If so, he is before his time. She opens the kitchen door to look up into the hallway and sees him moving slowly towards her, behind him a large dark-haired woman.

My mother calls out "Is anything wrong?" *In her voice is the beginnings of panic. My father doesn't look at her, but walks into the kitchen, forcing her to retreat, the fat woman following and pushing past my mother.* "You can go" *my father says truculently to my mother, refusing to meet her eyes.* "Phyllis will take care of the children." *My mother looks at my father's stubborn face and shaded eyes. She examines the large woman.* "Another earth mother" *she says to herself.*

"And then Mum was very clever" *says my sister. My mother speaks calmly and with an effort shrugs her shoulders.* "I'd better show you where everything is kept" *and she exhibits the nappies to be washed, the sink, the bottles to be boiled and the milk to be prepared, my special toddler diet, the floor cloth, the broom, the dustpan and brush, the gas copper, the saucepans, the larder, the vegette in which lie vegetables to be peeled and cooked, the beds to be made... until 'the fat woman' takes fright and runs out of the house calling out that Charlie had made a mistake and she can't stay.*

How that left my parents I do not know, but they survived somehow, pushing the incident away to be remembered only on odd occasions, my father more successful in this than my mother.

My sister makes no effort to forget. She has brooded on the matter for more than forty years, this story related to her by my mother growing in her concern as one year piles on another. Desperate to discover the secret of 'the fat woman' shortly before my father's death in 1971 she has spent her days in diligently searching my father's mail, both past and present. At last she is rewarded with a carefully folded yellowing letter in his trouser pocket and as she touches the creased paper a thrill of anticipation runs up her finger-tips, into her hand, up her arm, across her heart to culminate who knows where? It is a letter, affectionate, even loving, signed 'Phyllis'. My sister has struck oil.

By now my father is confined to one room, surrounded by newspapers, books and letters going back half a century, dusty heaps littering the room, yellow mouldering paper, fading ink. His legs ulcerated, his energy failing. "Would you like Phyllis Marshall to visit you?" my sister asks him. "Who? I don't know what you mean" my father growls, looking away and ducking his head. "Phyllis Marshall" my sister says, implacable, almost spelling it out. "You're both old and don't have much time left. She could come over to *visit and talk about the past. Cheer you up." "I don't know what you're talking about"* my father says. *"I found a letter from her in your trouser pocket"* my sister says patiently. *"I've had no letters"* my father insists doggedly. My sister can go no further with my father, but she will not leave the matter alone. She must track down 'the fat woman' to her lair. To tell her of my father's condition and the little time left to both of them.

The address written at the head of the letter is in Russell Square, and so my sister checks the telephone book to ascertain that 'the fat woman' still lives there. Thus armed, she then dials the number. *"Yes?"* replies a cautious voice. My sister announces herself and the connection is immediately broken. She phones again and again with the same result until P. Marshall's phone registers a permanently engaged number. It, and she, off the hook. My sister rethinks the matter. If the mountain won't come to Mahomet, Mahomet must go to the mountain. She takes the 'bus to Tottenham Court Road and walks through side streets to Russell Square. The flat in which Phyllis Marshall lives is in a block and at its entrance my sister is faced by an interphone. She presses the buzzer. *"Yes?"* asks a cautious voice. My sister announces herself and adds quickly *"I only want to see you for a moment to speak about my father."* There is no reply. She pushes and pulls at the entrance door, but it will not budge. She presses the tradesmen's and other buzzers to the flats, with no result. She is locked out. What can she do? She goes to see Rhys Davies who lives close-by and he operates his buzzer on her behalf. She walks up the stairs to his flat where he is waiting by the open front door. She stands in the hallway. *"I only want to speak to Phyllis Marshall"* my sister explains. *"To invite her to visit my father now that they're both so old and don't have much time left."* Rhys, himself old and frail, promises to see what can be done. He is puzzled. Why has Oonagh called upon him? Why, after all these years, should she want Phyllis to visit Wilton Road? My sister returns home and waits and waits, but Phyllis never arrives and my father dies leaving my sister frustrated and unresolved.

To my mother, the knowledge that up to the time of his imprisonment my father had continued the liaison with 'the fat woman' makes her very bitter. Especially so when she begins to realise that he has been oiling the relationship with money—small sums to be sure, but in times of hardship an additional commitment has taken the very food from out of her children's mouths. She knows now why they were always so desperately short of money, for not only was my father paying towards Phyllis' support, but dribbling money away on drink. Often he had arrived home late smelling of beer, to meet my mother's aggrieved look. Her mouth drooping, her eyes accusing. Old-fashioned. He feels her unspoken censure and mumbles, his expression sulky. *"I stopped on the way home for only one pint. I saw a customer and he paid for it."* Or sometimes, but not too often, *"A good customer asked me to have a drink with him while he wrote out a big order."* *"What big order"* my mother asks, but she never gets to the end of this story.

Of course, my sister and I know that my father likes a drink for each week on our way home from Alexandra Palace, he disappears through the doors of each pub on the route, leaving us to wait for him on the step. Occasionally, he reappears for a moment to thrust at each of us in turn his beer glass so that we can sip a little of the brown liquid. Then once more he vanishes through the swing doors. This becomes our usual routine until a neighbour living opposite one of the pubs, complains to the police that each Sunday she witnesses the corruption of young souls from demon drink. After that none of the pubs will serve my father. I wonder what all the fuss is about for I don't even like the bitter taste of the stuff and sup it only to please my father whom, I know, has offered it so as to reassure his children that they are not forgotten.

How long my father would have borne this walk from the Palace each Sunday without sustenance I do not know, for his conviction intervened and later he was to say that imprisonment saved him from alcoholism. Although, to the end of his life he enjoyed a glass of beer, never again was he to drink excessively. Instead, he would go into a pub, buy one pint only and putting the glass to his lips, perform the act of swallowing quickly without once removing the glass from his lips. All eyes upon him while the brown beer vanished down his gullet.

My mother might have been able to hide my father's drinking and love affair from her mother and sister, but she could not, and did not attempt to hide my father's arrest. Instead, in her distress she runs to my grandmother who, putting aside all dissatisfaction with my mother's life-style, rushes to sustain her hurt child. In the short story about the court case in *Something Short and Sweet*, Bates describes my grandmother as *"a dusky Jewess with sausage hands and a mouth wracked by the immemorial pain of the race."* Not a picture I recognise, for my grandmother was fair, blue-eyed and slight of build and, if her mouth was 'wracked' at the time, it was in misery for and sympathy with my mother.

My mother might not have to worry about her mother's reactions, but those of Becky are to be dreaded. However, as it happens, at this time my Aunt has troubles of her own so that she barely notices those of the Lahr family. The nineteen year old Florrie is pregnant and unmarried. 'In trouble' as the vernacular put it. *"She's in trouble... trouble... trouble..."* the word becoming synonymous for me, when a child, with pregnancy outside marriage. Now this 'trouble' has become personified for me in the thickening form of my cousin Florrie, for she has 'loved unwisely and too well'. She has met a suave older man, several years her senior, in fact, probably old enough to be her father and she has believed his professions of love, his plans for their future together, his intention to open a business with her as a partner. Now he, Raymond, tells the gullible girl that he is married, and makes use of the male get-out *"How do I know it's my child you're carrying?"*

I had met Raymond shortly at a time when Florrie had brought him to Wilton Road to parade him before my mother as her intended. He sits in a wooden armchair to the side of my mother's pride and joy, the Ideal Boiler. His crumpled face grins at us wolfishly. Florrie, a plump girl whose straight brown hair is twisted into curl, her pale face marked by the excrescences of acne, sits at the table watching him anxiously, hanging onto his every word. When Raymond, with Florrie trailing after him, has left the house, my mother says firmly *"He's a white slave trader."* My mother knows about such things for East End girls have taken in this knowledge with their mother's milk, have breathed it in with the air of the streets, have whispered bed-time stories which tell of how many an immigrant girl arriving alone at the docks, confused and unable to communicate, has been trapped into a life of shame. Girls walked a tightrope between poorly paid exploitive wearisome work regarded as respectable, and a life in the gutter. As women hurry through the streets, a white slaver takes shape on every street corner, waiting to lure, or abduct, them away from family and friends. For, as William Fishman writes:

> *Here (in England) young men were employed to pick up lonely girls embarking at the dockside and inveigle them to a place of refuge which soon revealed itself as a brothel. Within the ghetto*

the single girl, living alone provided a permanent challenge to the seducer-cum-procurer.[1]

Even Sylvia Pankhurst and Nora Smyth are caught up in this panic on 3rd January while walking to Hackney through Victoria Park. Sylvia is liable for arrest and imprisonment under the Prisoners' Temporary Discharge for Ill Health Act 1914 (known as Cat and Mouse Act). They keep a sharp look out for police and when they are confronted by plain clothes detectives turn to run, but at that moment, from all four corners of the park a crowd comes hurrying. Word had gone around that 'white slave traffickers' are at their nefarious work. The crowd shout and threaten the men, getting between them and the two suffragettes, to push the men away. Until, to the crowd's delight, a uniformed Constable arrives. *"Go with him, my dears"* the crowd calls. *"You'll be safe with him."* And so Sylvia is seized and taken to Holloway prison.[2]

However, it is beside the point as to whether, or not, Raymond is a white slave trafficker, what is more to the point is that Florrie is pregnant and he doesn't want to know about it. Weeping, she comes to my mother. She has told her own mother, my Aunt Becky, but both of them are frightened of Gussy's reaction. *"He won't let me stay at home. He'll throw me out!"* Florrie cries. *"I can't have this baby."* This at a time when many an unmarried mother was certified as 'morally defective' and confined to a lunatic asylum for life, or sent to a colony for the feeble minded. Her child taken away at birth to be lost in the labyrinths of institutions. But my mother will not see this child harshly ejected from the womb while yet an amoeba—the victim of castor oil, slippery elm, Bols gin, a knitting needle or concoction from a sympathetic chemist, to bleed into the white bath and be swirled down the plughole, glug, glug, glug, into the seething sewers. Instead, she makes Florrie a promise that if her father turns her out she can stay with us at Wilton Road, where she sits around for most of the day growing bigger and mourning her lost love and listening to the wireless playing that year's top of the pops, 'Smoke gets in Your Eyes':

> *They asked me how I knew*
> *My true love was true*

1. William Fishman, *East End* (1888), Duckworth 1988.
2. From *Women's History Walk: Tower Hamlets Local History Library* No. LP4350 015, 29-07-79.

My sister and I, boarding at the Convent, see Florrie only on a Sunday, my sister sharing her bed for the night. Perhaps in frustration at this enforced proximity with a comparative stranger, or in a dream, one early morning my sister kicks out at her bed-mate, hitting her in the belly. Florrie gives a loud cry and my mother, entering the room at that moment, hurries to her side *"What's the matter? What's wrong!"* she asks, alarmed. Florrie sniffs, sitting up in bed and nursing her swollen stomach. *"She kicked me!"* she complains. My mother, exasperated by the daily toil of her life and a myriad of worries, turns on my sister who by now is sitting on the edge of the bed, sleepy and confused. *"You kicked Florrie!"* she accuses. *"You could have killed her baby!"* My sister says nothing, but for the rest of her life never puts herself into the position of responsibility for the survival of a foetus.

It is during these months of Florrie's confinement that my Aunt Becky and her family decide to move to Barnet—a bus ride away from Muswell Hill—for they must escape from neighbours who know of their daughter's disgrace. My Aunt is the mainspring in this move, for Gussy's first reaction is against it. He feels safe in these East End streets which he has come to know. Here he lives among Jewish people, many from his own shetl and has their recognition and respect. He works as a presser and has seen no need learn to read and write, therefore the unfamiliar remains a perpetual threat. He knows of no Jewish community in Barnet and his experiences in Poland have given him no trust in gentiles. However, at last he gives way and so he, my Aunt, and their family move away from Stepney's long history of refuge for those seeking shelter from oppression; the Hugenots who weaved their silk in the 17th Century, the Irish escaping the potato famine and the Jews freeing themselves from pogroms.

The child born, my mother has to convince Gussy that he must provide a home for Florrie and her infant and so she calls him over to Wilton Road where Florrie sits in an armchair in our living-room, her baby in her arms. *"There is your grandchild"* my mother says, pointing at the baby, Florrie looking away and not meeting her father's eyes. My mother continues, throwing her arms wide, her voice rising *"Do you want to turn your own daughter and your grandchild out on the streets?"* No, Gussy doesn't want that, and so he picks up the bag which my mother has packed in preparation, and Florrie, clasping her bundle to her bosom, follows her father home to Barnet on the 134 bus. There, where the family is unknown, the baby can be brought up as a late child born to my Aunt.

These troubles and her dependence upon my mother's support has meant that, in my mother's presence at least, my Aunt holds guard over her tongue and does not express the censorious thoughts passing through her mind with regard to my father, or the attendance of my sister and me at a Convent. On the other side of the family, my Aunt Mary also has her troubles, and just at a time when she had expected her life to improve, or at least be straightforward. For my Aunt had at last managed to provide a home for her boys by taking out a mortgage on a leasehold property at 3 Leathwaite Road, Battersea and it was to this address that in their early 'teens Cecil and Ted return from the Paris orphanage referred to by their mother euphemistically as a boarding-school. Most of the house my Aunt lets out as furnished rooms so as to provide the family with an income, while she and the boys live in the basement. And it is from here that Cecil is to stagger through his days, control continually slipping from his grasp, while my Aunt, in love and bitterness, does her best to guide and contain his every movement. Foster mothers, an English Catholic Orphanage and the Paris Orphelinat have disciplined away Cecil's identity and he does not know who he is.

"Cecil was so clever" says an old nun from the English Orphanage. With a younger nun she has attended my Aunt's funeral and now my husband and I are taking them back to their Convent. *"We had to stop him reading and asking questions. We thought he'd have a brainstorm if he learned too much—made his brain work too hard."*

Ted exorcises the pain of the Orphelinat by writing about his and Cecil's days there, in a short story published by the Henry Thornton School Magazine, *The Thorntonian*, in the summer of 1932, for at the time he is a pupil at this Grammar School:

Immediately the two offenders made to jump out of bed, but to their surprise, the usher stopped them from doing so. The latter began to gesticulate and speak hurriedly. The brothers just looked at him guiltily, unable to understand. As they were still unused to the abrupt manner and quick speaking of the French, they imagined that they had committed a grave offence. Then Monsieur Rose, exasperated, made another boy get back to bed with his trousers on and, making sure that Edward and John were watching, he made him take his trousers off under the sheets,

let them drop to the floor, pick them up again, and put them on
again under the sheets. Then, and only then, did he allow the boy
to alight from the bed. Having understood, the English boys got
up in the required way. Such modesty astonished them.

Ted describes the dormitory as 'poverty-stricken', the corridor
'dilapidated', the stairs 'rickety', the plaster-work 'cracked and
broken in several places':

> *The most remarkable feature of this repulsive sleeping room was*
> *a metal trough over which water-taps were suspended from a*
> *horizontal pipe and which stretched from one end of the room to*
> *the other. This was the dormitory's wash-basin. In rows on both*
> *sides of it were small beds.*

Ted soon realises that on their first visit to the school with their
mother a week before, they had been shown only that part of
the building reserved for the sick—visited regularly by the doctor—and inhabited by '*Messieurs les Professeurs*'. This because the
Directeur, "*a sly and unscrupulous man*" thought only of the fees
received for the boys' keep. Ted continues his story:

> "I want mummy", *he would keep repeating between sobs. Edward*
> *feeling miserable himself kept quiet. He placed the paper on the*
> *desk and began to write. His letter was cheerful from end to end.*
> *He told his mother untruthfully that they were quite happy, that*
> *the food was nice, their guardians good to them. Just as he fin-*
> *ished writing John began to cry out between his sobs:* "I'll tell her
> everything, the nasty rooms, the sloppy food, you wait! She'll
> have to take us away from here!" "Please don't," *Edward plead-*
> *ed.* "Mother's far away and worse off than us. It'll only make
> her sadder. She can't do anything for us, being so far away. The
> boys will make friends with us".

John, of course, is Cecil and soon the waters from his eyes flow
into the river of his body and he awakes each morning in a soak-
ing wet bed, so that each day he is forced to wash through bed
sheets in cold water at the metal trough. Cecil runs away from
school and on each occasion is found sitting on the doorstep of a
Frenchman appointed by my Aunt to be the boys' Guardian. And
he is returned to the school in disgrace.

I have a photograph of Cecil and Ted taken at this time. They
stand in front of a gateway, leaning against a wide stone post.
Cecil holds his right hand to his heart. They are dressed in navy

blue uniform, the coat adorned by gold buttons. They wear long trousers, black shoes, collar and tie. Cecil's peak cap seems to be too large for his round face. Ted holds his cap in his hand to reveal well-combed dark hair, an oval face, a set mouth and a high brow. Ted looks boldly upon the world. Cecil's eyes are veiled. Both boys have the Lahr protruding ears, 'Schlappohren' my father called them. Now the boys have been at home for some five years and my Aunt Mary has on one occasion called together with Cecil at the Convent on a Saturday while we are boarding.

We are in the Assembly Hall and I am kneeling on a table, gazing with longing out of the window, to look over the gravelled triangle, searching past the lime trees, straining to see the pavements outside the narrow gate. Around me older girls are chatting desultorily. Suddenly, the gate opens and two figures appear, one following the other. The first, a large woman dressed in loose flowing garments, a pork pie hat, hair falling untidily to her shoulders. Behind her a stooped boy dressed in a dark suit, the trouser legs flapping around his ankles. He is carrying a heavy bag. My mind whirrs round and into gear to encompass a life outside the Convent and I recognise my Aunt Mary and Cecil. With mixed feelings I watch their progress across the drive and round to the side of the house where I know that my Aunt will ring the front doorbell.

"Look at that couple of tramps!" says one of the older girls scathingly. *"I wonder what they want!"* The girls giggle together and I creep away from the table to sit on a bench, curled into myself to hide.

Soon a nun appears to call my sister and me to the parlour, a room of plush settees, stiff-backed chairs and a large dining-room table. A place where visitors are entertained. My sister and I stand hovering at the door which we have opened timidly once Reverend Mother has called out *'entrez'*. My Aunt and Cecil sit at a table on which two square boxes lie. We go into the room and stand to the side of the table. My Aunt is talking to Reverend Mother, Cecil gazes moodily at the floor and does not greet us. Perhaps the Convent reminds him of the Paris Orphanage school, or maybe his voices have told him that one day in the future I would call him untidy: *"Why did you say my room was always untidy?"* he grumbles. *"You could have said that it was only like that on that particular day."*

I had been a witness for the defence at his trial at the Old Bailey. The police had produced a photograph of Cecil's room piled high with books and papers as if he were preparing for a bonfire. This is after my Aunt's death at the age of almost eighty years. *"Was his room always like that?"* ask the Counsel for the Defence. *"Yes"* I reply truthfully *"I have never seen it any differently."* Cecil in the dock cringes. I have returned him to the institutions of his childhood when the worst crime was to be accused of untidiness. He is never able to understand that I have saved him from a possible life sentence for arson, following a localised accidental fire in his room.

My Aunt takes the cardboard boxes from the table and presents one to me and one to Oonagh. They contain dolls' bakelite tea-sets, blue for me and red for Oonagh. I feel grateful and at the same time guilty for I resent the appearance of these relatives in my life. Cecil must accompany his mother on her visit to Oonagh and me at the Convent, for she dare not let him out of her sight. Ted at this time is a waiter. *"All that education,"* remarks my mother, *"and she lets him leave school to become a waiter!"* My mother has forgotten that Ted's father was a waiter. Later Ted is to thrust away his father's inheritance to become a Merchant Seaman. While Ted waits, Cecil walks tortuously in a strange land through a maze, a confusion.

Ted, who even as a boy in his photo looks outward, determines to work towards changing a society which forces mothers for financial reasons to give up their children to the uncaring and demeans the mass of the population into a nothingness. He joins the Communist Party and spends his weekends standing on street corners to sell the *Daily Worker*. *"He's exchanged the Pope for Stalin"* growls my father. The Lahr family is *Evangelisch*, but my Aunt Mary is a Catholic convert. My father can understand the need for my sister's and my conversion, but cannot understand that of his sister. And so while Ted who is not to live long in this world, works for its salvation, Cecil is caught up by the spirits and demons of the next. Perhaps even then he saw himself in middle-age painting out in red or green all the signs in Battersea reading 'Way Out—in care parks, supermarkets, church entrances. But this is to be many years later, and for now he searches for a way through, walking between darkness and light, the depths and the heights, celibacy and the sinful call of the flesh, between a sense of *anomie* and a yearning to belong, between alienation and conciliation, timidity and assertiveness, amity and enmity, aggression and pacifism, between life and death. And at last his path leads him to the lunatic asylum, Colney Hatch at Friern Barnet—to become in 1973 Friern Hospital, and to be closed down by the 1990s when plans are made for the development of its grounds by storehouses, supermarkets and housing.

> *Colney Hatch Asylum was opened in 1851, the year of the Great Exhibition, as Europe's largest and most modern Institution.* "Here society's impossibles, victims of the double misfortune of lunacy and pauperism, found asylum whatever the disease that made them so."[3]

The admissions register for 1851 includes among the reasons for Lunacy, 'Socialism and Extreme Arrogance'. Hunter and McAlpine write also that nurses and attendants worked a ninety hour week, from 6 a.m. to 8 p.m. *"after which they were allowed out till 10 p.m. except when on call 'for the reserve'."* Nurses who were late on duty were fined and should it happen more than twice in a twelve-month period were dismissed and a nurse found negligent in allowing the escape of a patient had to pay the expense of 'recapture'. It is no wonder that Hunter and McAlpine add *"a few Attendants have been guilty of roughly using the patients"*, 90% of whom, some 2,000 in the 1920s and 1930s, lived in locked wards and for fresh air were confined to ward gardens. The asylum was paralysed by sheer weight of numbers of patients and the financial stringencies of the recession.

My Aunt takes my sister and me to visit Cecil in the Asylum for we are staying with her for a week or two during the Easter holidays so as to leave my mother free to work at the bookshop all day without worry. We ride on the bus past Wilton Road and I reach out my hand to touch my own home, but the bus speeds away too quickly: down to the North Circular Road, past the sewerage farm, the smell of which permeates the district and which the residents tell each other is 'healthy', on past the high Asylum wall, to the Orange Tree. We sit at a table in a long ward, Cecil opposite us, and my Aunt places before him gifts of food, a cake, some fruit, a pot of jam. Around us shuffle aimlessly, or walk purposefully from wall to wall, male inmates, some mut-

---

3. Richard Hunter MD FRCP and Ida McAlpine, *Psychiatry for the Poor: 1851 Colney Hatch Asylum, 1973 Friern Hospital—A Medical and Social History*, William Dawson and Sons Ltd., 1974.

tering, others calling across the ward to unseen protagonists or antagonists. A boy, not much older than me, dressed in his own clothes of shorts, shirt, pullover, appears from a cubicle to call out excitedly *"I'm going home!"*

Cecil sits slumped over the table, shutting himself away from the ward which has been presented to him as his world. Perhaps his voices tell him that this is the first of many such incarcerations for the future holds Tooting Bec, Springfields and a short time on remand in Brixton prison. I visit him in this last place to find a large waiting room, the floor of which is pitted with cigarette burns, the walls are filthy and the visitors, most of whom are young women holding crying children, in despair wait to be called. Decorating this scene of misery and hung high on the dirty wall is a reproduction of Constable's 'Hay Wain'.

While with my Aunt and sister visiting Cecil at the Asylum, I fail to see my mother working around the wards, for she will work here as an orderly after the Second World War. Nor do I see my Great Aunt Railer, my grandmother Rachel's sister, confined to the Asylum in old age because she has grown old and difficult. And it is in this Asylum that she will die. This Great Aunt had lived through the 1905 revolution in Poland, having left an orthodox Jewish home to live with an anarchist, a lover shot down by the forces of law and order during the revolution and whom she found among the dead. Her sisters settled in England brought her over where, for ever after, she was given the reputation of 'not being quite right in the head'. For she espoused atheism and the necessity for the abolition of government. *"I can't offer you a cup of tea"* she says worriedly when I visit her on one occasion with my mother *"but take one of the blankets."* She speaks in Yiddish and my mother translates. We are sitting in a long ward beside her narrow bed and my Great Aunt is obviously concerned that she is not in a position to offer us hospitality.

At last, we bid good-bye to Cecil who has paid my sister and me no attention, his thoughts all being upon his own predicament and his claims upon his mother, and once again we board the bus. Now we pass Wilton Road from the opposite direction and again I stretch out my hands to hold the house, but my grip slips and we travel on to Battersea. My eyes following the roads I know so well until we are in strange and unknown territory.

And so we are caught up in time. A time marked out by John Harrison also of Holborn and a resident of Red Lion Square, whose gravestone in a Hampstead Churchyard states *"worked without instruction on a time-keeper for fifty years and died in 1770 aged 83"*. Time having caught up with him.

Time, time, time—a time in which my father, his daughters and his nephew are all separately institutionalised.

Holiday Task

A Haslemere Children's Home: My father suffers his release: East Chaldon, Sylvia Townsend-Warner, Valentine Ackland, T.F. Powys, Malachi Whitaker, Gay Taylor and A.E. Coppard: An unhappy journey home.

That year my sister and I spend the long summer school holiday of eight weeks at what was known as 'a children's hotel' at Haslemere, Surrey. As it happens, we were sent to the same Home during the summer holidays of the following year, for although my father was now at home, we remained boarders at the Convent while my parents sorted out their lives. For me, these two breaks at the Home run into one so that it is impossible for me to separate the incidents into their chronological order.

I recall waiting with my sister in the dining-hall of the Convent for my mother to collect us both and take us to this place in Haslemere and I view it with dread. In fact, I would have preferred to go to Bognor Regis with two of the nuns and the boarders, such as Joan Batchelor, unable to go home for the holiday. For the devil one already knows is said to be preferable to the devil yet to be met. My fear originates from a similar 'children's hotel' to which I had been sent two or three years previously, my mother at the time intent upon building up my health by sea air, having taken me to a Home at Whitstable in Kent. From the Home, a large house, we are directed to the beach to find The Matron and a party of children sitting on the stones and so we walk along the hard, concrete promenade to look down upon the pebbles until we spy two large women and a small group of supine children, each child forming a separate island. *"Hurry!"* my mother bids me, herself descending, legs, body and lastly head disappearing. I hasten to catch up with her and follow her along the strand. *"I don't want to stay here"* I whine, for hasn't she promised me that if I don't like the look of the place, or the people, she will not make me stay. *"I don't like them"* I moan. My mother takes no notice of me, she is not listening. I hang back as my mother greets the women in charge, one of them rising to meet her, then my mother beckons me. Hoping against hope that these sorry children and their keepers will prove to be a mirage, I walk up to my mother. She pushes me forward and a woman takes my by the hand. My mother walks away, turning once to wave. I watch her out of sight. *"I don't want to stay here,"* I whimper. But she has gone.

Cold stone floors, washing in cold water in a stained butler sink, queuing each morning at a hatch for two slices of bread and paste to take to the beach. I am hungry, hungry, hungry. My mother visits and I complain that I don't have enough to eat. She speaks to one of the Attendants, but then tells me that here I have tea at dinner-time and dinner at tea-time, no more than a substitution of meals. I am making a fuss about nothing. I feel betrayed, unsatisfied, hungry.

This Whitstable is very different to the Whitstable I come to know and love as an adult while staying with Maude Ehrenstein, wife of Carl and sister-in-law of the poet Albert, who discovered Kafka. And yet when, at this sea-side place, I borrow from Maude's shelves and read Nathanael West's *The Day of the Locust*, once more the place takes on for me a macabre, unreal aspect. Whitstable is no more than a film-set, the houses and shops tacky frontages, the shop signs borrowed, the people in the street transient actors and extras. All is outward show. Top show.

The Home at Haslemere in Surrey is an old rambling house set at the top of a hill in extensive grounds. A long steep driveway closed in on each side by dense shrubs and trees, leads to and from the village. A village foreign to the children at the Home. The driveway winds up to a large lawn on which during the summer we spend our days. Dressed only in a swimming costume I burn and it seems that I am crawling out of my peeling skin. There are many children on this lawn, the majority of whom are permanent residents. *"I came for a holiday when I was little"* a teenage girl tells me *"and my mother died while I was here, so Mrs. Lee said I could stay."* I hear the girl's words and I am sick with apprehension. Could my mother die while I am no longer at home to keep a guardian eye upon her? Am I never to leave this place?

Mrs. Lee, a large, middle-aged woman wearing a floral dress is called 'Mother' and each morning after breakfast at refectory tables arranged in a line in a long dining-room, she holds Assembly in a large hall. We children, some two or three hundred, line the walls in a semi-circle while at the end of the room Mrs. Lee presides over prayers. This is the only time we see her officially, although I often pass by her empty office and, if the door is open, leave on the desk a letter to my mother begging her to come and fetch me home, hoping against hope that it will be posted.

I go out onto the lawn where an Attendant holds on reins made from webbing a mentally handicapped boy of about eight years old. His eyes are wild as he strains against the restraint, he screws up his face, makes strange noises, throws out his arms, drums his feet. Sometimes he slips the reins, or the attendant loosens her hold, and in sudden joy the boy runs pell mell down the long incline of the driveway. At this all the children leave their games and whooping and shouting with excitement, together with the attendant, chase after the boy, the stony ground crunching under our feet, our eyes on the manic running of our quarry who must be captured before he reaches the village. At last he is taken and confined. I am at the Home when this boy's parents visit, bringing with them a younger son, a three-year-old. The parents, smartly dressed, softly spoken, have with them a pedal car into which the younger boy climbs. The older son, unrestrained for the present, grabs hold of the back of the car roughly to push it forward. At once the parents become alarmed, their faces and arms jerking in agitation until an attendant grabs hold of the afflicted child and he is once more put under restraint.

A small blind boy with curly black hair feels his way about the house and grounds and I watch him from a distance.

Those children who live at this Home receive their schooling within it and a day or two following my arrival a girl comes up to me where I stand on the grass and grabs my arm. *"School's started, you've got to come to the schoolroom"* she says bossily. I argue *"I'm here on holiday, my school's broken up!"* The girl confers with an older girl and it is agreed that I am not at the Home for schooling. Later on, when I learn that classes have been discontinued for the past six months during the absence of the teacher, an old lady, I almost regret having been so precipitate, for surely I would have been top of the class!

If my sister and I wander away from the lawn into areas of bushes and pampas grass, sooner or later we are sure to be trapped by grinning twelve or thirteen years old boys who demand that we take off our bathing costumes and let them "*have a look.*" We refuse and run away from their side of the bush, shouting insults at them once we are in sight of the populated lawn.

My mother comes to visit, bringing with her treats, fruit, cakes and sweets. We sit on the grassy lawn for a picnic while around us children play, leaving us to our family grouping, except for one little girl named Helen who joins us, sitting cross-legged alongside me on the grass. My mother reluctantly includes the girl in the share-out of goodies for she cannot bring herself to send the child away. On the following Sunday Helen's parents visit, but no such kindness is extended to me and I feel cheated.

I become attached to a little girl of about my own age, named Kathleen. She has rounded face and limbs, is friendly and talkative; everybody's favourite. I follow her everywhere and she kindly lets me play with her. Then, suddenly, she announces that she is going on a fortnight's holiday with her parents. She is happy and excited, but I am desolate. I cry bitterly and to comfort me she gives me a rubber doll to keep for her until she returns:

> *My mother told me if I were good-y*
> *That she would buy me*
> *a rubber dolly*

I carry the doll about with me as a badge of Kathleen's favour, but one day in the grounds a group of boys approach and before I can run away a grinning youth grabs the doll and pulls off one of its legs, slinging the doll at me, but throwing the leg to make a wide arc and fall into the undergrowth where it is lost. What am I to tell my friend? At night, in the long dormitory in which Kathleen's bed is empty, I agonise over her return.

At last Kathleen arrives in a flurry of excitement, other girls gathering to greet her, to examine the toys and presents with which she has returned. I wait on the outside of the circle until at last I screw up courage and approach timorously, holding out the damaged doll. I say haltingly "*a boy pulled her leg off.*" She looks at the doll without interest and seems hardly to know me. Sadly I understand that she has forgotten we are friends.

Once I am home again, and some time later, I am happy to hear from my mother that this Home was closing down and moving in much reduced form to Regent's Park, for surely I would not be sent there for a holiday. My mother adds that she suspects Mrs. Lee's motives in keeping the older girls, and she hints at 'white slave trading'.

"Your father's been in prison" calls out Ena Macfarlane from her first floor bedroom window, to me standing outside in the street. She is a pupil at the Convent and lives almost opposite to us in Wilton Road, but while proximity dictates that we play together, we are not friends. Today we have quarrelled. Wilfully misunderstanding her I pretend that she is referring to my father's internment and shout back *"only because he was German. He was interned."* My father has been home for some months and yet not home. He has suffered a 'sea change', a change in emphasis which makes him creep out of the house to go about his daily business. His newspapers—for he reads several every day and carries two or three with him wherever he goes—have to be purchased by us, or bought farther afield, as he refuses to enter the newsagents, Torrys, at the top of Wilton Road. He is certain that the shop assistants spend their days in searching the newspapers for local gossip and know of his conviction.

> *Dear Charles* (writes James Hanley) *Glad to hear you are set-tled at Red Lion Street again and that Hitlerland is far off. Well I must say I admired your letter for not many people who have been in prison can escape pitying themselves. Yes, I admire your courage.*

Once again, my sister and I are day-girls at the Convent, no longer boarders, but the fact of my father's imprisonment continues to make waves.

We visit the Foreman family at Camden Town where we are invited to sit down to tea. At the table are Bill Foreman, whom my parents refer to as 'the gas man' because he is a meter reader, Lydia, his wife, a lugubrious Russian woman some years older than her husband, and Audrey, their daughter, a blonde, ringletted child a little younger than myself. The grown-ups are talking and somehow the subject of porridge enters into the conversation. Prison porridge is mentioned and my sister pipes up *"My Dad had that!"* Absolute silence. Embarrassment, for if the Foreman family know of my father's sentence, it is unofficially. *"Don't be silly!"*

I snap *"that was when he was in hospital!"* Everyone relaxes and my parents are delighted with my quick wits. My father speaks little of prison, but he closely monitors each postman who walks by with a mailbag thrown over his shoulder. My father dogs his footsteps, peering at the stitches in the sack's seams for he sews with his left hand (although he had been taught to write with his right hand at school)—lefthandedness regarded at that time as 'sinister'. *"My stitches go in the opposite direction to everyone else's"* he explains *"and I will always recognise my own work."*

> *It is not linen you're wearing out,*
> *But human creatures' lives!...*
> *Work–work–work!*
> *From every weary chime,*
> *Work–work–work -*
> *As prisoners work for crime.*[1]

In time, however, the family settles into a kind of normalcy and my mother stays home within the four walls of Wilton Road where I know always where to find her.

That year my mother takes my sister and me on two holidays, one to Leigh-on-Sea where we lodge for a week with a Mrs. Thomas, and a second to East Chaldon, Dorset, near to the homes of T.F. Powys, Sylvia Townsend Warner and Valentine Ackland. My mother has fond memories of East Chaldon for before my sister and I were born, she and my father, attracted by the writers living in the vicinity, had spent much time there and my mother had also holidayed in Dorset with Sarah Roberts, on one occasion staying in T.E. Lawrence's cottage near Bovington while he was away. My father claimed T.E. Lawrence, the uncrowned King of Arabia, as a friend and my mother insisted always that on the day on which Lawrence was killed on his motor-bike my father had been invited to Dorset. *"If he had gone"* she says *"Lawrence wouldn't have been killed."* Sarah and my mother were able to relax in Lawrence's cottage, the interior faded, a strip of coconut matting in an unswept hall-way, a room in which all four walls held bookshelves with books closely packed from floor to ceiling. A garden grown half-wild into which my mother and Sarah pulled two old, shabby armchairs, for my mother to sit and read

---

1. Thomas Hood (1799-1845), *The Song of the Shirt*.

while Sarah lies back to feel the sun on her face, a sun which warmed and shone upon the whitewashed exterior of the cottage.

With regard to East Chaldon, this is described by Wendy Mulford as "*a tiny village, its cottages grouped around the green: at one end lies the pub, at the other the church, and in the middle the village store and post office. The writers and intellectuals who stayed there made up a fairly right-knit group of which Theodore Powys was the pivot.*"[2]

On this holiday, we stay with my mother in a large bleak house named 'The Hut' which during term-time houses a progressive school. Stone floors, bare boards, sparse furnishings, no cooking facilities—or perhaps both gas and electric had been disconnected. To cook we use a small primus stove in which must be inserted two large white flat tablets, the embossed lettering of which warns 'Not To Be Handled By Children'. My hands behind my back, I examine them with my eyes, a thrill of fear running me through. What would happen should I touch them? Would I immediately drop down dead? Or would I sicken and fade away by degrees? How old must I be before I develop the invulnerability of an adult? Water we draw from a pump at the back of the house, pulling the handle down, up, down and watching the cool water gush into a clean bucket. For lighting we have an oil lamp which shines out upon the table as if we own our own special moon. My mother does find a box of candles, but refuses to use them because, she says, a candle could fall over and start a fire. I love this pioneer living for to me it spells romance and, anyway, the spartan conditions inside 'The Hut' are nothing to me against the field outside in which wild flowers grow, and the stream over which is a rickety wooden bridge where we can play that we are crossing into an exotic foreign land.

Sylvia Townsend Warner and Valentine Ackland call upon us, one very tall, cropped hair and dressed as a man in a smart suit, collar and tie. I can hardly believe my mother when she tells me that this is a woman. At that time for me 'clothes maketh the man'. The other is a shorter woman with pretty dark hair. As it happens, until fairly recently I had assumed that the male dresser was Sylvia and the obvious woman, Valentine, which says something about the unconscious brainwashing I had undergone over

---

2. Wendy Mulford, *This Narrow Place: Sylvia Townsend Warner and Valentine Ackland: Life and Letters and Politics 1930-1951*, Pandora, 1988.

the years which made me believe that male clothing indicated the greater achievement. While Sylvia and Valentine are being entertained in the house by my mother, my sister and I outside in the field, set up on a card-table a stall of wild flowers placed in jam jars and paste pots:

> *It fell between her and the dirty brown face of a woman who was selling mimosa and who, scenting a foreigner, hurried forward, her earthy face peering behind the soft golden plumes. On Sophia's skin at the same moment fell the powdering snow and the soft tickle of the mimosa blossom. The shaken pollen made her sneeze, the touch of this cold and this soft falling together sent a thrill through her flesh.*[3]

At last Sylvia and Valentine emerge from the house, walking together as if one person. *"Would you like to buy some flowers?"* I ask, from behind my temporary stall, and keeping a sharp look-out for my mother who disapproves of such entrepreneurship. The two women look at one another and the small dark one smiles. She passes a sixpence to the tall woman who hands it to me and I present both women with small posies of wild flowers.

"There was once a little girl" T.F. Powys says to me. We—my mother, sister and I—are walking along a country lane with Theodore and his wife Violet who is wheeling their adopted fair-haired infant daughter Susan in a push-chair. *"And each time she looked in the mirror she grew uglier."* I recognise this as a Convent-type moralising against vanity. *"Why?"* I ask myself *"should looking in the mirror make anyone ugly?"* I am angry at this white-bearded Patriarch who is 'getting at me'.

> *He read the lessons in Chaldon Church on Sundays, in a deep booming voice... Sylvia... attended church on her first visit to the village... for which occasion Theodore searched for an appropriate passage in the Scriptures, about a young lady coming down from London, musing* "perhaps I may find you in the Apocrypha."[4]

"The house is in a terrible mess" Violet says to my mother who is visiting the Powys house, Beth-Car, which Wendy Mulford calls *"an ungainly red-brick villa,"* *"but we've got the baby and that's all that*

3. Sylvia Townsend Warner, *Summer Will Show*, re-published Virago Press, 1987.
4. Wendy Mulford.

matters." Susan is the daughter of the woman the Powys son, Francis, is to marry and the self-styled claimant to the throne of Poland, Count Geoffrey Potocki de Montalk, son of a New Zealand milkman. Potocki walked the streets of London dressed in a red cloak which we were always sure he made from a curtain, over a tunic on which glittered a 'gold' medallion. He wore also open sandals. His dark, straight hair falling over his shoulders. He, Potocki, was publisher of the *Right Review* which propagated his own monarcho-fascistic views. Having abandoned a wife and daughter in New Zealand, when Susan's mother announced her pregnancy, he ended their relationship. Potocki comes into the bookshop at the time of the accession of George V1 in 1936 and browses among books looming on all sides and above him, until he turns to address my parents with a panegyric upon the Royal Family. My republican parents are embarrassed, uncomfortable. They know that this man is baiting them, but do not want to argue with him. He turns to me. Do I like the little Princesses? *"I like the princesses in fairy tales better"* I say seriously, for I have been disappointed in photos in the press and on film of Margaret Rose and Elizabeth dressed in pedestrian clothing and wearing their brown hair short. *"In fairy tales princesses have long fair hair and beautiful dresses"* I explain, and my parents are delighted.

During the Second World War, Potocki appears overnight in a battle-dress of dark green trousers and jacket resembling a soldier's uniform. On his head, hair now cut short, he wears a black beret. Suddenly, the impressive appearance betowed upon him by the eccentricity of his long garments and long hair vanishes, and he now appears as small, middle-aged and insignificant. No wonder, that on returning to New Zealand some years after the war, he assumes once again the cloak, tunic and long hair. In his home country, he continues to present himself as a poet, for while visiting New Zealand in 1993 my daughter, Addie, reads in the local newspaper of a newly published book of poems by Count Potocki, now in his eighties.

In London, pre-war, Potocki had been charged with obscenity following his submission of a poem to a publisher. The publisher had taken this poem to the police, and although it was never published Potocki was tried and convicted. My father who was against all censorship, had befriended Potocki at this time and my mother bailed Potocki out previous to the trial. Later, she was to say that this was because she wanted the anti-semitic

Potocki to be beholden to a Jew. She assumed, of course, that he was capable of gratitude.

Towards the end of the Second World War Potocki comes into the bookshop my father had set up at 12 Little Newport Street. I am sitting typing in a room upstairs and Jack Carney, a journalist, is sorting through books when Potocki appears. *"Did you see the picture of Susan in the newspaper?"* he asks Carney. A photo of the half-grown Susan had appeared in a newspaper article about T.F. Powys. *"I asked (he names a journalist) to get me an original copy and he refused."* Potocki's lower lip drops. *"Don't you think that's mean?"* he whines *"After all, they do say she's my daughter."* Later, when Susan is an adult, I hear that Potocki, whose means of support were obscure, but who was reputed to have benefited from various Wills, has made contact with Susan who, apparently, welcomed the advances of this long absent putative father.

However, to return to the text. We meet two other writers who are on holiday in Dorset. Gay Taylor, whose short stories have been published by my father in *The New Coterie*, and Malachi Whitaker, the better-known writer of the two women. Malachi has with her an adopted son, two years of age. Within the last few years, Malachi's short stories have been read on Radio 4, but Gay, author of a novel entitled *No Goodness in the Worm* and a number of short stories, is now forgotten as a writer. And yet her own story could be written as a block-banger-buster! Gay, whom I remember as a slim woman with fairish shoulder-length straight hair and green eyes, had married a wealthy man much older than herself. Suffering from premature ejaculation, or perhaps quirky in his sexual tastes, he agrees that Gay can have affairs provided he, her husband, whom I shall call Clifford, first vets such a lover. This works well until Gay falls in love with the writer A.E. Coppard. She becomes pregnant and is preparing to leave her husband for Coppard when both men disown her. The child is aborted. A sorry, wiser, Gay has to pick up the pieces of her life. Not long afterwards Clifford dies, leaving Gay a small income, but the bulk of his wealth to his relatives. Bitterness enters into Gay's soul and if only she could have drawn it into her heart and consciousness, to escape through her fingers as words, this might have resulted in her writings living forever. As it was, Gay lives out her drama from day to day, drifting in and out of love affairs and never, during the time we knew her, giving, nor expecting, too much.

I cannot forget Gay, for a constant memorial to her stands in my bedroom. This is a limed oak chest of drawers, darkened by the years. This chest was left with my mother at the beginning of the war when Gay moved out of London, and for many years afterwards my mother worriedly expected Gay to descend upon us to reclaim this now necessary piece of furniture. But we were never to hear from her again.

At East Chaldon, my mother, sister and I walk through the village, blackberrying, dodging out of the way of a line of mooing cows being herded along the road, the last cow flicking her tail into Oonagh's eyes, so that she cries and my mother must comfort her. Teenage girls pass by and one turns to look at my mother. My mother approaches her hesistantly until the girl makes it clear that she remembers my mother as having stayed at The Red Lion some years before. The girl is the older daughter of the Inn Keeper. *"It's your curly hair I remembered"* the girl explains to my mother who is delighted at being recognised. We go into the Red Lion for a light lunch, to be greeted by the inn-keeper and his wife, and my mother invites the younger daughter of the family, a girl of about my age, to The Hut. There we spend the afternoon dressing up in my mother's clothes, smearing on lipstick, and for a few short hours we are ladies. We are film-stars.

Most of the time we eat out, sometimes at the Inn, but more often than not at The Sailor's Return, a cafe, in which there are reputed to be secret smugglers' passages leading from the coast:

Five and twenty ponies,
Trotting through the dark -
Brandy for the parson,
Baccy for the Clerk:
Laces for a lady; letters for a spy,
And watch the wall my darling while the Gentlemen go by.[5]

However, one morning my mother decides to cook on the primus stove and, in spite of all her precautions, it catches fire. Whoosh! Red and orange flames shoot up into the air, out towards the confining walls, up towards the ceiling. My mother sees her half-sister Flora together with her dead children in the flames, and shouts to my sister and me to run outside. Pale with fear my sister and I hurry into the field, screaming in unison. Screaming,

---

5. Rudyard Kipling, *A Smuggler's Song.*

screaming, screaming, fearful that my mother will be devoured by the fire and we will never see her again. Screaming, screaming, screaming so that we are heard for miles around. By T.F. Powys, by Sylvia Townsend Warner and by Valentine Ackland. At last my mother puts out the fire and the primus stove is pushed to one side, not to be used again by us.

My mother takes us to Weymouth, where I am fascinated by the white sand, running it through my fingers, making patterns which are too dry to stay in place. My mother is tense. She murmurs that we are to meet someone my father knows, a customer at the shop, and soon a shifty-eyed little man dressed in black approaches us and hands to my mother an envelope. These are our rail tickets to return home. My father has sent us down to Dorset on day tickets, cheaper than a monthly, and now we must return in the same way. My mother is worried and unhappy with this ruse.

Before taking our leave of The Hut, my mother writes a letter of apology to the proprietor, one of my father's customers, and pins it above a crayoned picture with which my sister has brightened up the bare walls. She has drawn directly onto the wall a picture of a lady dressed in florid mauve triangular skirt and with much yellow hair. Her red mouth a red half crescent of laughter, her eyes and nose shiny black. Around this she has drawn a thick brown line to represent a picture-frame. My mother pins her letter of contrition under the picture and murmurs *"after all, this is a progressive school!"*

Lugging suitcases we travel by bus to the station and this is where the holiday goes horribly wrong. For when we arrive on the platform with our large cases, an Official calls us out of the line of those waiting to board the train, insisting that our luggage must be weighed. The ticket for a day visitor allowing a certain weight of luggage only. My mother agitatedly tells my sister and me to stay in line and asks those adults nearest to keep an eye on us. Then she runs madly, her small frame almost bent double, to disappear into an office. As she disappears, my sister and I surrounded by tall strangers, begin to cry. *"Your mummy will be back soon"* those nearest assure us kindly. I do not believe them. I know that I will be taken onto the train which will speed away with me. Widening, widening, ever widening, the distance between me and my mother. I will never find my mother again. The line is moving slowly, but inexorably into the train and I am stiff with anxiety, until my mother appears at my side, lugging our cases. I am ecstatic with relief, but she is crying bitterly at this humiliation. She has paid for excess weight, but must have feared discovery and prosecution. My mother cries all the way to London, her head held down as the tears flow and my sister and I, jerked out of our own distress and happy to be with her once again, spend the journey in trying to cheer her up by singing songs, making funny faces. Asking her to be happy again. So that later she tells us that the other passengers of whom we, locked in our own personal drama were oblivious, said that we were *"good children."*

Escape

Cecil's escape: I am a day girl: The Wilsons and Twi: The Spanish Civil War.

I n the meantime, Cecil is languishing in the Colney Hatch Asylum. Opened in 1851, Prince Albert, the Prince Consort, had laid the foundation stone for what was to become the largest mental asylum for pauper lunatics. My Aunt has applied several times for his release into her care, but on each occasion it is refused. Refused. Refused. At that time the insane were regarded not merely as ill, but as morally defective. They had offended against the puritan ethic which demands that we rise above adversity, as did Job, who, sitting on his dunghill, responded to disaster and tragedy by declaring that God knew best in the best of all possible worlds. Therefore, an unbreachable dichotomy existed between the mad and the sane, with no possibility of redemption from either condition.

My Aunt becomes more and more agitated at her son's incarceration in such a place and takes her distress to a Catholic Church where she kneels in the confessional box, the face of the priest barely seen behind the grille. *"Bless me father for I have sinned"* she says and having told him of her son's agony, confesses more than she ought. *"My daughter"* says the Father *"you are being punished for your sins. Say ten Hail Marys."*

My weeping Aunt comes to my mother who, indignant at such harshness and superstition, offers comfort and then together the two women hatch a plot. Cecil must be helped to escape:

> *Harriet S… escaped from the attendant in charge whilst walking in the village.. owing to a thick fog, and not being re-taken within fourteen days was written off the books.*[1]

This was the regulation—if a patient escaped from an Asylum and was not retaken within fourteen days, he or she remained free.

Cecil must be sprung from the hospital to be hidden away and so my Aunt will apply to take him our for the day on a Saturday, the day on which privileged patients were allowed out with their families:

> *As usual all the patients desirous of so doing, and being in a tranquil state have been permitted to visit their friends in London.*[2]

But my Aunt's request is refused, as if the Asylum authorities guess that she will not return her son to their mercies. My Aunt knows now that she must get Cecil out in some other way, and she traverses the confines of the Asylum, past the high walls, the locked iron gates, searching for a breach in security. At last she strikes pay dirt in the form of two loose boards in the wooden fencing edging the hospital farm and opening onto an alley off the North Circular Road. First swiftly looking about her to make sure she is unobserved, my Aunt pushes the boards apart to reveal a field of cabbages. She measures the gap with her hands. It would be impossible for her to climb through, but the 19-year old Cecil with his slight frame could make it sideways, one leg at a time. Her head filled by plots and plans, my Aunt walks away smartly, first neatly pushing the boards together again.

My Aunt must now obtain Cecil's co-operation, for while he is sure that he wants nothing more than to be out of the Asylum, to be obstructive has become part of his character. To cause annoyance and anger in others is the only manner in which he can assure himself that he possesses some power and control.

The Cecil I know is in late middle and old age at a time when he is plastering Battersea with slogans a foot high in red spray paint, one of which reads "**MOTORISTS—SPEED IS GREED!**" This on the brick wall at the back of my Aunt's house and facing the South Circular Road. He walks over the zebra crossing, which leads to the common, backwards and forwards, Canute-

---

1. LCC 1890. From *Psychiatry for the Poor.*
2. From *Psychiatry for the Poor.*

like, and then stands in the middle of the crossing, his feet firmly planted, his arms crossed, an expression of devilment upon his face, while the traffic masses in impatience along the busy thoroughfare. Horns hooting and motorists shouting.

Or he dresses in a curtain for a cloak and holding a small plastic bowl before him in both hands, walks through the traffic of Battersea Rise. He is the Pope, or a prophet, and is invulnerable to the danger posed by the work of secular man.

I sometimes think that Cecil, dubbed insane, enjoyed acting madness as if he were on a stage and the public his audience. For not only did it provide him with the attention of others (not least his mother) but it gave him a freedom of action denied to those of us intent upon presenting ourselves as sane. It was not these actions which declared Cecil insane, but his inability to structure his life, an ability lost for him by the imposed structures of the orphanage and boarding school; at home, in the care of his mother who has compensated herself for the loss of his childhood by returning him to infancy; and in regimented Asylums and mental hospitals.

Cecil's main frustration was that he, an educated man, widely read, was forced, because of his record of mental illness and a lack of formal qualifications, to work at menial occupations under the supervision of the barely literate and alongside the almost illiterate. His wide knowledge of poetry and literature cut no ice here, like them he was at the bottom of the heap, and yet unlike them he recognised his situation. It could be said that he had been 'educated above his station'—so-called education in our society concerning itself with the vocational only and not with the whole man or woman.

A debasement which broke out in Cecil in bouts of aggressive behaviour, especially when he suspected that he was being laughed at or put-down. Making others fearful was the only way in which he was able to decalre his humanity. Not that Cecil was easy to live with. Following his mother's death, at the end of a dramatic scene including a social worker, policemen, ambulancemen and a carpenter, Cecil, my Aunt and me, Cecil persecuted his tenants, tenants nurtured by his mother for they were her living. Now Cecil walked up and down stairs all night long playing loudly a transistor radio. He argued with the tenants, searching their rooms in their absence, impressing upon them that he, Cecil Ernest Vivian Stone, was the landlord, they were in his house living there on his bounty. The tenants fled and, in any event, this leasehold house was soon lost to Cecil, so that even the role of Lord of the Manor escaped him.

However, perhaps at the age of nineteen he still has hopes for his own future and my Aunt is able to easily convince him that he must apply to work on the farm:

> The farm account was an important item in the asylum's balance sheet. In 1853 the cost of feeding a cow was 'not less than 4s per week'—about the same as providing food for a patient at 2s 2d. weekly.[3]

Cecil must work outside and during the lunch break make his way over the cabbage patch to where the garden wall meets the wooden fence. My Aunt would be waiting. She whispers this information quietly while visiting Cecil, sitting at a table in the ward, looking about her warily to ensure that she is not overheard. But the male nurses and orderlies are at the other end of the ward and the patients and their visitors are intent upon their own troubles, or lost in the general hum of noise. "Working on the farm might not be allowed." Says Cecil, for he cannot resist playing devil's advocate. My Aunt laughs sourly. "They'll be glad of another pair of unpaid hands in the fields" she says. And so it proves.

On the Saturday on which the escape is to take place, my Aunt waits at the fence, a change of clothes for Cecil in a carrier bag for in the Asylum he must wear a uniform and only those patients selected by the Medical Superintendent for going beyond the bounds of the establishment are furnished with ordinary clothes.

My Aunt paces the alley, each second a minute and each minute an hour. One or two people pass and she feels that they look at her curiously. She stiffens. At last she hears the signal she has arranged with Cecil, a tapping on the wooden panel, for she has warned him that he must not climb through until she has assured him that no one else is around. She looks this way and that. No one in sight, and so she pushes back the two boards and Cencil's pale face peers out at her. "Say the password, mother" he demands in a low, deep growl. "We cannot surrender without the password." "Quick, quick, quick" my Aunt almost shrieks, catching his arm and

---

3. From the stewards annual report, CHA 1854: From *Psychiatry for the Poor*.

pulling him through onto the pathway where he puts on quickly, and over his Asylum clothing, an ordinary shirt and suit.

It is not until they are on the 134 bus to Wilton Road that my Aunt realises that she has forgotten to bring Cecil a change of socks and that the striped socks of the Asylum are in clear evidence beneath his ridden-up trousers. And what is more, they are sitting on a long seat in the 'bus opposite to a nurse from the Asylum. A nurse who at one time worked on Cecil's ward. My Aunt sweats with fear while Cecil's striped socks seem to fill the whole 'bus and the Wilton Road 'bus stop moves farther and farther away. However, the nurse, tired after a long shift, pays no attention to the couple ,and when at last my Aunt and Cecil alight at Wilton Road no hue and cry follows them.

"A looney's escaped from Colney Hatch" parents warn their children. *" Don't go near the woods or onto waste ground. We must keep all the doors locked."* The children shiver with excitement, expecting at every turn to be met by a madman with a long, glinting knife and staring eyes. At night every noise is the sound of this crazy forcing his entry into the house. The children walk by day and night in delicious fear. My sister and I over the years sharing in the excitement of this community hysteria.

The next stage of the journey for Cecil has been arranged by my mother and is to be to a boarding-house run by a Mrs Thomas at Leigh-on-Sea, where my mother, sister and I had spent a week. From the first day of this holiday my mother had not been happy. Perhaps she had brought with her unhappiness emanating from a situation at Wilton Road, only to find the truth of the old adage *"No problem is escaped by running away, because you must take yourself with you."*

Mrs Thomas is a small, grey-haired, sharp-featured, sharp-eyed, woman to whom my mother takes an instant dislike. Each morning we sit quietly at a breakfast served sourly by Mrs. Thomas and then go out for the day, although the only such outing I can recall is the three of us sitting on a park bench. Boys rollerskate around us on paving stones laid out in a square. They come close, nearly knocking into our bench. My mother, perhaps feeling threatened by these half-grown boys, or needing to let out pent up emotions, harangues them. Calling at them in her sharp, adult voice. They skate around us and away, and from a distance make rude gestures. One, who himself wears glasses takes his index finger around his eyes to indicate that my mother's glasses make her a 'four-eyes'. The incongruity of this making my mother even more indignant.

While at Mrs Thomas' establishment my mother suddenly misses her Waterman's fountain pen with gold band and gold nib. A day or two previously Mrs. Thomas had admired this and now my mother is certain that she has stolen it. My mother cries, she shouts and she screams. She will not leave the house until her pen is found. Mrs. Thomas, white-faced, denies all knowledge, but at last the pen is produced, the landlady saying that she has found it in the ashes of a fireplace, where, she says, it must have fallen.

Therefore, my mother has no compunction in sending Cecil to Mrs. Thomas and involving her unknowingly in his escape. My Aunt has telephoned Mrs. Thomas to say that the doctor had advised a holiday for her son because he was recuperating from pneumonia. And when she takes Cecil to Leigh on Sea, my Aunt makes all kinds of promises of reward if only Mrs. Thomas will take good care of Cecil, who, for the next fortnight will be called 'John'.

For the next fourteen days information on Cecil's progress is to leak out to my Aunt through the medium of coin phone boxes. During one such phone call, with much amusement, he tells his mother that he has helped to load onto an ambulance from the local Asylum one of Mrs. Thomas' long-standing tenants, an old lady now judged to be a little senile:

> there appears to be a gradual increase in the proportion of aged and infirm to the other patients noted the comissioners in lunacy.[4]

Towards the end of his stay Cecil is convinced that Mrs. Thomas is beginning to suspect that he is in hiding. She is watching him closely and questioning him about his supposed illness of pneumonia. But at last, with a sigh of relief from all concerned, he completes the necessary 14 days and is a free man!

The newspapers tell his story, presenting Cecil as the 'great escaper'. He is photographed holding a violin under his chin, the bow in his right hand about to strike. It is news to us at Wilton Road that Cecil can play this instrument and my mother murmers that my Aunt must have received it from a tenant in lieu of unpaid rent. The article exhibits him as a talented, educated,

---

4. CIL 1894, *Psychiatry for the Poor.*

gifted, bi-lingual young man shut away in the Asylum for no good reason. And so for a short time Cecil gains the celebrity he craves and for once is 'among the angels'!

As for me, at last I am happy, or at least, happier, for home life is more settled and at school I have found friends. At the end of each school day, together with my sister and Zara and Mervyn Wilson I gallop home, Zara's and my girdles from our gym slips held around our younger siblings as reins. Down the road we trot, geeing-up or halting our 'horses' who for the most part appear to be perfectly content to clump along in accord with our demands. Only Mervyn would sometimes whine that surely it was his turn to be the driver.

At home I hear talk of the Spanish Civil War and the bombing and destruction of Guernica by German planes sent by Adolf Hitler in support of Franco:

> *In the city soldiers were collecting charred bodies. There were flames and smoke and grit, and the smell of burning human flesh was nauseating. Houses were collapsing in the inferno.*[5]

"*This would be a good place to hide from bombs*" says my mother. We are making one of our pilgrimages through an empty house and have at last descended to the basement. "*A war?*" I ask tremulously for some time previously I have watched the film of H.G. Wells *The Shape of Things to Come* and burned into my memory is the sight of a small child in a still road, crying and staggering under an attack by poison gas. "*It would make a good bomb shelter*" says my mother. "*they say there's going to be a war.*" She breaks off, becoming aware of my distress and adds quickly, "*Perhaps it won't come, or not for a long time.*" I breathe a sigh of relief, but the small, dead child stays in my mind to become at one with my own later expectations and memories of war.

However, for the most part, encompassed in my child's world I can push aside tales told of persecution and murder in Nazi Germany, the use by Mussolini of poison gas in Abyssinia, the death and prison sentences on Old Bolsheviks by Stalin, the Sino-Japanese war, and an agreement between Germany and Japan "*to protect European culture and save world peace from the Bolshevik menace.*" In those days when it was not usual for the mass of the population to travel abroad, it seemed that these horrors were

---

5. *20th Century Chronicles*, published by Longman.

happening far away. Perhaps for a moment I leave my games to listen to adult talk of the machine-gunning of seventy Palestinian Arabs by the Royal Air Force, or nearer to home, the long march to London of the Jarrow Hunger Marchers, and the Battle of Cable Street, but I am soon caught up again in my own immediate concerns.

Innocently, my sister and I and the Wilsons play our games on our way home from school or out of school, in an inverted version of Virtual Reality—a world which reflects the real, but over which we ourselves exercise control. Our games integrating into fantasy our own direct and indirect experiences, the life around us and what we have read in books or watched in films. An incline becomes a mountain, a few trees a jungle, androgynously we girls transmogrify into cowboys, Indians, detectives, Musketeers or animals.

Zara is one month to the day younger than me, and Mervyn a year younger. Zara is a slim, pale girl whose hair fades into the colour of her skin. She is a pale reflection of her slightly built dark-haired brother who is all sharp points. They are always together, in and out of school, or if Zara joins in a game with classmates, Mervyn wanders unhappily on its periphery. Unlike myself, Zara has no fears of lost status if seen continually in the company of a younger sibling. It is as if only together can they form a complete person and a barrier against a hostile world. For a certain cynicism in the Wilsons makes them regard even professed friends as potential enemies.

Perhaps because of the Wilson's antagonism to their fellows, or defensiveness, they love practical jokes; the kind that makes the other person look foolish. And for some reason, even if the joke is against myself I go along with it.

"*Have you got a penny?*" Mervyn asks. "*Yes*" I reply cautiously. "*Well, we've found out about a lovely sweet*" he tells me, half grinning. We are standing outside a sweetshop in Colney Hatch Lane near Buyansave. "*Go in and ask the man for a pennorth of sweet nut-things, you get a big bag for a penny*" Mervyn instructs me. "*Go on!*" Zara adds to her brother's urgings. Both of them attempting to hide their anticipation. I know that their intention is to make a fool of me, but in a spirit of bravado I take the penny from my pocket to enter the shop. "*Can I have a pennorth of sweet nut-things?*" I ask the gray haired man behind the counter. He looks surprised for a moment and then sees the grinning faces of the Wilsons as they poke their heads around the door to enjoy the joke. The man chuckles and I retreat in pretended embarrassment. I have made their day.

Although I spend much time with Zara and Mervyn, I am never invited into the Wilson home. Should I call upon them, knocking at the door of their first-floor maisonette in Bedford Close, I am told to wait outside until they are sent out to me. But the Wilson children are often at Wilton Road where Mervyn joins us girls in our games of dressing up in my mother's discarded clothes, putting on lipstick, the girls attempting to comb our hair into Hollywood styles, while Mervyn decorates his short back and sides with a hair ribbon.

My mother regards Mervyn with disquiet as he acts out the starring role in *Snow White*—large blue bow on the top of his head, a cotton dress sheathing his body, the skirt of which he holds with one hand as he minces about the room, tossing his head and fluttering his eye lashes.

Sometimes, Zara says to her brother *"come on boy!." "Don't call me boy!"* he sulks. In those days, Mervyn regarded boys with animosity and had no wish to join in their boisterous games. To keep them at bay he had developed a vitriolic tongue. The boys, for their part, regarded Mervyn and his rejection of them with puzzlement. Especially when he, feeling threatened by their uniform behaviour on the playground in which they seemingly rush at him in an intimidating group, lashes out at them with his tongue. At those times, as they stampede past him some of the boys turn and shout back the only insult to hand *"You're a sissy—you play with girls!"*

This perception of prejudice had developed in Mervyn a cunning which made of him a sound strategist. For instance, on one occasion when we had raced our sibling horses along one of our many routes home—this one down Pages Hill, past the suburban houses and their neat gardens, up through the garage with its work area and petrol pumps and out into Colney Hatch Lane—a thickset, stolid boy dressed in school uniform and a little older than us, shouts *"You're not allowed through here it's private!"* Mervyn calls back promptly *"Who said! Not you Fatty!"* The boy in fury picks up a stone. We girls turn and run, Mervyn behind us until, calling upon us to wait, he turns to our adversary and baits him once again. *"Fatty, fatty, fatty, ugly face, looney..."* pulling faces and poking out his tongue. Once more the lad chases us, aiming stones as he runs. Each time he tires and seems about to give up, Mervyn makes sure to provoke him further and soon Zara, intuitively understanding her brother's purpose, joins in until at last our antagonist is in Wilton Road itself. Whilst Mervyn and Zara engage the enemy in insults, my sister and I run indoors to call our mother who, at our impassioned tale of having been attacked by a 'big boy', hurries out of the house to insist that the boy take her home to complain to his mother. Sadly and sulkily the boy leads her up the road to his house in Pages Lane. *"The foreman told me to chase strangers off from the garage"* he mutters, creeping into his middle-class suburban home, shoulders bent, tail between his legs, his mother's outrage at his conduct striking his bowed back and making him stumble.

On Saturdays we make a Virtual World from Weddells Builders Yard, to the side of Bedford Close. This was surrounded by a wire fence over which we could easily climb, to jump down to a place filled with bricks, drain-pipes, guttering, roof tiles, chimney pots, window frames, doors, porch posts, fencing, bags of cement—an ideal landscape for acting out, under the Wilson's direction, *The Four Feathers*, *The Three Musketeers* or any other Hollywood epic of this nature, viewed during the week by the Wilsons, who were avid filmgoers.

We also make a camp in the wasteland behind Pages Hill which runs between the fenced back gardens and a railed off allotment. At the edge of this wasteland a hollow concealed by bushes seemed an ideal hiding place, and even the railings on its other side and bordering the allotments appeared to provide security. We furnished our camp with one or two books and a doll's teaset, our minds' eyes transporting us a hundred miles from our own homes. Untroubled by danger, we light a small fire made from twigs and paper and lit by a match. We make sure to stamp out the fire before leaving, for we know of forest fires and my sister and I, at least, have been brought up with the story of the death by burning of my mother's half-sister Flora. We have seen also the colourless rendering of fires in black and white films, the glorious and fascinating red, blues and oranges supplied by our imaginations and yet it is clear to us that fire possesses an all-consuming passion. But our fire had been seen from the allotments and complaints made, so that on one of our visits we find the books torn and the teaset broken, the pieces scattered. Joan Richards, who lives in Pages Hill and is in my class at the Convent, tells me next day *"some boys broke your things. A man on the allotment saw the fire and told the boys to stop children playing there."*

For a time, after this incident, we walk home through Creighton Avenue and down Tetherdown, or along Pages Lane and down Colney Hatch Lane, until we are once again secure enough to take the Pages Hill route. Names fascinate me and I am sure that the houses in this road are at the bottom of the hierarchy of Muswell Hill's roads and these small bright, three-bedroomed houses, all pages, stand at the ready to serve the larger and older housing in Kings, Queens, Princes and Dukes Avenues. Therefore, I have with this road, and Pages Lane, a sneaking sympathy. But now, instead of galloping through the garage, we 'jump' our 'horses' over a fence to one side of it and drop down onto Greenham Road, accompanied in this exploit by the angry shouts from a side window of a woman living in the house standing alongside.

However, turning away from our games and into actual reality, at times I must walk through Sydney Road past the crumbling cottages, now replaced by an equally crumbling Council estate, past the marginalised and disaffected dwellers who are unemployed or in low-paid casual work. Penurious people. *"Go back to where you live!"* shout the pinched ill-clad sullen children as I pass through wearing my school hat, velour or panama, with band and badge. Sometimes a child throws a stone towards me to emphasise his, or her, shouts of outrage. When alone I flinch and hurry on my way, my shoulders hunched, my back tense. I am more secure, and therefore happier, when I make a foray into this district in the company of Zara and Mervyn. It is then that I appreciate Mervyn's vicious turn of phrase and the fact that both Wilsons will return in kind any stones which come hurtling at us from across the road.

Sometimes when out shopping with my mother at the Broadway we meet the Wilson children with their mother. Mrs Wilson is a sallow-faced woman, hair pulled back into a bun, mouth discontented. Immediately she begins to complain about *"'im."* Her husband was never other than *"'e"* or *"'im." "'E"* was lazy. *"'E"* drank too much. *"'E"* kept her short of money. The only time we ever met 'im', a fresh-faced and thickset bus driver, he had set up a cricket pitch for his children in Bedford Close and was trying to interest them in the game. They co-operated reluctantly as if in some way they were betraying themselves, and certainly their mother, by accepting pleasure from this man.

The last time I saw the Wilsons was during the war when I, at home for a weekend from evacuation, found them playing ball in the middle of Wilton Road. They had ceased to go to school from the outbreak of war and spent their days wandering and playing in the streets. Keeping to the pavement, I pass by. I have other interests now and other friends. Mervyn throws a ball to his sister and she returns it carefully. *"You home?"* Mervyn shouts at me. *"I'm going back tomorrow"* I call in return. *"Lucky devil!"* he yells, batting the ball with his hand.

At the end of the war the Wilson parents move out of London, but my mother receives occasional news of them from Mrs Wilson's sister, also sad and sallow. Her son, another fat boy, had at weekends followed us at a distance and been the butt of Mervyn's spiteful tongue. *"Mervyn goes with men"* says Mrs Wilson's sister. The word 'gay' had not yet been invented and she did not know what other word to use. *"Black men"* she adds, more outraged by this latter fact than the former. The Wilson parents had opened a general store in Deal and wanted nothing more to do with their 'errant' son, he must never darken their doors again. Fortunately, Mervyn was not penniless, for the paternal grandfather, a farmer, had left his money and property to his two grandchildren. As for Zara, she married a man some years older than herself.

Another friend of those days is Twi Carson. The Carsons lived in the house behind ours, in Sutton Road, our gardens separated by a fence. Twi, short for Twilight, and whose real name was Violet, was exactly five days older than me. Her hair is light auburn and her skin freckled. I have played with her out of school for years, but she comes to the Convent at the age of eleven as she has failed to pass the scholarship for Grammar School. Twi is the youngest of four children, all born in India where her father, a tall, dark, cadaverous, dour man and an Oxford graduate, had been Headmaster in a British school under the Raj.

Arriving home in the midst of an economic slump and following a long period of unemployment, Mr Carson could find nothing more than a teaching post in a Council school, a post for which he had no leaning and in which he felt undervalued. Perhaps it was then that the canker which was to destroy his body began first to eat away at his soul. In the meantime, to assure himself of his worth, neither at home, nor school, would he allow himself to relax, or surrender the cane of office. Therefore, Mrs Carson, a soft-voiced Northern Irishwoman and the children, lived their lives around him.

The Carsons occupy the upstairs flat at 19 Sutton Road, the downstairs flat and garden belonging to its tenant, a Mr Adams. Mr Adams is one more adult who objects to me bridging fences, especially as, having alighted on the ground, I run across his carefully tended garden. But his animosity adds to my excitement. "*Quick, quick!*" I shriek, should Oonagh be with me, both of us expecting this elderly gentleman to pounce on us at any moment. He is the ogre, or the monster of our story-books. Generally he contents himself with shouting imprecations out of a window and it is only occasionally that lying in wait he catches me and directs me back to my own side of the fence. When this happens I am forced to take the much longer trek up Wilton Road, past the shops and down Sutton Road.

Twi's flat is a place of long corridors from which the rooms open out, a short flight of stairs leading up to the front room. Her bathroom has no pedestal basin, but only a bowl fitted over the bath and in some way I know that this proves the superiority of the Lahrs, for we have a pedestal basin with its own taps. Sometimes we play in the flat, or at other times in the front garden, but more often than not we go to Coldfall Woods.

Coldfall Woods forms a haven between the Council estate of houses built some time between the wars to provide just enough room to eat, sleep and procreate, the Finchley cemetery and the solid, roomy middle-class housing of Creighton Avenue. Entering the woods by a tight passage in either Everington or Barrenger Roads, we make for the narrow stream which zigzags across the woods to end in a man-made waterfall at the main entrance in Creighton Avenue. Often we follow the stream to its source, stopping every now and then to dip our hands into its yellow mud which Twi calls sailor's soap, and then rinse them in the sparse stream water. We are explorers trudging to the end of the world, in front of us marvellous lands of mountain and lakes, magic forests and enchanted castles; behind us dense jungles, wild animals and hostile peoples.

Our secret call to each other in the woods is "*Ooook, ook, oo*" sung on an ascending register. Many years later, when I had been dragged into adulthood and had children of my own, I often wondered with yearning as to whether the old familiar cry would result in an answering shout, so leading me back to an inevitably discarded childhood.

Our imaginations exhausted for the moment, we play 'He', chasing each other around the trees and bushes, or hide-and-seek, until we come to an open space bordered by blackberry bushes behind which the fence edges the cemetery. There we lie down on the rough grass until becoming bored, we jump up and start our games all over again.

My friendship with the Dawson boys who continue to live above us, is interrupted by the first intimations of adolescence. Now I am shy with them, the biological differences between us suddenly making a barrier. For instance, on one occasion I am upstairs taking some clothing from the linen cupboard, behind me the bathroom door. "*Alf!*" shouts Mrs. Dawson from the kitchen door on my right. The room in which I had fallen onto the black staining when we first moved into the house. The bathroom door opens and Alf stands there, naked. I am concealed by the cupboard door and shrink even further behind it, holding my breath. I can see clearly his boy's testicles and am filled by guilt. At last Alf retreats into the bathroom and closes the door, when I, in panic, rush downstairs, hugging to myself my knowledge and discomfiture.

"*Jump up and down*" Alf instructs Oonagh and me. My sister and I are in our nightdresses, sitting on the big double bed which we are sharing. We have been playing cards with 'the boys', but the game has come to an end. My sister and I jump, banging down on the mattress, up high, our feet in the air, banging down again. "*Pull up your nightdresses*" says Alf. I jump less readily and more gently keeping my legs together and pulling my nightdress around my knees. "*Go on!*" says Alf. I shake my head and sit down and my sister, puzzled, does the same.

Not only sex, but class entered into our relationships with the Dawsons, my mother intent upon maintaining the educational differences between us for she needed to cling to a conception of cultural superiority in or to maintain respect for herself in poverty. Therefore the Dawsons suspected us of being snobs. On one occasion, while we are boarding, my mother sends Alf and Fred to the Convent with a message. It is early evening and we are watching a magic lantern show—postcards of mountains and distant places. A nun asks the boys in and invites them to watch. My sister and I sit on a hard bench opposite the boys, a narrow gangway between us. We gaze at them without speaking or acknowledging their presence for it is as if we are looking through a window into another world. When the boys arrive home they tell their mother in disgust that we wouldn't speak to them. We think we're too good for them.

However, all my friendships pale into insignificance in comparison with my passion for Colleen Sullivan.

Holding My Breath

Colleen becomes my best friend: Confession, Communion and other religious rites: Girl Guides: The IRA in London: A school stockings strike: Swimming and Roller Skating: Racism: I develop asthma and miss school: I am demoted: A few words on Humility.

Colleen Sullivan is the most popular girl in the school. She is straight out of an Angela Brazil novel. She is plump and freckled, but her thick auburn hair reaching way down her back to hang in shining ringlets, is the envy of other girls. Each morning Colleen's mother releases her daughter's hair from rags and brushes the locks around a copper stick and I, having called for her early in the morning, watch enviously. If only my hair would grow long and change colour overnight so that my mother could do the same for me. But to my mother, bobbed hair represented women's emancipation and so my hair was never allowed to do more than touch my shoulders. In fact, on one occasion during the long school holidays, my mother cut my hair so short, largely in an attempt to even up both sides, that for weeks I refused to go out without a hat. Colleen had no such problem, and on the strength of her golden locks and a commanding presence had gathered around herself a group that was recognised by the rest of us as at the summit of the pecking order. All of us left out stood alone on the periphery looking in, for to group together with other rejects would confirm in us our lowly status.

Then, all of a sudden, as if it were one of the Miracles enumerated by the nuns, Colleen deigns to invite me into her charmed circle. It happens like this. One morning I am jumping up and down on the steps to the side of the triangular driveway, waiting for the narrow school door to open. Colleen and her friends are playing on the self same steps, and while I am alongside them, I am alone. *"Let Sheila play"* Colleen commands and the group opens to allow me in. Soon we are walking home together, for Colleen lives in Greenham Road which runs parallel to Wilton Road. Colleen! I can hardly believe my luck. Colleen, whom all our classmates admire and whom the nuns respect. And yet she does not see my family as odd and unacceptable, nor does she despise our house which is dilapidated when compared with her own. She never mentions that my mother often dresses in ill-fitting second-hand clothing and that, unlike Colleen who is always smartly turned out, my sister and I wear our school uniform until they are shabby or obviously too small. She does not care that my father wears open sandals without socks: this latter of concern to me, and if my father is to come to a school event I plead with him *"put socks on Dad.,"* for I hope that socks will cover the fact that he is not wearing shoes.

This is not to say that at times Colleen does not attempt to make me over in her own image. *"You can't say 'school' properly,"* she says. *"It's not 'skoool', like you say it, it's 'skul'."* She pronounces the 'oo' like the 'u' in pull. At the time we are walking home accompanied by Betty Scott who lives opposite Colleen in Greenham Road. Betty, a tall, sallow, girl with spread nose, remarks *"her way might be right, but who's Sheila Lahr to be right!"* BC—Before Colleen—that had been the general consensus of opinion: *"Who's Sheila Lahr. Who and what does she think she is!"*

Together, Colleen and I go to Confession, discussing, on our walk up Colney Hatch Lane, the sins we should enumerate to the priest. We giggle over 'adultery' for we are not supposed to know about that. At last we settle for three or four lies, stealing a pencil, losing our tempers, and being rude to our parents. All safe bets. At last it is my turn to enter the confessional box where I kneel facing the grille behind which the priest can barely be seen. *"Bless me Father, for I have sinned. I last went to confession one, two, weeks ago."* To assure us that it is never too late to receive forgiveness and grace, at school we are told the story of a sinner who after many years repented. Kneeling in the confessional box he informs the priest that he last went to confession twenty years ago! *"What kind of penance was he ordered,"* I wondered. *"How many rosaries, how many Our Fathers and Hail Marys! Maybe it would take him a further twenty years to say them all!"* I snigger. However, in the confessional box my sins are simple statements. They are practical and reveal nothing of the physical, sexual and emotional turmoil of the pre-pubescent. I had made my first confession at the age of seven, shortly after my baptism, and my First Communion a year or so later. For this latter I was dressed in white dress and veil, on which my mother spent hard-earned money, rushing madly about for the best bargain to ensure that I was dressed appropriately. To this day when I look at the veiling—which I use to cover exposed food—I say to myself *"that would have done for First Communion or the Corpus Christi procession!"* At this June procession, those who had recently made their First Communion were given cardboard boxes of rose petals, a ribbon attached on both sides of the box and around our necks. As we walked, we scattered rose-petals over the pathways. A year or so later when Oonagh made her First Communion, I was happy to be allowed once more to importantly bedeck the pathways around the Church with these pink rose petals; petals which appeared to come straight from God at that time. But now, instead, I see a group of nuns deliberately gathering roses for mutilation. He loves me, he loves me not.

Colleen takes me along to the Catholic Girl Guides meeting at Our Lady of Muswell church hall, where I promise, with some reservations, to do my duty to God and the King. At Guides I join in camp fires in the hall, several Companies of Guides meeting together to sit cross-legged around a virtually real fire made from twigs and a light behind red paper. *"Little Liza Jane"* we sing, banging the metal ends of our belts together to maintain the rhythm. We are on a scavenger hunt and I am racing against time to find all the items on the list. We are taken on a trip to the Home Farm at Arkley, walking from Chipping Barnet. The day is sunny, the sky blue and we walk along chatting happily. *"How far do you think you've walked?"* Lieutenant Weber, a dark woman somewhere in her thirties, her black hair worn cropped, asks me suddenly. The way has seemed so short I have no idea. *"About half a mile"* I say blithely. She frowns. *"You've walked a mile in twelve minutes"* she says *"you've passed that bit of the test, but you don't know how to estimate a mile."* I hear only that I have passed a test, a mile in twelve minutes! Alongside and in front of me Roger Bannister runs a four minute mile in 1954. But I am never to receive the appropriate badge to sew onto my uniform; a uniform which my mother has bought for me at Arthur Humphreys, darker and thicker than the washed out blue cotton worn by the other guides, even by Colleen, for mine is winter weight. Colleen and the others need to wear jumpers under their uniforms during the winter. But I am not at all grateful to my mother for I want to be the same as my peers. The Guide hat, both winter and summer, was made of navy blue felt with a brim. Ena Macfarlane, also in our Guide Company, could pull her hat into wonderful shapes, which on our way home, she perched on her head: a skill denied me.

At Home Farm we visit the cowsheds where the cows stand quietly in their stalls and I breathe in their sweet smell of milk, straw and dung. Men milk them by hand and one such milker turns to smile at us. He holds a white blue rimmed enamel mug which he dips into the bucket of milk beneath the cow and invites each of us to drink. The milk is creamy and pleasantly warm, but I sip it guiltily. Milk, my mother has told me, must be pasteurised to guard against tuberculosis which is endemic to cows. For days afterwards I watch myself for symptoms, hearing them in every cough and sneeze. It is several years before an X-Ray indicates that during my childhood my lungs had been attacked by tubercular bacilli although this had nothing to do with unpasteurised milk. Tuberculosis was common in those days.

At the Farm on this balmy day, we play team games in the field and in the afternoon, after we have eaten our sandwiches, Captain instructs us to take an afternoon rest in one of the few tents set up in the field. A few of the older girls rebel. They are not tired, why should they waste the day in resting, or sleeping? They go off together in a group and climb trees. For a time I lie down on the palliasse, but soon I am bored and leave the tent to explore the terrain. It is then that I find my mother has arrived and brought with her Alf and Fred Dawson. Alf is perched on the branch of a tree surrounded by these older girls and I feel left out. He has no interest in me, now he belongs to them, and it is not possible for me to stake my claim.

Guides is not all pleasure, for even here we are affected by the arbitrary decisions of authority. We sit cross-legged on the floor in the hall and the Captain addresses us. She is flanked by Lieutenant Weber and the Ranger, Gwen, who is a plump, placid girl. The two Officers are dressed neatly in military style with navy blue skirts and fitted jackets. A reorganisation is to take place. Girls are to be moved from one patrol to another. Also, the policy which put sisters together is to be changed. They are to be separated. I glance at Oonagh who has recently joined the Guides. She is to be moved from out of the Poppy to the Rose patrol. Neither of us care, for our paths have already diverged. But the girls around me are crying, some quietly, the tears running slowly down their cheeks; others such as tall, dark, slim, 14-year-old Josephine Wilde, with abandon. She sobs into clenched fists, her head bent in grief. She rocks backwards and forwards, cries out hysterically. I find tears in my own eyes. Loyalty given to a patrol, work to obtain marks in competition with the others in order to make it the top patrol, have all gone for nothing. At last we are dismissed and return home sullenly, many vowing never to go again to Guides. But, the intervening week and parents' urgings result in adaptation to the new regime. On returning home from the meeting I had complained to my mother, but she could not understand why anyone should make a fuss about such matters. *"What does it matter which patrol you're in?"* she asks reasonably. *"Anyway, Josephine has the right surname!"* At the Home Farm she had taken a dislike to Josephine Wilde, finding a threat in her loudness and unrestrained energy.

Colleen and I form our own club—the Daredevils Association—for Colleen is a devotee of the Saint, Biggles, and Bulldog Drummond. We make ourselves badges from a piece of oblong metal covered in blue silk embroidered with the letters 'DDA' and to prove our daring, we walk along the scaffolding of a deep trench which takes up half of Greenham Road—a roadworks temporarily deserted by the workmen. I hold onto the sides and try not to look down to the gravel and water below. We climb trees and jump from walls. Later, during the war when I am evacuated, memories of the DDA encourage me to walk along the outside of a bridge across a railway line, the metal rails far below, the threat of a smoky steam train under my carefully moving feet.

Colleen's mother always makes me welcome and sometimes we play in her garden. Mrs. Sullivan is a home dressmaker, an activity which adds to the family income. The Sullivans also let a room to an old man named Mr. Hodges, grey haired and wearing side whiskers. His one claim to fame resides in his description of the loss of a watch: *"There it was, gone"* he is reported to have said; a statement repeated by Mrs. Sullivan to Colleen who in repeating it to me with much glee, adds by way of explanation *"If it was there it couldn't be gone!"* Mr. Sullivan, a short, broad, sandy-haired man, born in England of Irish parents, is a building trades foreman and his job takes him away from home for long periods. Colleen's brother Terence, four years older than her, is away at a Catholic boarding school and so Colleen is in the position of an only child. Colleen adores this plump, stocky, freckled boy, but to me he is no more than someone Colleen talks about, for even in the school holidays, I am separated from him by his seniority. At last, when he is brought home to live and sent as a day boy to St. Ignatius College the reason given to me by Colleen is that she made herself ill with excitement each time he was expected home.

"My mother was the girl next door" Colleen tells me. *"She lived next door to my father when they were children, then they went out together and got engaged and got married."* Mrs. Sullivan is half Jewish, her hair dark and a little frizzy, although not as curly as my mother's hair. Colleen, with an Irish name and colouring, favours the Irish side. *"The men in the IRA are lining up and wanting to be hanged and die for Ireland,"* she tells me proudly. I see a long line of men pushing and shoving each other in their eagerness to be first on the gallows. There have been a number of bomb incidents in London involving bridges. Colleen repeats also tales of the Black and Tans, the British force raised in 1920 'to put down insurrection in Ireland'.[1] *"They boiled prisoners in oil"* says Colleen. Later, my mother tells me that Mr. Sullivan had been a Black and Tan. She is scathing. *"What kind of Irishman does he call himself!"* But his experiences have confirmed in him a nascent Irish patriotism which has been passed on to his daughter.

It may well be that it was Colleen's revolutionary emotions in this direction that led her to be one of the leaders of a school stocking strike, or sock sit-in. For while we are allowed in summer to wear a navy and white cotton school dress, we are forced winter and summer to encase our legs in beige woollen stockings. We are ten to eleven year-olds and the day is hot, the sun striking the large classroom windows to bathe us, sitting targets, in perspiration. The murmur begins. *"Why can't we wear socks?"* We scratch ouir legs, the wool in this heat having set up an irritation. Our grumbles and discontent culminating in an instruction flying about the classroom from girl to girl *"tell everyone to come to school in white socks tomorrow."* Next day I wear my badge of courage on my feet. We are defiant. Sitting at our desks, our faces

---

1. *Longman's Encyclopaedia.*

resolute we declare stubbornly, "*we ought to be allowed to wear socks when it's hot.*" The sister is agitated. Her whole class is out of control. She cannot cope with children resolute upon an unapproved cause. She sends for Reverend Mother. Reverend Mother enters the classroom to sit at the high teacher's desk, her lined face smiling, her sharp eyes behind the wire-rimmed spectacles watching us closely. "*I know*" she says in honeyed tones "*it is very hot weather. Your legs become very warm and you do not like a little discomfort.*" Her eyes flick towards the picture on the wall of St. Catherine tied bravely to her wheel, arms and legs extended, whirling round and round to be consumed by fire; then to the crucificx of Jesus nailed to the cross, thorns piercing his bloodied head, his poor hands nailed to the wood. We fidget in discomfiture. Reverend Mother continues "*We like our girls to look smart so that Convent girls are respected... always properly dressed... proud to belong to us...*" her gentle voice presenting us to ourselves as soldiers in the battle, soldiers in the struggle for recognition and veneration of all our school stands for. And a promise to the Catholic girls of a heroic martyrdom in defence of our religion, besieged by evil forces.

Outright or threatened punishment we could handle, meet with fortitude, but sympathetic words and a call to duty we are unable to withstand. "*But*" Reverend Mother concludes, just in case any doubters remain, "*We will look into the matter if you all come in stockings tomorrow. Perhaps in the future we will make socks part of the uniform for hot weather.*" She has won. Next day we wear woollen stockings and offer up our discomfort to God. We hear no more about a relaxation of the school uniform.

During the school holidays I go swimming together with Colleen, at Durnsford Road Open-air Swimming Baths, Bounds Green. A wonderful swimming pool, the fifteen foot deepest end reflecting a blue floor, and the shallowest end three foot six inches. There are also sun roofs and there we sunbathe once we have had enough of the water. The baths are entered by a swing door and once in the lobby we pay 6d for a private cubicle and locker, or 2d to undress and dress in the Common Room, receiving in both cases a coloured elastic band to wear on an arm. Then, pretending a pleasure of which I am not certain, I enter the water, uncertain in my enjoyment for I always feel cold. Surely I had not struggled out of the fluids of my mother's womb to be engulfed in these less accommodating waters with their smell of killer antiseptic. I have learned to swim only because I fear that otherwise Colleen will go to the baths without me. When we have had our fill of the water, we climb the wide stone steps up to the sun roof to lie on our towels.

Should the pool be especially busy, which is mostly throughout the summer, swimmers are culled by the colour of the band on their arm. *"Blue* (or red, or yellow, or green) *bands, out of the water"* the megaphone blares. Therefore we never know how long we will be able to stay at the pool, but on a 'good' day we can spend all day there, from morning until tea-time, taking with us a sandwich for lunch and, if we have any money, buying a fruit drink, or a chocolate bar, from the kiosk.

I am an indifferent swimmer and on one occasion almost drown, for Ena Macfarland, at home in the water, grabs me from out of the shallow end and, swimming on her back, pulls me, also on my back, out to the deep end. My face is under water and at first I struggle, but soon a delicious dreaming comes over me and I am at peace. When suddenly, as if from a distance, I hear Oonagh's voice cruelly breaking into my reverie: *"Leave her alone, Ena. Let her go,"* I find myself dumped. There are no arms around me. I am on my own. I reach out for Oonagh, but she is swimming away. In spite of myself, self-preservation takes over and I struggle to the side of the baths, grasp the rail and climb out to bring up 'bucketfuls' of water. *"You nearly drowned me!"* I say fiercely to Ena, but she laughs and quickly runs away. Nowadays, the swimming bath is a nursery and growing plants send their tentacles into the confined lockers, to drag over the tiled surround and to lurk on the floor of the pool in the place of my almost demise.

Colleen and I go roller skating at Alexandra Palace, walking up Goodwyns Vale, along Grosvenor Avenue, stepping in the footprints made together with my father a few years before. Under the archway the echoes of years past call out to me, up the wide stone steps to the side of the Palace and into the rink, to be assailed by the noise of metal wheels striking a hard surface, a colour of skaters whirling in a circle, circle, circle. At first I must hire skates, strapping them across my shoes, or tightening a metal grip with a key, sometimes not tight enough so that one of them loosens, and hangs from the strap around my ankle, and I fall. But soon my mother is to buy a secondhand pair screwed to boots, the boots too small. However, the skates are extendable and so my father screws them onto an old pair of my walking shoes. For the learners, a number of spaced horizontal bars have been provided nearby the rink and at first I practice down these alleys, my hands poised over a bar on each side in case I start to fall. Until, at last, my feet obey directions from my mind and soon I am flying like a bird. 'Fast Skaters Only' announces the roll down, or over, board lit up and situated over the rink. When the board announces 'Dancers Only' I watch the girls in their colourful short skirts and the nicely dressed boys skating together around the rink to the *Skaters Waltz* and other such music. One day I too will dance on skates.

After skating, and on our way home, Colleen and I stop to talk to friends, standing outside a house to the side of the archway entrance, and there we attract the enmity of an old woman who, disturbed at the presence of several pre-nubile girls, calls to us repeatedly from a window *"go away—go away from my house."* So incensed is she at our aimless chatter and youthful pleasure, that she doesn't see or hear the bomb which during the Second World War whines down to fall upon her house, levelling it out of existence. *"She wasn't a nice old lady"* we say, with the callousness of youth and inexperience.

Although Colleen considers herself Irish, her awareness of her mother's heredity means that she makes a friend of any Jewish girl attending the Convent. There are not many and are generally identified by their withdrawal from class during lessons on the New Testament. The only Jewish girl in our class is Stella Friedlander whose father owns a small grocery shop, Colleen drawing this small, dark-eyed girl into all of our games at school. As it happens, at St. Martin's Convent I never heard an antisemitic remark, although antisemitism was much in evidence in the surrounding neighbourhood. *"You're Jews"* accuses a boy aged about ten, and flanked by several companions. They have cornered me, my sister and my cousin Seema in the yard off Wilton Road. We are pressed against the wall, our tormentors lined up in front of us. My only instinct is to deny everything. *"I'm not!"* I reply vehemently. *"I'm a Catholic."* *"Cafflicks are Jews"* retorts the boy.

"My best friend at home is Jewish" says Colleen angrily. She is referring to Stella Friedlander. This is during the Second World War and we are evacuated with Our Lady's Convent to Welwyn Garden City. Loud-mouthed Pamela Bloomfield has made an antisemitic remark to small, neat, quiet Zena Platter, the only Jewish girl in our class. Colleen stands in the classroom, her eyes blazing and the other girls, silent spectators to the scene, melt

away. Fully confident of her own worth, in those days Colleen had greater courage than me. For I was never sure who I was and clung to what I was meant to be within the majority group. For otherwise:

> *O.U.T. spells out*
> *And out of this game you must go*
> *Because my mother told me so*

It is ironic that while I look back at this short space of time before the Second World War as happy because I am at last at home with my mother, and Colleen, the most popular girl in the school, is my best friend, it is during this period that I develop asthma. While I was boarding at the Convent, there had been moments when my breath was caught within my body and I could neither inhale nor exhale. But such experiences lasted only moments and then, of its own accord, my breath moved in and out again and I forgot the feeling of stasis, until it happened once again. But suddenly, for long periods normal breathing which accompanies us at birth, fails, and to breathe I must painfully force air in and out of my lungs. The breath entering harshly, but losing itself on its way out. I walk bent over, my hands pressing on my hips, I hold onto furniture, clinging to tables and chairs. If I go to school I stagger along grasping at garden walls, stopping frequently and making slow progress. Sometimes, fortunately, by sitting down for the morning in the classroom my difficult breathing eases and I am able to walk home almost normally. My mother buys me Potters Asthma Cure for use at home, and I light a mound of the herbal mixture with a match, to breathe in its smouldering smoke. Later, my parents buy me an atomiser, a plastic cup with glass funnel attached to a rubber ball which, when pressed, releases a spray of Riddobron, this latter bought in a small, dark bottle. For many years I sleep at night with my atomiser by my side.

My mother blames my asthmatic attacks upon the shock of my father's imprisonment and the upset which it caused in our lives. In those days asthma was considered to be an entirely psychosomatic illness. Therefore, my mother takes me to hospital after hospital where we sit on hard benches for five, six, seven hours, waiting in a large, drab, noisy open room, the monotony broken only by the occasional appearance of a large, trundling tea-trolley. First, of course, it is necessary to lay bare our financial circumstances before the Lady Almoner, for some payment must be made for treatment. We sit in a small office and I feel my mother's embarrassment as she reveals our poverty. The Lady Almoner sits filling out a form while my mother tells her *"we're not selling very much now. I have to pay the mortgage, the coke bills, the electricity, the gas, the rates, the water rates, the school fees and so on and so on."* At last the sum total of our existence is set down in black and white and with any luck my mother will have to buy no more than one or two sixpenny stamps to stick on a card. When at last we see a doctor, he has various theories about me: spoiled children develop asthma and need to be sent away from home. Others understand vaguely about allergies and blame our cat or hay fever. I am to develop hay fever a little later, but that is as the result of lying in the straw-like grass of the garden of a nearby empty house in Wilton Road, my mother intent at the time upon collecting some admired plants. As for our cat, well, I suppose it didn't help, but we had always kept a cat at home. Our visit to the hospital generally results in a carton of powder or crystals with instructions to dissolve in water and breathe in as a nose wash. Eventually, after many such visits and hours and hours and hours of waiting time, I refuse to enter another hospital and my mother at last accepts my asthma as a given fact which can be ameliorated, but not cured.

It is not until 1968—a year in which the American military continued to lay waste to Vietnam, a year in which the man with the dream, Martin Luther King, was murdered, a year in which Enoch Powell forecast 'rivers of blood' should black immigration continue, a year in which the students of Paris went to the barricades, a year in which Russian tanks crushed a move to liberalisation in Czechoslovakia—that researchers announced much asthma was caused by an allergic reaction to the dust mite. Billions and trillions of these microscopic ugly mites having invaded my respiratory system from the hundreds and hundreds of dusty books amidst which at night I sleep, until my body, in defence, closes in upon my breathing apparatus. Soon I am missing out on school for weeks at a time and sometimes, especially in winter, bronchitis accompanies the asthma. At these times I am confined at home to lie in a bed around which a tent, made from sheeting, has been erected while I breathe in friars balsam issuing in steam from the spout of a tin kettle. Days, weeks, months, years, I spend, lying in bed and watching patterns on the walls and ceiling made by staining and changing light. On one side of my bed in the downstairs front room, the wallpaper is torn and reveals broken plaster. I lie back on raised pillows, I draw the fingers of my left hand across the pitted wallscape to enjoy the harsh tactile experience.

While I lie in bed struggling to breathe, at the Convent lessons are continuing, the class being taught as an entity and the lesson given only once. On each occasion when I return to school following an absence, I find chunks of knowledge have been dealt with and put away, and I must proceed without them, much as if I am putting together a jigsaw from which many pieces are missing. For instance, during the term in which we begin upon algebra I am fortunate enough to remain well until the very end of term, when I miss the exam. However, my report says 'Algebra-Very Good'. Unfortunately, during the succeeding terms I am ill with asthma for several weeks and suddenly I have become a dunce—at Algebra, Arithmetic, Geometry, French, Geography. *"Does not concentrate—does not listen—must work harder,"* declare my school reports. My parents are disappointed in me and begin to concentrate upon the academic prowess of my sister. The class is streamed by age and performance into two divisions and suddenly I drop from among the first three in exams to last. I cannot understand how this has happened to me and yet vaguely I connect this to my absences from school. But no one else appears to recognise the effect these absences are having on my school work. Apparently, I am expected to rise above them and do as well as ever. I am the same person as in previous terms. An avid reader, a writer of stories and poems, interested in ideas and the world around me and yet here I am, dubbed supid, a thickie. Years later my cousin Cecil is to give me a book—*I am Jonathan Scrivener* by Claude Houghton[2]—which divides persons into those who have brains and those who have minds. The former are good at learning facts and the latter able to put together knowledge and experience to form concepts. With relief I class myself among the latter and this provides me with some consolation. School, of course, is interested only in those said to have 'brains', those who can learn by rote and regurgitate knowledge. Imagination and curiosity are dirty words. Children are inadequate adults to be disciplined to fit into an irrational society and indoctrinated with disinformation. In fact, while on teaching practice in an in-

2.Claude Houghton, *I am Jonathan Scrivener*, Penguin Books, 1936.

ner city infant school in the early 1970s, I conclude that children are sent to school to be made stupid.

The nuns especially distrusted 'precocious' children and no doubt their belief in divine intervention left them a little short in an understanding of cause and effect. It may well be that they saw my descent as a fitting punishment for my family, God being just. This because my mother would boast to them about the family's literary connections and her glorious plans for her children's futures. *"Do you think we're foolish?"* Reverend Mother demands of me. Her eyes glinting behind wire-framed spectacles. I have been called to her office to face both her and Sister St. Francois, the latter standing alongside me and nodding her head, while Reverend Mother interrogates me from behind her desk. Reverend Mother thrusts a piece of paper at me and I see it is a poem written by Oonagh, beginning *"O moon, O stars."* *"Oh,"* I say to myself *"why did my mother send it to them?"* I look at Reverend Mother without speaking, for I do not know what to say and at last she instructs me to return to my classroom. And as I leave the office she sends after me a parting shot *"We know Shakespeare when we see it—we are not stupid."*

Since that time I have discovered that I and my sister were in good company, for Anna Wickham writes for the Centenary of her birth:

> *Often during this time I would write a poem for my father. This got me little credit with the nuns, who thought it queer. We wrote our home letters on Sunday afternoons in the large classroom, and we always had to show what we wrote to the nun in charge. On one occasion I had written in reply to some sad word of his, a very inspiring poem on the beauties of hope. Sister Mary Aden looked up at me virulently from the verses and said 'I have read this before in a book'. That was the cruellest thing the nuns ever did to me.*[3]

For the religiose Humility is the greatest of Christian virtues and the words of the poet William Blake have no meaning for them:

> *Humility is only doubt and does the sun and moon blot out*

---

3. Anna Wickham, *The Writings of Anna Wickham: Free Woman and Poet*, Virago, 1984.

nor do the words of Charlie 'Bird' Parker, the Afro-American Jazz musician:

Humility won't take you nowhere

I cannot fathom why my parents made no connection between my absences from school and my lack of scholastic achievement. Whatever the reason, they accepted the assessments of my ability—or inability—set out in school reports. *"Does not concentrate"* leads my mother to take note of advertisements flooding the newspapers for 'Pelmanism', a pseudo-science which claims to train the mind. While she cannot afford to send for the course, she can at least pounce upon the words *"Do you have a butterfly mind?"* That, she decides, is my problem: a butterfly mind. This fluttering mind alighting on friends such as Colleen, or playing when I should be studying, resting on a thousand and one interests which take me away from proper attention to my school work. I, at her words, as if in a distant screen see my mind with gossamer wings of light blue, flitting from table to chair, to the bookshelves, out into the garden to land on the blood-red peonies, then down to lie out flat on a grey stone, transparent wings outstretched, drifting to sip nectar from the mauve buddleia, rising to soar into the cloud-streaked sky—up, up, up this ephemeral creature. What if there is no return? And I see myself as living in a kind of no-man's land.

The Wilton Road Story

The romances of the Misses Vernons: Mrs. Sargie and Guy: The Reeves: Old Vinegar: The Pearces: Our shed theatre: I am punished for lying: Visitors: Rhys Davies and a doll's funeral: Lawrence and Maud Jones: Johanna Lahr.

M y mother, exiled from the busy-ness of Holborn, the customers and the browsers coming in and going out of the bookshop, must now transfer her interest in people to our neighbours. Opposite to us at No. 14 live the Misses Vernon, Dolly and Nellie, residing in the house in which they have grown into adolescence, maturity and now late middle-age. Their parents and siblings leaving the girls one by one until the two women are left together as if shipwrecked. Aware of the value of money, Dolly Vernon, whom we call always 'Miss Vernon', has let the ground floor, which means that the parents' heavy furniture and numerous ornaments must be crowded together in the upstairs flat. Tables, sideboards, whatnots, old clocks, rugs, faded prints in dark frames of sweet obedient Victorian children, simpering china shepherdesses, candle sticks with and without used and unused candles, bowls of all shapes and sizes, the list is endless. All these objects pushed together in this flat where over the years the dust collects to hang over the rooms so that Dolly and Nellie grow older every day in mustiness.

Miss Dolly Vernon comes often into our house for my mother's proffered cup of tea and toast. She is a short, dumpy figure, her mousy hair worn in a bun, her nose doughy, her complexion high, but the general effect is not unpleasing, for her brown eyes are soft and her manner gentle. Nellie, for some years we know only from a distance as a thin bird-like witchy creature, clutching at the evergreen for support, as she traverses the length of the outside garden wall only to turn at its end and hurry back into the house. We watch her progress from our front window. *"She's got a corset on over her dress!"* says my mother. *"Miss Vernon says Nellie does it to embarrass her—whenever they quarrel and Nellie can't get her own way!"* I watch Nellie uneasily for her actions smack of infirmity which frightens me. At that time I could not bear to see the odd, the deformed, amputees struggling on crutches, or standing on the remaining stumps of their legs and begging in the streets, twisted bodies in wheelchairs, the blind. These deprived human beings threatened my completeness. *"She's been no further than the front of the house for thirty-two years!"* says my mother. *"Thirty-two years!"* To me, several lifetimes. I look across at No. 14 and imagine Nellie waiting behind the drab curtaining. Day after day, week after week, month after month, year after year, awaiting the ending of youth. The changes of middle-age. The failures of old age. Awaiting death. How could she bear it? What did she do all day in that gloomy house?

"Years ago Nellie used to lie with any old tramp in Lovers Lane" gossips our next-door but one neighbour from No. 13, Mrs. Sarginson (whom we call 'Mrs. Sargie'). She is sitting in our living-room sipping at a cup of tea. Lovers Lane was an unmade-up road off the North Circular. *"It were a scandal"* says Mrs. Sargie. In time, my mother hears from Dolly herself the Vernon story. It seems that years before when the Vernons had occupied the whole house they had been a family of mother, father and four children, two girls and two boys. *"A brother was killed in the war, in France"* my mother tells me and the screen in my head shows him lying on the field of battle. His face is pale, his eyes closed, his arms outstretched, around him gather grieving comrades. Perhaps Sir Philip Sidney himself is there to offer his sacrifice of a drink of cool water: Thy need is greater than mine;

> Not a drum was heard, not a funeral note,
> As his corse to the rampart we hurried,
> No soldier discharged his farewell shot
> O'er the grave where our hero we buried.
>
> We buried him darkly at dead of night,
> The sods with our bayonets turning,
> By the struggling moonbeam's misty light
> and the lantern dimly burning.[1]

---

1. Charles Wolfe, *The Burial of Sir John Moore after Corrunna.*

"*Miss Vernon's other brother*" says my mother "*was wounded very badly and wears a metal plate in his head.*" I wince and feel my own head to assure myself that its bone structure remains intact. If I suffered a terrible injury and my head was held together by a metal plate, would I be able to think for myself? Could thoughts and ideas pass through metal? I see this brother of Miss Vernon's as a kind of zombie, but my mother tells me he is married and has children. "*He never comes to visit Miss Vernon or Nellie*" says my mother. "*His wife's a snob and wants nothing to do with them.*" I take it for granted that this brother must do as he is told by his wife, for I had heard of a blind man claiming that his wife was his 'eyes'. This wife must be the man's mind. My mother continues. "*Miss Vernon's fiancé was killed in the war and that's why she never married.*" This is the stuff of romance, but try as I will I cannot equate the stubby Miss Vernon with a romantic heroine. "*Their father, James Francis Vernon Esq., was very strict, but he spoiled Nellie because she was delicate.*" I see a young girl languishing on a couch, dressed in long garments, her hair tumbling about her shoulders. She calls for smelling-salts and they are brought to her in a cut-glass decanter. "*So Nellie stayed at home and helped her mother who was a quiet, sad woman, a semi-invalid.*" On screen: A woman still and faded, lies on the couch alongside Nellie. "*Their father was something in the City.*" On screen: Dark suit, watch-chain across an ample abdomen, bowler hat, furled umbrella. "*The mother had money of her own and when she died she left it to be divided equally between her daughters and son.*" On screen: everyone dressed in black. The curtains at No. 14 drawn-to. The solicitor reading the Will to the mourning relatives. "*Miss Vernon banked her money because she was earning a salary by writing the* Children's Corner *and an advice column on a local newspaper.*" My mother's voice indicates her admiration for Miss Vernon in undertaking this almost literary occupation. "*But Nellie, a week or two after receiving her inheritance, disappeared.*" Disappeared! The screen flickers. "*It was some months before Nellie returned, and she was penniless!*" On screen: Nellie dressed in rags and singing in the streets. "*Where's the money mother left you?*" her father and sister demand. "*Tom's keeping it for me*" Nellie replied simply "*he said I could have it back when I wanted it.*" Neither Tom, nor Nellie's money, is ever seen again. "*Didn't they try to find him?*" I ask. "*I dare say they couldn't risk too much of a scandal*" replies my mother. "*A scandal would have ruined the family's good name.*" I recognise that we are back once again at sex outside marriage and suppose it fortunate that Nellie had not landed herself 'in trouble'. *"Mr. Vernon, the father"* adds my mother *"decided that Nellie was weak and couldn't be trusted with money, so he changed his Will. Everything was left between Miss Vernon and her brother, with the proviso that Miss Vernon, the younger of the two girls, take care of Nellie for the rest of her life."* My mother's voice shows her disapproval of this arrangement for in this manner were the two sisters locked together. And Nellie completely dependent upon her sister.

However, if Mrs. Sargie is to be believed, for some time after these events Nellie continued to walk the neighbourhood, making her way down Colney Hatch Lane and across the North Circular to Lovers Lane. Maybe she is sure that one day she will find Tom waiting for her and together they will walk off into the sunset. Instead, she finds passing travellers, itinerants on their ways from one place to another, and each one plays his part in regaining for her the ecstasy she had known with Tom. Her journeys to Lovers Lane are of hope and serendipity. What later makes her cease her wanderings and shut herself away in the house? Continual disappointment, tiredness, illness, disillusion, bitterness? Who can tell. But this is not to be the end of the Vernon story.

Mrs. Sarginson was a countrywoman, a comfortable body who bustled in and out of our house, offering assistance and advice. She wore her grey hair screwed back, her complexion was high, her nose beak-like resembling that of the green budgie which flew about her living-room. Her father, a poor farm labourer, had resented every morsel of food his children fed into their mouths. *"It's time she put her feet under someone else's table"* he had grumbled when Mrs. Sargie was but ten years old. And at the first available opportunity she had been put into service. *"The children of the house taught me to read and write"* Mrs. Sargie tells us. She claims to have had virtually no schooling; possible I guess in an isolated country district where the provisions of the various 19th Century Education Acts trod softly into force. Over the years Mrs. Sargie progressed as a domestic servant, to be employed by County families. *"Edward the Seventh used to visit one house I was in when they held balls, big occasions. Me and the other maids watched over the banisters. It were lovely"* she says. I hear the horse-drawn carriages draw up with a clatter and see the ladies entering into the mansion to remove their long velvet cloaks under which they wear long satin dresses. Their hair swept-up and beautifully coiffured bearing diamond tiaras. Around their throats jewelled necklaces; golden bracelets, rings set with precious stones. The men in black evening dress, starched white shirt fronts, bow ties, long coat-tails. I hear soft voices and laughter. All in a kind of haze as the music plays and the company move to the *Blue Danube* in a dream-like Hollywood sequence beneath the sparkling prismatic chandeliers. *"I had to show my mistress my diaper with blood on every month"* Mrs. Sargie tells my mother *"to prove I weren't pregnant. All the maids had to do that, in all the houses I were in."*

Mrs. Sargie and her husband, who is a bus conductor, have one son, Guy, born on a Guy Fawkes Night. Outside Mrs. Sargie's bed of pain, and throughout the land, beacons burn, effigies in the red and orange flames are consumed and fall to ash. Fire-works explode reverberating in and rending the cold night air to shower the darkness with golden sparks. Golden rain, whirling wheels, shooting stars of green, purple and scarlet! To be born on such a night! It was difficult to equate the lanky, slightly stooped man peering through wire-rimmed spectacles with such a mag-nificent entrance. However, there must have been more of the 5th November burning in Guy than showed on the surface, for against parental advice he married lively and fiery Iris Blackwell, her long hair black, her complexion dark and in her ears dangling gold rings. Guy and Iris have a baby son named Allan, about whom Mrs. Sargie worries constantly. For Mariella's next door neighbour, a Mrs. Jones, had told her that when Guy was working on late shift, Iris would go out all dressed up and leave the baby alone in the flat. Sometimes she heard him crying. Mrs. Sargie had made up her mind not to interfere in her son's marriage, but tentatively she asked Guy whether Iris sometimes went out on an errand in the evenings, leaving the baby alone. *"She wouldn't do that!"* he replied shortly and Mrs. Sargie does not know what to believe. But it is not too long before we are to find out the truth of this matter.

Mrs. Sargie tends to malapropisms and always speaks about knitting her son a 'gherkin'. This gives us a vision of a green pickled cucumber emerging from her knitting needles, so that we are almost disappointed when she exhibits the finished article and we find it to be no more than a plain, dull jerkin! My mother is often amused by this novel use of words, but hides her smiles out of politeness and in admiration for Mrs. Sargie's good nature. For it is Mrs. Sargie who goes into the Reeves who live in the downstairs flat in No. 11, taking with her a shovelful of coal, a tin of soup, a loaf of bread, a few vegetables.

The Reeves family had moved into No. 11 two or three years before WW2. Mr. Reeves is unemployed, but his wife earns a little money from home dressmaking. The remnants from orders she makes into dresses for her two small daughters Sylvia and Shirley, so that the two blonde curly-haired children are always beautifully dressed. *"He lies in bed most of the day,"* Mrs. Sargie says in disgust, speaking of Mr. Reeves, a man of middle height, his shoulders broad, his arms muscular. *"I were in there this morning and she were in tears. There weren't a scrap of food in the house, nor coal, it were bitter cold in there. She'd wrapped the little girls up in blankets! She'd got a bruise on her cheek and she didn't say, but I'm sure he hit her."* During the war, the Reeves are to cause my family problems and a great deal of anger, but at this time we know them only to nod to and pass the time of day over the garden fence. And, of course, from Mrs. Sargie's account of their lives.

Our next door neighbours at No. 7 are the Lazenbys, separated from us by a right of way, the intention of which had been to allow the dustmen and tradesmen access to the back of houses from Nos. 1 to 7. Chestnut fencing marks off our garden from this grassy strip entered by a high wooden gate facing Wilton Road: a gate which the Lazenbys keep locked so excluding us from entering. My mother grumbles that on buying the house we had been promised the right to make use of this strip of ground. Often I and Oonagh scale the chestnut fencing and lay claim to this land, only to be chased away by Mrs. Lazenby, whom we call 'Old Vinegar'. *"Get back on your own side!"* she snaps. Her mean mouth hissing; her small eyes angry; her long thin figure towering over us. Quickly we climb into our garden and once on our own side shout in fury *"It's a right of way. My mother says we can play there. It doesn't belong to you."* She makes no answer, but triumphantly passes through the gate which forms part of the high fence which surrounds her garden. *"Old Vinegar face!"* I shout. With what glee we read the name of the Lazenby house, declared in gold letters on the glass above the front door 'Foulden', and from our point of view, she couldn't have moved into a house with a more appropriate name! We, of course, separate the syllables.

I have no memory of Mr. Lazenby, but my mother who gleaned information from the air, tells me that the Lazenby grandfather had been a trade union official for the Railwaymen's Union. *"And now his son and son's wife are Tories!"* My mother could never understand these transmogrifications. Sometimes now I wonder whether the Lazenbys were in reality the family of old Samuel Lazarby of the Amalgamated Society of Railway Servants who had walked Fairbridge Road so proudly, on his head a high hat. The Lazenbys have one son, Peter, a small blonde boy, a little younger than me and older than Oonagh. A lonely child, he stands in 'no-man's land' and watches us through the palings of the fence. But because of his mother we will have no truck with him.

At No. 41, in the upstairs flat, live the Pearces, husband and wife. That is the old No. 41, not the postwar house which replaced it. And sometimes I wonder whether the present residents feel the presence of the former home, the rooms at times seeming to take on different sizes and altered shapes. Do they lose their way down a passage, or find themselves in the wrong room? Or conversely, had the old No. 41 ever felt insubstantial to the Pearces, the new house shaking it apart as it grew up in its midst? Or had Mrs. Pearce ever sensed the children of later generations making their home in the space of her flat—the children longed for by her, but denied? Mrs. Pearce I remember as a tall, over-thin young woman, dark hair, green eyes, long dangling ear-rings and a face on which the expressions were mobile. Mr. Pearce of stocky build, average height and ruddy face. The Pearces make local children welcome in their home and Twi visits them often, so that I am jealous. After all, it is I who live in Wilton Road! At last Mrs. Pearce invites me and Oonagh to tea. We sit at a table next to a window which overlooks the back garden—to be the scene of the future tragedy. I look out at the tall line of poplars in the background, each one at that time standing firm and straight as if they are soldiers on guard. We eat bread and jam, cakes, drink lemonade. Mr. Pearce smiles at us and Mrs. Pearce shows us her collection of long ear-rings of all colours and shapes, and lets us try on shiny bead necklaces, gold and silver bracelets.

At the last house in Wilton Road, No. 94, live the Spurgeons, a stage family. The son and two daughters are all dancers. Mrs. Spurgeon herself being an old trouper. How my mother admires Elsie and Marie as they walk with a dancer's lilt down the road. Their backs straight, their legs moving from the hips. My mother sees her might-have-been if only she had been allowed as a girl to join Hayley's Juveniles. As she watches the passing-by of the young women, my mother straightens her own back and holds in her stomach. For a time I attend ballet classes in the Spurgeon home, held by Marie, the younger and taller of the two sisters. A fair-haired friendly girl, slim and long-legged. Elsie we watch from a distance for she has no interest in neighbours. Her face over made-up, her nose in the air.

Above one of the shops in the parade in Colney Hatch Lane, the back windows overlooking the yard off Wilton Road, live the Willis family. From our back garden we can see the Willis flat rising with those alongside, chimney pots, windows, back doors leading to flat roofs, dwarfing our small suburban houses. Eva, a girl small for her age with straight short brown hair and wearing glasses, enters the front door behind which are the stairs leading up to the Willis flat, by pulling the key attached to a length of string, out through the letter-box. Mrs. Willis, a small, dark, pretty woman had lost Eva's two younger brothers within a week of each other—one from diptheria and the other from scalds. The little boy having fallen, or climbed into, a tin bath filled with boiling water before the distracted Mrs. Willis could add cold water. For the flat was without a bathroom and water was brought from the floor below. I can barely comprehend this tragedy. Two such small bodies to drift onto the pile of history. Covertly, I watch Mrs. Willis for an ineradicable mark which set her apart from more fortunate mothers. Eva, for a year or two, remains an only child, but then a baby girl named Freda, for her dead brother Fred, is born. On meeting Mrs. Willis in the street with the baby, I say blithely *"I bet you hope what happened to the other children doesn't happen to her."* Then I turn away in confusion. I have spoken out of turn. Mrs. Willis, a pleasant, gentle woman, is taken aback, but says nothing.

At another time, I take Eva's education in hand. Having learned that all my friends and acquaintances apart from Eva have learned how babies are born, I try to explain the process to her. She doesn't want to know; isn't interested—Eva, the only one of us whose mother has been recently pregnant. I am determined that she shall learn the facts of life and put a book written on the subject for children through her letter-box, pushing it past the string and the key at its end: a book showing illustrations of spermatozoa and ovula, the foetus developing in the uterus and the struggle of the baby down the birth canal. Mrs. Willis returns the book to my mother. She is not angry, almost apologetic as she tells my mother that Eva refuses to look at the book. She does not want to know about the process of conception and birth. Does she know then that she, when married some years later, will give birth to a chiild with cerebral palsy? A photo in my album shows Eva, my sister and me together with Ena Macfarlane, standing to the front of our open shed at the end of the garden, a shed which we call a theatre. My sister and I wearing my mother's dresses hitched up in the middle by a belt, Eva and Ena wrapped in curtain cloaks. Here we play games which we call 'plays' and on one occasion my sister and I, having recently seen the film of *A Midsummer Night's Dream*, act out the film, taking all the parts, and watched by visitors to our home.

We climb also onto the flat roof of this 'theatre', sometimes taking a chance by jumping up and down, for my father's hasty building methods have left it unsafe. Two small pale faces watch me from the upstairs flat of No. 11, and I wave to these young daughters of an Austrian family, refugees from Nazism who are to live there for a short time. My parents take an interest in this deeply unhappy and unsettled displaced family who bring with them an air of desperation. My mother, having visited their flat, tells me that they have barely a stick of furniture, the children sleeping on a folding camp-bed and the parents making do with mattresses on the floor. As winter approaches and with no warm clothing, the two children become prisoners in the flat.

My mother knows Mrs. Macfarlane only to nod to and perhaps pass the time of day when meeting in the street. Mrs. Macfarlane, a tall woman with light brown wavy hair and a mouth which twists cynically, is wary of us Lahrs; we are not what she is used to. But she has no objection to Ena, an only child, spending hours in our house. Ena can be a bit of a madcap, her movements quick and often unrestrained, however, she will settle for the day with Oonagh and me to play Monopoly. On one such occasion, when we have sat at our living-room table in front of the board for several hours, my mother complains that we have had no 'fresh air', and so the three of us run across the road and back again claiming. "*We've had some fresh air*" and get back into our game. At another time, I have assured my mother that we have been given a day's holiday from school. My mother, unsure about this, sends me across the road to check with Mrs. Macfarlane. I stand in the Macfarlane porch and then return to tell my mother that

Mrs. Macfarlane has agreed that today is a school holiday. Of course, I am found out. My mother has met Mrs. Macfarlane in the street and she says "*no*," I have not knocked at her door. She knows nothing of a holiday. My mother is furious; not because I have missed school, but because I have lied. She hates liars. I am ashamed. After that, I creep shamefaced past Mrs. Macfarlane when I meet her in the street.

The day's holiday takes place in the following week, for one saint's day or another, and as a punishment my mother delivers me to the Convent. The nuns receive me with an expression which tells me that they are aware of my sin—venial, but a sin nevertheless. I spend this warm, sunny, day on a daisy-covered lawn in helping the boarders to clear away the sweet trimmings of May blossom from a Hawthorn hedge. Nevertheless, it is a punishment to be exiled for the day from home. A photograph of me on this same lawn, dressed in white and standing second in a line of children, is shown in the *Highgate and Muswell Hill: Compiled for the Archive Photographs Series* by Joan Schwitzer and Ken Gay.[2] The small child sitting on the ground, I believe to be my sister, Oonagh.

Over the years, even when I am an adult and have left home, I am to hear from my mother stories and snippets about neighbours' lives: the woman in the bottom flat of No. 11 whose partner, a married man, has deserted his wife and children on her behalf. She finds a second lover and becomes pregnant by him. "*Guess what! She's living with two men!*" says my mother. The woman throws out the first lover, but the second lover leaves her. The first lover, whose wife refuses to take him back, kills himself by carbon-monoxide poisoning, sitting in the back of his car to breathe in the fumes from a hosepipe run from the exhaust. And my mother, like me, brought up on morality tales, feels that this is a fitting punishment for this woman whom she finds rude and unpleasant. There had been a dispute over a tree. One of the poplars had fallen in a storm—an occurrence which reminds us of the Pearce tragedy. The tree decimates everything in its path, including part of the fence and our peach tree, which is never again to bear fruit. My mother, intent upon helping, offers to claim for the fence on Lahr insurance. "*What do you think we're*

---

2. Joan Schwitzer and Ken Gay, *Highgate and Muswell Hill: Compiled for the Archive Photographs Series*, Chalford, 1995, p. 131.

doing!" the woman snaps impatiently. *"We've got our own insurance."* Her look at my mother is one of suspicion. When the fence is renewed, not only the part broken is replaced, but the whole length of fencing. *"She thought I wanted to claim and do her out of some money!"* my mother says angrily.

Mrs. Ridgeway, Miss Vernon's downstairs tenant at No. 14, locks her little boy in a dark cupboard when he is naughty. However, there is a problem. *"The little boy likes being in the dark cupboard, so she's got to think of another punishment!"* my mother says wryly. I shudder at this tale. To be locked in, all alone in the dark. My worst nightmare! When I see the little boy out playing I look at him with respect. Mrs. Ridgeway's mother, Mrs. Walker, like her daughter tall, thin and yellow faced. Mrs. Walker runs Vi's Cafe at the Orange Tree, Friern Barnet, and one Christmas attempts suicide by putting her head in the gas oven. This because her frequent borrowings from the Christmas Club, saved by her on behalf of customers, had dribbled all the money away. Attempted suicide is to become a residential hazard at No. 14.

Our involvement is not entirely in the immediate environment, for frequently we have visitors to our home from the world outside. On becoming friendly with a customer in his shop, my father invites them for Sunday tea. Often not telling my mother about the expected guest until the day in question, when she panics, hastily constructing a salad and what we would now call 'a buffet'.

For years, Bob Mauker, whom my parents refer to as 'the wireless boy', a man in his early thirties, calls upon us at least once a week and often twice, or more. He spends his time in tinkering with our wireless housed in a home-made wooden box and run by accumulators. On each visit taking it apart and then putting it back together again. Therefore, our wireless is in a constant state of flux, thus proving the theories of Heraclitus. Unemployed, this is how Mauker spends his time. Mauker had first been wished on my mother by my father when they lived at Roseberry Crescent. *"A boy's coming to put a wireless together for us,"* announces my father. While, at that time, Mauker, born in London the illegitimate son of a German girl, tinkers with wires and accumulators, my mother sits reading. I, her infant daughter, am abed and my father is out on business of his own. She feels no compunction to entertain him. For to pull a wireless apart, and then, like a conjuror, to restore it as if it were his world, is for

Mauker entertainment enough. These visits continue until war is declared, when Mauker is one of the first to enlist and comes to see us dressed in Air Force uniform. He walks me up the hill to the Convent and I feel proud for my schoolmates to see me with an airman.

A second regular visitor is Joe Cohen, a chemist. Dark curly hair, small of stature, sallow of complexion. He arrives every Saturday evening armed with a 1lb bar of milk chocolate. After a time, we become bored with this excess of chocolate, and so my mother melts it down and we drink it as cocoa. My parents and Joe Cohen spend the evening in playing cards, a game called Hearts. Sometimes, when Oonagh and I refuse to lie in bed and invade the living-room where the adults play their hands, the card table is set up in our bedroom. Unknown to all of us at the time, as Joe shuffles, tuberculii microbes are at work tearing apart the lungs in his slight frame. When Joe dies my mother is distressed, but she shudders at the realisation that she has brought her children into close promimity with a contagious killer disease. She runs her fingers down the light-brown wall-paper in our bedroom and then, holding her hand away from her, hurries to the bathroom to scrub the hand clean.

My parents' friends, can be divided into the literati, the left-wingers, the lame dogs and customers for whom my father has a liking, several falling into more than one category and a few into none. While I am astute enough to determine the differences in acceptable behaviour at home and school, unless warned otherwise, I assume that visitors to the house share my parents' political views. This leads me into error. For instance, with regard to the Boylans. This aged husband and wife are frequent visitors, he with grey mutton chop whiskers and wearing a dark suit and tie, white shirt, broad-brimmed black hat. She, dressed in a long frock of indeterminate colour, her grey hair worn in a neat bun. Tortoiseshell spectacles across her face. My sister and I like Mr. Boylan for on each visit he gives to us a shilling, and immediately we run up the road to spend it at Torrys which stocks also a few toys. With one of these shillings we buy a tin drum and my mother grumbles at such waste, for a shilling would buy the ingredients for a meal. *"He means you to give the money to us"* she says. However, we have a child's view of our parents' parlous financial state and so we continue to spend the shillings on ourselves. Mr. Boylan plays the piano and on one such visit he sits at our Stromenger to play *Marching Through Georgia*, to which I sing the only words I know:

The land, the land, God made the land,
The land, the land, the land on which we stand,
Why should we be beggars with the billets in our hands,
God made the land for the people.

My mother becomes agitated. She calls to me and my voice wavers and then dries up. I go over to her. *"Those are the wrong words"* she whispers, one eye on Mr. Boylan at the piano. Later, she explains that the Boylans are conservative church-going Catholics and all mention of politics should be avoided while they are in the house. As it happens, Mr. Boylan is a diabetic who falls into comas while he and his wife are out shopping. If they are in separate stores, she tells us, she waits hours for him unaware that he is being ambulanced to hospital; until, worried at his prolonged absence, she at last wanders the streets, to ask passers-by if they have seen a small old man with grey whiskers and wearing a black broad-brimmed hat.

I wander to your graveside,
And place each flower with care,
For the Husband I love so dearly,
Is peacefully sleeping here.

I read on a gravestone in Finchley Cemetery. Gay Taylor has called upon us and Oonagh and I have taken her for a walk. We enter the cemetery through a hole in a broken fence in Coldfall Woods. For slim, tense Gay winds in and out of our lives and we take her for restless walks. The headstones are heaped around us, white and shining, marking out the individual gardens under which the dead lie mouldering. We wander here often with my mother, who in January 1970 is to end her days here. However, when a child on one of our visits to this cemetery I spoil for her a phantasmagoric love affair. My mother, longing for romance to overshadow the realities of her life, had invented a phantom lover named 'John'. Kind, attentive, rich. She and I make up stories about him and my sister listens. One day, or once upon a time, while wandering in the cemetery I notice a new headstone, the name of the deceased etched deep into the stone—John. *"John's dead!"* I say teasingly to my mother. *"Look! Here's his grave!"* She blenches. I have killed him for her, reminded her of unromantic

inevitability. We never play the game again although in repara-
tion I try to substitute a 'Rudolph' equally kind and rich, but my
mother rejects him. And ever since John has followed me to cast
his shadow. However, I say nothing of this to Gay, in whose life
romance has figured too largely.

One long-term affair entered into by Gay was with Alec Bristow, also an aspiring writer and a customer in my father's bookshop.[3] A tall young man, brown haired and smooth complexioned,
some years younger than Gay. He is to marry eventually a young
woman who, following WW2, and having produced six children,
is to write articles for the *Daily Express* to complain bitterly about
the difficulties of bringing up a family under a Labour government. Before the planned wedding takes place, my father advises
Alec to warn Gay of his impending marriage. But she takes Alec's
letter badly for she sees him as bragging of his intended betrayal.
I meet the new Mrs. Bristow only at a distance. The Bristows live
at Barnet and my father who takes invitations to call as if they
are meant, insists that Mrs. Bristow would welcome a visit from
my mother. We take the bus to High Barnet and in the heat of
the summer traipse along several side roads. At last my mother asks a passing postman for directions, which he gives, at the
same time passing to my mother a letter for delivery. On arrival,
we see a woman sitting at an open upstairs window, a baby in her
arms. *"We have a letter for you"* my mother calls out, holding it out
and looking upwards. *"Put it through the letter-box"* is the curt reply.
A reply which sounds so final that my mother does not know how
to proceed with the visit. Therefore, we leave and trudge back to
the High Road and the bus which will return us to Wilton Road.

Alec and his sister had been orphaned at an early age, his mother dying as the result of a kick received from an anti-suffrage yob
at a suffragette street meeting and his father dying soon afterwards. Left in the care of a solicitor, the two children are sent to
separate boarding schools. However, part of the holidays they
spend together in the house of the solicitor's two maiden sisters.
"Wasn't that Alec Bristow I saw in your garden?" one of these two old
ladies, both now living in Sutton Road, ask my mother on meeting her at the shops. *"Ask him to call on us."* My father relays the

---

3. Short stories both by Gay Taylor and Alec Bristow are contained in
Charles' Wain, a book of short stories put together for my father by
his writer friends and proteges, published by Mallinson, London, 1933.

message to Alec, but he refuses such contact. The solicitor had swindled him and his sister out of a substantial inheritance.

For a time, Alec is the Zoo Man on *Children's Hour* radio. Desperate to retain and advance his position, he gives my father the answers to the programme's quiz, together with a request for the competing child to name their favourite programme. My sister and I reply 'Zoo Man'. I demur. *"I might like something else better"* I say to my parents, who are a little shamefaced at involving their children in this subterfuge. However, as I rarely listen to *Children's Hour*, I know of nothing better. In due course both my sister and I each receive a prize of a box of chocolates.

Rhys Davies visits us occasionally, a gentle spoken man bringing in his train the argumentative, devious characters from the Welsh Valleys who swagger down Wilton Road. And while Rhys visits with us, their sharp challenging eyes watch us from the four corners of the room. I show to Rhys an unfinished story which I have written in response to urgings from my parents. I never finish them and spend most of my efforts on the illustrations. Rhys, having little knowledge of a child's interrupted span of concentration, expresses surprise and disappointment over my sparse entry, so that once again I feel guilty. At another time, Rhys calls upon us to find my sister and I performing the rites at a doll's funeral. The broken china doll laid out carefully in a shoe box and a grave dug in the earth of a small part of the garden allowed us by my father. Peter Lazenby watches us through the chestnut fencing, his face pressed against the struts. His light eyes in his pale face following our every move:

> *And if today my tide of life*
> *Should ebb away,*
> *Give me the sacraments divine,*
> *Sweet Lord, today.*

Oonagh and I intone over the grave, dug by use of a metal seaside spade held by its long wooden handle. Rhys the observer sees not only Oonagh and me in this play, but Peter's vain endeavours to be included. Returning home he writes a sombre short story based on our game.[4] Rhys, I always claimed as my beau and said that I would marry him when I grew up—a promise neither of us took seriously, especially Rhys, as he was a homosexual.

---

4. Rhys Davies, 'The Funeral'—short story included in *The Things Men Do*, Heinemann, 1936.

At another time, I stand beside the piano, violin under chin, wielding my bow. At the piano sits Beatrice Hastings, one-time model for Modigliani and also his mistress. Together we work over the libertarian democratic anarchist songs, words and music written by herself. Beatrice, her head of short, straight, greying hair, nodding in time to the music. Her dark eyes flashing, the fingers of her hands giving each note its true worth as she sounds clearly and tunefully each revolutionary word. When she goes, leaving for us a copy of the music, I will turn the page upside down and play it back to front. A possibility that I have only recently discovered. Beatrice visits us quite often for she is fond of my mother. Frequently, she spends the greater part of the visit on annotating her grievances against Sylvia Pankhurst. *"She's not coming here again to talk about Sylvia Pankhurst!"* I exclaim to my mother when I know that Beatrice is expected. I am never to learn the reasons for Beatrice's grievances, for by the time I am old enough to ask and understand I am caught up in my own life. It is I who spoil a holiday for Beatrice, so that when, during the war, she commits suicide by gas in her Worthing home, I am sure that in some way I have contributed to her death. Now, when in galleries, I avoid the eyes of Modigliani's paintings of women with long necks, in case one of them should prove to be Beatrice. For I could not face the reproach in her eyes.

Welcome visitors are always the young Jones's, Lawrence and Maud. Lawrence—tall, gangling, auburn haired, a librarian who plays the violin, a vegetarian, pacifist, and a quiet gentle man, as if the cancer which is to kill him many years later has already sapped at his energy. Maud, however, has vigour enough for two, but as her accent identifies her as a Londoner my mother's feelings are ambivalent towards her: *"Some of these left-wing people like to sound working-class"* she says. Maud had been a dancer and loves ballet, so when we visit them in their Stoke Newington flat she entertains us by exhibiting her ballet shoes. I stroke the long, shiny pink ribbons, wishing the ties on my ballet shoes were not black tape. My mother enjoys this part of the visit, but is not so happy when the Jones introduce us to their pet white rat kept in a wire cage, removing it from its prison to allow the rodent to run back and forth over their hands. In 1940, my mother in a letter to my Aunt Mary, is to call the Jones *"good, honourable and sincere friends"* and in the same year, Lawrence is to enter Oonagh's and my lives briefly in the performance of a kindly act.

The brothers Philip and Eugene Lahr visit us several times a year. They are not relatives although they share our surname. In the future, both are to become engineers. Eugene emigrating to Brazil with his wife and two children, Philip to work for the Rockwell Group. At this time they are very young men and while Philip has dark hair and eyes, Eugene's hair is blonde and his eyes blue. Explaining the difference in appearance between the siblings, my father blithely tells me *"their mother Johanna was an anarchist and she had a number of lovers and children by all of them. None of them are really Lahrs."* I eye these young men, the fruit of her womb, with interest and envision their progenitors as shadowy men who pass in and out of Johanna's life while she sits writing pamphlets.

> *The journeymen bakers of London are at last making themselves heard, being urged on by the lessons taught by the skilled and unskilled Labour Strike of the dockers, and the sweated tailors in the East End, which showed what can be done if workers are united and organised... Do you toil and suffer such lives under these wretched conditions for yourselves and your families, or your masters? Where are the fruits of your labour? What hopes have you when you are past work? Have no trust in your Houses of Parliament. The sooner they are turned into a washhouse or bakehouse the better for the workers. I am with you heart and spirit, and will never tire of helping you to a brighter future, where freedom, love and harmony shall reign; where the dawn of the morning shall be greeted with gladness, and work be only a pleasure; and where the burden of life and sorrow-stricken faces shall disappear like a snow-white mist in the morning.[5]*

A little while ago, I asked Oskar Lahr, Philip and Eugene's brother, about Johanna. *"I know very little about her"* he says. *"She was not my mother. Johanna died when her own children were very small. My father's second wife was my mother and we were a large family as my father had children by both marriages."*

---

5. Pamphlet written by Johanna Lahr at the end of the 19th Century.

Dancing and Playing

I try to learn the violin: Ballet School: William Roberts RA, Sarah and John: Memories of T.E. Lawrence: The London Zoo: A visit to H.E. Bates: A paedophile in the bookshop: I run away from a holiday at St. Leonards on Sea: The Crisis—Chamberlain and appeasement.

Some time previously I had begged my mother to allow me to learn the violin instead of the piano. And, no doubt hoping to spawn another Menuhin, she had agreed. My mother loved music, and when young queued for hours outside the Queen's Hall waiting for admittance to a concert. She had also been an enthusiast for opera and sang to us often snatches of arias from various dramatic scenes. At first I go to a studio in the Athenaeum Buildings, a number of studios being provided on the first and second floors, above what had once been the cinema. I know these studios well, for by now Gabrielle Rowley's ballet class is held in one of them. Nowadays, the shoppers in the supermarket which squats on its space are too deafened by muzak and intent upon consumerist requirements to hear the lingering clash of fencing sticks, straining of muscles at the barre, fluttering hands on piano, cello, violin.

Later I go for violin lessons to Mr. Franks, a professional violinist whose two daughters are pupils at the Convent. Winifred, my sister's age and Mary, two or three years younger. The Franks live on Muswell Hill and so carrying my black wooden violin case for all to see, I walk up Colney Hatch Lane to the Broadway. Past the Express Dairy (now a Swiss Chalet cafe), this an ornamental building with a forecourt, where my mother sometimes takes me out to tea—a plate of cakes, those uneaten returned and not charged for—and for children a glass of milk with a dash of coffee. Past the Ritz cinema, its tenuous hold upon the hill to give way to the present heavy brownstone public house and offices, over the bridge under which lie the railway tracks, out of which will rise a primary school and on to the Franks' house half-way down the hill. There, in their sitting-room I scrape a bow across a violin which my mother has bought me secondhand. At the Academy I borrowed a three-quarter size violin on which the finger spacing was marked out by different coloured strips. At Mr. Franks I find my own notes.

Violins in various stages of manufacture hang about the walls of the sitting-room, some plain wood and others on which the varnish is not yet dry. For Mr. Franks, a slightly built man under average height, is also a violin-maker. Carefully, he cuts the wood from a pattern and assembles it piece by piece. Taking special care with placing the sound post which must stand upright within the violin. *"Mr. Franks is a socialist"* says my mother to me as she bustles about in the scullery. *"He's a Trotskyist. I told him your father and I have no gods."* Anti-Stalinism had not led my parents into supporting Trotsky, for they could not forgive him for the annihilation of the mutinous sailors at Kronstadt:

> The fortress... must be seized before ice floes barred the approach. In feverish haste picked regiments and shock troops were dispatched to reinforce the garrison of Petrograd... White sheets over their uniforms, the Bolshevik troops... advanced across the Bay. They were met by hurricane fire from Kronstadt's bastions. The ice broke under their feet: and wave after wave of white-shrouded attackers collapsed into the glacial Valhalla. The death march went on. From three directions fresh columns stumped and fumbled and slipped and crawled over the glassy surface until they too vanished in fire, ice and water. As the successive swarms and lines of attackers drowned, it seemed to the men of Kronstadt that the perverted Bolshevik revolution drowned with them and that the triumph of their own pure, unadulterated revolution was approaching... The bitterness and rage of the attackers mounted accordingly. On 17th March, after a night-long advance in a snowstorm, the Bolsheviks at last succeeded in climbing the walls. When they broke into the fortress, they fell upon its defenders like revengeful furies.[1]

---

1. Isaac Deutscher, *The Prophet Armed: Trotsky 1879-1921.*

Mr. Franks takes great pains with me, but I am never to progress very far with the violin, although I long to play vibrato—fingers and wrist shaking on the strings to give the notes an almost broken quality. However, political events are gathering force which will put an end to my violin and ballet lessons.

With regard to ballet lessons, I will record here that it is at Miss Rowley's ballet class at her home in Woodberry Crescent that for the first time I stand with shoulders back, so that with some surprise I feel my spine and attendant skeleton shifting into its proper place. And this miracle is to continue at an Academy studio to which Miss Rowley moves once her ballet school is under way. Miss Rowley is very English middle-class and her tall slim figure is stiff and unbending. No more than twenty or twenty-one in years, she has no natural rapport with children and yet by dint of sheer energy and determination she works her classes into a knowledge of movements and technique. Each year she produces a show for the public at a church hall where I dance the role of a gnome, or a doll, or a butterfly, or a fairy, although my greatest triumph is as the god Pan for which I am dressed in an artificial animal skin slung across one shoulder, my legs and feet bare. I dance threateningly and disturbingly among the rest of the ballet class, dressed as nymphs in short silk dresses. But it is my mother who has to point out to me that this role is an honour, for I would have preferred to dance in the same role as my peers.

My mother bustles about to find materials and patterns to dress me for the various roles. I am measured, the fabric is cut and pinned together, I try it on and feel unfamiliar dress material such as American cloth, smooth and shiny on the outside, but rough against my skin., My mother threads her treadle sewing machine—the machine under which I play at pretending that its wheel guides a ship—and the costume is soon sewn together. Sometimes my mother and the other mothers form a sewing party at the home of one of them, while we children play together in the garden.

My mother also encourages my sister and me to sing, teaching us old music-hall songs:

I'm Henry the eighth I am I am…

or —

Mother I love you, I will work for two
Don't let the tears run down your cheek,
I'll bring my wages to you every week.

And she loves opera, reminding herself of the days when she queued to go into the opera house, by recounting to us the stories of Aida, Rigoletto and many others: Humming a tune and snatches of the words.

In one of the years before the war, I join other girls from Miss Rowley's Dancing School for a fortnight's stay at Joss Bay, Broadstairs. We stay at North Foreland House, which I surmise is a private school vacant for the summer. Almost a mansion and with large well-kept grounds. The afternoons we spend on the beach, a sandy cove bordered on one side by the sea and on the other by cliffs. I perch on a rock, holding my penknife firmly in my hand, to carve my initials among the many on the cliff face. I am recording for posterity that I was here and I am me. A magic penknife, for I lose it on this beach and while digging in the sand a few days later, find it again. Every afternoon we walk down an incline to the Bay and every day an ice-cream tricycle waits at its base: **STOP ME AND BUY ONE** painted on the large fixed ice-box to the front of the handlebars. This year a glut of jelly fish floats in the sea and settles on the shoreline, to form small glutinous mounds. I slip on one of these creatures, my foot sliding on its gummy side and I want to vomit. But I am relieved to have escaped its painful sting and disfiguring scar. The transparent appearance of these marine creatures impresses itself so deeply on my mind that on returning home, and for some time afterwards, I cannot see a glass bowl, or any glass of a similar shape, without it taking on the appearance of a jellyfish, *Scyphozoa* or the phylum *Coelenterata*.

At the house, I sleep in a room with four other girls, none of them close friends for they are at different schools and for the most part friends are chosen from among schoolmates. I am acquainted with Emily Heath, a year or two older than me, a platinum blonde who wears her shining hair hanging loose on her shoulders. She lives on the Council estate off Tetherdown and Mrs. Heath, while on her way down Wilton Road to the shops, stops to talk to my mother who is in the front garden, or standing at the gate. *"Your Emily is a beautiful girl"* says my mother, for apart from her fine hair the child has large brown eyes and a well-proportioned straight nose. *"When I was carrying her"* confides Mrs. Heath *"I used to gaze at a very handsome Jew who worked in the shop. I looked and looked at him."* My mother is ambivalent about this story, for she is contemptuous of Mrs. Heath's belief in Old Wives Tales, and yet pleased at this indication of philosemitism. *"Does your father like the fascists?"* Jean, plump and confident, asks Emily. Jean is the daughter of a local builder who is a member of the British Union of Fascists. We are walking in pairs down to Joss Bay. *"No he doesn't!"* Emily replies vehemently, and I love her for that. Ballet lessons take place each morning, for which we wear a rose-coloured short silk tunic, split at each side; *pliez, jetez*, pointing our toes, positions of the feet, the arms. For luncheon we change once more for the evening meal. I seem to be whipping my limited number of dresses on and off all day long! Sometimes, if we are being taken out to a theatre or show, a fourth change of dress is made. Previous to the meal, we collect together on the lawn and on passing through the dining-room I am tempted by the bowls of brown pieces sugar set out on the tables. Miss Rowley considering this unbleached sugar preferable to white, for she is intent upon healthy eating. But to me it is sweeter than any sugar I have ever known. Quickly, I grab a spoonful and shove it into my mouth. Almost immediately Miss Rowley appears before me. She is outraged. *"Have you been eating the sugar?"* she demands. I try to speak through the gooey mess clinging to the roof of my mouth and covering my teeth. I blush, mumble, stammer. She says nothing more, but stands tight-lipped. Sheepishly, I make my way out onto the lawn. A holiday which lacks the anxieties normal to me on being sent away alone from home, for I know that we must all return to Muswell Hill and that I will once again be at Wilton Road.

Apart from ballet, we, at Wilton Road, are interested in Art, which for us is represented by William Roberts, who designed the cover for *The New Coterie*. William is an upright dour man who in an industrial age sees human kind as extensions to machines, their limbs performing the roles of pulleys and hoists, cantilevers, joints and belts and braces. His men on canvas are faceless and robotic. However, his portrait of my mother as a young woman is in a different style and presents her as ageless, or of an age, so that as the years pass by my father, glancing at the portrait in its frame hanging on the wall, says *"She grows more and more like it with every passing day!*"[2] In the portrait, my mother's large, bright blue almond-shaped eyes look away from the viewer, her mouth is shadowed and her hair a solid fuzz. The cupid bow of her mouth is beautifully shaped, and in spite of her brooding expression it seems as if she might smile. Following my mother's death, my sister, intent upon some of the immortality with which the portrait endowed my mother rubbing off on herself, insisted that my father present it to the Tate Gallery, where it now rests.

The Roberts—William, Sarah and their son John, the last some seven years older than me—live near to Regents Park. Their house is light and airy, containing little furniture; the furnishings and decor in a mode well before its time. On our first visit there my mother sniffs and says *"when Sarah visited us her first words in that lilt of hers were* 'Esther, I thought you'd live in a house without curtains!' *It's her who has no curtains!*" My mother and Sarah go back a long way and my mother tells the story of the day it was decided that my grandmother Rachel and Sarah's mother, Mrs. Kramer (the mother also of the artist Jacob Kramer) should meet on a Saturday. Mrs. Kramer who is Orthodox trudges on foot together with Sarah to this rendezvous in Regents Park, for Jewish law forbids the faithful to travel on vehicles during the Sabbath. At last she arrives and sits herself down on a seat, declaring that she has travelled the permitted number of miles. My grandmother arrives with my mother, the two of them having come from the East End by tram and bus. Entering the park, my mother spies Sarah and her mother a short distance away. Now, as it happens, my grandmother is fashion conscious, taking much care over her clothes and appearance, her trim figure always neatly dressed and her hair well-groomed. To Mrs. Kramer, clothes are no more than a necessity with which to cover modesty and, to my grandmother, she looks like what we now know as a 'bag lady': a dark crumpled dress, the hem escaping from its stitches to hang unevenly, a shawl over her head, shoes scuffed and run-down at the heel. My grandmother takes one look at this woman and immediately sits herself down on a bench, announcing that she too has walked the number of miles permitted. For an hour or more, the two old women sit a short distance from one another while my mother and Sarah run backwards and forwards, from one mother to the other, in an attempt to induce

---

2. See the portrait on p. 251.

one of the women to walk a few feet to where the other is seated. To no avail. At the end of that time, both women return home without having met. Sarah's mother on foot, my grandmother by public transport.

Sarah and my mother at one time went about together and on holiday, even though, as my mother said *"Sarah had been married since the year dot."* However, William's preoccupation with his painting and a spinal injury to John when a baby, which confined him to an Orthopaedic Hospital for some years, left Sarah a free spirit. I spent at least one holiday with my mother and Sarah, in a cottage at Rye Harbour. Of course I have no recollection of this, but I grow up with the nostalgic story of our stay, and especially of the afternoon when my mother comes out of the cottage to find a snake mounting my pram. I identify with Eve in the Garden of Eden, and wonder why she, like my brave mother, did not hit out at the serpent with a stick and scream blue murder. It would have saved a lot of bother.

William Roberts is a Fellow of the Zoological Society and so passes to my father free permits into the London Zoo to which my mother takes my sister and me quite often. In those days the Zoo was always packed with people and for an elephant or camel ride we had to queue for an hour or more. However, the most memorable visit to the Zoo is a visit I made together with Colleen. We stood for two or three hours in the Reptile House to watch a python in its glassed cage swallow its six monthly meal of a whole dead goat, the mouth of the snake stretching itself elastically over the bulk of the ruminant to draw it into its length in slow motion. Fascinated, we mark out the shape of the goat's horns and hoofs journeying under the skin of the python's long body. Until, at last the goat has vanished into the snake's maw and the reptile lies supine. Sometimes, my father takes my mother and we children out for the day. And I can remember one visit to H.E. Bates and his family in Ashford, Kent. *"The house is a converted barn"* says my mother. I had seen barns in the countryside, filled by hay and smelling of manure and I could not understand how a barn could be a house in which people lived, for to me, in those days, uses were static. On viewing Bates' imposing home I found it even more difficult to envisage it as anything other than a house. Bates writes in *The Country Cottage Life Book*:

The house was finished in a little over six months... a beautiful neat snug place that looked as if it had never been a farm build-ing... where the wind once howled bitterly through the wheels of dung carts and that my books should sit under the beams where birds nested.

In Bates' country garden I pick peas, working up one row and down the next as if this were a supermarket which provided food from off the vine. From this visit I am left with no more than an awareness of a table in the open air and chattering adults. I have a clearer recollection of Bates from his visit to my father's book-shop at 12 Little Newport Street during WW2. Bates, a short man dressed in uniform as Flying Officer X.

Other friends are the Petersons who, for two or three years, take us on an annual outing in their car. In those days a rare method of private travel. Impatiently, I wait in our front room, peering from behind the curtains at the street, starting up at the sound of every vehicle. At last they are here! Mr. Peterson small and quiet, a shadow of his large, lively wife who is auburn-haired and ruddy of face. My parents and we children pile into the back of the car, Mrs. Peterson maintaining a flood of conversation as we purr towards our destination. I bathe in the River Thames at Runnymede on a warm sunny day, its banks covered in tall purple Willowherb which grows to the edge of the waterline. On the opposite bank stands King John, his regal robes worn heavily. A gold crown rests lightly upon his head. Defeat and humilia-tion show upon his face. On his forehead, the mark of Cain. I see King John from the corners of my eyes and hide behind the Willowherb.

The Perersons live in a flat in a block in Gray's Inn Road, and following my fortnightly visit to the Edmonds Dental Clinic, my mother, Oonagh and I call upon Mrs. Peterson, who has obvi-ously forgotten her invitation and nothing is prepared. But she makes us welcome, and ever resourceful, amuses Oonagh and me by offering us sips from a vast array of miniature liqueur bottles, soliciting our opinions on each taste. Years later, my mother, re-membering the occasion, is to remark wryly that this was an odd way in which to entertain children, but I demurred. I had enjoyed the variety of tastes, receiving each one on my tongue before swallowing, and Mrs. Peterson treating me as if my opinion of her liqueur was worthwhile. When the Petersons no longer come to take us on our yearly outing it is not as a result of threatening war clouds, but because, so my father says, *"they think we don't appreciate or enjoy the outings."* I am perplexed. What should I have said to assure them of my pleasure? The Petersons are childless and their only niece had been run down and killed by a bicycle: a puzzling end to me for both my parents and myself are cyclists and I regard these machines as familiar objects and as friends. I touch my father's upright bike, pressing down on its pumped-up tyres and try to envisage the slain niece crushed beneath its light wheels. Had they hoped that Oonagh and I would be substitute nieces, and had we in some way disappointed their hopes?

Of course, we also visit relatives. My grandmother Rachel is not happy visiting our non-kosher household and so we go to her. For even on those few occasions on which she called on my Aunt Becky in New Barnet, she insisted on bringing with her pots and pans and food from her own house. I see her now, a small, neat figure, bright blue eyes and a fuzz of white hair, pots and pans strung together and dangling from her arm as she stops passers-by in East Barnet Village to ask them the way to Netherlands Road. She might be willing to break Sabbath travel laws, but food was a much more emotive subject. And so we call upon my grandmother at her small house in the East End where one day we will sit shiva. While my Bubba speaks to my mother in a mixture of Yiddish and broken English, I open the isolated, unused front room in which stands an unopened piano, a mahogany table, a cloth hiding its high gloss, and four matching stiff-backed chairs with leather seats, lined up against the wall as if waiting to be called. The table and chairs we are to inherit, but the table comes to us without the chenille cloth from which hangs scarlet tassels, for this is claimed by my mother's Aunt. *"She grabbed it from off the table and ran out of the house with it!"* wails Becky to my mother. *"I tried to keep it for you!"*

Bubba calls me to the wooden table in the kitchen where she is ladling lokshen soup into plates. *"Eat! Eat!"* says my Bubba, placing a plate before me on the table. Her lokshen soup is good, thick, with small pieces of chicken and vermicelli floating on its surface. *"Your Bubba makes her own vermicelli"* my mother tells me proudly *"with egg."* Before we leave, Bubba bids us wait while she runs to the market to return within a few moments holding two shiny golden toffee apples on sticks, presenting one to me and one to my sister. I am shy with my grandmother for I feel foreign to her and this district of grey mean streets in which nothing grows. Strange clothes, strange smells, strange voices—a world away from the suburb of Muswell Hill.

However, my Aunt Becky and her family live now within our ken and my mother, whose ambivalence towards to her sister, does not extend to her nephew and nieces, frequently takes us over to New Barnet to visit them. Sometimes, of course, they come to us and I can remember Helen, a year older than me, staying with us over Christmas, sharing with Oonagh and me the double bed in our downstairs front room. And on Christmas morning we watch her surprise and pleasure on finding, in a pillow-case tied to the bed-post, a box of chocolates labelled "*for Helen*." At my Aunt Becky's house, my sister and I play in the garden with Seema who is my sister's age, and Helen, making our home in the circular summerhouse. My Aunt Becky sometimes takes advantage of our game of keeping house by presenting us with a box of cutlery to be cleaned. First we must cover each knife, fork and spoon in white Silvo and then vigorously polish. At other times, we run down to the village where relatives to my cousins run a grocery store. Two boys belong to this household, one of them a little older than Helen, who is supposed to be in love with him. Seema makes up teasing songs about this supposed infatuation and we all annoy Helen by singing them at her. The boys' mother has been widowed recently and my cousin Woolfie, then about sixteen years of age, goes to work for her. Soon she has seduced him and later claims that he has made her pregnant. They marry, a marriage doomed from its start. It takes Woolfie many years to extricate himself from the failure of this relationship and its aftermath. (The child of this union is to emigrate as a young man to Australia and an aftermath in 1998 is a letter from his daughter—a TV Production Assistant—to one of my cousins, enquiring about the family and her grandfather. As Woolfie eventually denied paternity, this letter has put the family in a quandary. Such are aftermaths.

Sometimes my Aunt Mary calls upon us at Wilton Road, squatting her large bulk on one of our narrow chairs. For a time, my Aunt Becky and Aunt Mary are on friendly terms, visiting one another. And my mother says wryly that they deserve each other. But our most frequent family visitor at Wilton Road is Cecil. My mother tolerates these visits for while it is possible to forecast and trust the likely responses of most of us, the behaviour and responses of the insane are unpredictable. And my mother was of a generation which equated mental illness with moral turpitude. *"He hunches himself up and makes terrible faces"* she once told me *"and when he's into madness he eats his food like an animal, picking it up with his hands and pushing it into his mouth!"* Uneasily, my mother takes from Cecil the clear soup sent over by my Aunt in a beer bottle. Later she will release the liquid from the bottle and run it down the plughole in the sink. She cuts up the cake made by my Aunt and encourages Cecil to eat as much of it as possible. For her idea of hospitality, inherited from the East, determines that to swallow an enemy's food is to cement a friendship. Years later, when the breach between my Aunt and my parents is complete, my Aunt is to remind my mother of these donations of soup and cake. *"Didn't I always make him eat that cake before he went home!"* rages my mother to Mrs. Dawson. *"You know, you saw him eating it! As for the soup!"* My mother pulls a face. *"It looked more like dishwater—or urine! Anyway"* continues my mother *"she only sent him over to us while she was busy with a lover. The lover wouldn't have Cecil around because he was afraid of blackmail!"*

Towards the end of WW2, my mother is to work at the Colney Hatch Asylum for three or four years as an orderly, tending the elderly and confused, cleaning up the incontinent and worse. Working within the hospital she develops some sympathy for these patients incarcerated in the Asylum because of the lack of other facilities to care for them:

"They had in mind old folks homes which are so desperately needed today when the proportion of over 65s in the general population has increased so much and among long-stay patients (at the Asylum) has risen to 75%." Write the Commissioners in Lunacy in 1894—quoted in *Psychiatry for the Poor.*

Working at the Asylum is not a pleasant occupation for my mother and, what is more, she is shocked by the violence of some of the staff towards patients, especially those inmates who have been abandoned by their families. My mother tells me: *"The old lady wept because her husband told her he'd had enough of visiting her in such a place and he wouldn't come again. And, anyway, there was someone else. The next time I saw her the Sister had blacked her eye. So I phoned the husband and said 'I can't tell you my name, but I work at the hospital. It's vital you visit your wife this week.' He did and there was a row about his wife's injuries, her mouth had swollen up as well."*

This is not the only occasion when my mother calls in a husband, son, daughter to visit an abused patient. However, the above is to take place in the future and, anyway, she is never to work on a male ward among young men suffering from suppressed masculinity and sexuality. Therefore, she is wary of Cecil, for he arrives bringing with him the threat of chaos in a disordered world.

Sometimes, we visit my Father at the bookshop and I play with his typewriter, the old Underwood, pushing down one key at a time to make the mark of a letter on a piece of paper; the typewriter which my sister is to donate to the Church Farm Museum, Hendon:

> *The typewriter, upon which the typescripts of stories by Bates, Lawrence and Rhys Davies were produced, has been generously donated by Charles Lahr's daughter, Oonagh, whose own poems were published by Blue Moon Press. The typewriter will be displayed, with a small selection of books by the many writers associated with Lahr, and portraits of Charles and Esther Lahr by Jacob Kramer, at South Friern Library—just around the corner from Lahr's house.*

On one such visit, my sister and I stand in the bookshop at 68/69 Red Lion Street alone, my parents in the small room used as a storeroom. A man enters and greets us. all at once I feel hands and fingers at the back of my neck, massaging the top of my spine. exploring hands stretch down the back of my dress. He stands between my sister and me, a hand on both of us, sometimes relinquishing one to concentrate both hands upon the other. I squirm, I want this man to take his thrusting hands away from my person, but what can I do? This is an adult and a customer, the word customer being synonymous with family friend. Suddenly, my mother erupts into the shop and the man hurries out into the street. Some time later, my mother tells me that Gay Taylor, about to enter the shop, had seen what was happening and hurrying to the second entrance had warned my parents *"Ross Nichols is doing terrible things to the children!"* Nichols is a well-known paedophile. In fact, his landlady on one occasion had entered the shop in great agitation to tell my mother *"he did something terrible to my son."* But, in those days, and sometimes perhaps today, Victorian virtues made both women and abused children into the guilty parties: the child must have tempted the adult man. One time, my mother and I call upon Nichols' Holborn lodgings to deliver a book he had ordered. We walk up a narrow staircase, the stairs covered in cheap lino into a room filled by heavy furniture. Nichols dressed in a Scoutmasters uniform sits in an armchair, his bare legs spread wide. With a grin he informs us that he is awaiting the visit of a Boy Scout. A good many years later, I read in a national newspaper gossip column a 'puff' for a preparatory school for the young sons of top people. The name of the headmaster: Ross Nichols. The rich are not like us.

Inescapably, the years pass by and in 1937, the year previous to the Crisis, and yet at a time when war clouds threaten, I am sent on a holiday to Hastings with orphans from an Automobile Association funded Home named Willoughby, based at Crystal Palace. My mother has prepared me for this fortnight's holiday weeks ahead and she has promised me a ten shilling note for pocket money. Ten whole shillings to spend! Twi spoils my anticipation a little when, my feet balanced on a strut, my hands clinging to its edge, I lean over the fence which divides our two gardens to boast of my expected new wealth. Twi had been given ten shillings to spend on holiday and *"it hadn't gone very far"* and then, in mitigation, she adds *"of course, I did have to buy plimsolls and they cost* 2s6d." Quickly I add up sums in my head. She had only 7s6d. I would have ten shillings!

The day arrives and my mother and I take the 134 bus to Victoria, past the equestrian statues—military men balancing stiffly on horses made rigid in motion as if turned to stone by a gorgon. Past the grey cenotaph and the mouldering wreaths at its base; past the Houses of Parliament, its flag at half-mast, past St. Margarets, Westminster Abbey, to the station. A sober-clad group of children of mixed sexes and ages, in the care of two women, await us on the platform. These are the inmates of Willoughby and all have lost one or both parents in a car accident. The holiday has been arranged by Arthur Dawson—referred to in letters by James Hanley and in whose house I spent my days while my mother was in hospital to undergo surgery and receive the disfiguring red scar which stretched down her abdomen. Arthur Dawson is a trustee of the orphanage. He had become interested in this charitable work following the death of his twin brother and sister-in-law in a car crash. He and his wife childless, they had adopted their orphaned nephew John, some three or four years older than myself. During the time when I had visited the Dawsons daily, they had expressed an interest in adopting me also, but my mother had refused. These early encounters with this family forgotten—to me Arthur Dawson is no more than a vague figure of a customer in the bookshop, a thickset man of medium height and raspberry coloured nose. Seemingly, Arthur Dawson maintained an interest in me, for on hearing of my asthmatic condition and general poor health he suggested a holiday at the seaside. It may be that to explain my presence to the Willoughly authorities he insinuated that I was to become a future inmate of the Orphanage. Whatever, this is the information imparted to me by the children; "*You're coming to live with us at Willoughby.*"

I look at these alien beings who have no place in my life and deny this future they claim for me. But, I am horribly frightened. What if my parents have agreed with Arthur Dawson that I should live at Willoughby! Behind me line up all the places to which I have been despatched from Herne Bay onwards. But strenuously I continue to deny that I have been abandoned by my parents:

> *There's my ballet lessons…*
> *You can learn ballet at Willoughby.*
>
> *My violin lessons…*
> *You can learn music there.*
>
> *My school…*
> *We go to school.*

I become more and more alarmed and my behaviour more and more bizarre. When I can put this threat to the back of my mind the holiday is happy, for I learn to play Pit and other board games. I find an old xylophone which has on it the old scale including the 'H'. Therefore, when much later I learn that Bach wrote a piece of music using the notes B A C H I feel a proprietal interest. I am able also to go down to the pier and flip pennies onto a side stall to win cheap gifts of tin brooches or chalk ornaments. However, these pleasant occasions become less frequent as I become more distressed. Every day I write to my mother and this thin thread of blue-black ink maintains my only contact with home.

The large house in which we are holidaying is a private Residential Home and across the passage from my bedroom which I share with five other Willoughby girls, is a bedroom for the permanent residents. Fascinated by their predicament and the vacuum of their lives, I visit them on most evenings. Soon they lie in bed waiting for my entrance. And yet their situation exacerbates my fears, for it seems that they will spend their lives within these walls, and perhaps in this very room. They provide me with puzzling information: *"My grandma said I'm not my mummy's little girl"* an eight-year-old tells me earnestly. This is an enigma, for surely she must mean that she's not her father's little girl? I am aware that of the two parents it is the mother who cannot deny the fruit of her womb: *"My grandma pushed me when I was getting off a ship"* the child continues and I see a small girl with short brown hair descending the gangplank of the 'Queen Mary'—which I have seen on newsreels—followed by an old lady with white hair. The old lady pushes the child who falls into the water.

Perhaps I too have been deserted, abandoned by my parents. I cry and cry until all the older girls gather around the bed on which I am lying, eyes red, face tear-stained and they assure me that it is all a mistake. I am not to go to Willoughby after all. However, the damage has been done. Whom can I trust? A latent paranoia takes hold and a certain amount of grumbling from the older girls about the quality of the food leads me to pick at it. Perhaps it is poisoned? The clear drinking water in my glass on the table, I pour into the vase of flowers for the same reason. I cannot eat or drink this nourishment which is aimed at my destruction.

Arthur Dawson and his wife live in St. Leonards, but I see nothing of them. During this holiday they invite some of the older girls to tea, but not me. Something must be wrong. One of the girls invited is 14-year-old Biddy, brown-eyed and black-haired. A girl who is afraid to open an umbrella in the house lest someone dies as a result. She enumerates for me the number of persons within her family who had died because they had ignored this superstition: Umbra—total shadow. Biddy speaks bitterly of her mother. *"She never visits me and only writes sometimes. She doesn't care about me, so I don't care about her!"* I ask myself *"If Arthur Dawson likes this odd girl and invites her to his home, why not me?"* He cannot face me! He had wanted to adopt me when I was a baby, now he plans to confine me to his Orphanage! *"You're coming to live at Willoughby!"* jeers a small boy. We are walking in a loose crocodile in the park. In a temper, I rush at the boy and push him over. He picks himself up without crying and I watch the blood run down his leg. I feel myself wrapped in the disapproval of the group and determine to return to Wilton Road, come what may. Where is my return ticket to London? I search through the case stowed under my bed and cannot find it, but miracle of miracles, I make the same search a day or two later and there lies the green half ticket! Hastily, I throw my clothes into the case, shut it and lifting it to the balcony opening off the French windows of the bedroom, drop it over the side where it bounces onto the stony driveway. I wish that I could jump or drop after it, but the ground is too far away and so I hurry down the stairs and out of the front door, only to find the suitcase surrounded by a small group of Willoughby children. The eldest girl, a trusty, carries the case back upstairs. *"You'll be going home next week"* she tells me, but I do not believe her.

I will not stay here, case or no case, I am determined to leave. I refuse to be incarcerated within Willoughby. My eyes red from weeping, nonchalantly I walk down the drive watched by the curious eyes of children. *"I'm going for a walk"* I call out as a cover and while I continue to feel their eyes on my back, no one stops me from leaving. Whether I travel by bus, or walk to the station I cannot remember. In those days the places at which I arrive make the impact. All I know now is that I sit on a bench alongside two comfortable looking middle-aged women and await the London train. *"Travelling on your own, dear?"* asks one of the women. *"My Aunt's meeting me"* I lie. She offers me an apple. This is the first of nine or ten apples I am to eat on that day, for everyone in the small Pullman carriage espying a child travelling alone wants to give me something. And all they have are apples.

Unknown to me, my mother has planned to take Oonagh to Worthing on the following weekend to spend a week with Beatrice Hastings at her tiny flat, but now a telegram arrives to tell my parents that I have left St. Leonards and am on my way home. This information having been gleaned from enquiries made at the station. *"She said she was meeting her Aunt,"* says one of the two women sitting on the bench and this perfidious untruth is later related to my parents. It is dusk when I arrive at Victoria to hear the noise and bustle of a busy station. *"Where's your Auntie, dear?"* asks one of my benefactors. *"Over there!"* I reply, jumping from the train and running for it. I find the 134 bus and am home within the hour, to find my parents agitatedly waiting for me. Relieved that I am safe and yet angry. My mother scolds, my father sulks. I weep and at last my mother relents. *"Would you like an apple?"*

she asks. That night I am ill with stomach pains and diarrhoea for which the plethora of apples takes the blame. Next morning I go around the house searching for minute changes which have taken place during my absence—I examine the Japanese prints hanging on the wall, touch ornaments and the bulbous blue pair of vases on the mantelpiece, find a new cushion cover, run my eyes along the books on the shelves.

"Oonagh and I were going to stay with Beatrice at Worthing" my mother says reproachfully *"but I've had to write and say we can't go, her small flat can't house more than one other person and a child."* I hardly hear her for I am home. But Beatrice sends a bitter letter to say that she hopes I will be made to understand the unhappiness my selfishness and thoughtlessness has caused. A lonely woman, she must have looked forward with great pleasure to my mother's short stay. My friends are the young Jones's who listen to the sorry tale over tea at their flat. *"Good for her!"* says Maud *"if she didn't like it there, she was right to come home."*

Arthur Dawson does not give up on our family, however, for the following year my sister goes on the Willoughby holiday at St. Leonards. On the morning she and my mother are to leave for Victoria Station, our black and white cat gives birth to kittens so that my mother and sister almost miss the train. My mother travels with Oonagh to St. Leonards and the other passengers in the coach hear of how my sister had comforted the cat by talking to her gently while she gave birth. *"The passengers were very impressed,"* says my mother. And, of course, Oonagh returns from St. Leonards triumphant. Everyone had liked her! They had all said how awful I was! This year there had been another fussy, miserable girl staying there and they had all said we were two of a kind. I shrug away these criticisms for while I now feel guilty about my behaviour and will never be able to meet Arthur Dawson without feeling an acute chagrin, I have friends who like me. And this I see as the natural order of things.

In those days I hated to go away from home. I was unaware that soon I would be caught up in economic and political forces over which my family had no control, the family unit to be tossed aside and our lives and aspirations regimented.

Exodus

My Bubba is run over and dies: We all sit Shiva: My Uncle Marky the boxer: Miss Stranger and tactical marches: The Nazis invade Czechoslovakia: In Great Britain men of twenty are conscripted: The Hitler-Stalin Non-Aggression Pact: I am evacuated to Preston Park, Brighton.

"*Good old Chamberlain*" shout the Wilson siblings "*we don't want war!*" We are walking along Colney Hatch Lane towards the North Circular Road and they are answering my criticism of Chamberlain's appeasement policy. A criticism relayed from parents, as, of course, was the Wilson defence. I had written a poem in response to the events at Munich, a poem much appreciated by my parents, two lines of which read:

With two flights of an aeroplane
England was put to shame

"*Chamberlain's a silly old sod*" I reply to the Wilsons, not understanding that this is swearing, but the Wilsons know. "*What did you call him!*" Mervyn asks me in delight. "*Silly old sod,*" I reply uneasily, adding "*it doesn't mean anything—it's just a word.*" "*I dare you shout it out*" Mervyn challenges, Zara adding her voice to her brother's, "*go on!*" she urges. "*Silly old sod*" I shout defiantly and the Wilsons, hooting with laughter, look around in the hope that I have been heard by passers-by.

Whistle while you work,
Mussolini bought a shirt
Hitler wore it,
Chamberlain tore it,
Whistle while you work.

sing the children in the school playground, paraphrasing a song from the film of *Snow White and the Seven Dwarfs*.

In the year of the Crisis, my Bubba, Grandmother Rachel, dies in the London Hospital. This on the 21ˢᵗ October, 1938 and my cousin Flo's twenty-third birthday. Bubba's spare figure hurries across the Commercial Road. It is Friday evening and she is on her way home from Schul where she has been bargaining with God for a prolonged and active life. As she nears the kerb a lorry swings around the bend and runs her down. *"In collision with a motor vehicle"* the Official Police Report records. As if fragile skin, bone and blood is the same in substance to harsh crafted metal. The driver climbs out of his cab and stands aghast at the sight of my Bubba's broken body around which a crowd is collecting. The family is summoned, perhaps by telephone. My Uncle Marky is in Rotherham, my Aunt Becky in New Barnet and my mother in Muswell Hill. Or possibly they were summoned by telegram:

COME AT ONCE STOP YOUR MOTHER IN LONDON
HOSPITAL STOP

Or maybe a policeman knocked on doors with the bad news. My grandmother lies in bed at the end of a long ward, the iron headrest against the wall. Her broken leg in traction. Her blue eyes light up at the sight of her children, two daughters and one of her two sons, gathering fearfully around her bed. *"I will be all right"* she says *"I want to live!"* She says this in Yiddish for the violence of the accident has sent out of her head the little English gleaned over the years. *"Your mother's in good shape for a woman of seventy-two"* the doctor tells my Aunt Becky. My grandmother has recovered enough English to give the doctor her official age. *"Seventy-two!"* says my Aunt Becky to the doctor, *"my mother's eighty-four!"* My grandmother had always felt it incumbent upon herself to reduce her age by twelve years— as widow at the age of thirty-two she had married my grandfather, then a boy of eighteen, and in her early thirties had become once more a girl in her twenties, deferring in its turn middle-age and old age. But she could not defer death, and she died in the London Hospital from pneumonia brought on by shock. As it happens, in spite of my Aunt Becky's revelation to the doctor of my grandmother's true age, the family agreed to honour her by recording her age on the Death Certificate, and subsequently the grave-stone, as 72 years. They dared not do anything else.

During this shocking time, I had seen a great deal of my Uncle Marky and Aunt Becky and the house seemed to be always full of people. *"Your Uncle seems to be very sure your grandmother isn't blind"* says Twi to me earnestly. We are playing outside the kitchen window where raised voices of adults can be heard. *"Bubba has cataracts over her eyes"* says my mother. Maybe she had crossed the road in front of the lorry because she could not see. My Uncle will have none of it. The mother who had raised him, fended for her children and a sick husband, whose foresight had surmised their every need, could not now be blind. My mother does not argue too fiercely with my Uncle because she feels close to her brother and she sees in him what was left of their father. *"Uncle Marky was like our Tsaider"* my cousin Flo tells me. *"Gentle and a gentleman."* Flo remembers my grandfather, for he had not died until she was eleven years old. She would meet him from the barber-shop in Aldgate and he took her for an ice-cold milk with soda water. This was her treat and he needed this beverage to wash from his mouth the taste of hair and the smell of scalps. Half-an-hour on a stool to quieten his hair-filled lungs.

It was in his temperament that my Uncle Marky resembled my grandfather, for whereas my Tsaider had brown eyes and a dark complexion, my Uncle like my mother and Aunt Becky had their mother's colouring. *"The gentleman boxer"* my Uncle was called when he had fought in the ring as a Welterweight under the name of Fred Archer. Boxing was an ability he had developed at the Jewish Boys' Club, and economic need had driven my Uncle into this, for him, unlikely profession. My mother tells me that he had fought Ted 'Kid' Lewis and lost on points, only because the bandages to protect my Uncle's hands had not been tied properly, nor his gum shield inserted correctly. This meant that he had been forced several times to stop the fight for these technical repairs, so throwing his boxing out of sync. *"The betting was on Marky"* my mother says, *"so the organisers wanted Lewis to win."* Lewis was a fool, what his family would have called 'meshuga' for before Mosley had officially adopted anti-semitism as part of his programme, Lewis had been employed to teach Mosley's thugs how to fight, and had also stood as a Mosleyite candidate in the East End. He had received very few votes and those he did receive, it was surmised, came from relatives.

My Uncle had killed a man in the ring. My mother could barely express in words my Uncle's grief. *"The man had children"* my mother says *"and your Uncle gave the widow £100—a lot of money in those days."* My mother remembers the end of my Uncle's boxing career when he was out of the big-time. *"All he could get for a fight was £9,"* she says. *"I'll never forget the look on his face."* In later years, my Uncle expressed a distaste for the violence of the ring and those who practiced it. And in exculpation he became a faith healer and spent his time mending broken bodies. By that time he had married Passie and they had two children, a boy and a girl. Passie, whom my mother despised. *"She was a Kitter"* says my mother *"we Argebands come from the tribe Ben Shia, but the Kitters come from nothing at all."* In her view, they had no refinement nor learning. Maybe they were Dutch Jews who, having arrived in England much earlier than the 19th Century immigrants from Poland and Russia, had become integrated into the English working-class, their religious practices differing and becoming less orthodox than those of the later Jewish arrivals. At one time, when my Uncle and his wife are having marital problems, my mother takes their wedding photo from out of the album. A photo which shows my Uncle in bow tie and tails, a smile on his face, and Passie in long white dress and veil, her eyes and hair dark. With sharp scissors, my mother cuts through the photograph to surgically remove Passie from this marriage. She then tears into pieces the strip of Passie and pokes the bits into the Ideal Boiler. And yet Passie was the archetypal Jewish matriarch who possessed the *nous* that not only kept the family solvent, but made them well-to-do. For Passie's knowledge of the clothing industry led to her opening a workshop to produce children's clothing, which soon developed into a small factory; my Uncle, no businessman, working with her only on the periphery and spending much time in occupying himself with his own interests.

My Bubba had also been forced to supplement her family's income and because of my grandfather's poor health, at times support the family financially. During the years at Portsmouth she had worked on the market stall selling sailors' hats, collars, navy blue jerseys, gold buttons, insignia for the sailors themselves and, child-size, for boys and girls; clothing designed to advertise the Imperial might of the British Navy. *"Rule Britannia, Britannia rules the waves."* *"We always had good food to eat,"* says my mother *"even during the war when butter was five shillings a pound, my mother found the money to buy it."* This praise of my grandmother coming from my mother is rare for often it seemed to me that my mother had rejected her own mother along with her rejection of her religion. We are visiting my grandmother in her small house and she sits before us at the table to speak haltingly of dying and heaven. *"Superstition!"* snorts my mother *"There's no God, no heaven!"* *"She's very old,"* I remark on the way home, sitting alongside my mother on the tram. *"She might be going to die soon and wants to believe in God."* My mother is disconcerted. She feels bound, when in the environment from which she has escaped, to justify the opinions which have severed her roots.

Therefore, it comes as a surprise to me that my mother takes my Bubba's death so hard and that she reproaches me for a lack of caring. For on the day my Bubba died my Aunt Becky comes to the house and my mother, in a sudden rush of goodwill towards her sister, gives my Aunt two rag dolls given to my mother for my sister and me. Dressed in long clothes and with old faces they remind me of my Bubba's two younger sisters, Shindel and Railer. I burst into tears and my mother comforts me. But after my Aunt has left, my sister whispers to my mother that I had cried because she gave the dolls away. My mother reproaches me: *"You weren't crying for Bubba!"* She is disappointed in me. I do not know what to reply. I cannot make my feelings plain even to myself. Perhaps for me the loss of the dolls stood in for the absence of my Bubba, the old lady in the hospital.

The family sits shiva and my mother takes me to my Bubba's house where a thick candle in a glass burns in the small front room; a candle to represent the spirit of immortality. This candle must stay alive throughout all the days of shiva. What will happen if it blows out accidentally? I hold my breath even when on the other side of the room, for I see the light flickering under my breath and extinguished. What would that mean for my Bubba? For me? For all of us? I leave the adults and go into the back room, my Bubba's bedroom and climb onto her high feather bed, falling into its centre, but soon I become bored and struggle down onto the floor to examine the heavy furniture. Behind the solid overmantel fronted by a high mirror I can spy a piece of paper. I try to push my hand between the wall and the back of this structure, but the aperture is too narrow. I cannot reach. What might it be? A lost will? A map to treasure? A secret my Bubba has hidden away? After the funeral, after sitting shiva, my Bubba's belongings are parcelled out and it is then that her mahogany table and chairs are delivered to Wilton Road—minus the chenille cloth promised to us by my Aunt Becky, but claimed by my Great Aunt Railer. I have a sudden vision of my Great-Aunt and my Aunt Becky playing tug-of-war with the plush red material with its hanging tassels, my Great-Aunt proving to be the more determined of the two.

My Bubba's small, neat body lost in a mound of history, my mother's ambivalence towards her is quietened, so that when she looks into the mirror resting over the mantelpiece in our living-room, she sees looking back at her the face of her mother. Mother and daughter have become one. *"My grandmother died"* I say to Colleen. I would never call my grandmother 'Bubba' to my classmates for this would have thrown me into a separate culture. *"She was run over and died in hospital."* We are walking along Grove Road on our way to the Ally Pally skating rink. Sometimes on our way into the Palace along the pathway close to the old tram lines, teenage boys attracted by Colleen's auburn hair and sturdy figure call out to us. Colleen takes no notice for she never flirts with boys. She treats them all as if they were no more than her brother's friends. I know that the boys are not interested in me, for at eleven years of age I am skinny and my chest development negligible. And yet in the year of the Crisis I begin to menstruate.

"When I started my periods and told my mother I was bleeding she slapped me round the face" my mother tells me. *"I cried,"* my mother continues, *"because I thought I must have done something wrong. But then my mother told me the slap was to ward off the devil!"* The curse! Unclean! Only men's bodily emissions are a matter for pride. For some time during the war we are to have a nurse from the mental hospital as a tenant, a Mrs. Taylor, and she advises me never to wash my hair while menstruating. Otherwise the blood would rush to my head and leave me mad. This, she has no doubt, diagnosed as the cause of insanity in her patients. However, my mother, remembering her own ignorance and fear, had prepared my sister and me for the event, but I am taken aback when she says *"you mustn't go skating today—the exercise might be harmful."* *"I'll just play at Colleen's house,"* I lie, for I have every intention of going skating with Colleen. Anyway, I cannot tell Colleen I am menstruating, for both of us are reticent about bodily functions. And so we set off for the rink and a slight show of blood has no impact upon my activity.

At the Convent, several of the girls gather at times to whisper recently gleaned information on physiological developments and processes. I am left out of these huddles for my small skinny stature makes them regard me as 'too young'. However, when menstruation for me has become a regular occurrence and between lessons the girls sitting next to, and around me, whisper, whisper, whisper; heads bent towards one another, a sharp eye kept on the door for the teacher's entrance. I, annoyed at my exclusion, whisper to my neighbour, *"I've started my periods."* She looks at me in disbelief, but passes on the information and the girls gaze at me in amazement, astounded that such a shrimp should beat them into womanhood!

With regard to the year of the Crisis, the events to us children are no more than a blip in our pattern of life, disturbed temporarily to resume its normal flow for the first nine months of 1939, during which the war was in its final period of gestation. At the Convent, a whiff of militarism in the air, combined with the influence of Hollywood spectaculars, results in Miss Stranger, the games and drill mistress, introducing tactical marches. At our annual display in front of the parents we fan out on the Convent lawn into long lines meeting each other at the centre. Slowly, we walk round, keeping in our line, so as to give the impression of an enormous wheel turning. Photographed from above, no doubt, the exercise would have appeared impressive, but denied the resources of Hollywood , every parent watches the lines for a sight of their own child. My one fear in performing is that I will move forward at too quick or too slow a pace, so drawing upon my head Miss Stranger's wrath. She a short, stubby figure, greying eton-cropped hair, dressed in a plain suit of straight skirt and man-like jacket, stern and quick to anger. She is much feared by the children. I have reason to fear Miss Stranger, for two or three years previously she had trained us to dance around a maypole, for a May Festival to be performed in front of the parents. For this dance we hold onto a red, white, or blue ribbon, which becomes plaited as we weave in and out. It is not easy for the girls, to whom the process has not been explained, to always remember their part: 'do I go inside now or outside?' And so at practice, Miss Stranger stands shouting *"blue ribbons out, white in, red under..."* Several times she loses her patience with us. *"The next one to make a mistake is out of the dance for good!"* she threatens. In trepidation I move round, weaving in and out, meeting on the way Madeleine McCormac who dances round the wrong side of me. *"Sheila Lahr, you're out!"* shouts Miss Stranger *"we'll*

find someone else to take your place!" Crestfallen, once again out of
step and separated from my peers, I creep away. My mother has
bought me a white dress especially for the performance. What
will she say? A few years later, Madeleine and I are to go about
together, but neither of us ever refers to this incident. *"What a
cow that woman was!"* my mother is to say several years later. *"You
arrived home heartbroken and threw yourself into my arms."* But, my
mother would never have gone to the Convent to protest, for my
mother did not expect justice and knew that while the workings
of authority were strange, they had their own inexorable method.

In that last year before the war Miss Stranger's infant nephew
and niece become pupils at the Convent. She brought them to
school each morning in her care and took them home again at
the end of the school day. Maybe she expected her own flesh
and blood to excel, but she was certainly tough on those kids.
The little boy's head lay on one side, and because my mother
had described to me the symptoms of John Roberts' spinal injury
I understood that this little boy had a similar condition. Miss
Stranger preferred to believe that he drooped his head wilfully.
She is walking a circle of infants sitting on the floor and comes
to this small nephew, *"keep your head up!"* she snaps, emphasising
her words with a swipe round the side of his head. The boy's
face crumples and he cries soundlessly. The niece, Heather, a
pretty little girl with auburn hair receives also the expression of
Miss Stranger's ire. *"Did you see?"* the children whisper *"she hit
Heather round the head with a tin box!"* It is not until after the war,
and following deputations from parents to complain about Miss
Stranger's treatment of their children, that Reverend Mother
dismisses the woman, in this way ending for Miss Stranger a
lifetime association with the Convent: although she was not a
Catholic, she had attended there as a child and at the end of her
schooling had been promoted into teaching.

When I consider the negative experience school was for me, I
wonder why in 1971 I accepted a place at a Teachers' Training
College, having first sat and passed three 'O' Levels. Of course, I
had enjoyed teaching my own children and foolishly had equated
teaching with schooling. I told myself school had changed since
'my day'. However, my return as an adult to school left a terrible
taste in my mouth, not least because of once more undergoing
the traumas I had suffered as a chiild. In an inner city infant
school in the 1970s I found that the teachers zig-zagged in and

out of self-control, sneering at, slapping, and punishing children for fancied misdemeanours, without even the saving grace of the nuns' belief that suffering, humility and penitence were necessary to save souls. The teachers found it impossible to enter into the thought processes of a young child, no doubt due to the loss of imagination during their own 'successful' school days. And this together with a lack of understanding of the backgrounds of pupils within their care, meant that the teachers could grasp only at inculcated feelings of class, imperialist and nationalist superiority with which, often unknowingly, they had been fed since birth. Opting for discipline and control of children from ethnic minorities or poor working-class families, many of the latter in hostels for the homeless, and bullying these children into a simulation of behaviour attributed to the English middle-class—the only type of schooling acceptable to the educational bureaucracy, backed by government. For the second time in my life I was glad to leave school.

However, that is for a future not yet caught up with me. In the meantime I must make the best of school and involve myself in living outside that institution in my child's world. Unaware that outside both these parts of my life, political and economic events are reaching out to take control and shape my future. As early as 1937 the House of Commons had voted in favour of a plan for air-raid shelters to be erected in most of Britain's towns and cities. In April 1939 a Bill is promulgated to provide free air-raid shelters and to evacuate the children. And yet in May 1938 the British government had signed a pact with Italy, Chamberlain at the time praising Mussolini. The British government having ceded Czechoslovakia, the Nazi armies invade in October, 1938. In November 1938 Nazi thugs smash the plate-glass windows of Jewish owned businesses in Berlin—known as *Kristallnacht*. *"They should have killed more Jews and broken less glass"* Goering fumes, annoyed that replacement of glass, to be imported, must be paid for in scarce foreign currency. In March 1938 Hitler enters Prague to raise his standard on Hradzin Castle. In the same month Chamberlain pledges to defend Poland; Nazi troops march into Austria; Japanese bombers mercilessly batter Shanghai and Canton, which they occupy; The Duke and Duchess of Windsor meet Hitler on cordial terms.

The British government orders the building of more weapons factories, more camps and vast supplies of boots and uniforms.

The House of Commons endorses the government's decision to conscript men of twenty for military service. In February 1939 the British government recognises Franco, the opposition greeting the Prime Minister with cries of *"Heil Chamberlain."* In April 1939 Mussolini occupies Albania. In July 1939 Polish dockworkers in Danzig, part of Poland, are arrested and sent to German concentration camps. On 23rd August, Hitler and Stalin sign a non-aggression pact; Ribbentrop for Germany, Molotov for the Soviet Union. Stalin proposes a toast: *"I know how much the German people love their Führer"* he says. Not so long before, in December 1938, Orson Welles in a rendering of H.G. Wells' *The War of the Worlds* on the radio had panicked listeners who in terror fled into the streets or made for open spaces. Virtual Reality.

During all this upheaval, I, in my child's world, continue with my ordinary daily activities. I go to school, I come home again, I go out with Colleen to Guides or to the skating rink, or play at her house, or play with Twi or the Wilsons. Christmas 1938 my sister and I buy a small 6d Christmas Tree and ornaments, the latter from Woolworths. Having set the tree with earth in a flower pot, we find the clip-on candle-stick holders bought for previous Christmases and having clipped them onto various branches, carefully give each one a coloured spiral-patterned candle. We buy coloured strips of paper from Torrys and sit at the living-room table making them into chains. We are unaware that this is to be our last peace-time Christmas for some years. Somehow we hope that the world will solve its problems without involving us. But, in the summer the population is issued with gas masks. *"It's only a precaution,"* we comfort ourselves and each other as we make our way to church halls to be fitted and issued with this protection. Our gas masks are handed out at St. Peter le Poer in Colney Hatch Lane and I try on the rubber protuberance which is tight upon my face, the nose hanging heavily. Then it is declared *"a good fit,"* boxed and I take it home with me. Towards the end of the summer the newspapers report:

> *31st August 1939: "Britain's Cities and towns are strangely quiet today. The children are leaving, clutching their few personal possessions and gas masks. Over 1.5 million of them are being evacuated to safe areas in the country. The great exodus began at 5.30 a.m. yesterday and will continue for the rest of the week. Schools have become reception centres with fleets of buses—taken*

off their usual route—conveying the evacuees to the main line sta-
tion. 72 London underground stations have been partly closed to
the public to speed the long planned operation. Few parents know
where their children will end up finally although the government
says "they will be told as soon as possible."[1]

Small feet were pattering, wooden shoes clattering
Little hands clapping, and little tongues chattering,
And like fowls in a farmyard, where barley is scattering,
Out came the children running
All the little boys and girls
With rosy cheeks and flaxen curls
And sparkling eyes and teeth like pearls,
Tripping and skipping, ran merrily after
The wonderful music with shouting and laughter.[2]

My sister and I caught up in this valediction, trudge up Colney
Hatch Lane, hurried along by our mother, our gas masks packed
in their square cardboard boxes hang on a string over one shoulder, to bang against our sides. We have been up and about very
early. Time enough for me to pull from out of my mouth the
fixed restrictive brace and prize off the tin surrounding the two
molars to which it had been fixed. My front teeth are almost
straight now and I want no more of this painful dentistry. The
bad news is that I am lamenting the loss of a silver ring which I
have owned since birth. Too small, I have continued to wear it on
a little finger. But, my mother has sent me on a last minute message to the shops and in pulling off a glove the ring has vanished.
    However, I cannot dwell on this loss for too long for the chara-
banc has arrived and stands waiting outside the Convent. A small
group of parents stand in the road, watching their children board.
I spy both Colleen and Twi and tell myself that this is an adventure on which I am embarking with my friends, but the confining
presence of the nuns tells me differently. A week or two previously, Colleen had said confidently *"there won't be a war—it's just a*
repeat of last year's Crisis. My Dad says the Germans are only celebrat-
ing the anniversary." Now, it appears that both Colleen and her
father had been wrong. Don't worry, it may never happen. You
die if you worry, you die if you don't, so why worry? The human

---

1. *20th Century Chronicles*, published by Longman.
2. Robert Browning, *The Pied Piper of Hamelin*.

capacity for optimism and blindness. And yet war has not yet been declared. Can it be averted? I could not accept the threat to myself. I would not be crushed by the rhythm of the mechanical jackboot. Others were menaced, not me. For somehow I had retained a belief in the capacity of my adults to protect me. I did not see us as threatened by the macho men in dark uniforms, carrying murder, hunger and disease, populations dispossessed. Genocide. And yet now I have been caught up in their mad rush by the appearance of a softly purring charabanc in Pages Lane.

The seats all occupied, we wave goodbye to our parents who stoically watch our departure as the coach sets off for Preston Park, Brighton. As this is a private arrangement we know our place of destination and it is not about us that the newspapers report:

> *Already reports are coming in of country folk shocked by the verminous condition of some children from city slums, and equally horror expressed by city children at their strange surroundings. For many it was their first sight of cows and other farm animals.*

Little of the journey remains with me now; the ride through drab London streets and out into the countryside. Sometimes, we pass other charabancs bent on the same mission and the children wave to us. Other children not yet caught up in the migration, stand and stare from pavements and playgrounds.

Mrs. Bennett—she who went up and down Wilton Road knocking on doors to collect money for Franco—is accompanying us. She has been employed by the nuns as a cook. She weeps hysterically while we children around her stir uncomfortably. A nun attempts to soothe her, but Mrs. Bennett continues to explode into tears and laments all the way to Brighton. *"She can cry!"* I say to myself. I have no sympathy for this pro-Franco Spanish woman married to an Englishman. *"Anyway, she's not leaving her children, she's coming with them!"* Adding (raised as I was on Saki and other satirical literature) *"maybe that's why she's crying!"* Subdued, the children sit in the coach barely speaking. All outside passing us as if viewed through a kaleidoscope. In this speeding coach our future travels with us and at last we turn into a long driveway, at the end of which stands an impressive building. A building which I sometimes remember as a castle and sometimes as a church. But most probably it resembled neither of these. We have been evacuated to a Convent in Preston Park to occupy part of its extensive premises. Staircases, corridors, rooms and more rooms.

I touch the silver medallion hanging on a silver chain around my neck, which I wear as a talisman, although it is a First Communion medal. This medal was bought for me by the boarders at St. Martins and, shortly after making my First Communion, I hear an argument at breakfast between Renie and Sister St. Francois. Renie is complaining about the depletion of her pocket money. *"You forget you gave towards Sheila's First Communion medal,"* snaps the nun. I sink down into my chair and hope to avoid a glancing blow from the girl's contemptuous eyes. But now the medal has lost all past associations and I wear it as a sign that nothing will hurt my mother and soon I will return home.

Dark Nights

On learning of my imminent evacuation, one of the few pleasures I had anticipated was the sharing of a dormitory with Colleen and the group around her. For I am an avid reader of schoolgirl stories and tell myself that we will all have midnight feasts, whisper to one another after dark, form a tight-knit group by night as well as by day. This in spite of all the evidence to the contrary while I boarded at St. Martins. *"I was younger then"* I tell myself *"now I am one of the older girls,"* for the teenage boarders had not come with us. I rejoice in my newly acquired status. The nuns decree otherwise. Sisters must stay together whether they like it or not. Therefore, I find myself sleeping in a room in the next bed to Oonagh, together with three other pairs of sisters, including Miss Morant and her younger sister, Valerie. Miss Morant, a fat woman who has a large mole on her chin, was a pupil at the Convent and is now employed as an uncertificated teacher. She believes in ghosts, expressing this belief to us during a lesson at St. Martins. When I relay this information to my rationalist mother, she snorts with disgust. However, when other arrangements have been made for my sleeping, I yearn to return to this dormitory of sisters.

Torn away from my friends as well as my home, I am desolate, the breath knocked from out of my body. Day after day in the small room of eight beds, I wake up gasping for air. I creep along the long, dark corridors and the narrow staircases almost bent double, my arms hooked, my fists pressed into my sides. *"She needs extra pillows. She should sleep sitting up,"* says Sister St. Brigid, the Irish nun. I have met her and Sister St. Francois in one of the musty passages. *"Non, non!"* retorts Sister St. Francois, shaking her head. In her eyes to provide an extra pillow is to spoil a child. God in his infinite mercy has visited this affliction upon me and like Job I must bear it with fortitude. *"It could help,"* mutters Sister St. Brigid bravely. She is chagrined, her face reddening, but as the junior nun she can make no decision on her own. There is always some difference of opinion between the older French nuns and the younger Irish nuns as to the upbringing of the girls. *"Come down from those trees, you are not boys! Come down from there!"* shouts Sister St. Francois, her red face redder than ever. We are playing on a grassy strip in the grounds of our host Convent at the end of which grow a line of trees. Several of the girls are mounted on the lower branches until the nun intervenes. *"Modern girls do climb trees,"* Sister St. Brigid says timidly, but the rule 'no tree-climbing' prevails.

Separated from newspapers and radio it is some time before we become aware that war has been declared. Of course, from the first, at Morning Assembly, we pray for 'the dead and the dying', the girls and nuns standing in a large circle, the nuns presiding. But there are always dead and dying in one place or another. It is not until a wailing siren rends the air to declare an air-raid alert that we realise that the country is at war. We are hurried to a shelter in the Convent grounds, where for an hour or more we sit in a concrete bunker, tense in anticipation for we expect to find on emerging that the world as we know it has vanished. But, the alert turns out to be a false alarm, for the first eight or nine months after the 3rd September, 1939 is to become known as 'the phony war'. This due to the fact that actual hostilities between Great Britain and Germany are on hold. However, we sing the current song from 'top of the pops':

> We're gonna hang out the washing on the Siegfried Line,
> Have you any washing mother dear,
> We're gonna hang out the washing on the Siegfried Line,
> If the Siegfried Line's still there.[1]

---

1. Jimmy Kennedy, Michael Carr, *The Washing on the Siegfried Line*, 1939.

At Morning Assembly once we have said a prayer for the dead and the dying we are warned not to speak to the pupils of the host Convent, most of whom are boarders. This segregation had been one of the conditions of St. Martin's stay. The girls at St. Martins are mainly the daughters of tradesmen and artisans, while the pupils at the host Convent are from the upper Middle Class and the nuns are intent upon maintaining the social divide. However, with regard to Convent snobbery, I don't think anyone has written about it more cleverly than Antonia White in *Frost in May*. Sometimes, we pass our host Convent's pupils on one of the many corridors twisting and turning in this old building and leading to countless staircases and endless doors. Under the strict observance of both sets of nuns, we avert our eyes from one another. However, Sheila Pauley, a fair-haired girl in my sister's class, tells the St. Martin's nuns that her cousin is a boarder at this Convent. The St. Martin's nuns intent upon proving upper-class connections, and also to encourage the cohesion of the family, obtain a special dispensation to allow the two girls to meet—until it is discovered that the so-called cousin is no more than the adopted daughter of Sheila Pauley's so-called Aunt, a family friend, at which the intercourse between the two girls is ended. *"She is not your cousin!"* storms a Sister.

In spite of this segregation my sister and I do speak to a girl named Nonie; thick chestnut brown hair to her shoulders, dressed in the light blue smock which is part of this Convent's uniform. Holding herself and speaking with the confidence inculcated from birth into the middle-class. Nonie appears before us at odd moments, on a pathway, in a doorway, and always when we are in the grounds. She introduces to Oonagh and me her younger sister, a girl very like herself, but I cannot now remember our conversations. All that remains is the pleasure of her speaking to me for I felt chosen.

During this time I am plagued by asthma, day after day, and cope as best I can. And then, one evening I am in the Hall with Colleen when Sister St. Clare enters, trailing behind her the infants, for it is their bedtime and she is taking them to the dormitory which she supervises. *"Sheila Lahr,"* she calls out. Girls nudge me. *"Sister St. Clare wants you."* They are curious. I walk towards her. What have I done, or not done, now? *"You are to come with me,"* she says, a half-smile upon her flat white face. *"You must go to bed early, you are not well."* I protest feebly. I am twelve and a half, I am one of the older girls. I hang back. But it is no use and at last I follow Sister St. Clare and the infants up the stairs and along a passage to the infants' dormitory where a bed has been made up for me in their midst. Night after night, Sister St. Clare shames me by calling me to bed with the little children. How I long for the room in which I slept with Oonagh and the other pairs of sisters; a room where my bed was next to the window, so that once the light was extinguished by Miss Morant I could pull back the curtains a little and assure myself that the darkness had not left me blind. In the infants' nursery Sister St. Clare sleeps behind a screen in front of the windows, guarding this opening to the outside world, the blackout curtains firmly in place. Bedtime becomes a nightmare to me for once the light is doused and my sight blacked out, I panic. Sister St. Clare, ensconced behind her screen, I creep out of bed to stand before the fanlight over the door through which artificial light percolates while others in the Convent are awake. Until, cold and tired, I climb once more into bed and agitate myself into sleep. Once, waking in the night to strain my eyes against the blackness, I climb out of bed only to find the fanlight invisible in the darkness. I move my head this way and that, in a vain attempt to catch one point of light, and at last, in terror, throw open the door to run down the long passage to the room where my sister sleeps. There I climb under a blanket on the unmade-up bed, to be found almost immediately, for my hurried entrance has awoken Miss Morant, who sounds the alarm and a nun hauls me back to the infant dormitory.

I see little now of Colleen and my peer group and savour each moment I am with them. We meet, of course, at lessons which for the most part are aimed at keeping us busy. And we meet in the Chapel for a morning service, evening benediction and mass on Sunday. Following this mass we walk in a crocodile to take the non-Catholic girls to an Anglican Church. On first arriving at the host Convent, the nuns, sitting at a desk in the classroom, had discussed how to provide the protestant girls with a religious education which would not offend their parents. We had two Jewish girls with us, Stella Friedlander and her older cousin, June Nyman, a slow girl whom we regarded as a bit soft. Should they be taken to the synagogue? This would have to be on a Saturday, one nun pointed out to another, it would interfere with the week's routine. The nuns hummed and ha'ed over the matter, but at last Stella and June are allowed to be relatively free from religious indoctrination. When the nuns, leading a crocodile, arrive to deposit several pupils at the Anglican Church, the Vicar is delighted at this increase in his congregation. He is also impressed by this example of Christian unity and often waits outside the Church to thank the nuns profusely. While the protestant girls are on their knees, we trail around the neighbourhood of Preston Park, past hedges and houses, one suburban street much like another.

My one clear recollectiion of Colleen from this time is of both of us bathing in adjoining wood partitioned cubicles. Overjoyed at being so near to my friend, I climb onto a chair to peer at her through the glass fanlight and look down on her plump, completely naked body as she climbs out of the bath. Guiltily, and in embarrassment, I jump down to the floor. I have sinned. I remember Josephine Kenny, a girl some five or six years older than me, who lives in Wilton Road, telling my mother that when she boarded at the Convent the girls were expected to bath while wearing a long, loose gown, in this manner avoiding the sight of their own nakedness. How much worse to view the nudity of another and violate their privacy. Anxiously, I pray that Colleen has not seen me looking down at her, but a certain coldness in her manner towards me makes me suspect that she knows of my intrusion.

My mother visits to take Oonagh and me out for the day. As the three of us gather together in the driveway, Nonie in her blue smock appears at the side of a building, a low wall separating us, and I proudly introduce my friend to my mother. They talk, but I take in little of what is said for I am assessing my mother's appearance. She has a sore upon her face—the bitterness and sorrows of her years often breaking out in such excrescences, just as mine stifled my breath. In later years, a longing for the sweetness withheld from her in life enters my mother's blood-stream and she is diagnosed as *zucker-krank*, or diabetic. Nonie will notice this sore and think my mother ugly. I examine my mother's clothing. Is she dressed smartly enough? She wears a black pill-box shaped hat and a loose black coat. Her shoes and stockings also black. Will she say the wrong thing—something that will reveal our family as poor, odd and undeserving? I am on tenterhooks and Nonie's voice comes over to me as no more than a collection of beautifully sounded vowels. The conversation over, "*h-mm*" says my mother as we walk down the driveway, "*Well spoken, but a snob. Did you hear her say that Brighton is not a good place to live because there are too many Jews?"*

We take the bus down to the sea-front and stand indecisively as my mother decides what we should do next. *"Ted is in a sanatorium near here"* she says doubtfully; *"Perhaps we should visit him. Your Aunt Mary asked me to go and see him."* I do not know my cousin Edwin Stone well, for he is twelve years older than me. But the little of him I have seen I have liked. Unlike his brother Cecil who is locked away in his own world, Ted has always taken notice of my sister and me, even when we were quite small. Only a few months previously, Ted, as a member of the Communist Party, had sent us a letter in which he praised Stalin. In replying to this missive, and in a spirit of mischief, I had written that I'd seen a flock of 'starlings' flying over our garden. *"What's a sanatorium like?"* I ask my mother. *"All the windows are kept open both Winter and Summer,"* my mother replies *"because people with TB must have plenty of fresh air."* I try to envisage this place where the outside is inside.

I have two photographs of Ted at the sanatorium. In the first he stands half-smiling, cloth cap on his head, outside the building and in front of an open window. He is dressed in dark clothing, a corduroy anorak zipped up three-quarters of the way, to reveal curled-up collar and dark tie. Next to him stands an older man, strained face, black hair. He leans forward to place a hand on my cousin's shoulder. Two of the sitting patients smile, while the fifth, standing, rests his hands on the shoulders of a sitting young nurse as if for support while she with her left hand adjusts her hat. A second nurse stands, a melon-like grin upon her face. In the second photo, my cousin dressed in similar clothing, sits on a chair. His head leans backwards so that it appears to be resting against the chest of a headless man behind. My cousin's eyes are closed.

However, my mother decides not to visit Ted. Perhaps she revolts against taking her children into this environment of sickness and death. Instead, we catch the bus to Ovendean to visit Dr. R.L Worrall, he of *Time and Lifetime*:

> *Time is the one thing on which we cannot experiment. It is either all in the past or all in the future... But do not imagine that the past is passive. The past never ceases preparing fresh sets of possibilities for the future... even as we move and measure we are in*

*a past that is on its way out, making the way for a later past that
we shall not live to see.*[2]

A little while ago, before his death in 1996, I spoke to Dr. Worrall on the phone and reminded him of this visit to himself and his wife. *"Yes"* the old man replied *"who was I married to then?"*

*Even now time is ageing and slowly changing our surroundings, to
be replaced eventually by other things and perhaps other people.*[3]

At Ovendean we alight from the bus and walk past a high building casting its shadow upon all around and because of isolation appearing even taller. *"That's St. Dunstan's"* says my mother, *"where
the soldiers blinded in the war stay."* Fearfully I view this monumental tower and its surrounding kitchen gardens. All is quiet. There is no sign of life. We walk past rows and rows of cabbages standing green and firm in the dark soil. How, I wonder, can blind men plant cabbages in such straight lines? For I see the blind as lost in a dark world where all is chaos. We walk on, leaving the building behind us and I resolutely look straight ahead feeling its shade upon my back so that I am not happy until I know I am out of its grasp.

Of the visit itself, I remember little, the impression remains only of a tall young man, a woman and chatting adults in a light airy house. My pleasure is being with my mother and away from the supervision of the nuns. The visit over, my mother returns Oonagh and me to the Convent. But before she takes her leave I tell her that if I put three large crosses, masquerading as kisses, at the end of a letter it will mean that I want to return home. We are allowed to write home once a week, but the letter must be handed to Sister St. Wilfrid for vetting. On one evening when I am in the Hall, she comes towards me, in her hand the missal

---

2. *Adscene*, week ending 13th January, 1969.
3. Dr. R.D. Worrall was Brighton's Medical Officer of Health and was very opposed to children being evacuated to Brighton, which, he said, was in the front line. He produced a leaflet at his own expense to oppose this 'lunatic move', the result of which was a fine of £100 and dismissal from his post. But, Churchill, on a visit to Brighton remarked that he had come to 'the front line' and, in addition, a bomb exploded in a cinema at a children's matinee, killing many of the evacuees. Dr. Worrall was reinstated and his fine reduced to £5.00. See Ray Challinor, *The Struggle For Hearts and Minds: Essays on the Second World War*, Unkant, London, 2011 (1995), p. 50.

which I have written an hour or two before. Her pale face is stern and I tense in apprehension. What have I done now? *"We do not send love to a cat"* the Sister says coldly. *"A cat is an animal without a soul and cannot give, or receive, love."* Years later, I am to hear the words of William Blake, *"Everything that lives is holy"*; which puts into words my own feelings in the matter. Fortunately, the three large crosses at the end of my letter to my mother, Sister St. Wilfrid will not censor. Ignorant of the code she will accept these Judas-like kisses at their face value. To such extremities are we driven by authority.

It is not long before I am pressing down hard at the end of a letter to make three large crosses, for an added worry is my thinning hair. Once a week Sister St. Wilfrid gathers up girls to wash our hair in a bowl set out on a table in a bathroom. She scrubs and pulls at my hair until it is declared clean, rubs it dry with a towel and then parts it into two bunches tied by thin ribbons. As the weeks pass the bunches become skimpier and skimpier, and the girls call me 'Keyhole Kate' after a character in a comic strip who has a long sharp nose and short skinny plaits. What is more, I develop an inflammation at the back of my head, under the hair-line. A redness which is to plague me to this day. *"What's that at the back of your neck?"* I am asked occasionally by a hairdresser. *"Only some sort of nervous trouble"* I reply placatingly, to assure the young woman that my condition is not contagious. I am not the only girl to lose her hair while evacuated to this place at Brighton, for others find their hair thinning and Ruth Lindsay (cousin to Madeleine McCormac) is almost balding, as if she were suffering from alopecia. We are all Samsons.

I continue to make crosses like mad on my weekly letters home, and my mother sends down to me my violin and stand, the latter of dark wood. Music, she is sure, will soothe my savage breast. The nuns twitter around these musical accoutrements. Why should I require them? Didn't I learn all that I needed to know at the Convent? Anyway, if I spent time in practicing, the even flow of daily routine would be interrupted. Therefore, both violin and stand are put away and I do not see them again while I am at Brighton.

At last, my mother writes to say that she is collecting Oonagh and me from the Convent to take us home. I meet Nonie in the grounds and happily give her my London address in an attempt to meet her on her own ground. I return to Wilton Road the

original name of the house, a name expunged by my father—
'Suffolk House'. Except that I get it wrong and write 'Somerset
House'—the name of the Records Office in those days. On arriving home, I write to Nonie and correct the error in the head-
ing, without comment, but receive no reply.

And so, I leave behind morning chapel, where the nuns from
both Convents hiss *"ora pro nobissss,"* Mrs. Bennett's Friday fish
pie, the shame of my demotion to the infant dormitory, and the
long black nights. Within a few weeks, other girls follow me and
soon it becomes unviable to maintain a separate establishment
at Preston Park. Therefore, all, including the nuns, return to
Muswell Hill; a wise move, for when the bombing starts, coastal
towns are a target.

I return to school at the Muswell Hill Convent, but now we
must enter by the front door, walking a little way up the hill and
into the grounds by the second entrance; or, by walking at the
side of the triangular driveway, crunching the gravel beneath our
feet. The shame of tardiness no more than a memory when I enter this front door, to step along the polished lino of the corridor
and breathe in its cloying smell. In passing I glance at the picture
of St. Martin transfixed in time as he offers half a cloak to cover
the nakedness of the beggar at the gate.

For Assembly, those pupils remaining—for many have been
evacuated privately or under government schemes—gather in
the dining hall, as the main Hall has been requisitioned for Civil
Defence training. School itself has acquired a state of impermanence, a transitoriness—nuns, children, building evanescent—all
in a state of flux; a lack of permanence compounded by Reverend Mother who announces at Assembly that school fees are to
be paid weekly instead of termly. Every Monday, the girls take
their envelopes containing a few shillings to the nun sitting at her
desk in the classroom. I have no such envelope for my mother's
arrangement is to pay from my Life Endowment policy once this
becomes due. A year or two previously, it had been a matter for
pride when it was announced at Assembly that I was that year's
winner of a scholarship which allowed the parents of the most
promising pupil to pay half fees only. At the announcement of
my name my classmates had looked at me in amazement and I
carried off the situation as best I could. For, cynically, I considered that this was a deceit to save the Convent from losing half
the fees of a paying pupil. To be said to pay half fees in those cir-

cumstances was an honour, to be seen to pay no fees at all was a matter for disgrace. Such are the muddied reactions in which we are trained—the giver exalted, the receiver despised. But, with an unexpected sensitivity, the Sister announces that if girls were not seen to pay weekly, it was because their parents had made other arrangements for payment.

Because of the lack of pupils, classes have been telescoped and the pattern of form-mates with whom I have travelled through school has been shaken up, to fall into a design to include girls from both lower and higher forms. Jean Wilson and Doreen King are now in my class, sitting behind me, and I am uncomfortable at feeling them on my back. A year or two previously, Jean Wilson, then in the form above, during the school holidays had made a great friend of me. She lived in Creighton Avenue, the road leading from Pages Lane to Tetherdown, the only road in Muswell Hill on which we tread pink paving stones. We children looked upon this road as a special place. Should a house stand empty in this Avenue, we saw it as haunted and children on their way home from school would dare each other to walk up the path and touch the front door. I am honoured to be the friend of this dark-haired, dark-eyed girl, the daughter of a French mother. But, when the school holidays come to an end and Jean's classmates have returned from wherever, she is no longer my friend. In fact, she doesn't want to know me and passes me by at school as if we are barely acquainted. Doreen King, a blonde girl who lives in a cottage in Tetherdown, has never liked me and has often flung at me insulting remarks, to which I have replied in kind. Now I have the two girls on my back.

At Wilton Road my father digs a deep trench in the garden to partially sink our shelter, provided free by the government to those earning less than £250 per annum. Whether or not my father fell into this category I am not aware. Anyway, we have a steel-built, tunnel shaped shelter, made in sections and measuring six foot by six foot; a shelter which later is to cause much dissension. My father has firmly planted this DIY protection and covered its part protruding above ground with earth and seedlings. In time it will blossom as a kind of beacon. The shelter is not named for its designer, but is called an 'Anderson' after the Home Secretary and Minister of Home Security 1939-40 and Chancellor of the Exchequer 1943-45, John Anderson First

Viscount Waverley. The designer, the engineer William Peterson is later to be knighted in compensation.

While on the surface life goes on much as before, in reality it is only a reflection of our former life; it were as if the usual is struggling to maintain its normality. For instance, Guides. There are only enough girls left in Muswell Hill to form one Company and so we are combined to meet weekly at the Methodist Church Hall in Coppetts Road. Colleen and I transfer although not altogether happily. After school, or at weekends, I go to Colleen's house, or we go out somewhere together. *The Wizard of Oz* takes over the devotion we have given to *Snow White and the Seven Dwarfs*, and we sing 'Somewhere Over the Rainbow' and 'Follow the Yellow Brick Road': the latter along any path which we are walking, whether yellow or not:

> *Follow the yellow brick road,*
> *Follow the yellow brick road,*
> *Follow, follow, follow, follow,*
> *Follow the yellow brick road.*

My father develops an intense interest in the news. In the evening and at weekends, on the hour, his ears are glued to the wireless and we dare not speak.

Ration books are issued:

> Butter—4^{ozs} per person
> Sugar—12^{ozs} per person
> Bacon or ham uncooked 4^{ozs} per person
> Meat also to be rationed

Each household registering with local shops. Later these rations are to be reduced. The ration of meat during the course of the war varied between $2s\,2d$. per person and $1s\,2d$. per person per week, and we ate unfamiliar meats, such as whale steaks, its taste oily. (Save the Whale!) Some said that we ate horse meat, and two or three years later when I and some friends had waited almost an hour in a cafe to be served, and on finishing our meal found that the horse which had been standing outside when the entered the restaurant was now missing from its cart, we joked that we must have eaten it. For our cat we bought horsemeat from the butcher's shop and this was dyed green to show that it was unfit for human consumption. The butter ration was to come down to two ounces per person per week, and to this day I can estimate two ounces of butter by sight.

"*This is the first time many families will taste butter*" says my mother, for many working-class families can afford only margarine. Butter is a status symbol. Even Twi's family never buy butter. My mother whispers this latter information to me as if some shame is involved. So, to assuage Mrs. Carson's guilt, if she gives me a piece of bread and margarine I always compliment her politely on the taste of her 'butter'. Of course, if my mother had said nothing I would not have known it was margarine! Can you tell Stork from butter? "*I do like a little bit of butter on my bread*," my mother quotes from an A.A. Milne poem. My father brings home potatoes from his allotment and my mother follows a recipe published in the newspapers for 'Woolton's Pie', named for Lord Woolton, the Minister of Food. My father brings home cabbages he has grown, but also collects dandelion leaves for salads and nettles to cook as if it were spinach. Our neighbour, Mrs. Sarginson, keeps chickens, but we are not registered with her for from half to two eggs per week per person, but with Stevens and Steeds. Failing fresh eggs, we use dried egg.

Sometimes, Oonagh and I go to a Civic Restaurant for a meal, the nearest to our home being at the Orange Tree, Friern Barnet, in a church hall. There, for a shilling, I buy a main meal and a sweet, and to the assistant behind the counter serving the latter, I say "*no custard*" in memoriam to the lumpy custard at St. Martin's Convent!

Notices appear outside church halls to inform the public how to recognise the spread of poison gas. With the film of H.G. Wells' *The Shape of Things to Come* continuing to loom large in my mind, this makes me apprehensive. I know something about the effects of gas from the old caretaker at Monkswell Court, a stocky man with wispy grey hair who often offers me and the Wilsons 2d each to weed the grounds. The Carsons have moved to this low rise block of flats in Colney Hatch Lane shortly before the beginning of the war. When I go to Monkswell Court, sometimes with the Wilsons, the caretaker comes out of his house to regale us with stories of mustard gas. He had been in the army, in France, during WW1 and mustard gas had crept behind his eyes. Every now and then, he says, his eyes had to be removed from their sockets for scraping. Although it is obvious to me that his greeny-blue watery eyes have been returned to their rightful place, I shudder at the idea of my own suffering such a fate.

> Arthur: *Must you with hot irons burn out both mine eyes?*
> Hubert de Burgh: *Young boy, I must.*[4]

The popular press is full of stories about whole families in Europe displaced from their homes and desperately seeking refuge. Stories about refugee children arriving in Britain veer from the sentimental to the sneering. One boy allowed sanctuary arrives clutching a violin case. This would-be musician is lauded to the skies by the press, only to be pilloried a few weeks later for reportedly remarking that he hated music—he had brought the violin only because his mother had said it would ensure him a good home. *"Just like those Jews, lost everything and still crafty!—They never learn!"* Short stories, plays, a dance performed at a local show in which the teacher mimes the despairing mother and Ena Macfarlane the refugee child. Refugees become part of cultural perception, so that Britain offered to settle refugees from Germany in different parts of the Colonial Empire. Announcing this in the Commons, Mr. Chamberlain had said that the number of refugees Britain could accept was limited and that 11,000 had come from Central Europe since 1933. On 29th June 1939, 206 German Jewish refugee schoolchildren had arrived in the UK and the Convent had taken a German Jewish girl of about 13 years. I watch this stockily built girl with short curly brown hair from a distance as she passes down the corridors. Sometimes she practices the violin alone in a classroom, drawing the bow back and forward over the strings, her fingers moving in accord with the black notes on the sheet of music before her on a stand. I want to speak to her but she never acknowledges my presence. It is as if she walks surrounded by impermeable glass.

A talkative, French refugee family of mother, Aunt and lively young daughter of eight or nine years come to stay at the Convent. For some reason which I cannot remember, I am sitting with the mother, Aunt and a nun in a small room overlooking the lawn. Before us on the table are plates and a salad made from dandelion leaves. The little fair-haired girl comes to the window and holds up a white handkerchief: *"Bourgeois"* she laughs!

---

4. Shakespeare, *King John*.

Nicole Mittelstein, the daughter of a French mother and English father is put into my form. A pretty girl, dark hair and eyes, effusive in manner, so that although I never count myself as one of her friends, if we meet in the street she greets me as if I am a long lost companion. This makes me uncomfortable, for in spite of my continental background, from somewhere I have absorbed the English attitudes of reserve and understatement.

Renate, Renate
Tomate, Tomate

The children call after another refugee girl who attends at the Convent for a short time. I have little memory of her except that she flits through my mind as a slim figure with shoulder-length brown hair. Good-naturedly she puts up with the children's teasing. However, recently I met her again in *Collar the Lot*, a book by Peter and Leni Gillman about the internment of aliens in the UK during WW2.[5]

---

5. Peter and Leni Gillman, *Collar the Lot: How Britain Interned and Expelled its Wartime Refugees*, Quartet Books, 1980.

Philipp Lahr
father of Charlie Lahr

Barbara Lahr
mother of Charlie Lahr

Rachel Argeband

Charlie Lahr

Charlie Lahr
photographed by Douglas Glass. Taken in the 1930s

Esther Lahr *as a teenager*

Esther Lahr
1920s

Charlie Lahr: P/W 789 at the Alexandra Palace Registration Office with military warders. Interned as an alien for four years in Alexandra Palace during WW1.

Head Study (Charles Lahr)
by Jacob Kramer from The New Coterie No. 6
Summer & Autumn 1927

Esther Lahr
by Jacob Kramer from The New Coterie, No. 2, *Spring 1926*

Esther Lahr
Painted by William Roberts

Charles Lahr
outside his bookshop at 68-9, Red Lion Street, London WC1

Charles Lahr *(centre) with two German POWs*
stationed in Muswell Hill: "We were allowed to take them out for a day"

**Cecil Stone, Günther Gerhards, Oonagh,
Sheila,** *in front;* **Esther** *(Sheila's mother)*

Charles Lahr *on the steps of St Pancras Station, delivering the Independent Labour Party newspaper* Socialist Leader.

Back row: **Onkel Ludwig, Charles Lahr**; *middle row:* **Tante Anna, Marienna, Helga**; *in front:* **Hans-Dieter, Klaus Lahr.** *Mainz, October 1953.*

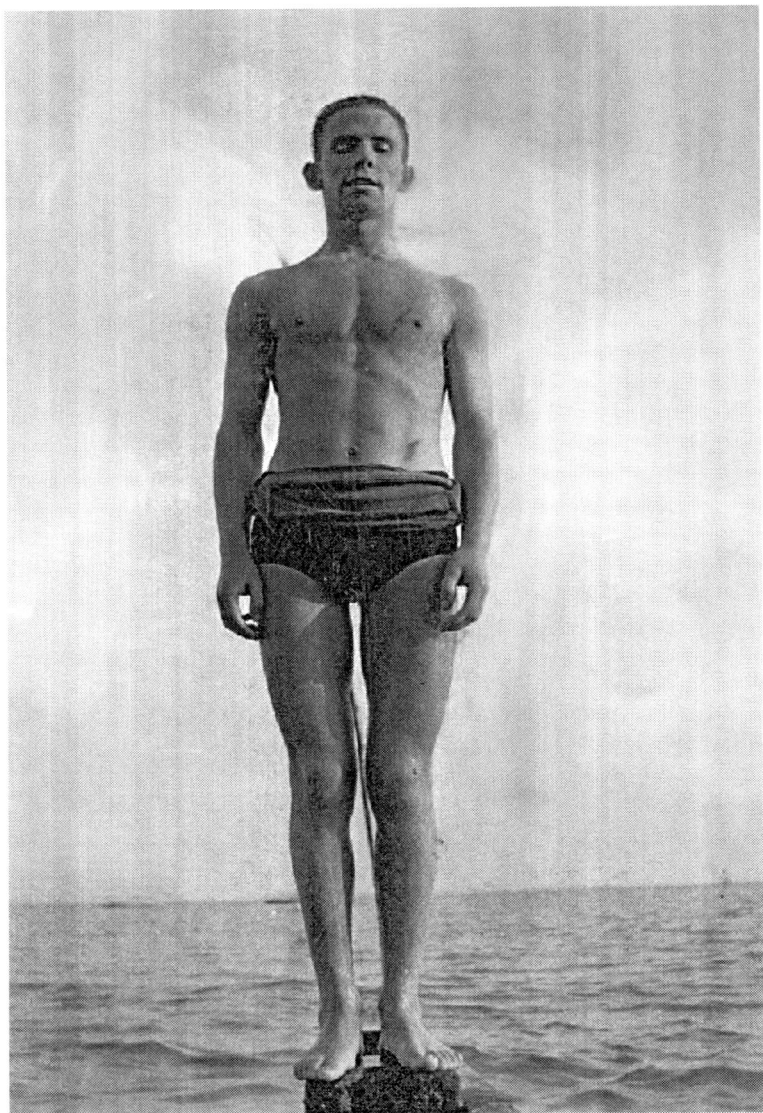

Edwin Stone
Cecil's brother, who died of tuberculosis in 1943, at the age of 28

Uncle Marky
(Esther's brother) who fought under the name Fred Archer

Sheila
1944

Werner Lahr *on motorbike;* Heinrich Lahr *to right;* Georg, *Tante Maria's husband, on far right;* Anne Liesel Lahr *and* Onkel Ludwig *at the back;* Sheila *(in glasses, at back); other two ladies unknown.*

Alien

The press spread fear and alarm against 'aliens': Tribunals are set up:
My parents are interned: I become a police evacuee: My father goes
on hunger strike in the IOM: My Aunt Mary does her worst: Renate
Scholem again: Dunkirk: The sinking of the Arandora Star.

**THE GREAT ALIEN SCANDAL OUR MONEY FOR COMMU-
NIST PROPAGANDA**, screams the *Dispatch*, followed by, **RED
CELLS FORMED BY SUBSIDIZED REFUGEES**: both stories
attacking Czech refugees in Britain. "*Hitler*" blares the *Dispatch*,
has a Fifth Column in Britain: "*made up of Fascists, Communists,
peace fanatics and alien refugees in league with Berlin and Moscow.*"
The Peace Pledge Union (a pacifist organisation) is presented as
an underground political force "*which endangers the very life of the
nation.*" *The Daily Mail, The Yorkshire Post* and *The Daily Express*
take up the cry, *The Daily Mail* headline blazoning:

DISQUIET ABOUT BRITAIN'S
FIFTH COLUMN IS GROWING

However, for a short time, while Lord Beaverbrook is having a
love affair with a Jewish woman refugee, the *Daily Express* back-
tracks a little by publishing an editorial against a witch-hunt.
How often does policy depend upon the itching of the genitals?
At last, the politicians, who for the most part take their remit
from the mood of the press, join in. Tory MPs complain about
aliens, communists and pacifists. Labour MPs concentrate upon
Oswald Mosley and fringe movements on the far right.

On the outbreak of war the government had been faced with
the question of what to do with non-British residents, dubbed
'enemy aliens', especially having regard to the fact that so many

Germans and Austrians in the UK were Jewish refugees from Nazism. On 24th October, 1939, Viscount Cobham, Parliamentary Secretary of State for War, in answering a question in the House of Lords on internment, says that the government had decided not to indulge in mass internment. He deplored the 'spy fever' of the First World War, which had gained momentum following the sinking of the Lusitania. Viscount Cobham concludes that no more than 1,000 to 1,500 enemy aliens should be interned in this war, as against 29,000 in the last war. He reckoned without 'campaigning' newspapers and the military reverses which made it necessary for the government to be seen to be doing something.,

As it happens, internees during WW1 had been divided into camps by social status. Class 'A' denoting past or present Army Officers, senior government officials and others of 'good social and financial standing'. Those dubbed 'A' had been permitted to pay 4s 6d. per day for high-class food and accommodation. The rest—A.N. Other—had been placed in Class 'B' and allowed to work as Batmen for those in Class A. WW2 'enemy aliens' are a different matter, for there are few Officers and it is not easy to identify gentlemen in the 55,000 refugees forced out of Germany and Austria. The men from the Ministries deliberate and at last agree to set up two types of camps, the one divided by social status, the other for refugees. Tribunals were set up to decide the relative danger each individual 'enemy alien' posed to British security. Those dubbed:

A–to be interned
B–to have restrictions placed upon their freedom
(a ban on travelling more than five miles, owning cameras or large-scale maps)
C–dubbed friendly and to remain at liberty

The tribunals were to be held in secret and the members drawn from the legal professiion—Barristers, JPs, the occasional Judge. The aliens would not be allowed a solicitor, but were able to bring a 'friend'. The War Office had warned that the categories should not be applied too vigorously although a refugee classed 'C' could be interned because he, or she, was of 'bad or dubious characater or repute'.

"*Do you own a car?*" asks the Chairman of Sutton Tribunal. "*Yes? Well you'll need to drive, so you'd better be in 'C'.*" Or if the answer to this question is 'no', "*Oh well, I'll put you in 'B'. If you buy a car later, apply to be put in 'C'.*" "*Better to be safe than sorry*" says the Chairman of Reigate and also Leeds "*put 'em in 'B'.*" "*I see you're down here as a domestic servant*" says another Chairman to a refugee woman. He knows from the complaints of his wife and the wives of his colleagues that servants are notoriously unreliable. "*I'm putting you in 'B'.*"

Other Tribunals place a political interpretation upon the clause 'dubious character and repute' and intern refugees who are socialists and communists, including veterans from the International Brigade in Spain. And it was this last interpretation which did ultimately for my father, my mother, and Renate Scholem.

"*Here there are more than 2,000 subversive agents acting on instructions from Moscow*" blares the *Sunday Dispatch* on 4th February 1940: Attacking the Independent Labour Party and the Peace Pledge Union, the *Sunday Dispatch* says: "*They disguise themselves as peace societies or genuine working-class organisations. It is time they were shown up for what they are.*"

The *Sunday Dispatch* and the *Daily Mail*, both owned by Lord Rothermere, had in the 1930s openly supported Hitler, Mussolini and Oswald Mosley as 'bulwarks' against Bolshevism. Now the Hitler-Stalin Pact of 23rd August 1939 enables them to continue to present extreme right-wing opinion as patriotism, in the process muddying the waters by confusing all strands of liberalism and socialism with Stalinism.

In the month of May 1940 the knock at the door comes very early in the morning and my father is taken. A month in which we sing at the Convent:

This is the image of the Queen
who reigns in bliss above;
of her who is the hope of men
whom men and angels love.

Most holy Mary, at thy feet
I bend a suppliant knee;
in this thy own sweet month of May,
do thou remember me.

On that morning when I at last open my eyes it is as if our home has been touched by a cold draught which moves about the house until it gains the momentum of a whirlwind which takes us into its centre, twisting and turning our everyday lives and our perceptions inside out and threatening to let us fall. The four walls, at times so hated by my mother, now join her in shouting out their misery and outrage. For my mother, once again there looms the prospect of stepping in as breadwinner, and this following a break from the bookshop during which she has lost all contact with the book trade. But she sends Oonagh and me to school as usual. She has much to do. *"My father's been interned"* I tell Colleen and the other girls assembled in the dining-room. It is as if by saying these words I can really believe in what has happened., I am not proud that my father has been taken away for internment, and yet I am not ashamed. Unlike his prison sentence, this imprisonment is not for what he has allegedly done but for what he is—a man born in Germany. What could he have done about that? My anger and disgust is reserved for the government. *"My father's friend was interned last week!"* says Pearl Bangerter offhandedly. My news is old hat.

Worse is to come. *"The wives of aliens are being interned"* my mother tells me glumly. In those days British women married to foreigners lost their own nationality. This because women were regarded as their husband's property. *"They're being sent to the Isle of Man, but children under sixteen can go with their mothers."* *"I'm not being interned"* I retort angrily. No government was going to decide my fate. *"I'm British!"* I surprise myself, for here I am for the first time agreeing to be parted from my mother. My mother broaches the question once or twice more and again I am adamant. *"I will not be interned!"* My sister is not asked. It is taken for granted that I make the decision for both of us.

ACT! ACT! ACT! DO IT NOW! screeches a headline in the *Daily Mail* above an article by George. Ward Price:

> In Britain you have to realize every German is an Agent. All of them have both the duty and the means to communicate information to Berlin.

"Arrests should be carried out as a rule in the early morning" state Home Office guidelines, announcing the decision to intern 'enemy' alien women. The only women to be spared were those who were invalid, infirm or in advanced pregnancy, or mothers with children who were dangerously ill—the police to search the women's homes and tell M15 of *"any information suggesting the existence of plans for assisting the enemy."*

My mother approaches the Catholic Church to enquire about the Father Craven Homes, for she realises that our care could be long-term. With much hesitation, the priest tells her that he would not recommend them for the children of educated persons. They were for the children of 'poor' people and the girls were trained for domestic service. My mother in great distress calls at a Citizens' Advice Bureau, recently set up to present government information to the public. A Mrs. Shillan listens sympathetically to my mother's tale and promises to take my sister and me into her own home should my mother be interned. She had listened forbearingly while my mother poured out her fears and anxieties and she must have been impressed by my mother, or perhaps something in her despair touched Mrs. Shillan's heart. The Shillans were living in Hampstead Garden Suburb, but within the next week they would be moving to Gloucestershire.

The knock at the door comes before 6 a.m. Two male detectives stand to watch my mother as she runs to and fro agitatedly, collecting together clothing:

> *Women should be given reasonable time to pack their requirements for the journey, and they should be informed that it might be two or more days before they reach their destination.*[1]

Oonagh and I dress ourselves. My sister had been reading a *Billy Bunter* book when the detectives come for us, and now she places it under her pillow, in the belief that it will remain there until our return. The cases packed, my mother runs upstairs to speak to our tenants, a young couple named Rowley who have occupied the upstairs flat for weeks only: while I was at Preston Park, the Dawsons, whose name had been on the Council list for fifteen years had been rehoused and now lived in a self-contained maisonette in Alexandra Road. These Rowleys, husband and wife, are ex-pupils of our local Grammar School, Tollington (known as Tolly) and have pretensions. He, a tall well-built ruddy-faced man—later to join the Grenadier Guards—she, almost the twin sister of her husband. Now, my mother dependent upon her nearest neighbour, rouses the Rowleys to give them the keys to the bookshop and addresses of people to contact. The rent to be paid into my father's bank account.

---

1. Peter and Leni Gillman, *op cit.*

While my mother is so occupied, I scribble a note to Colleen to say *"my mother is being interned and I, and Oonagh, are going to stay with people in Gloucestershire. I'll write you."* Then, murmuring to the detectives that I am going to the outside lavatory, I duck down past the kitchen window and run out of the side door and into the street, up to Colney Hatch Lane, along to Greenham Road, up to the top and push the note through the letter-box of No. 91 and dash home again. One of the detectives and my mother are out in Wilton Road searching for me. *"Where have you been!"* my mother cries as I come into view and I mumble that I went to put a note through Colleen's door. The detective says nothing, but it must have been this fear that given a chance I, and perhaps Oonagh and my mother, will abscond, that results in a detective shadowing all three of us at the police station whenever the cell door opens in answer to our ring, and we make our way to the WC.

However, at last we are ready to leave the house and it is only when we are in the police car and half-way up the road that my mother remembers that she has left her hand-bag on the kitchen table. A bag holding money and keys to the house. But the detectives refuse to return. Neither gas nor electricity have been disconnected and the flat is wide open.

Unknown to me, at about the same time on 27th May, 1940 Renate Scholem, seventeen years old and dressed in school uniform, opens the front door of her lodgings to find standing on the step a policeman and policewoman. She must pack a suitcase and go with them. Renate, who has been in England since the age of eleven, is confused. Why are they taking her? And the reply given is that she has been reading left-wing literature—*The New Statesman* and the Left Book Club. Renate Scholem is the daughter of Werner Scholem, one of the founders of a breakaway socialist party, the USPD, and was among the revolutionaries who formed the Spartakus League. He had edited the Communist Party paper *Die Rote Kapelle* and at one time sat in the Reichstag. However, he had returned disillusioned from a visit to Moscow in 1925, which had turned him away from active politics. Instead, he had put his energies into private living and into studying to become a lawyer. Of course, Werner's past political history and the fact that he was Jewish made him 'an enemy of the Reich'. Therefore, barely a week after the burning of the Reichstag, a gang of men in brown shirts burst into the Berlin apartment and took both Renate's parents away. Renate, who had been largely brought up by her non-Jewish grandparents in Hanover, once again lived with them until her mother was released. Eventually, both she and her mother escaped to England to join an older sister in north London. On leaving the Convent, where Renate passed by me briefly, she went to live at Carmel Court with Naomi Bentwich, the sister of Norman Bentwich, a leading figure of the Jewish refugee and welfare movement. Renate's mother remaining in north London and disappearing for a time to fight with the International Brigade in Spain. On the outbreak of war, Naomi Bentwich decides to move to Devon, but Renate, intent upon finishing her schooling, stays in Kent and lodges with a local family. Now Renate, dressed in green school uniform, is taken to the local police station and then by car to Holloway prison in London:

> *It was dark when they eventually found the prison, one of the largest and most forbidding of all those the Victorians built. Its enormous studded front gate appeared to Renate like a dungeon, and when she stepped inside, she could see two arms reaching out from a barred window high above.*[2]

"*Don't worry*" she is advised by Minna who had been a teacher at Carmel Court. "*The British aren't Fascists, it will all be cleared up.*" But, it is here, in Holloway, that Renate comes to understand that she must shed the Englishness learned during the past years and for her own survival accept that she is a German, a prisoner and an enemy alien.

ALIEN WOMEN IN LUXURY

Proclaims a headline in the *Sunday Dispatch* on 7th January 1940, above a story about internees in Holloway prison:

> *The alien women, Germans, Austrians, some of them Jewesses, used to march round the exercise yard singing German songs.*

While our lives are being disrupted at Muswell Hill, my father is on his journey to the Isle of Man. First to Kempton Park race course where he sleeps in a stable, drawing into his lungs the smell of horses and manure. Then onto a derelict old mill in Bury, Lancashire, described by Peter and Leni Gillman in *Collar the Lot*:

---

2. Peter and Leni Gillman, *op cit.*

> Cotton waste littered the entrance and the floor was slippery with
> oil and grease. The mill was lit only through the glass roof; as
> many of its panes were broken or missing, it also let in the rain
> which collected in large puddles below. There were eighteen cold
> water taps for each 500 men and the lavatories were filthy... the
> food was sparse: the evening meal consisted of a lump of bread,
> a small piece of cheese and a cup of tea. There were few mat-
> tresses at first and most internees slept on boards covered by two
> or three blankets, some of which proved verminous. At night they
> could hear rats scuttling among the remnants of the mill machin-
> ery. The entire building was surrounded by two fences of barbed
> wire, with armed guards patrolling in between... The Red Cross
> (was) performing its traditional neutral role of trying to secure
> the best conditions for the captives of war... singled out the di-
> lapidated conditions, the absence of lighting, and the poor hygiene,
> which included the small number of taps, the absence of hot water
> and the dirty lavatories... the delegate to Britain of the Geneva-
> based International Committee of the Red Cross, also criticized
> the camp's inadequate sick-bay, with only thirty beds for the 250
> internees who required treatment.

Interned Italian doctors lead a protest to the Commander, Major Braybrook, who calls the prisoners together. Climbing onto
a wooden box he addresses his audience. "It is not so bad here,"
he thunders, "there are much worse conditions in other places." He
emphasises his words with gesticulation of hands, arms, body
and the prisoners watch his movements, his mouth opening and
shutting, hear his voice hitting and bouncing off the mouldering
walls and pitted floor. Suddenly, behind him a water-pipe bursts,
knocking him from his perch and almost burying him under a
weight of water.

This incident, and the lack of hygiene, reminds my father that
in the shock of his arrest he has come away from Wilton Road
without a towel. Malachi Whitaker lives in Yorkshire, the neighbouring County, and so he writes to explain his predicament and
to ask that she send him a towel. Malachi responds immediately,
but held up by bureaucratic procedures, it is several months before the towel comes into my father's hands.

My mother, my sister and I sit in a cell in Fortis Green Road
police station. My mother sits slumped on a red shelf-like bench
against the wall. Her face bleak. She is despairing for her life

has once more been snatched away. There is nothing she can do. She must resign herself to being at the disposal of blind authority. We watch her crying, aware that we must soon leave her and in an attempt to make her happy, I begin to sing the Vera Lynn favourite:

> *We'll meet again,*
> *Don't know where, don't know when,*
> *But I know we'll meet again,*
> *Some sunny day,*
>
> *Keep smiling through*
> *Just as you always do,*
> *Till the blue skies drive the darkness*
> *far away.*
>
> *Please say hallo to the folks that I know*
> *Tell them I won't be long,*
> *They'll be happy to know that as you saw me go,*
> *I was singing this song.*[3]

My sister joins in and we tap dance in the confined space as if we are performing in a Hollywood film, or a latter half of the 20th Century song and dance routine in a Dennis Potter play. My mother at last begins to smile and then to laugh. For a short while she has forgotten our parlous situation and sees only its humour.

A policeman opens the cell door. The Shillans have been contacted. They are about to leave for Gloucestershire and we should join them immediately. A detective drives us to Hampstead Garden Suburb where we find Mr. and Mrs. Shillan waiting with two cars, a large Wolseley and a small Fiat. Now everything happens at breakneck speed, there is barely time for greetings or to effect introductions. Our luggage is placed into the boot of the Wolseley driven by Mr. Shillan and my sister and I climb into the back seat of the Fiat. Mrs. Shillan drives, her maid Dorothy sitting next to her.

By that time, my father has crossed on the boat to the Isle of Man. As he gazes over the side of the churning water, he remembers his crossing from Germany to England thirty-five years before. In fact, if anyone should ask him his age, he would

---

3. Ross Parker, Hughie Charles, *We'll Meet Again*, 1939.

reply *"thirty-five"* for he considers that he remained unborn until he settled in London. Then it was to escape the confinement of military conscription, now he crosses the water as a prisoner of the military. But, what worries him most is that he does not know what has happened to my mother or his daughters. He has heard that the women, including the wives of 'enemy' aliens, are being interned, but whenever he makes enquiries from the Officer in charge, he receives the stock reply *"you will be informed in due course."* Tough measures are required and so once on the Island, my father declares a hunger strike. In my mind's eye, I see my father lying out on the grass in front of the small boarding-houses requisitioned for an internment camp and surrounded by barbed wire. There he lies, stiff-faced, his teeth clenched, his limbs tense, refusing to reply to commands or entreaties from faceless authority which requires him to eat. But he could equally have declared this hunger strike while lying on his bed in one of the boarding-houses, or sitting in the dining-room and refusing to look at the food laid before him.

Maybe I think of my father and grass because he told me that when he and the other internees arrived and were led into the compound around the boarding-houses, local Manx people gathered together on the other side of the wire to gaze at the prisoners as if they were strange creatures or aliens from another planet. My father feels it incumbent upon himself to put on a show. Therefore, he bends down, yanks out of the ground a large tusk of grass and chews it voraciously as if he were a ruminant. But, of course, these surprised spectators of my father's antics must themselves have been disconcerted at this invasion of their island, for the Isle of Man had not been included in the list of camps drawn up by the War Office in August 1939. And yet, on 12th May 1940 the boarding-house keepers receive a letter from B.E. Sergeaunt, Secretary to the Island government, on behalf of the Lieutenant Governor, acting on instructions from the British War Office, ordering them from their premises within six days. They must leave behind *"all furniture, bedding, linen, cutlery, crockery and utensils."* This order being first given to boarding-housse keepers in Ramsay and soon afterwards to those in Onchan, north of the main town of Douglas, Isle of Man:

I haven't had a line from anybody except your parcel. I don't know where Esther and the children are, but have been told that they have been interned so they are 10 to 12 miles from here.

writes my father to my Aunt Mary. He continues by asking her to contact several of his friends—Dr. Sekar, Mr. Chapman, a retired School Inspector and John Amphlett, his solicitor and friend. At one time, Dr. Sekar had owed my father money. Unable to pay, he had sent a friend into the bookshop to inform my father that Sekar had died of TB. When Dr. Sekar reappears in the shop at the beginning of the war, my father growls at him *"you're a very substantial ghost!"* My father concludes his letter to my Aunt Mary:

we have a lovely view over the sea and Douglas and if I could have my family here I would enjoy the holiday.

Within the boarding-house, my father, his hunger strike behind him, has taken on the job of Cook, feeding each day 26 men. The weeks pass, and at last my parents are able to write to one another. Two letters per week, each one of no more than 24 lines. But there is no restriction upon letters received from outside. Letters show my parents as worried, for Aunt Mary has said that she is closing down the bookshop. This is not only their life's work, but their living. My father writes:

Dear Sister, Esther sent me your letter. We both appreciate what you are doing to save something for us out of the wreck, but I am sorry you are closing the shop. I had hoped that Burrows, to whom three shelves of fiction in the shop belong and a lot of whose books are stored in the basement, would pay the rent of the shop and carry on till I am out again. The war can't last very much longer and it would be an expensive job to buy shelving and open a new shop. And even if you closed the shop you could have kept the first floor. The rent is only 7s 10d a week, Miss Carson[4] pays 5s. for the little room and Mr. Michel pays 2s 6d. a week for storing the Cut Glass. This leaves 4d. If Miss Carson gave up, Burrows would take the room and pay enough to cover the whole. You would have stored the glass-case with the expensive books from the shop upstairs till I'm back. What were you going to do with the shelving? You couldn't store it at Wilton Road. I got a letter from Burrows to the effect that he is willing to carry

---

4. This is Twi's older sister, Amy (stage name 'Sorrell').

*on. He is honest and would have kept the shop going. The land-
lord wouldn't have worried about the few weeks unpaid rent. If
the books are dumped in the middle room at Wilton Road and
the war lasts over the Winter, in an unheated room, the damp
will make them valueless. Your letter is dated 3-6-1940 so I may
be too late to prevent the closing down of the business. There
are many valuable things among the effects upstairs, there is the
Roberts painting of Esther worth £50[5] and an early drawing by
him, etc. If you kept at least the upstairs part on, it would help
me a lot and save you any amount of work. I want all my letters
kept intact no matter whether they are from famous people or not.
Thanks for the parcel and the 10s. Will write again soon. Hope
Cecil and Ted are well. Love from your brother Charles.*

A letter from John Amphlett, Solicitor, to my Aunt Mary:

*I am rather worried about Charlie's affairs. As you know, when
he was interned, his wife kept the shop open for a few days, but
now she has also been taken off and the shop has been shut for
some time. I called there this afternoon and there was a Mr. Rowley there. He seemed a very decent sort of fellow and told me that
Mrs. Lahr had handed him the keys without any instructions as
to what to do. I believe he is seeing you on Sunday. There was
also a Mr. Berridge[6] at the shop who seemed to be suggesting that
the best solution would be for him to try and keep the shop open.
My own opinion is that it would be hopeless to try and keep the
business going. It was all that Charlie could do to pay his rent
and make something for himself and if somebody is put in charge,
I feel that all they will do will be make something for themselves.
Furthermore, I believe there is a substantial amount of rent owing
in respect of the shop.*

*Upstairs there is apparently a lodger and I have a strong sus-
picion that a good deal of the more valuable stock which is there
may not remain there for long unless the rooms are kept properly
locked. It would, I am sure, be better to move the more valuable stock to Charlie's house and dispose of the rest at the best
terms possible and give up the shop. This would save rent. So far
as the house is concerned, Mr. Rowley told me he thought there
was £20 owing for rates and probably a certain amount to the*

---

5. This is the painting of my mother by William Roberts, now in the
Tate Gallery: see p. 251.
6. This must be 'Burrows', referred to in my father' letter.

Building Society. If the Borough Council and Building Society are approached, it might be possible to arrange something and we are far more likely to do this if all further expense in connection with the shop is cut down. I understand that no-one knows where Charlie or his wife are and it would pressumably be necessary for somebody to get authority, such as Power of Attorney, to act for them. If, however, you like to take the responsibility, it could probably be done without any such authority and I have no doubt that Charlie would approve afterwards of anything you do.

With such friends, who needs enemies?

A letter from my mother to my Aunt Mary sets out money owed, payments to be made, incomings expected. My father's life policy for £400 is held by the bank as a security for an overdraft of £78, the Manager advising that the policy be not surrendered as to do so would raise only £160 minus the overdraft. Two quinquennial bonuses from the policy would, however, cover about three years payments so that there were now only seven more quarterly payments to be met. My mother continues:

Here is the children's address. The thing that worries me is that I sent them without proper clothing. If you would be so kind and post them anything you find of theirs, Oonagh went off without her real shoes, only in sandals. I had a good weep at your letter. Yours, Charles and Mrs. Rowley were the first communications with the outside world. Give my heartfelt greetings to Mr. Hanchant and to Maud and Jones (Librarian). These are good, honourable and sincere friends… My morning job here is brushing the stairs and scrubbing the hall. We all have a little work to do but are otherwise free to lead our, at present, aimless lives. It's very much like being on a seaside holiday, except for the air of depression and sadness.

The above letters from which I quote, I picked up from the floor of my Aunt's house at 3 Leathwaite Road, Battersea, following her death; a place where she lay, aged almost eighty, surrounded by mouldering and stained papers, newspapers, fallen books, torn rags, scraps of rotting food, dirty crockery, stained cutlery, crumpled religious pictures, broken ornaments and these letters. As if Cecil were intent upon showing his mother a prevision of the heights of past history onto which her earthly remains would soon fall.

However, in internment my mother does not allow depression to immerse her for too long. She remembers the words of Joe Hill, the American Syndicalist framed and executed for murder; *"Don't mourn—organise!"*; she remembers her days as a suffragette working alongside Sylvia Pankhurst; she remembers her days as a union organiser; she remembers her days as a socialist agitator. And so she contacts other interned British wives to present a petition demanding their release and for the return of their lost British nationality. My mother opens also a class to teach English, a continuation of the teaching she had undertaken in Berlin for six months during the 1920s.

Renate Scholem, whom I had last seen at St. Martin's Convent, imprisoned also in the women's camp, makes a fiery speech outside the recruiting room run by the Women's Army Corps. Freedom being offered to those 'enemy' aliens enlisting in the armed forces. *"Freedom must be enlisting from our own choice, not as a condition of release,"* she thunders. Hauled before the Camp Commander, Dame Joanna Cruikshank, Renate is threatened with reclassification from 'B' to 'A' and imprisonment on the Island for the duration of the war. Soon afterwards, the Red Cross tell Renate that her father has been shot in Buchenwald for leading a protest against food racketeering.[7]

On 10th May, following Dunkirk, Churchill had succeeded Chamberlain as Prime Minister and set up the Home Defence (Security) Executive. This had a remit to act on the prediction made by the Chiefs of Staff that 'Alien refugees' were a most dangerous source of subversive activity and recommended that they all be interned. In consequence a terse note sent to Chief Constables requested them to intern any German and Austrian men and women of Category 'C' where they had grounds for doubting the reliability of an individual. This meant that M15 were able to nominate its own arrests and local forces follow their own initiatives and prejudices. No one was safe. Maybe it was this blanket internment and the crowded camps which decided the government upon deporting internees to the new world. A policy always favoured by Churchill who would have preferred no aliens to remain within the UK. As early as November 1938 the government had proposed settling refugees in the Empire. Now, into the camps, news seeps of the sinking of the Aran-

---

7. Peter and Leni Gillman, *op cit.*

dora Star on its way to Canada, loaded with 1,700 internees and guards in addition to the normal ship's crew. 374 British men, 712 italians, 478 Germans—1,864 souls compressed into a ship built to take 250 passengers and extended to take 200 more. The majority of the Italian expatriates who had lived in Britain most of their lives, the Germans a mixed group of Jews, Nazis and merchant seamen.

The *Arandora Star* on its second day out from Liverpool, somewhere off the west coast of Ireland, slowly swims into view and frames itself on the crossed hairs of the periscope sights of a German U-boat's Captain:

> *The torpedo struck the Arandora Star fair and square amidships, erupting in a roar of sound and a towering wall of white water that cascaded down on the superstructure and upper decks, blasting its way through the unarmoured ship's side clear into the engine room. Deep inside the ship, transverse watertight bulkheads buckled and split under the impact, and the hundreds of tons of water, rushing in through the great jagged rent torn in the ship's side, flooded fore and aft with frightening speed as if goaded by some animistic savagery and bent on engulfing and drowning trapped men before they could fight their way clear and up to freedom.*[8]

Not enough life-jackets had been provided, the rafts were lashed immovably to the ship, there had been no life-boat drill and all decks were partitioned by impenetrable barbed wire, cutting off access to the life-boats. The Captain, named Moulton, had protested resolutely against the erection of this wire:

> *You are sending men to their deaths, men who have sailed with me for many years. If anything happens to the ship, that wire will obstruct passage to the boats and rafts. We shall be drowned like rats and the Arandora Star turned into a floating death-trap.*[9]

The Captain's plea is ignored. The government knows better. Prisoners must be surrounded by barbed wire at all times, even when on the ocean. Therefore, 1,000 men drown, including brave Captain Moulton who goes down with his ship together with Second Officer Stanley Ransom and Fourth Officer Ralph Lid-

8. Alistair Maclean, *The Lonely Sea: Collected Stories*, William Collins 1985, Fontana Paperback 1986.
9. Ibid.

dle. The three Officers standing together on the sinking bridge-wing to await death. At last the *Arandora Star* was gone,

> but almost a thousand of its passengers, guards and crew still lived, scattered in groups or singly over several square miles of the Atlantic... but the sea was bitterly cold. Before long the number of swimmers and those supported only by planks and benches became pitifully fewer and fewer... Their pathetic cries of 'Mother', repeated over and over again in three or four languages, grew fainter and fainter and gradually faded away altogether.[10]

That evening the first news of the sinking is broadcast on BBC's nine o'clock news, the number of dead explained away by a claim that the Nazis on board had swept everyone aside in their rush for the lifeboats. The *Daily Express* states that *"the scramble for the boats was sickening."* All reports give the impression that the *Arandora* Star had carried only Nazis and Italian Fascists, there was no suggestion that there were refugees on board the liner. And for the population as a whole and for the families of internees, this was the first intimation by the authorities of the deportations.

Most of the 800 survivors picked up out of the ocean by the St. Laurent are to spend two nights in a draughty warehouse where for almost 24 hours they stand and sleep barefoot on cold concrete. A local priest in Greenock hearing of their plight, brings to them buckets and soap and towels and on each subsequent trip he carries buckets filled with hot water supplied by local housewives. This priest and clergyman assisted by Salvation Army workers and Red Cross officials. After that, still numbed by shock, the prisoners are taken to Edinburgh where they are shipped aboard the Dunera sailing with internees to Australia.

"The whole camp grieved" says my mother. Each woman mourns for a husband or son, or both, she sees as drowned. A pall settles over the camp, the houses and streets falling into an unnatural silence and the women go about their daily tasks heavily and with bowed heads. A verse of chilling beauty from Shakespeare's *Tempest* runs continually through my mother's head:

> Full fathom five thy father lies
> Of his bones are coral made
> Those are pearls that were his eyes

---

10.   Ibid.

Nothing of him that doth fade
But doth suffer a sea-change
Into something rich and strange,
Sea-nymphs hourly ring his knell:
Hark! now I hear them—ding-dong bell.

Fostering

The journey to the Cotswolds: I must learn to live with the Nouveau Riche: The Library and H.G. Wells: Rationed reading: Cascara: My Aunt Mary again at her worst: St. Clothilde's Convent: S'il vous plait: Lechlade and Reginald Arkell's mother.

Dr. Foster went to Gloucester,
in a shower of rain
He stepped in a puddle,
right up to his middle,
And never went there again.[1]

Oonagh and I drive with Mrs. Shillan to Gloucestershire and meet up with Mr. Shillan in Burford. There we stay for the night in an hotel. I have never stayed in an hotel before and so it ranks as another first, almost equivalent to learning to tell the time or to swim. A strange bed, but I sleep well and awaken to a bright day. Having washed and dressed, I sit on a padded stool in front of the long mirror of the dressing table and comb my short hair as if it formed a cape about my shoulders. Behind me, in the mirror, I see the tumbled beds in which my sister and I have spent the night. Under my feet I feel the luxury of soft carpeting. Over breakfast in the hotel dining-room, I observe the Shillans. Mrs. Shillan, tall, almost willowy, hair brown with auburn high-lights, bright in manner, somewhere in her middle forties. Mr. Shillan, some fifteen years older than his wife, square-faced, square-figured, thinning light brown hair, horn-rimmed spectacles. Stolid. At an adjoining table, almost abutting onto ours, sits Dorothy, the maid, nervously nibbling at a slice of toast. A thin, tense

---

1. Nursery rhyme.

woman in her early thirties, dark brown hair pulled back into a bun at the nape of her neck. She is obviously uneasy at such close proximity to her employers.

We climb back into the car for the five-mile drive to The Vicarage, Filkins, a model village in Oxfordshire, but on the borders of Gloucestershire. The *Shell Book of English Villages* says:

> *FILKINS: on the eastern edge of the Cotswolds, listed in 1675 by John Ogilby in 'Britannia' (our first genuine road-book) as on the route from Salisbury to Chipping Campden; Salisbury—Marlborough—Highworth—Lechlade—Filkins—Burford—Stow—Campden. Almost certainly based on the carriage of wool from the Cotswolds to the Channel ports.*
>
> *A lane winds through this village of mainly modest houses and cottages, all stone-roofed, many with upright stone slabs as fences, but F.E. Street's mid-nineteenth-century church is out of key, with its pink tiled roof."*

Since our stay at Filkins, Sir John Cripps and COSIRA[2] have supported the conversion of a large 1720 barley barn into an excellent art gallery and centre for local crafts: wool-weaving, rush-weaving, wood-turning, as well as other stable and wood-crafts and stone work. The guidebook remarking that William Morris, who had lived down the road at Kelmscott, would have given his approval to this exhibition. While at Filkins, Oonagh and I remain unaware that William Morris had lived nearby. If his name had been known to the Shillans, they would not have found him a person worthy of note, William Morris prints not becoming fashionable until the 1960s. The John Cripps referred to is the son of Sir Stafford *"the austere Chancellor of the Exchequer in the post-war Labour government."* The Cripps lived in Filkins and played a benevolent role in village life. But, while Oonagh and I were there, Sir Stafford was away in Moscow as Ambassador, leaving his large house for us to gaze at across extensive and cultivated grounds.

A further guide-book is equally disapproving of the usurper church with its *"hexagonal E and French Gothic windows and… steeply-pitched tile roof,"* the guide book adding that *"Even the council houses are built of stone with natural stone roofs."* The Vicarage, which has been leased by the Shillans for the duration of the

---

2. Council for Small Industries in Rural Areas.

war, stands next to this despised church and until the bells are silenced to be rung, or tolled, only in the case of invasion, we are awakened each morning by their loud insistent clanging. The previous incumbent, Reverend Austen, a white-haired, ruddy-faced widower, had moved with his only daughter, Elizabeth, a tall, thin, pale girl in her twenties, to a prestigious, but much smaller house nearby called St. Peters. Perhaps the Vicar and his daughter had become lost in the old Vicarage, the many deserted rooms and spreading grounds which widened out into infinity, so that he and she moved silently as if two postulants in a ruined Cathedral. These Austens claimed to be kin to Jane Austen, a matter for pride, but they whispered the name of a more direct ancestor, John Hampden, for to Elizabeth, an obedient daughter and communicant of the Church of England, Hampden's defiance of Charles I presented itself not only as disobedience, but ingratitude.

The Shillans soon brought the rooms deserted by the Austens in upon one another, making them part of a whole by designating and furnishing each one for its expected use. The library held floor to ceiling book-shelves and books on all four walls, a small room off the library which becomes Mr. Shillan's study, the dining-room, the breakfast room, the drawing room, the kitchen with its stone floor, large cupboards and an Aga cooker on which Cook never learns to bake cakes. Off the kitchen is the servants' sitting-room, used by Cook and her husband the gardener. On the first floor of the house are bedrooms and on the second a number of adjoining attics. I don't think that I ever entered all the rooms in that house.

Oonagh and I sit at the long refectory table in the dining-room, Mr. Shillan at one end and Mrs. Shillan at the other. This room, Mrs. Shillan says, dates back to Saxon times. There are also priest holes, Mrs. Shillan proudly exhibiting to us the blocked entrance to a secret passage at the back of a cupboard. On a flight of stairs, an inside window opens onto a window on the outside wall, a space between in which to the side can be seen the beginnings of a tunnel.[3] I have a snapshot showing the side of the house and it is clear that over the centuries the house has been extended by a number of wings, but always in the original grey stone. The incline of the stone roofs is gentle, so that later in our stay I climb along them, an activity which brings me into disgrace and I defend myself by claiming, unkindly, that Miss Moss, the greying, timid governess Mrs. Shillan has by then hired for us, agreed that we could climb roofs. The truth of the matter is that she knew about this substitute mountaineering, but even more at a loss in this environment than me, and not especially competent at her job, she was lost for words. In the same snapshot can be seen open French windows, small white-framed windows above, an added wing jutting forward, with a window set in its side, this wing itself largely obscured by a bushy tree, roofs one behind the other. In the foreground my sister in bathing-costume lies on the lawn, her back towards us and she is reading. Mrs. Shillan sits in a garden chair sewing, while Gwenda Coy perches on her lap. Gwenda Coy from Coventry, blonde-haired and younger than Oonagh and me, has arrived in answer to an advertisement offering a home to evacuees. In the photo, the Shillan dog—Buster—approaches. He is an Airedale who delights in fighting the baker's bulldog and returns to The Vicarage to proudly exhibit his war wounds.

I had lived in buildings of equal, or even larger, size, but they were schools occupied also by many others, so now I relish the space around me. Room upon room, each one of a different size or shape. To live in such a house as a family home, I know means that I have 'gone up in the world', but there are none of my school friends present to see my sudden rise. The Vicarage and its grounds form a world in itself, for Mrs. Shillan, intent upon maintaining the social divide, makes it clear that she is opposed to us becoming acquainted with village people. This means that

_____

3. Judith Fay and Richard Martin, *Jubilee Boy—The Life and Recollections of George Swinford of Filkins*, Filkins Press, 1987. Swinford remarks *"I have heard that the Old Vicarage was built for a hotel, but was never used as such. It was to be named The Green Dragon. It was taken over for use as a Vicarage when the church was built."* Swinford also writes that from a bakehouse in the village, dated 1626 a tunnel runs by the house into a deep pond at the far end of the orchard; *"The tunnel was used, they say, at the time of the Civil Wars as an escape route."*

at first we pass through the village in Mrs. Shillan's small red Fiat, on our way to somewhere else, looking out at the unfamiliar stone houses and village people from behind a glass shield. But I do remember visiting, together with Mrs. Shillan, the village pocket-handkerchief swimming-pool. There I look with interest at a girl of about my own age whose eton cropped hair and round freckled face gives her the appearance of a tomboy; a girl I would like to know. I see her also waiting at the village bus stop but I can never pluck up courage to approach her.

At the beginning our days are spent in the grounds and, of course, the Shillans' library. Neither of them are great readers, but their library includes all the acclaimed writers which, I remark to myself cynically, are obviously bought by the yard. Today, perhaps as a result of the blurring between literature and the mass best seller, the library would have contained block-buster-bangers and instant history based on recent dramatic events or the breakdown of a Royal marriage. But at that time, although trashy novels were published they were not confused with literature. Therefore, the Shillans' library contained books by eminent 19th Century and 20th Century writers and included only the odd novel which purists such as my parents would have dubbed 'trash'.

It is at Filkins that I go on a 'bender' with novels by H.G. Wells, perhaps at first because his name is a link with home, but afterwards from sheer interest and enthusiasm. I have a photo of myself sitting on a swing in the Vicarage grounds, and in my hands I hold open a thick book which I know to be *War of the Worlds* by H.G. Wells. Behind me is the Yew Tree which I climb often, mounting by way of wooden struts nailed against its trunk for the use of generations of children before me. There I sit in my own private space, reading or writing, hidden by the needled branches of the Yew. In front of the Yew runs the brick wall which surrounds the Vicarage.

I read also several books by Joseph Hocking, an author of whom I have never heard previously, and whom I suspect my parents would dub 'trash'. But his titles fascinate me. Titles such as *All Men are Liars* appealing to the anger I hold inside because of my family's predicament, while the emotion in which the stories are steeped, answers some need. I now know Hocking to have been a Christian writer and it seems to me that the sensual hymn by Charles Wesley, 'Wrestling Jacob', will better explain his plots. I quote the last stanza:

> *What though my shrinking flesh complain,*
> *And murmur to contend so long?*
> *I rise superior to my pain,*
> *When I am weak, then I am strong;*
> *And when my all of strength shall fail,*
> *I shall with thee God-Man prevail.*

Fortunately, the Shillans are not possessive with their books and have no objection to my sister and me taking them from the shelves. Unfortunately, after a while they become concerned at the rate at which we devour them and are in their view, lost and isolated. Mrs. Shillan especially, as the person more involved in our upbringing, watches this endless supply of black print feeding into our brains to stain them as sin darkens the soul. A little reading encourages basic literacy and is a quiet pastime, too much holds back a child from natural activity. Mrs. Shillan calls Oonagh and me to her in the large drawing-room where she stands at its centre. I feel beneath my feet the soft brown carpeting and see from the corner of my eye the brown velvet drapes hanging each side of the French Windows. Mrs. Shillan looks at us seriously, her tall body leaning over to address us more directly: *"Mr. Shillan and I feel you are spending too much time in reading."* I press my lips together in a grim line and hang my head to hide my disgruntled expression. *"It's such a lovely summer"* Mrs. Shillan continues brightly. *"We think you should be out playing. There are badminton rackets and shuttlecocks in the house, and I might be able to find a cricket bat."* I have no objection to badminton or cricket. However, then she continues by informing us that if we are forced to stay indoors because of rain, we should tackle our mending, sewing or knitting. *"I'll show you how to put a patch on a worn garment"* she promises *"you'll find it very useful one day."* That I doubted. Mending! Sewing! Knitting! My least favourite activities. But I say nothing for here whenever I open my mouth I tend to put my foot in it. Soon after our arrival I have shown disapproval of Mrs. Shillan buying tins of red salmon for her two ginger cats, Senior and Junior, while at home we had been able to afford only pink or grey for ourselves. A remark which brought from Mrs. Shillan an angry reaction. And only that morning, I had annoyed both the Shillans when at breakfast by insisting that it was the British soldiers and not the German internees, who had smashed up the pipe organ in Alexandra Palace during WWI. Having been brought up in an articulate household where discussion was overt and received opinion open to criticism, I tended to take statements at face value and, of course, I had definite views of my own. To the Shillans I appear as rude and ungrateful, but what is worse, as critical. Without faith, without trust. It takes me some time to understand that the Shillans' ways are not those of the Lahrs, a fact which should have become obvious when shortly following our arrival, Mr. Shillan teaches us to say:

A socialist is a man who's willing,
To share with you his ha'penny
and collar your shilling.

Oonagh, more introverted than me, is prepared to be seen and not heard, or when heard, to behave deferentially. On one occasion I hear her, in imitation of Dorothy, call Mrs. Shillan 'Ma'am'. Once out of sight of that lady, I hiss *"don't you dare call her 'Ma'am'! We're as good as she is!"* All these thoughts go through my head while Mrs. Shillan continues to speak. *"Of course, we don't want to stop you reading altogether, but Mr. Shillan and I think that fifteen minutes reading each morning, in the library, immediately after breakfast, is quite long enough."* I am shocked. I have never heard of rationed reading. Suddenly the dark drapes, carpeting and furniture of the drawing-room move to crowd me in and miserably I creep away.

It is Oonagh who finds the solution. My quiet, good, sweet sister, the child preferred by the Shillans. We have been playing together chasing each other up and down the paths and round the vegetable garden. Oonagh is obviously tiring, stopping every now and then, not seeming to care whether I catch her or not. *"You've got to keep on running!"* I complain. *"I'm going to the lavatory"* she says abruptly and hurries off in the direction of the house. I stand waiting, watching the cabbages and admiring the straight rows produced by Robertson, the gardener. a day or two previously, Oonagh and I have picked from their leaves more than fifty green caterpillars and put them into a tin biscuit box. What happpened to them after that I cannot remember, but we were hoping that some of them would turn overnight into crysalides and then into butterflies. But, cabbages can bear only a certain amount of contemplation and I am beginning to understand why a boring person is referred to as 'a cabbage' when it occurs to me that Oonagh should have returned by now. *"Where is she?"* I ask myself. *"Gone off on her own somewhere?"* I am annoyed and make my way to the house and through the library to the downstairs WC to find the door locked. *"Oonagh, are you there?"* I shout, banging on the door. *"I'll be out in a minute"* she calls and I give the door another bang. The door opens and under Oonagh's thin summer dress I spy an oblong shape. *"What have you got there?"* I ask, knowing the answer and quickly she pulls out a hardcover book and replaces it on the shelf. I am amazed at her ingenuity. After that, we take it in turns, first one of us grabs a book, shoves it down her knickers and makes for the sanctuary of the WC and, on exiting, the other takes her place. Perhaps this added danger of discovery lending a piquancy to our reading. This works well for a time, but one day Dorothy comes into the small room where Oonagh and I eat when not dining with the family. *"Mrs. Shillan would like to see you"* she says quietly. *"What now?"* I groan to myself. *"Why does she want us, Dorothy?"* I plead hopefully. Dorothy says nothing. She always treats us kindly, but is careful to maintain between us the same sense of distance that she has with her employers.

My sister and I hurry to the dining-room where Mrs. Shillan stands erect by the long refectory table. We stand before her. *"I have something to say to you"* says Mrs. Shillan, lowering her voice mysteriously. I look past her at the large, stone fireplace on which at one time whole carcasses were roasted. She appears to hesitate, as if she is searching for words. *"There's something I must ask you."* Will she ask us outright whether we are taking books into the WC? What will I say? I am cold with apprehension. At last she says *"you haven't taken any purgatives since coming here, have you?"* adding in explanation before we can reply *"a medicine to regulate your bowels."* *"No"* we reply enthusiastically, thinking of syrup of figs and senna pods and happy at being able to reply truthfully. She looks away. *"Dorothy tells me you are both constipated and spending too much time in the bathroom."* I glance at Oonagh out of the corner of my eye and she stoically stares ahead. Mrs. Shillan picks up a large jar from off the table and takes out of it two small white sugar-coated pills which she presses into our hands and watches while we transfer them to our mouths. *"Cascara is very good for you"* she says and turns to leave the room, calling out over her shoulder *"report to me here every Friday at about this time for a cascara."*

I know that I am not constipated and while very occasionally my mother had found it necessary to purge us, for the most part she had relied on natural methods; roughage and fruit. I remembered also a very bad experience I'd had with Exlax at Wilton Road, a free sample having been put through the letterbox. Having found it on the mat, I assumed from its appearance that it was chocolate and greedily ate all half a dozen squares. Therefore I do not intend to swallow this cascara and with Mrs. Shillan out of the room, I look for somewhere to hide the tablet held in my mouth. *"Under the carpet!"* I say and pull back a corner of its plush redness. Both Oonagh and I transfer the sticky pills to the floor and let the carpet fall over them. And this becomes our Friday drill.

My parents take it in turns to write and we receive letters each of 24 lines from one or the other, on Army issue notepaper. A regulation endorsed by a stern warning by Onchan's Commander Captain The Lord Greenway: *"Writing across the lines is forbidden and the writing shall not be unduly close... Any infringement of the above orders is an offence which will be punished."* My mother's 24 lines say less than my father's, for his writing is the smaller. My mother confines herself to instructions with regard to our behaviour, health and hygiene, as if even from a distance she cannot bear to relax her role as mother—or perhaps she writes in the knowledge that her letters will be read not only by the censors at Liverpool, but also by the Shillans. My father's letters are always sanguine, reassuring, rejoicing in the lovely summer, the beautiful surroundings, tanning in the sun... This infuriates the Shillans, Englishmen are facing death while aliens are being cosseted by a soft British government. Mrs. Shillan does not hesitate to express her feelings on this, which I feel unfair as I am always in such trouble for expressing mine. But, I steel myself to listen without comment, while inside I simmer, become hotter and hotter, redder and redder, until I am sure that my head will explode to shoot out anger, hate, disappointment, longing, bitterness, vituperation—drenching both Shillans and staining the polished oak refectory table, the off-white walls, the plush carpet and the old fireplace. Perhaps we would all drown in what flew out of my head. At last, the meal over, I am able to run into the library where I stand gritting my teeth, clenching my fists and shaking with loathing until I regain some equilibrium.

My Aunt Mary writes to the Shillans, the letter enclosed in a parcel. Mrs. Shillan reads out the letter while we are at breakfast, her voice registering different degrees of surprise as she repeats my Aunt's words. For here we are playing at happy families, and there is my Aunt who has dipped her pen into venom to pour onto the page bitterness, spite and malice against her brother and his family. My Aunt declares that she is sending this parcel from a sense of duty only and because my father is (unfortunately) her brother, otherwise she would refuse contact with him and his wife. My father wasted his money, was an atheist, drank too much and had been in trouble with the police. What was more, he mixed with disreputable persons, most of whom were communists. My mother's home was filthy because she considered herself too intellectual for housework, was unfriendly, unhelpful and a fool with money. Their children were both badly brought up and Sheila was especially badly behaved and rude: she needed to be brought down a peg or two and be shown she wasn't the only pebble on the beach. "*Well!*" says Mrs. Shillan, on coming to the end of the letter, rolling her eyes "*She certainly does love her brother and his family!*"

During this recital, I can hardly believe that the letter referred to my parents and me, half wondering if this was some deception on the part of the Shillans, but at last I accept that these are my Aunt's words. Flushing, I duck down my head as if I am counting crumbs upon the table and tell myself that I will never forgive my Aunt and that I never want to see her again. I write nothing of this to my parents, for I do not want to worry them. Also, I cannot bear to set down on the page my Aunt's calumnies to be read once more by Mrs. Shillan who reads through all our letters. "*That fat creature, Mary, said terrible things about you*" says my mother, her eyes blazing "*and the first words Mrs. Shillan said to me when she called were 'oh! your house is clean!'.*" This is when we are all together again as a family and it is my Aunt's letter together with other occurrences in my parents' absence from Wilton Road, which is to separate them from my Aunt for the rest of their lives.

Some four weeks after our arrival in Filkins, Mrs. Shillan decides that Oonagh and I must go to school. During our first weeks, Elizabeth Austen had taken us for lessons, gently asking us to write a composition about the beauty of the countryside or the seasons. She takes us for walks to local beauty spots, pointing out wild flowers on the way, which we pick and on our return to The Vicarage press into an exercise book, hard-back books piled on top until all the flowers' natural sap has been evacuated. Then we stick the flowers down on a page with a little glue and neatly label them. I feel sad for the flowers, plucked from their natural habitat to be pressed into unnatural shapes, all the life ironed out of them.

And yet I welcome learning, for I am beginning to worry about my education. How can I become an important literary or political figure without education? I have even taken away with me an arithmetic text book, shoving it into my suitcase before leaving Wilton Road. But, the pale old-before-her-time Elizabeth is not alone in attempting to educate my sister and me, for Mrs. Shillan takes a hand in this by correcting our elocution. *"Neither of you sound your 'R's' properly"* she declares and makes us say *"the ragged ruffian runs round the rugged rock." "The wagged wuffian wuns wound the wugged wock"* we repeat dutifully and I am never to learn to say it any differently. *"If you don't speak correctly, you won't cope socially"* says Mrs. Shillan. *"Mr. Shillan copes socially"* I say artfully *"and he doesn't speak correctly."* I had noticed that Mr. Shillan, a self-made businessman who had invested his fortune in glacé cherries, often said 'me' instead of 'my'—unacceptable in the Lahr household. Mrs. Shillan is furious. *"Mr. Shillan wasn't born with a silver spoon in his mouth"* she snaps. *"He's had to pull himself up by his bootstraps."* I get a visual image of Mr. Shillan walking along, bent over and holding onto his shoe laces. Later, I am to say to Oonagh *"lucky for him he wasn't born with a silver spoon in his mouth—he might have choked on it."*

Of course, Mrs. Shillan will not risk sending my sister and me to the village school where we will meet with village children. Instead, aware that we have been brought up Catholics, she approaches the Reverend Mother of St. Clothilde's Convent, evacuated from Eltham, South London to a Manor House at Lechlade, and begs for us to be taken in as non-fee-paying pupils. Convent schools at that time always willing to take in one or two charity pupils should they be in danger of corruption by dreaded protestantism. But, recently I have discovered a further point which argued in our favour and this refers to the Saint herself. For St. Clothilde, born in Lyons in 474 AD, in her old age retired to Tours. She was a Queen and daughter of King Chilperic, King of

Burgundy. Married to Clovis, King of the Salian Franks, she converted to Christianity. In Tours, worn out by the incessant quarrelling between her three sons, she died by St. Martin's tomb. This would have been the first tomb, to be destroyed by the Normans in the 14th Century, the spirit of St. Clothilde wincing at every blow against the basilica. The shrine levelled, the shade of the now homeless St. Clothilde wanders the face of the earth until it is taken into the Convent that bears her name. Oonagh and I coming from St. Martin's Convent must have been received as a sign from heaven by the Reverend Mother of St. Clothilde's and, therefore, she agrees to accept us as day pupils.

In preparation for our entry into the Convent, Mrs. Shillan takes us shopping for clothing at Cheltenham, a visit to Cheltenham Ladies College preceding this expedition. Mrs. Shillan's daughter by her first marriage—both Shillans having been widowed before they met and married—had received her education at this College. Now, in her late 'teens she has been evacuated to Canada, from where she sends her mother and step-father badly spelled letters. *"Look how Margaret spells beat!"* laughs Mrs. Shillan *"B E E T!"* I wish that she were so tolerant of my own inadequacies. I am interested in visiting the Ladies' College for upon the wall of my bedroom at The Vicarage hangs a photograph of Margaret with her year group and taken a few years previously. But it isn't Margaret, a fair-haired nondescript girl, who interests me. I feel a kinship with a dark-eyed gypsy of a girl sitting on a low bench in the front row, looking directly into the camera and grinning mischeviously. On this Saturday visit, no girls are in evidence and the many corridors and rooms through which we pass present themselves as cold and austere. Oonagh and I follow behind Mrs. Shillan and our guide, a smartly dressed middle-aged woman, or, I suppose, lady, until arriving again at the main entrance, we make our departure. Mrs. Shillan takes us to Marks and Spencer, remarking as we enter its portals *"the College girls aren't allowed to come here, or to Woolworths."* These stores are too downmarket for College girls. At Marks and Sparks, Mrs. Shillan buys both Oonagh and me a flowered summer dress with elasticated waist, both exactly the same as if we are twins. She buys me also a pair of cheap dark blue shoes which are going to become an inconvenience a few weeks later when the heel of one of them falls off, the heel catching on a step and rolling onto a pathway, just as I am about to commence the

four mile walk home from Lechlade to Filkins. Along the road I
hobble like 'dot and carry one', removing both shoes and socks
and walking barefoot whenever I strike grass.[4]

This four-mile journey is the most interesting and exciting
part of our education. But, as St. Clothilde's is situated outside
the town, we never go into Lechlade-on-Thames and, therefore,
I remain unaware that Percy Bysshe Shelley, having sailed with
Mary along the Thames and putting off at Lechlade, had written
in 1815 a poem entitled *A Summer Evening Churchyard, Lechlade,
Gloucestershire*:

*The wind has swept from the wide atmosphere
Each vapour that obscured the sunset's ray;
And pallid Evening twines its beaming hair
In duskier braids around the languid eyes of Day:
Silence and Twilight, unbeloved of men,
Creep hand in hand from yon obscurest glen.*

Shelley who a year or two later is to become my favourite poet.
And it is only recently that I have read a plaque on the brick wall
running alongside the church and leading to the graveyard, on
which is set out lines from the last verse of the above poem:

*Thus solemnized and softened, death is mild
And terrorless as this serenest night.*

School itself being much as I remembered it, except that at St.
Clothilde's once a week we sit as a group in a corridor to listen
to a recording of classical music. Beethoven, Bach... I watch the
black bakelite disc going round and round the turntable, wondering to what I am listening, for we listen blind, and deaf. We have
been told nothing about the composer or the music's history. No
doubt the nun in charge regards musical appreciation as no more
than listening, or takes it for granted that the pupils, all from the
upper middle-class, had drunk in such knowledge with the bottles of milk held by their nannies. Or perhaps she, herself, had no
specific knowledge of music.

The art lessons I enjoy for Art at St. Martin's had been represented by 'drawing with precision'. In fact, during the year when
Sister St. Alban, a crotchety old nun, took the class I spent a

4. 'Dot and carry one'—idiom for limping. Originally, someone with
a wooden leg (the wooden leg leaving a 'dot' in the sand, witht he
remaining foot 'carried over').

whole term sketching a fork, rubbing out bits of it, replacing them, rubbing them out again and so the torture continued week after week. My fork never passed muster, and I began to wonder whether Sister St. Alban wanted me to be able to eat with it. Fortuitously, the end of the school year arrived in mid-fork and I went into another class at the end of the summer holidays. At St. Clothilde's we are provided with powder paint of all colours, yellow, red, blue, green... and go out into the grounds to paint landscapes. With pleasure, I dip my brush into the mixture diluted with water and watch the colours spread across the page mounted on an easel. Under my brush grass, trees, flowers take shape, but I always feel that my paintings lack value because their production has been too easy and too pleasurable.

At St. Clothilde's we are also encouraged to learn by rote extracts from the New Testament, for which we receive extra marks. Oonagh provides an exact rendering every week, but I can never bring myself to memorise anything unless the subject matter interests me. As it happens, Mr. Shillan had offered Oonagh and me 6d each if we learned by heart *Corinthians 1:13*, which begins:

> *Though I speak with the tongues of men and angels, and have not charity, I am become as sounding brass or a tinking cymbal.*

Verses 11 and 12 making an impact upon me, even 'unto adulthood':

> *When I was a child, I spake as a child, I understood as a child I thought as a child. But when I became a man, I put away childish things. For now we see through a glass darkly, but then face to face.*

"*Seeing through a glass darkly*" has always meant to me hiding the truth from oneself, while seeing 'face to face' I interpret as having the courage of honesty.

Of course, 6d is a great inducement to learning these verses, but Oonagh and I take too long. So, by the time we beard Mr. Shillan in his den and recite them, he has long forgotten his offer and wonders why we are standing there quoting at him. I preferred to choose what I will learn and coming across the *Battle Hymn of the Republic* by Julia Ward Howe, caught up in its militant rhythm I learn it quickly. I quote the last stanza:

> *In the beauties of the lilies Christ was born across the sea,*
> *With a glory in his bosom that transfigures you and me,*
> *He died to make men holy, let us die to make men free,*

While God is marching on.

I was great on freedom! And two or three years later chose to
learn James Russell Lowell's:

Men whose boast it is of ye,
Come of fathers brave and free,
If there breathe on earth a slave,
Are ye truly free and brave?

Of course, in those days I did not feel excluded by the terms 'man'
or 'father'. Not yet out of childhood, I remained androgynous.

To return to the curriculum at St. Clothilde's. On Thursdays
we are expected to speak in French at the lunch table. This is possible because instead of the long refectory tables of St. Martins,
here the dining-room is set out with a number of small tables
around each of which five girls sit, supervised by a nun. Thursday
is also spinach day, and a dark-haired, soft-eyed girl named Naomi hates spinach. Every Thursday she cries *"I can't eat it!"* pushing away from her the green, congealed, soggy mess. *"Speak in
French!"* hisses the nun, her grey hair, parted in the middle, showing to the fore of her white bonnet. *"Je ne mange pas"* sobs Naomi.
"Regard eating it as a sacrifice for the dead and the dying" instructs
the Sister. She says this in English, probably because she is not
sure of being understood in French. *"No, no, no!"* cries Naomi and
then, recollecting herself *"non, non, non!"* Lunch on Thursdays
always ends with Naomi being chased around the room by the
nun until, captured and forced to return to the table and eat the
spinach, she is promptly and violently sick.

While this scene is enacted around us, we make valiant efforts to continue French conversation practice: *"Pass the bread s'il
vous plait; pass the salt s'il vous plait; it is raining n'est pas?..."* In this
way our childhood proceeds normally, unimpinged upon by the
horrors of war. But it is many years before I can face a plate of
spinach without suppressing a vomit! Certainly, the best part of
school for me is the getting there—stepping through the Vicarage gates each morning not caring that the four mile road to
Lechlade stretches before me as a long trudge, for I find distrac-
tions along the way. Bright wild flowers nod me forward, narrow
grassy pathways invite me to tread them, their secrecy defended
by nettles. I look for and find a dock leaf to rub over their spiteful stinging. Giant trees put out their limbs in greeting. I take

great gulps of the air and smell of the countryside. Birds whistle or fly across my path. Cars whoosh past to leave me behind: All these provide diversions so that the macadamed road beneath my feet springs me forward.

On the outside of the village in one of four stone Council houses up a bank and off the road, lives an elderly lady named Mrs. Keeps. Each morning when Oonagh and I pass by she waves or calls out pleasantries: *"You're looking better now than when you first came"* or *"Hurry, it's coming on to rain!"* Pleased at this kindly attention, I never walk by without returning her salutation and on return to London I send her a postcard. We came also to know familiar figures in the village, such as Mr. Gibbs who runs the sweetshop. The Shillans give us each 6d pocket money weekly and we see this amount as very generous. Mr. Gibbs is a slim, dark, middle-aged man of average height. From the first he shows some sympathy for Oonagh and me as evacuees, but when he finds that like himself Oonagh and I are Catholics, he extends his kindness by often popping an extra sweet or two into our purchases. Another friend is Mr. Pryor, the dairyman, who greets us whenever we meet his milk-float in the village or on the road.

On leaving St. Clothilde's at the end of the school day, to walk the path out of the grounds, trees and grass on either side of us, we are met by a Mrs. Arkell, a middle-aged well-built lady who lives in a house opposite the Convent. A pail in each hand, she walks towards us on her way to feed her chickens housed in St. Clothilde's grounds. Soon, Oonagh and I stop to help her, standing by as she empties the pails of boiled peelings with their strange smell, into the compound, and we watch the chickens, their red-brown feathers fluttering in excitement as they peck eagerly at the mess. On several occasions Mrs. Arkell invites us into her house to serve each of us with a glass of lemonade and all the time she talks. What she talked about I cannot now remember, although I do recall her informing us proudly that her son, Reginald Arkell, had scripted for the theatre *1066 and All That*, a comic history book by Sellar and Yeatman, which I had read and enjoyed. In 1941 he is to write, together with Noel Gay, a popular war song, *"Mr. Brown of London Town had a job to do, and he did it too…"* It seemed almost like home again to be in virtual contact with a writer.

Flagging

Before leaving for school, Oonagh always grabs a book from
the library shelves and shoves it down her knickers until
we are out of the village. Then she walks along reading
while I jump backwards and forwards over ditches, look for berries among the brambles, explore side lanes and greet passers-by.
By the time we have covered a mile or two, I begin to worry
about being late for school. Oonagh, head in book, is by now
dragging along several yards behind me and I call out to her *"I'm
not waiting for you!"* I am hoping that she will put away her book
and catch up with me, but usually she makes no sign of hearing my threat. And so I plod along purposefully, reducing the
distance between home and school and lengthening it between
my sister and myself. At last the Convent grounds come into
view and I heave a sigh of relief, at the same time wondering how
long it will be before Oonagh puts in an appearance. When, suddenly, a car draws up and out hops Oonagh. She has hitch-hiked.
This becomes a regular occurrence and soon I see myself as a
fool to trudge along so virtuously while Oonagh has the best of
both worlds, and so I join her in flagging down cars. Or if she
has trailed some way behind me and 'caught' a car, she asks the
driver to stop and pick me up. We see no danger in this for the
war is another country in which the government requests drivers
to make the best use of their transport. But, I do remember one
young man on leave from the RAF, warning us solemnly to be

careful from whom we accepted lifts. At this, I am returned to my mother's country in another time, another place, to hear her warning against strange men in cars.

One of our favourite lifts is in Captain Ponsonby's wagon, drawn by a sturdy brown horse. Sometimes the wagon is driven by Captain Ponsonby himself, and at other times by his son, either one of them stopping for us. Captain Ponsonby, a thin, wiry man with a nice smile generally makes a few pleasant remarks. The Ponsonbys are a County family, but there is no side with him. His son, in his late teens or early twenties, resembling his father in appearance, is wrapped within himself for he is still adapting to becoming an adult and a man. This makes him shy and silent with us. I approve of both of these Ponsonbys for they work as farmers and dress for the fields; very different to the other members of the family, for two of the Ponsonby daughters are at school at St. Clothilde's. Winifred Ponsonby, my sister's age, is a small, thin, sharp-faced quick moving, argumentative, aggressive child. June Ponsonby, a year or two older than me, is the exact opposite of Winifred for she is heavy of build, bumbling, slow moving. Her only claim to beauty is her bright blonde hair which frames a heavy plain face, and to me it seems that such hair is wasted on her. A Ponsonby cousin, Elgiva, the same age as Winifred, is also at the Convent for she is residing with the Ponsonbys for the duration of the war. Round-faced, pig-tailed and good-natured, she tells me proudly "We're half American." Both her own father and Captain Ponsonby had married American women. I have heard of the 'impoverished' aristocracy marrying American heiresses and wonder whether this is the case here. We come across the Ponsonby children whenever, after school, we have failed to stop a car and so walk past the Ponsonby estate. Winifred, Elgiva and Wilfred, Winifred's younger brother, or maybe twin, for he is so exactly like her in appearance and character, linger outside the high gates to their home and play in a small alcove. Oonagh and I stop for a moment to hear Winifred giving forth on one matter or another, or arguing with her brother, Elgiva standing quietly by, smiling. I can remember little about June, apart from her appearance, except that she was much given to emitting small screams when at play with the girls of St. Clothilde's, but this squealing was a general phenomena at the Convent—recreation passing as a number of shrieks.

On first gaining admittance to the Convent, Mrs. Shillan had nursed dreams of us being invited home for tea by a County family, an occasion which would lead to her introduction into such society. In this she was to be disappointed. *"You don't seem to have made any friends at the Convent,"* she remarks ruefully, *"I thought the girls would be more friendly."* Mrs. Shillan had phoned Mrs. Ponsonby to offer jars of jam made by Cook, only to be rebuffed. I wondered whether the situation might have been different if Mrs. Shillan had speculated to accumulate and bought Oonagh and me the various parts of the expensive St. Clothilde's uniform which made up the whole. However, I doubt it, for in that type of society one is either in, or out. It is not that the girls or nuns are obviously unfriendly, they merely sense that we come from an alien world and are not part of their scene. In fact, the Reverend Mother, an elderly nun, must have been concerned about us for on one occasion when I am walking with my class through a wide corridor, she stops and looks at me worriedly, to say *"this child doesn't smile enough!"* On another occasion, she stops both Oonagh and me on our way out of school to warn us not to become infected by the Shillans' protestantism. But to me the Convent and its surroundings could have been a stage or studio set in which I move around amidst the characters; the nuns in their habits and the pupils dressed in cambridge blue smocks and exhibiting a rosette of the same colour, pinned to one shoulder. The blue rosette is an important prop. An ex-pupil who had remained in London and now attended another school, says her lines. She is visiting for the day and sits at our table for lunch. *"All the old girls wore their rosettes on St. Clothilde's feast day. It caused quite a stir at school,"* she says. Sister Mary Raymond smiles benignly and on cue.

"We always wonder if she can hear thunder," speaks another girl, referring to her younger sister of eight years who is profoundly deaf as a result of meningitis. In the best Hollywood tradition, a storm rages outside and I look across at the afflicted child who is sitting with the younger children at another table. She turns her head this way and that, her eyes swivelling to scan all about her as if to determine the exact position of the universe and her place within it. When she speaks—for this she has been taught to do—her words come over to me as a series of disconnected odd sounds, each one divorced from the one before.

Towards the end of the term a new girl of about my own age arrives as a boarder at the Convent. She too has no school uniform, but wears that of a previous school, a white-collared navy dress. With large dark eyes and black wavy shoulder-length hair, she is strikingly attractive, but spoiled by a sulky expression and aggressive body language. Sensing that Oonagh and I do not belong in this place, she regards both of us with disdain, pushing past us, her eyes flicking over our clothes. Until, one day after school as I make my way down the stairs to the exit, she calls after me. I turn in surprise and she proffers a few coppers. *"I want you to buy me some sweets and bring them to school tomorrow,"* she says, looking at me as if she is doing me a favour. I refuse, for this is against Convent rules. *"I'll give you twopence for yourself,"* she promises. *"I don't want your twopence,"* I retort proudly and, to show the sincerity of my refusal to be bribed, agree to purchase for her the sweets without pecuniary reward. Once in Filkins, I buy the sweets in Mr. Gibbs' shop and on the following day thrust them at the unpleasant girl. And here the plot thickens.

On arriving home that evening, I am hauled up before Mrs. Shillan in the drawing-room, where she sits po-faced, tapping the fingers of one hand on the arm of the settee. The sweets have been discovered by one of the nuns and the miserable girl has blamed me for bringing them in for her. The Reverend Mother has phoned Mrs. Shillan to complain of my evil behaviour. In defending myself, I reveal too much about the kindness shown by Mr. Gibbs and immediately Mrs. Shillan accused me of being mercenary—I am exploiting the shopkeeper by being pleasant to him merely for extra sweets. I am horrified that she should think this of me, and dejected when on my next visit to the sweet shop Mr. Gibbs serves Oonagh and me in silence. Tacitly, I understand that Mrs. Shillan has 'warned him off'. What she has said to him I do not know, but our former happy relationship is ruined and to the end of our stay not resumed. No happy ending here.

To my surprise, towards the end of term I am given the part of 'Death' in the school play. It may well be that this was Reverend Mother's way of cheering me up. However, to me it was a play within a play, as if I were a Pirandello character. The play, adapted from a Hans Andersen fairy tale entitled *The Nightingale* is about a Chinese Emperor who values a jewelled mechanical bird above the plain brown nightingale. On his deathbed, however, with no one present to wind up the mechanical bird, it is the brown nightingale which sings the Emperor back into life. Death itself relinquishing his claim on the Emperor in exchange for the nightingale's song:

> *The poor Emperor could scarcely breathe; It appeared to him as though something were sitting on his chest; he opened his eyes and saw it was Death, who had put on the Emperor's crown and held with one hand the gold scimitar, with the other the splendid Imperial banner, whilst from under the folds of the thick velvet hangings, the strangest looking heads were seen peering forth; some with an expression absolutely hideous, and others with an extremely gentle and lovely aspect; they were the bad and good deeds of the Emperor which were now all fixing their eyes upon him, whilst Death sat on his heart.*

I am minus the crown, the gold scimitar or the splendid Imperial banner, and certainly lack the thick velvet hangings. Instead I must dress in a long black robe and monk's cowl. Assiduously, I set myself to learn the script, for this is not merely rote learning, but has an end in view. The part begins 'I am Death', but unfortunately, the rhythm of the words are the same as a quote learned over many years from the catechism:

> *Thou art Peter,*
> *And upon this rock I will build my church;*
> *And the Gates of Hell shall not prevail against it.*[1]

which means that I have to fight against combining the two speeches. As it happens, I can never truly get into the part, for although I am word perfect, the speech comes out of my lips woodenly and drops with a dull thud on the stage. *"I hope the little ones aren't frightened by the black figure"* I hear a sister whisper to another as I pass by. *"She doesn't act well enough for that"* says the other disparagingly, and in a stage whisper. She hadn't told me anything I didn't know already. But, on one occasion, the school watching, I provide an interesting, if unexpected performance. In this non-purpose built school, the stage is formed by putting together a number of tables and covering them with a heavy cloth. Unfortunately, a gap has been left between two of the tables. Of course, I walk straight into it as I exit stage left, and suddenly, with much clatter, the greater part of me falls down the hole, and I drag with me the stage covering. No one at

---

1. *Matthew* 16, 18-19.

the Convent reproaches me for this fiasco, and later in the privacy of my bedroom, I chuckle at the scene of myself dressed so sombrely and yet disappearing as if I were a pantomime Dame shooting through a trap-door.

The school term having come to an end, we are left with much leisure-time on our hands. Therefore, possibly influenced by the prayers said at the Convent for the dead and dying, Oonagh and I decide to do something for the dead, the dying being outside our scope. Several times a week we spend an hour or two in weeding the cemetery, crawling round very old graves that no one visits because no one is left to do so. We institute also a weekly ritual whereby we place at the foot of the village war memorial a jar of water and wild flowers plucked from the hedgerows. I carry the jam jar carefully, taking care not to spill the water, and Oonagh clutches the blue, purple, white flowers in a procession of two down through the village. On arriving at the memorial I take from her the flowers, put them in the jar and then bend over solemnly to stand the whole on the step. After that we read through the names on the memorial until they become those of old friends. Maybe this was our way of remaining in contact with the war, for at the Shillans we saw no newspapers and heard no radio. The last news I had of the war was the fall of France and the withdrawal from Dunkirk, this at a time when I was leaving Wilton Road to go to Filkins. The retreat of the British forces joined up with my hurried removal, and so I felt at one with the soldiers, many of them wounded, waiting on the beach for rescue.

At about this time, Mrs. Shillan decides to evict Oonagh and me from the two comfortably carpeted bedrooms which we occupy and spend some time in vacuum cleaning each Saturday morning. We are exiled to an attic, our beds set alongside one another. This, I am convinced, is a demotion, for the attics are the domain of the servants and it may well be that we took over the maid Dorothy's room, for she has by now quitted the Shillans' service. The attic is bare apart from two beds, a locker by each, an old-fashioned wardrobe and muddy brown floor covering. Beside the wardrobe and each side of the window hang shiny dark blackout curtaining. The adjoining attic, the door always open, is unused, but a double bed stands at its centre. A bed with iron bed-rests at head and foot. A narrow winding staircase leads from this adjoining attic to the floor below, while on the other side of our attic a corridor separates us from further attics, in one of which

Cook and her husband sleep. The wide main staircase is also on this side. Oonagh and I now lie with our heads under a sloping ceiling and on awakening in the morning, if I sit up without thinking, I give myself a bang on the head. On the locker beside my bed I place a photograph of my father's face, taken by Douglas Glass, a well-known photographer. In this photo, my father's head is turned slightly to one side, pipe in mouth (an indication that it was taken before 1938 for following that year's Budget increase in tobacco tax, my father renounced smoking for ever). In the photo he sports a small moustache and a few hairs above his chin pass for a beard. Deep lines run each side of his mouth, but his most prevalent feature is a long, straight nose, which seems to jut out of the picture. Good humoured eyes, black hair receding slightly and combed back, and a Schlappohr. My father's shirt is open at the neck and also a little of his dark coat can be seen. Cook, a short, squat woman in late middle-age, looks in on us and I show her the photo. She takes it from me to examine my father's face closely, concluding at last *"he's a very handsome man, your father!"* When, some months later, I repeat Cook's remark to my mother, she says, with some asperity, *"servant girls always fall for him!"* But I am pleased with Cook's praise, for I see it as spilling over onto myself.

In spite of my demotion, I find some pleasure in these attics. It seems that we are a long way above the main house and, therefore, the more private. We think up games to play and rig up two empty cocoa tins at both ends of a long piece of string as a telephone. Together with Oonagh, I pass one end outside the window to be pulled into the window of the adjoining attic. It is while I am involved in this that I see scratched into the slate of the short sloping roof at window-sill level, several names:

Alfred Willis
Kenneth Trinder
Charles Weston
Alec Adams
John Flux
Joe Swinford

Names from the war memorial! I am excited. Why are these names recorded at The Vicarage in this unofficial manner? I could have dreamed up all kinds of stories, but the most obvious was that the six men had been servants at what was now The

Vicarage before the First World War and had slept in these very attics. *"Just think of it!"* I say in awe to Oonagh, almost feeling the shadowy presence of men as they were in death, and yet dressed in khaki, their legs wound by puttees. *"They once stood here, where we are standing now!"* This discovery makes our weekly ritual at the war memorial even more compelling.

Of course, if any house should have been haunted, it was The Vicarage, for its walls had watched over the dying and the dead for many centuries. Therefore, it was no surprise to awake one night to the sound of footsteps in the adjoining attic. I am fearful and will not risk calling attention to myself by sitting up, or calling out. Instead, I lie and listen to the footsteps as they go on and on and on, as if someone were walking round and round, or up and down, until at last they come to an end and the springs of the double bed give a loud shriek. The bedclothes tucked firmly under my chin, I peer, straining my eyes into the darkness, but see nothing except blackness. Then I hear the sound of shaking and flapping and my eyes are drawn to the window of the next-door attic. where I see the blackout curtain moving backwards and forwards as if possessed. I tense, clutching the bed-clothes ever more tightly around me and at last the curtain stills itself. Then with a shock, I see that the black outline of the curtain no longer ends at the window-sill, but now continues to the floor. I lie without moving, desperately wanting to put out a hand into the night to feel for the torch on my bedside locker. And yet afraid of what my hand might meet in the darkness. Oonagh makes no sound but intuitively I know she too is awake and watching. At last I fall asleep, watching that long, black image and awake to brightness and seeming normality. The adjoining attic with its sparse furnishings and dull decor betraying nothing of the terrors of the night. Oonagh has also seen the ghost, she too unable to make a sound, has watched in fear the black cowled shape. We shiver with apprehension and all that day follow one another about the house as if stuck together by glue. For several days, neither one of us will enter the attic without the other.

I ask the Shillans if the house is haunted, and even waylay the Vicar outside the gates to put to him the same question. But the Shillans laugh in the superior way of adults who, imagining that children are playing a game, do not take such questions seriously. While the Vicar gazes at the two of us in perplexity and pats each of us on the head. After that, I take my torch into bed with me, determining upon finding the courage to shine it should the ghost return. But as the days and nights pass without incident, our terror subsides and the attic becomes once more no more than a barely furnished space, exorcised by our fast diminishing fears.

The Shillans go away for a few days, leaving Oonagh and me in the care of Cook who feeds us, but otherwise happily leaves us to our own devices. We are sitting in the library, able to read openly for more than our allotted fifteen minutes, when a knock sounds on the front door. I run to answer it and on pulling it back, find Lawrence Jones standing on the doorstep, his hair redder than ever, his smile just as wide. I throw myself into his arms and invite him into the house. Having questioned him as to where he is going and how he happens to be in Filkins, Oonagh and I take him to view the grand piano in the drawing-room. This because we know that Jones is a musician and we want him to feel at home. I have never heard this piano played, but it is unlocked. Jones sits himself down on the stool and charms music from the white and black notes, music which sounds throughout the old house, making the walls and floors sing and the furnishings dance.

Jones is cycling to Whiteways, north-east of Stroud. Whiteways being a village founded in 1898 by a Tolstoyan group of Anarchists who built their own houses—for the most part wooden shacks. The land was held in common and the inhabitants supported a few small workshops. Gillian Darley writes in *Villages of Vision*:

> Long after the Chartist land colonies had faded from public view, one practical attempt was made to set up a community based on a similar brand of self-sufficiency supported by home-based industry.

Jones would like to stay in Filkins overnight and asks if we know of any place he can pitch his tent. Proudly, Oonagh and I escort him to Mr. Pryor who offers Jones the field at the side of his house. Mr. Pryor smiling at Oonagh and me and speaking in a friendly manner to our friend from London. Next morning we watch Jones until he, his bicycle and the pack on his back, are out of sight. Later in the day, the Shillans return to be informed immediately that we had invited a strange man into the house, and what was worse, he had gone into the drawing-room to play the piano. *"How dare he!"* rails Mrs. Shillan. She is in a fury. Her face red, her limbs twitching. "*A stranger in my house, playing my piano! The man is obviously ill-bred, ill-mannered.*" I try to explain. "*He's our friend, our parents' friend, they asked him to call on us.*" "*He should have written for permission,*" Mrs. Shillan says grimly, "*and come only when I and Mr. Shillan are home.*" I want to weep, not on my own account, but for Jones who had come out of his way to do us a kindness and whose character is being scathingly denigrated by Mrs. Shillan.

Although the grand piano in the drawing-room is no more than a piece of furniture, Mrs. Shillan has some interest in music. One morning, from the confines of the drawing-room comes a loud rhythmic sobbing. I peer through the French windows from the garden side and spy Mrs. Shillan on a low armless chair, dressed in white blouse and bloomers. Across her knees she flexes a large saw with one hand, while in the other she holds a violin bow. She sees me peering through a window and beckons me into the room. There I listen to the loud crying of 'The Blue Danube'. Later, she tells Oonagh and me that Mr. Shillan had seen a busker playing the saw, and going up to him had asked whether he would be willing to give his wife lessons. The next day the busker came to the house to be greeted benevolently, if patronisingly, by Mrs. Shillan, who is proud of this example of Shillan democracy. The busker had brought with him a saw and after humming and ha'ing, asked Mr. Shillan if he would object to his wife playing dressed in bloomers. This because a skirt impaired movement. "*Mr. Shillan and I are both broad-minded*" says Mrs. Shillan "*and the man was married, so I didn't make a fuss about it. I took off my skirt and sat in my knickers.*" She gives a little smirk. In my mind's eye I can see the shabby busker secretly laughing at having reduced this well-heeled middle-class woman to her knickers. And in Mrs. Shillan, I sensed that to appear in her underwear before this strange, rough man, gave an added spice to the lessons.

Mr. Shillan's granddaughter Jean comes to stay, the daughter of his older son, now an Officer in the Navy. A bouncy, lively girl of about my age and very interested in sex. She asks Oonagh and me whether we have ever seen a man's 'thing' and tells us a story about a couple doing 'it' while standing up in a cinema. A story which puzzles me, for I, in my innocence, think 'sleeping together' necessitates lying down. "*I wish Jean were at a nice school like St. Clothilde's*", I hear Mrs. Shillan say to her husband, "*they send her to such odd schools!*" But, although the Shillans might disapprove of her upbringing, she was family, to be preferred, and believed before Oonagh and me. For while at The Vicarage Jean, sorting through a cupboard in the library, comes across a pile of bakelite records in their sleeves. She takes one out to examine it and, of course, drops it, the black, shiny record snapping into two halves. Guiltily, she returns both halves to the sleeve and says to me *"don't tell anyone, will you!"* The broken record she puts to the bottom of the pile. A week or two following Jean's departure, Mrs. Shillan tackles me about the broken record. *"If it were an accident,"* she says, trying to sound reasonable, her voice controlled, *"I know it can't be helped. But it was deceitful to put it back in the sleeve and hide it in the cupboard!"* She looks down at me from a great height, waiting for my apology. At last I say *"it wasn't me who broke it. Jean broke it."* Mrs. Shillan does not believe me. Jean was a Shillan and Shillans did not do such things and, anyway, why hadn't I said anything about it before now? *"She asked me not to"* I retort. Mrs. Shillan would have none of it. *"Jean wouldn't be so deceitful"* she says flatly and there is no way I can convince her otherwise. Some years later I read in the newspapers that Mr. Shillan's second son, Philip, was arrested in a tube station in London for travelling up the escalator and on the way pinching women's bottoms. Remembering this incident of the record, I was delighted that a Shillan had been caught out.

Gwenda Coy arrives as an evacuee in answer to one of Mrs. Shillan's advertisements and with three children in the house she needs to employ a governess. And so Miss Moss, a tall, thin, plain middle-aged woman now becomes part of our household. I can remember almost nothing of the lessons she gave us, apart from one story I wrote as an English composition. This was about the Severn flooding and families having to run for their lives to escape drowning. I had never been to the West Country at that time, nor seen the Severn, but both Miss Moss and Mrs. Shillan admitted the story read well and Mrs. Shillan promised to type it. Of course, she never got around to it, in spite of Gwenda's reproaches, for although several years younger than me, we were friends. Another story, which I wrote to please myself, resulted from watching Mr. Shillan cutting the grass with a motor mower; a powerful machine which he appeared to have difficulty in controlling. I envisioned it getting away from him to run amok in the grounds, out of The Vicarage gates and scything its way through the village. I show this story to no one, but a few days later Mrs. Shillan remarks, half-teasingly, *"so a fat old man can't control a mower!"* Embarrassed, I murmur an inaudible reply. At the time I assume that I must have left the story open to view. Now I am sure that Mrs. Shillan regularly examined our sparse belongings, letters and writings. This because Oonagh and I were dubbed 'police evacuees'. A fact which I, chilled by excitement on first hearing the term applied to me, recorded in my notebook in a code of dots and dashes which I had invented and used with Colleen. Perhaps the Shillans had been instructed by the authorities to maintain constant surveillance in order to ensure that Oonagh and I were not collecting or passing military information to Hitler—or Stalin!

As the eldest child at The Vicarage, I am expected to set an example to Oonagh and Gwenda, but I am not certain what type of example is required by the Shillans. However, I must have got it right at least once, for Mrs. Shillan added a 3d piece to my pocket money for that week. She says, handing me the coin *"because this week you have been so good and helpful to Oonagh and, especially, Gwenda."* I rack my brains to discover how my behaviour had differed during that week in comparison with all the weeks that went before and after, but for the life of me could find no answer. In those days I found the Shillans' antagonism towards me puzzling for in my own eyes I never did anything really bad, like stealing, or lying—well, perhaps the occasional white lie. I had soon learned to hold my tongue when opinions were expressed with which I disagreed, or if the Shillan activities amused me, but the expressions on my face gave me away. Rather like Bud Flanagan, of the Crazy Gang, who when in the army was charged by his Sergeant with *"dumb insolence and insubordination,"* the Sergeant accusing him of *"insulting me with his eyes."* And yet, of course, the Shillans had a legitimate complaint against my roof climbing. It is possible that the Yew Tree had whetted my appetite for this, for I scale the side of the house to perch on the gently sloping stone roof. And what is worse, I encourage the other two children to do the same. From the top of the roof I can see the world. I am a mountaineer, a climber of cliffs. Therefore, we slide down the inclines with no thought of displaced tiles or broken limbs. Miss Moss calling out to us ineffectually, to come down, to be careful, but we take no notice of her. How many times we climb these roofs I cannot now remember, but at last Mrs. Shillan catches us and all hell is let loose.

It is then that I sneak on poor Miss Moss. To me, in those days, adults were adults and held power. Theoretically, I understood that some were more powerful than others—the exploited and the exploiters—but I did not understand fully that in the hands of the employer, the employee is put into the position of a child.

"Would you like to join your mother on the Isle of Man?" Mrs. Shillan asks me. We are in the grounds, the Shillans sitting in wicker chairs while Oonagh and I chase about in a game of our own. Mrs. Shillan has called me over to put this question. I am taken aback. The question has come as a shock. I do not know what to say. *"I don't know"* I stutter *"I don't know what it's like over there."* To me this reply appears straight-forward and only common sense, but Mrs. Shillan reddens, her eyes giving out sparks. She has taken my answer to mean that I might be worse off on the Isle of Man. Once again I have proved my ingratitude and confirmed her view of me as mercenary. But, no plans are made for my removal to the Isle of Man, and a week or two later Mrs. Shillan calls me to her in the drawing-room. *"Sit down"* she says, patting the space beside her on the settee. Gingerly, I accept her invitation. She looks at me half smiling and says *"you haven't done too well at school, have you? I think you should go into a domestic science course when you're fourteen."* She explains that I would leave school to work in the kitchen of a College or other Institution which trained girls in domestic 'science'. I am outraged, but say nothing because I am lost for words. There is no point in trying to explain myself to this woman. Later, I fume to Oonagh *"she wants to put me into domestic service!"* For the following few days I stamp about The Vicarage grounds and even consider going to the Isle of Man. It is difficult for me to know now why I was so opposed to going there. Certainly, a few years later I am to regret a missed opportunity to learn German. But, I guess that at the time it stuck in my craw to be dubbed an 'alien'.

Fortunately, I do not have to agonise for long, for suddenly out of the blue a letter arrives from Twi, to whom I have written regularly: *"Your mother and father are home and I have been round to see your mother today. She looks very well and brown."* In amazement, I take the letter to Mrs. Shillan who, of course, has already read it. *"Isn't she a naughty girl!"* she says *"I'm sure it's not true!"* But I know Twi, she would not pull that sort of practical joke. Believing and yet disbelieving, I continue to ponder the conundrum until a telegram arrives:

BOTH HOME LETTER FOLLOWING

While I have been fretting and fuming, my parents, reunited on the boat, have been making the crossing from the Isle of Man to the mainland. As the boat rocks to and fro, once again my father remembers his first journey over the sea to England, the coast-line obscured by a yellow fog. For my mother, the journey evokes folk memories of the flight made by her people from Poland, persecution and pogroms. Both of them mourn those drowned on the *Arandora Star*. My parents have been released as a result of Fenner Brockway taking up their case and questions being asked in the House of Commons. On the inside pocket of his jacket my father nurses a piece of Army issue notepaper, on which his twenty-two fellow prisoners in House No. 8, Onchan, have writ-ten their names and addresses. On the other side of this paper is a poem by Dr. Willy Salomon in praise of my father. This my daughter Esther has translated from the German, and I have put into verse in English, maintaining the intention of the original:

RECOMMENDATION
Herewith upon my honour I testify
That should a cook to bake or boil or fry,
Be wanted then Charles Lahr is your man.
For he can magic soup from out the pan,
To feed the many from a pot so little,
Did he add to it his piss, or was it spittle?
And did he mix ingredients with bare feet?
Treading and splashing until the soup's complete?
But as he will not tell us what he did,
The secret of his recipes remain hid.
Whoever will employ this marvellous guy,
Will discover to his pleasure by and by,
That cooking is not his only gift,
For his wind music brings with it a whiff,
That makes you block your nose and close your ears.
Additionally Eine Kleine Nacht Musik blares,
With snores of a singing sawing sound.
Which shakes and wakes the neighbourhood around.
And so I swear there are these reasons three,
And I say again in all sincerity,
For anyone who will Charles employ,
His attributes will give perpetual joy!

At the news of my parents' release I am jubilant and even more so when in the following week Mr. Shillan, who is driving to London on business, takes Oonagh and me with him. As I enter home territory, and see the familiar landmarks and at last Wilton Road, I want to put out my arms to embrace houses, streets and people, all mine! Mr. Shillan sets us down outside No. 9 and, having said our good-byes, Oonagh and I hurry through the back entrance to find my mother busying herself in the scullery. I am home, home, home! I go from room to room touching furniture, books, ornaments, stroking them with my hands as if I am marking my territory. But there are depredations, for both my Aunt Mary and the Rowleys have been busy in our absence. The two weeks or so before sending for us have been spent by my parents in fighting for the return of their household goods.

Blitzkrieg

*My parents had returned to a house emptied of furniture and fight
for its return: My Aunt Becky has died: Colleen has left St. Martin's
Convent: The phony war comes to an end and the bombing begins:
Mr. Reeves and our Anderson shelter: Visits to the Nonnenmachers:
The artists interned in the Isle of Man: My mother lets to new tenants:
Wilton Road is bombed: I am evacuated to Welwyn Garden City: A
second bomb falls on Wilton Road.*

While at the Isle of Man, in my mother's mind's eye, our home at Wilton Road had appeared as when we left it, our furniture and furnishings standing still and caught up intact in time to await our return. Now she and my father alight from the bus at the top of Wilton Road and she rushes ahead of him. She can hardly wait to be in her own home. Impatiently, she stands on the step for my father has the front door key, but at last the door is open and they are inside. She hurries down the short flight of stairs to our living-room and throws open the door, her eyes immediately seeking the handbag left behind on my Bubba's magogany table. No furniture! Only a dartboard hanging on the closed scullery door and a number of empty beer bottles stacked in a corner. The room stinks of cigarette smoke. Panic-stricken, my mother hurries to our front bedroom and is relieved to find our beds still standing, although they have been stripped of bedding. Her eyes are drawn to the middle of the floor between the beds where piled together as if someone had intended to start a fire, lies torn up correspondence. Letters which my parents have received over the years and preserved, many of them from well-known writers. But, fortunately, the books remain on all four walls of the 'press' room and in piles on the floor. The overspill into our bedroom appears also to be untouched.

Neither the electricity nor gas have been disconnected, and with the connivance of the Rowleys, our living-room has been used by neighbours on ARP or fire-watching duties. Again and again my mother laments the loss of the Dawsons as tenants. "*They were honourable people, they would have cared for our property as if it were their own.*" Although, it could be said that my Aunt, our tenants and our neighbours had done exactly that. "*The Dawsons would never have allowed it to happen,*" my mother says bitterly as she gets together what little money she has to pay exorbitant bills for gas and electricity. Bills accumulated during our absence. As aliens, my parents are fearful of making complaints against neighbours and tenants and, therefore, must grin and bear it— maintain a low profile, not provoke hostility. Luckily, the Rowleys move out for Mr. Rowley is called up for military service and his wife decides to live with her parents.

By the time Oonagh and I return home, my mother by dint of argument and threats has induced my Aunt Mary to return most of our possessions. But there are some we are doomed never to see again. On arriving home, I go immediately to the drawer of the sewing-machine to find the cultured pearl necklace inherited from my Bubba, but the drawer is empty, and the necklace lost to me forever. My mother repossesses also toys, dolls and a child's desk and chair from our next door neighbours, the Reeves. Mrs. Sargie advising her where to look. But this is not all the Reeves have taken from us. My father calls upon my Aunt Mary to reclaim the back wheel of his bike. Opening the gate to No. 3 Leathwaite Road, he walks past the two grey dustbins, the successors of which, many years later, Cecil is to paint. One green and one red. In the Rise stands the Church which some time in the future will convert its apron to a car park. Cecil painting out the 'Way Out' notice when his mother becomes bedridden and he is unable to cope with the organisation of their daily lives. My father climbs the stone steps to my Aunt's front door and rings the bell. She watches him from behind the glass panel. He keeps his finger upon the bell so that it screams throughout her house, and at last she opens the door.

"*I've come for my back wheel*" my father growls, his eyes hard, his teeth clenched. My Aunt's face is red with temper as she glowers at my father. "*Sam!*" she calls, and from behind her appears a muscle man in shirt sleeves who moves to stand in front of my father, his fists raised. My father, no fighting man, is forced to retreat down the steps and out of the gate. *"You bitch!"* my father shouts at my Aunt from the safety of the street. That was the end of my parents' relationship with my Aunt Mary. Thereafter, my father had no further contact with either of his siblings in England. For he had quarrelled also with his brother, my Uncle Henry, before the outbreak of war. My Uncle Henry was sympathetic to the Nazis which disgusted my father, and additionally he had refused to cash a cheque, acting as if he thought my father was intent upon defrauding him. But my Uncle Henry had not been interned because he was a naturalised Englishman. Aunt Mary was British by marriage, such are the vagaries of nationality and who is, and who is not, alien. With regard to my Aunt Mary, later my mother is to tell me that her further plans (encouraged by Amphlett, although this latter fact was not known to my parents) were thwarted by their Bank Manager, the Bank Manager refusing access to my parents' accounts. In those days when Banks served only a minority of the population directly, Bank Managers were expected to show probity. In the 90s, and no doubt the years 2000, Bank Managers are no more than salesmen selling loans, insurance and savings schemes, many of dubious value. And, of course, they work on commission.

In spite of these setbacks my father soon regains his old place at the bookshop in Red Lion Street, for somehow or other it has been saved, at least for the present. There are restrictions placed on his liberty and he is not allowed to travel more than twenty miles. He is also subject to a midnight curfew. But he can live with this.

While we are away, my Aunt Becky has died on 26th June 1940 (my eldest daughter being born on the same day in 1955). She has died under a simple operation on a fallopian tube and it is difficult for me to equate the solidly built, loud-spoken woman—a rude version of my mother—with the fragility of death. For I was unaware that her seeming strength hid a weak heart. The doctor calls my Uncle Gussy into a side room and says, avoiding his eyes, *"I'm sorry I have to tell you…"* Gussy is taken to view his wife's body, her gown straightened, her curly hair combed, her eyes closed, her arms crossed. *"We are Jewish,"* he says, *"her arms must lie by her side."* He watches while an attendant straightens limbs which can no longer move under their own volition. My mother's feelings are ambivalent about the death of her sister. They were not friends and, in fact, a dispute, the cause of which

I cannot now remember, had prevented them from seeing each other for some months prior to my parents' internment. And yet my mother is in shock because her sister, her contemporary, who should have lived many more years, is dead. At the death of a person close to us we go through many phases of regret, the most important of these guilt, followed by attaching blame to the victim. My mother in the second phase says: "*Whenever she couldn't get her own way she clutched her heart and fainted. She gave herself heart trouble.*" This is how my mother rationalises and explains to herself the death of her sister. Florrie brings her younger siblings to visit us at Wilton Road, where they wander through our house and garden as if lost. Seema with her large, sad, brown eyes and shoulder-length chestnut hair, making the most impression upon me, so that I see her as an orphan child escaped from the stories of my childhood.

While I am away in Filkins, Colleen has left St. Martin's Convent and now goes to a grant maintained Convent, Our Lady's, in Amhurst Park, Stamford Hill. But, in the remaining school holidays I go to her house or out with her to the swimming baths, the cinema or we take the 102 bus to Epping Forest. But Colleen is to be evacuated with her school at the beginning of the new term. I blench, for life without my friend seems bleak indeed. "*Can't I be evacuated with Colleen and go to her school?*" I ask my mother querulously. I am not concerned with the difficulties, cost for instance. My mother is vague, says little, perhaps she would prefer now to keep us at home. But I nag and nag at her. Maybe my mother would have continued to put me off with bland replies, but the decision is taken out of her hands by the bombing of London which becomes knows as the Blitz. A bomb drops in Alexandra Park Road and I stand with a crowd to gawp in amazement at a house sliced in two, tables and chairs clinging perilously to sloping floors as if this solid brick, wood and plaster 19th Century home which had sheltered generations, were no more than a plyboard doll's house:

> On 7th September hundreds of incendiary bombs are dropped on London Docks, on Sunday 8th September the Luftwaffe bombs the East End. Throughout day and night fire-fighters battled to control 19 major, 40 serious and nearly 1000 small fires. Doctors, nurses, ARP wardens, policemen, rescue workers and a host of others fought to save lives, maintain order and offer comfort. 430

civilians died, 1600 injured and thousands more made homeless on this one night.[1]

And this scenario continues day after day, night after night.

For us at Wilton Road the Blitz brings with it a specific difficulty because during our absence from home, Mr. Reeves and his family have commandeered our Anderson shelter. The shelter planted so firmly and deeply by my father and covered with flowers. And for quick entrance to this shelter, Mr. Reeves had knocked down part of the fence between our two gardens. His own shelter he had taken the opportunity to sell for £1. Now our shelter houses not only Mr. and Mrs. Reeves and their two young children, but also the upstairs tenant of No. 11, a Mrs. Fairgrieve, and her baby of a few months. Her husband in the forces. There is no room within it for my parents, but once the sirens have sounded their long wail of warning, my mother hurries Oonagh and me outside to the Anderson. Oonagh pulled from bed and dressed in the siren suit recommended by the government and made by my mother on our sewing machine, a wool material, trousers and top all in one piece. Today we would call it a catsuit or a jogging suit. My sister never stays long in the shelter, for seriously overcrowded there is no room for us to sleep on the bunks. Because of this, we are forced to sit stiffly until the broken wail of the All Clear sounds. I remain in the shelter after Oonagh leaves, not because I am afraid of bombs, for after all, death and injury happen only to other people. I use the Anderson as a place of sanctuary away from my usual routine, a place out of time. Sitting on a hard chair I bury myself in a book and soon I am oblivious of the two families pressed up against me in this claustrophobic environment. In that shelter I read the whole of Hugh Walpole's 'Herries' series—*Rogue Herries*; *Judith Paris*; *The Fortress*; *Vanessa*—wrapping myself in these early blockbusters to avidly follow the lives of a family over the generations of love, death, jealousy and revenge.

In my private world I am deaf to the gunfire of the anti-aircraft batteries, known as 'ack-ack', shooting at incoming German planes. At that time we are unaware that this gunfire shot down few planes, but many civilians are killed by its shrapnel, for what goes up, must come down; the British government and the military apparently regarding the guns as a morale building

---

1. *The London Blitz*, published by Chapmans 1990.

exercise. Mrs. Feargrieve saw them as no such thing and as soon as the ack-ack fire booms out, its sound reverberating around the iron shelter, she panics, screaming in unison with the guns, laying noise upon noise. As the guns outside become noisier so does Mrs. Feargrieve and the panic taking hold of her, she finds relief in shaking, banging and slapping her nine-month-old daughter sitting in her lap. Jerked out of my book by her hysteria, I watch in fascination until at last Mrs. Reeves says *"Leave her alone, May,"* and forcibly removes the baby from her mother's hands, to cradle the baby in her own arms. I am not surprised to hear from my mother a few years later that this child, on going to stay with grandparents, refused to return to her parents. At last the All Clear sounds, or I become too tired to sit at my book, the print wavering before my eyes, so I return to bed in the house.

On Sundays, quite often we are visited by, or visit, friends my father has made on the Isle of Man, they now being released—those house-mates who have signed the slip of paper on the reverse side of the poem for my father. Dr. Bauer is a frequent visitor. He does not list his first name, but signs himself 'Professor Bauer', for although the Nazis have stripped him of his home, his nationality, his life, he refuses to relinquish an academic achievement worked for so single-mindedly. All I remember now of Dr. Bauer are his said brown eyes which mourn also for the gentile wife who took the opportunity offered by the Nazis to divorce her Jewish husband. But their adult daughter had travelled with her father into exile. Sometimes, Oonagh and I walk with Dr. Bauer to the allotment on a disused reservoir facing the North Circular Road, where my father Digs for Victory. My father has offered Oonagh and me a halfpenny for every bucket of manure we carry, to put around the potatoes, cabbages and beans. But, not even the offer of a monetary reward can induce us to carry more than one or two of such buckets. Walking back from the allotments, Dr. Bauer begins to speak to us in German until our blank faces remind him of his whereabouts. Straddled across two worlds there are times when he mistakes one for the other. Occasionally, we visit Hermann Nonnenmacher—also on my father's list—and his wife, who are both sculptors and have set up a studio in a house off Archway Road. Nonnenmacher had been a well-known sculptor in Germany and his works had adorned many public buildings. His wife being Jewish, he had chosen to go into exile with her. Therefore, the Nazis had tumbled and smashed his works from pedestals. In Britain, the ground floor of their Archway house forms one large studio in which stand figures emerging from the stone and those struggled out, set in one position as if frozen. And yet the sculptor's art makes it seem that many are about to move, walk forward falteringly, or smile at us behind our backs:

> *As Pygmalion in days of old,*
> *Clasped to himself the lovely statue, cold,*
> *Until the marble's graven form and face,*
> *Glowed to throbbing life in his embrace.*[2]

Many years later, Sarah Roberts was to take lessons in sculpting from the Nonnenmachers and we were told a story of how, in a fit of pique and dissatisfaction with her own work, she seized a head and threw it out of the window, only to find that the head which lie cracked on the pathway was not her work. Hermann Nonnenmacher was only one of many artists interned on the Isle of Man. For apart from those coming to Britain on religious and political grounds, Britain had accepted artists whose work had been branded by the Nazis as 'degenerate' at the notororious *Entartete Kunst Ausstellung* of 1937, and who had thereby lost their teaching posts. These artists were forbidden also to exhibit, sell, or even work. Banishment and imprisonment, the artists could withstand, but creation was their very life's blood. Therefore, for some time on the Isle of Man and until artist materials became available, the interned artists improvised, using oil paint made from crushed minerals, dyes abstracted from food rations mixed with oil from sardine tins, paint brushes from Samson Schames' strong and wiry beard. While artists Dachinger and Nessler collected gelatine from boiled-out bones and mixed it with flour and leaves to size newspapers, and so made paper on which to draw with burnt twigs for charcoal. The artists of Onchan used also the reverse side of wallpaper, and having stripped one room completely, formed a human chain along the walls with each artist drawing a portrait of his neighbour on the bare wall, to form a continuous frieze. Lino from corridors and kitchens was used for linocuts. And Weissenborn manufactured an enduring printing ink by mixing crushed graphite from lead pencils with margarine. Kurt Schwitters made use of ceiling squares of a com-

---

2. Friedrich von Schiller, *Die Ideale.*

posiste material to paint portraits and landscapes. He collected also discarded cigarette boxes, stamps, sweet wrappings, papers and throwaway detritus, these to become the ingredients of his collages. For panels, Schwitters dismantled tea chests. Lavatory paper became a sort of illuminated scroll. Tent pegs were shaped into animal letter openers, especially crocodiles. Regularly the artists held exhibitions of their works within the camp.[3] In this the artists were more fortunate than other professional people interned, who were unable to follow their callings.

Now released, many of the Nonnenmachers' commissions are for churches. On one visit in which we are accompanied by Dr. Bauer, the doctor provides a medical diagnosis of a Virgin Mary standing some three foot high on her pedestal. *"She's pregnant,"* he declares, examining her from all angles and for once his sad eyes light up in amusement. His stocky figure is placed firmly in the centre of the floor. *"And I would suggest an exopthalmic goitre."* He walks around the figure once more: *"Perhaps also a spinal problem."* Refused permission to practice medicine in Britain, Dr. Bauer can, at least, practice his craft on statues. The Nonnenmachers take it all in good part. They are childless and the stone people to which their hands give birth are more to them than flesh and blood. Until my father dies in 1971 he counts also among his friends Fritz Schönbeck, whose name is also on my father's list. Schönbeck ordered books from my father and, as a financial consultant, freely gave my father money advice. Towards the end of his life, my father, losing track of time and unable to sleep, occasionally phoned Schönbeck at 3 or 4 a.m; this early summons from his bed not appreciated by Schönbeck, now himself an old man.

At about this time, in response to the 'Flat to Let' board, which has stood at our gate for some weeks, a young couple take our upstairs flat. They are to be married and we are invited to the wedding reception in a house in Holloway. My mother, taking Oonagh and me to the 'do'. At the tall Victorian house, divided into flats, the wooden partition dividing the front room from the back of the ground floor, is flung open to provide one long room in which the table is laden with goodies. Little girls dressed

---

3. David Cesarani and Tony Kushner (eds), *The Internment of Aliens in Twentieth Century Britain*, published Frank Cass 1993: paintings also reproduced.

in frilly party dresses and little boys in clean shirts and short trousers, their hair slicked back unnaturally. Mrs. Higgs in tailored navy blue suit (which in those days we called a 'costume'). Mr. Higgs uncomfortable in a dark pinstripe suit, stiff collar and tie. My mother, never at home with the working-class *en masse*, is relieved to find that one of Mrs. Higgs' Uncles is a trade union official, which provides her with some common ground. Mrs. Higgs is ugly-attractive, flat-face, pug-nose, dark, small. Mr. Higgs, dark mottled skin, thickset. Mrs. Higgs is a cigarette maker and works at Carreras, the large factory at Mornington Crescent, the doorway flanked by two enormous stone, sitting, black cats. As my mother has also worked at cigarette making, she has some fellow feeling for Mrs. Higgs. Therefore, the two women sit in our living-room and exchange experiences and work stories. They speak often of the marriage bar, for in the days before the war once women were married they were expected to stay home 'and mind the ba-bee'. And this marriage bar was applied throughout the Civil Service, local authorities and industry. Women in need of money were forced to marry secretly, "*until a baby was on the way,*" says Mrs. Higgs ,"*and then they'd say they were leaving to get married. It could be embarrassing because their workmates would get up a collection and ask when and where the wedding was taking place.*" This marriage bar applied also to laundries, an industry widespread before the war, and prior to the introduction of launderettes and later household washing machines. Prewar, those needing to work to support their families, or add to family income, on applying to wash the neighbourhood's bedding, smalls, shirts and so on, must take off their gold bands and swear to be single.

My mother is not so fond of Mr. Higgs, for he likes a drink and on one occasion when Mrs. Higgs is at work he comes down into our living-room and says to my mother, "*sit on my lap girl!*" After that she is chary when she knows that they are alone in the house together. Whether the Higgs worried about our lack of a useable shelter I do not know. Perhaps they were able to make other arrangements. Certainly an above-ground brick built structure stood at the Tetherdown end of Wilton Road, although its only advantage to a house was that it had no windows. In fact, I seem to remember that some years later a corruption scandal broke in connection with the building of these shelters.

And so our weeks continue, with me occasionally asking my mother when I can go to join Colleen in Welwyn Garden City. Until one evening when I put down my book and climb out of the narrow opening and confinement of the shelter, to go to the WC. As I cross the garden, I hear overhead the whining noise of a descending bomb zooming through the air, aiming itself at me. At the same time, I hear at ground level, the noise of crockery breaking. This is Mr. Reeves, who has thrown himself down on the path, letting go of a tray of cups of tea and biscuits. A voice screams *"put out that light!"* Quickly, I push open the kitchen door, banging it shut behind me, and run across the kitchen and into our cupboard under the stairs, a cupboard in which the meters are situated and my father stores seed potatoes. Then the floor moves and shakes, the kitchen electric light bulb flashes on and off, on and off. I stand in the cupboard, the door slightly open, shivering with shock until the room ceases its spinning and the electric light remains constant. The bomb on this 24th November 1940 has fallen on the other side of Wilton Road and at the end near to Tetherdown.[4] Fortunately, no one is killed nor injured, for the occupants are all in their Anderson shelters, the shelter on this occasion living up to its name. But once again I view houses torn apart as if they were no more than cardboard. Afterwards, the Lazenbys are blamed for an inadequately drawn blackout curtain—for after all, someone must be at fault—an offence, for wardens trudge the streets each night to discover such illegal lights. Whether the Lazenbys were fined or cautioned I do not know, but I am sure that my parents in their situation were relieved that no such blame could be attached to themselves.

We are fortunate, for our house has remained unaffected, not even a window broken by blast and my mother gives thanks to the Ash Tree which spreads its branches over our front garden. Other houses in the road not only have windows blown in and tiles from the roof lifted to fall onto the hard pavement, but have been left without water, gas or electricity. As soon as it is light, my mother and I busily hurry up the road, carrying buckets of water and trays of tea and sandwiches, while workmen labour to restore public utilities. Wilton Road takes on the appearance

4. *The Archive Photographs Series: Highgate and Muswell Hill*, compiled by Joan Schwitzer and Ken Gay, 1995, states that this bomb was in fact a landmine—*"high explosive delivered by parachute by enemy planes."*

of a busy thoroughfare as the more fortunate set about helping the others. We carry refreshment to Mrs. Pearce at No. 41 and she asks us upstairs into her kitchen. I gaze out at the line of tall poplars standing in rank and look down on the mound of her flower covered Anderson shelter. Suddenly, I become aware of Mrs. Pearce saying agitatedly *"I had a terrible dream last night!"* I turn to look at her. She stands in her useless kitchen, her eyes wide, her hands pulling at the long green bead necklace around her neck. *"I dreamed it was all coming up over me, smothering me!"* She moves her hands upwards and down again, indicating envelopment. She is overcome, can say no more. *"It's the shock,"* my mother says soothingly, *"the bomb fell almost opposite."* *"It was pressing down on me,"* Mrs. Pearce almost weeps.

I walk with my mother down the road to find Oonagh playing with the two younger children in the downstairs flat of No. 41, Oonagh running with them round and round a van parked at the side of the road. One of these children, Molly, had appeared a week or two previously in a concert at Coldfall School, to which my mother had taken Oonagh and me. Molly had sung:

> *I'll walk beside you through the world today,*
> *Through tears and joys and sorrows come what may...*
> *And when the great call comes and the sunset beams,*
> *I'll walk beside you to the land of dreams...*

And she had extended the 'e' in 'beside', drawing it out. When I return home I mimic her by warbling: *"I'll walk beeeeeeeeeside you!..."*

Now, I say to Oonagh in a grown-up manner *"why are you running around the streets like an urchin?"* I am censorious for while I have been playing the role of adult, Oonagh, Pat and Molly have been chasing each other and laughing as if a bomb had not shaken all the street and beyond. Oonagh takes no notice of me and continues to play with her friends in the street, so I follow my mother indoors.

The second bomb falls after my sister and I have been evacuated to Welwyn Garden City and I can repeat the story only as told by my mother: night had fallen and my parents sit in the kitchen, the blackout curtains drawn over the window covered by patterned sticky paper to ensure that glass broken by blast remains in one piece. Outside the batteries of ack-ack guns boom and crack: overhead, the drone of planes. They do not hear the bomb whine down, but they feel its crunch as it sets the house swinging around them until they fear that it will shake loose from its moorings. My parents fling themselves down on the floor and wait until the house is once again quiet and still. Then they rush out into the garden, expecting to find a crater into which my father's planted vegetables and the pocket-handkerchief lawn have fallen. But they step onto firm ground. All at once, from a little distance away, they hear terrible screams rending the darkness: "*Get them out! Get them out!*" Sobbing, screaming, keening.

My father grabs a garden spade and runs up the road towards Tetherdown, Mr. Reeves not far behind and on the way they are joined by another man also carrying a spade. "*It's at number 41*" the man shouts at them. The Pearces! The front door is open, a distraught woman standing in the hallway. My father and his companions run into the back garden where another neighbour is already at work, standing on a bunk of the Anderson shelter and shovelling soil from out of it. The bomb has fallen in the garden, felling a poplar tree, its roots tearing through the ground to throw a heavy shroud of earth up into the shelter, burying Mr. and Mrs. Pearce and two of the children from the downstairs flat. Ten year old Molly, the child with whom Oonagh was playing only a few days before, and the youngest of four children, and Peggy at 15 years, the eldest. All four sleeping on the two bottom bunks. My father climbs through the narrow aperture and the two men stand on the top bunks on which the parents and two of their children have been sleeping, My father, the reverse of a grave digger. He must work against time for he must observe a midnight curfew. At last they uncover the two children and the Pearces. "*The Pearces looked so peaceful,*" my father tells my mother, "*lying side by side, half smiling. They must have died in their sleep.*" The older girl, Peggy, is dead when they reach her and Molly barely alive. My father and Mr. Reeves struggle to free the little girl from the shelter, which has shifted and is lying across her legs. "*Mum, oh Mum*" they hear her murmur as she dies in Mr. Reeves' arms. The clock strikes twelve and my father, exhausted physically and emotionally, bereft of words, passes the bereaved parents and siblings who are now standing forlornly outside the shelter, as if they do not know any more what is expected of them. He returns to Wilton Road.

The Garden City

Our Lady's Convent: I am reunited with Colleen: Billets: I get lost: The school curriculum: The Red Lion Street bookshop is bombed: We meet Bill Howley, GI: I run away from school.

Knighted in the year of my birth, Sir Ebenezer Howard, founder of the Garden City Movement, gazes benevolently at his 1920s creation from a stone plinth. This pedestal alongside Welwyn Garden City Department Stores, an emporium catering to all material needs, and a forum in which the pubescent girls of Our Lady's Convent are to pass love notes to the boys of St. Ignatius College, until several boys have confessed in turn the girls' perfidy. The priest, breaking his professed vow of confidence, lays a complaint before the Mother Prioress at Our Lady's Convent. She in turn spits fire and brimstone over us, her pupils, at Assembly. Sir Ebenezer sees none of this for he is an idealist influenced by Walt Whitman, Ralph Waldo Emerson and the socialist author of *Looking Backward*, Edward Bellamy. Sir Ebenezer's dream is of the urban environment transferred to the countryside—rows and rows of suburban type housing with front and back gardens—the City masquerading as rural by the addition of grass verges and tree-lined streets. One of Howard's principal goals was to curb the unplanned growth of the suburbs and confine the population of his Garden City to 30,000. Now, as he stonily surveys his universe he must see the Garden City itself spreading outwards. For at the end of WW2, local Councils laboured to fulfil housing targets and to accommodate inner city dwellers bombed out of, or decanted from, their former neighbourhoods. At the same time, all over the country there sprang up New Towns influenced by Ebenezer's vision of nature held without bounds by the restraining hand of idealism. However, in 1940 the extending Garden City cast only a shadow over the surrounding fields and Sir Ebenezer's dream appears to be entire.

My mother, Oonagh and I travel to the Garden City by train. Or was it by green line bus? No matter, it is my arrival that is important. My mother has been sent by the Convent the address of a Mrs. Brown, who has offered Oonagh and me a temporary billet. When, on 31st August 1939, the children had been evacuated out of the city *en masse*, they had been lined up for the inspection of the local population in nearby fields, as if they were livestock. Those chosen first possessed the most pleasing demeanour. "*Middle-class people chose girls because they thought they'd eat less, and could be made to help in the house,*" remarked Frances Smith, my auburn-haired friend who some years later worked with me at Transport House. "*That meant the working-class families had to take hungry boys who ate them out of house and home.*" At that time a sentimental story in the tabloids told of how a small black child remained unchosen, until a couple, taking pity on him, agreed to offer him a billet. On undressing the boy for bed, the couple found underneath his vest £100 in notes in an envelope addressed "*To whomsoever is kind enough to give my child a home.*" Whether this story unleashed a run on the very few black children available in those days, was not stated.

By the time Oonagh and I arrived at the Garden City, the home of the Shredded Wheat factory, whose long white building was reproduced on every packet, the first furore of billeting had long been settled. It was now necessary only to fit us in somewhere. As soon as we had called at Mrs. Brown's suburban home and made our introductions, I insist that we call upon Colleen. Colleen does not ask me into her billet, for that is not her 'lady's' way, and during my stay in the Garden City I am never to go into anyone's billet apart from my own or Oonagh's. Instead, Colleen comes out of the house, smiling. She greets my mother and Oonagh who wait in the background and then, with a wave and a promise to see me at Sunday Mass on the morrow, disappears into the house, for she says "*my lady's laying the table for tea.*" "*My lady this, my lady that..,*" say the evacuees, referring to the woman of the house, neither the child nor the woman having distinguished a more exact relationship. The man of the house is rarely mentioned, and if so only as *"my lady's husband"* or *"M—at my billet."*

Mrs. Brown houses two regular evacuees from the Convent, the Anglo-French Priestnoll sisters, one older and one younger than me. The sisters are refugees from France. *"Ou est le Parc?"* I say, practicing my French, and the two girls hoot with laughter. *"J'habite a Londres"* I say with some difficulty and once again they treat me as a comic act. It is while speaking in English that I discover that they are acquainted with Nicole, for the Mittelsteins had stayed with the Priestnolls while fleeing France. Madeleine, the older girl, pulls a face and I gather than Nicole is not her favourite person, or that the relationship between the two families had soured. However, to me, any relationship at all seems to be an amazing coincidence and I ask enthusiastically for Madeleine to write to Nicole. She shrugs *"If she writes to me, I might answer."* On a visit home to Muswell Hill I relay this message to Nicole, whose face registers astonishment. I am treading in deep waters. A further memory of this billet is tea-time on my first day when Mrs. Brown asks me if I take both milk and sugar. Impulsively, and for no good reason, I reply "no milk' and have to suffer the consequences for the rest of my stay. Engraved on my mind also is an abortive walk to Mass through Sherrards Wood one Sunday. I am alone and take the short-cut which I have been shown on the previous Sunday. This leads over the level-crossing and comes out near to the Church. Walking into the woods, I follow the wrong path, trees crowding me in on each side, the occasional bird noisily flapping its wings or screeching a warning note above me as I go deeper and deeper into the forest. I know that I am on the wrong path and yet a stubbornness insists that I continue on my way, for I blame not myself, but my environs, as if I were Alice in the Looking Glass and the paths were twisting and shifting to deliberately confuse me. I will not give in to them. I will walk on until before me on the other side of the trees the level-crossing decides to appear.

I must have walked a full half hour on this path of packed earth, grass and twigs and at last arrive at a clearing strange to my eye. It is then that I have to admit to myself that I have lost my way. There is now no point in going to Mass, so I walk back the way I have come and return to my billet. I allow Mrs. Brown to assume that I have been to Church, and as she is not a Catholic, she knows no differently. But then a nun calls later in the day to enquire the reason for my absence. Mrs. Brown is annoyed with me. I am deceitful. Where did I go? What was I doing? Lamely I say that I missed the path and lost myself in the woods, but I can tell from Mrs. Brown's expression that she does not believe me. This is not a good start to my stay in the Garden City and it seems to me that wherever I go I take with me confusion and misunderstanding.

Our Lady's Convent of the Servite Order, whose motto is *Alma Mater Dolorosa*, Our Mother, or Our Lady, of Sorrows—which should have warned me—is billeted on Handside Elementary School. A one-storey off-white windowed prefabricated building, stretching out in a long line, one classroom behind the other as if they were compartments of a train which had ploughed its way through town and country until, running out of steam, it has laid up at this place. The Convent occupies several classrooms and had its own Assembly Hall, so that we have next to no contact with the girls of the Elementary School. The only time in which I come into contact with the Handside girls is during an air-raid alert, when we are hurried into the hall to sit on the floor against a wall where a lesson in home economy is in progress. ironing boards open and girls industriously plying the irons back and forth. Apart from one girl of about my age, pert face, curly brown hair, who emphasises every action by lifting the iron high, examining it, pressing it down, pushing it across the garments in a skating movement, lifting the finished garment, looking at it from all sides, frowning, putting it back onto the board, pretending to lose the iron… Colleen and I laugh at her antics, for we enjoy not only her performance but the joke she is making of this lesson. Colleen asks the girl her name and she tells us 'June' and so, perversely, Colleen says we will call her 'July'.

If I meet 'July' while out with Colleen all is well, for we indulge in banter. But once on my own and walking behind her and a group of her friends who are all talking and laughing together, I try to give her a greeting when she turns restlessly to look behind, but all I can get out is a croak. And the girls laugh, not with me, but at me. It may well be that Handside School were able to accommodate us, because so many of their own pupils had been evacuated farther afield. For the area was under threat of air-raid and on my first day at school I see a Convent girl with bandaged head and an arm in a sling. A bomb whining its way down to its target had hit the house in which she was billeted. Bricks, mortar, tiles, plaster, furniture, all fell in upon themselves and her, burying this girl under a tomb-like pyramid.

After a few weeks in the Garden City, we are taken to a permanent billet, this with a Mrs. James and her husband 'The Captain'. To what he owed this title I remain unaware, but to Mrs. James he was always 'The Captain'. He is a thin man in late middle-age and some years older than his wife, stiff and unbending. In fact, I cannot remember him ever speaking to Oonagh and me. Mrs. James is his first chain of command. I pull out from the book-shelf in the drawing-room one of the leather-bound books by James Barrie, *The Admirable Crichton*, lined up with its fellows. Mrs. James is indignant. *"Put that book back! The Captain won't have anyone touch his books!"* I return the book to its appropriate rank.

Mrs. James talks a great deal, and when it is not to complain about my sins of commission and omission, she spills out over us grievances against her husband's first family. Grievances which building up within her over the years have inflated her into her present shape. Pouring out this bitterness might have benefitted her figure, however, I was not with her long enough to perceive this—grievances which she can voice to no-one else for she is not popular in the Garden City. *"She come from nothing,"* sneers Mrs. Harding, 'my lady' at my next billet. *"She were only Captain James' housekeeper. She got him to marry her when his wife died. She ain't nothing."* *"My family came over with William the Conqueror"* Mrs. James tells Oonagh. She is washing-up carefully blue and white china, while Oonagh dries. This is later when I am no longer at this billet and Mrs. James had introduced Oonagh to various areas of work in the house. *"My maiden name was Vallis,"* she continues *"which is a corruption of the French 'Valois'."* The Royal House of Valois rule France from 1328-1589. Oonagh listens to Mrs. James, but makes no comment. Instead, she hurries through her chores so that she can continue to read the treasure trove she has discovered of Sexton Blake magazines, hidden in a wardrobe. *"They saved me,"* she said to me only recently, *"they kept me sane, they took me into another world."*

Before my eviction from this house, Mrs. James tells me bitterly, as restlessly she tidies the room and I stand to listen: *"Tony and I were very ill a few years ago"*—Tony is her son by Captain James, now about fourteen years of age and away at boarding-school—*"and we were too weak to get out of our beds. Tony was in his cot alongside me,"* she says, her mouth a grim line, her eyes sharply looking back into the past. *"Captain James's son and daughter left us to lie up there,"* she indicates the stairs, *"neither of them came near us, they did nothing for us, they wouldn't make me so much as a cup of tea, or give Tony a drink of milk. If it wasn't for the maid bringing up soup and milk we could have died!"* I see Mrs. James lying on her sickbed, her face flushed, her pinched-back hair loose, wet from perspiration. Beside her bed stands a cot in which a fat pallid baby tosses and turns restlessly, whimpering. 'The Captain' locked in his study, the step-children laughing and talking downstairs, the daughter tittivating, preparing to meet a friend, the son on his way to play cricket or tennis. The maid creeps up the stairs, holding on a tray sustenance for invalids. The step-children ignore her. They have no interest in this interloper and her child lying above them and tidied away by illness. Captain James' son by his first wife is now in the navy, the daughter married.

Tony comes home for the half-term holiday, a fat boy and I am fascinated by the wobbling of his double chin. *"Billy Bunter!"* I whisper to Oonagh. He is shy of us girls, ducking his head, or looking away, whenever we meet him in the house. However, I am surprised to learn from Mrs. James that his boarding-school is situated in the former holiday home at Haslemere, a place at which Oonagh and I had spent at least two summer holidays. I see Tony plodding the grounds where I lie sunbathing, or puffing as he runs down the long sloping drive in pursuit of the afflicted child who has slipped his leash. I envision him gathering with his fellows in the Assembly Hall to hear Mrs. Lee's morning lecture and lying in the dormitory alongside my hard bed where I nurse my friend's rubber doll. Tony at home for the holiday, I must vacate my bedroom and sleep on a make-shift bed in the dining-room. The blackout in this room immovable, I find myself at night in complete darkness. Waking to find the room pitch-black, in a panic I rush into the hallway to switch on the light, then I return to bed, the door open a little, so that the light comforts me into sleep. The first time or two this happens, Mrs. James assumes that 'The Captain' has forgotten to turn off the hall light, but at last it strikes her that I am the culprit. She is not pleased. Electricity costs money and, of course, should the blackout not be secure in any part of the house, a light would result in a heavy fine. Mrs. James cannot understand my motivation and looks at me oddly, while I will not explain my fear for I am ashamed of such a failing in a girl of my age.

During my stay with Mrs. James, I am taken into the cottage hospital for removal of my adenoids, re-grown since last pulled some eight years previously. This second removal in the hope that I will be encouraged to breathe through my nose, instead of mouth. Colleen is taken into the hospital at the same time, for having suffered a number of sore throats she is to have her tonsils yanked out. Parts to precede us into infinity. *"When the doctor said she was sending in two friends together to keep each other company, I thought she meant two little girls,"* says the Staff Nurse accusingly, eyeing two thirteen year olds, myself small and thin, but Colleen sturdy and plump. *"We were going to let them share a bed!"* I am laid out on a hospital table, the mask placed over my mouth ready for the gas to be pumped into my lungs. A type of death, for I have no control over my lapse into unconsciousness. At the age of five I fought against the pressure of the mask and the noxious substance invading my body, but this time I am resigned and take long, deep breaths, drawing into myself sleep as if I were a prisoner in the American gas chamber intent upon ending the fiasco of life. My co-operation giving me some control, for the injection of Pethedine which, with the prick of a needle, put me out some years later as if I were the Sleeping Beauty, is far more terrifying in concept. I am almost surprised to wake in my hospital bed. My throat is not too sore and I am lively, but Colleen is a little collapsed and croaky. It is a relief when we are sent home. At Mrs. James' house I spend a few days in bed, happy to be waited on by her. She does her best by me, possibly remembering the distress of her own illness and to atone to herself for the inattention of her step-family.

But I am not to stay at Mrs. James' house much longer, for my changing relationship with Oonagh decides her to part with me. As the older sister I had become accustomed to making the decisions for both of us, and if Oonagh agreed only with reluctance, or ignored my commands, she made no violent objections. After all, I could remember a time when I had been able to convince her that she was wearing her socks on the wrong feet! I had taught her to skip and attempted to teach her to ride a bike, although in this latter endeavour I was unsuccessful. Now Oonagh is growing up and beginning to challenge me. To me it seems that she wants to overlay my personality with her own, an attempt to dominate which I resist. Rows erupt, the two of us screaming and shouting at each other. The argument raging back and forth so that the walls resound and throw back at us our squabbling, and the tiers and tiers of blue and white china standing to attention on the Welsh dresser, shake and clatter one against the other. This china Mrs. James has obtained from spending her days before the war by diligently cutting out coupons from Shredded Wheat packets, each coupon representing one cup and saucer, or a plate, their blue and white haze spreading throughout the house, subduing in its refinement all louder hues. The reverberations of our shouting now threaten to topple them. If her china is to be saved, one of us must go, and of the two of us Mrs. James prefers Oonagh, if only because she appears to be the more malleable.

From Mrs. James' house on the middle-class side of the Garden City, known as Cherry Tree, I go over the tracks to the Harding house on the Peartree side. An area which consists of Council houses and factories; Ebenezer Howard's dream distorted by the realities of a class society. The Hardings live in a 1920s Council house built as a plain square box and veneered with an off-white cement wash, each house the twin of its neighbour. Mrs. Harding is a twice married middle-aged widow, square figure usually covered in a sleeveless overall, untidy grey hair and a face lined by travail. She has two adult sons, Harry and Johnny, and three daughters, Doreen, almost fifteen, who works in the spring factory, Primrose who is my age and six-year-old Sheila. Two Sheilas in the house cause a problem and so I am forced to surrender my name. *"What's your second name?"* asks Mrs. Harding. *"Mary's my baptismal name,"* I reply. Mrs. Harding does not like the name Mary. *"I do have a name Joy"* I admit. The translation of my Hebrew name Simcha is 'joy'. And so to the Hardings I become 'Joyce'. Joy, gladness, delight, glee, cheer, sunshine, cheerfulness— all lost to me. Mrs. Harding is apprehensive at my arrival, fearing that I will compare her working-class home unfavourably with Mrs. James' house. We sit in the living-room, Mrs. Harding in the armchair, the girls either side of me on the settee, the boys out somewhere. A small coal fire warms the room. *"Mrs. James's house is bigger than ours,"* Mrs. Harding says tentatively *"I expect you got used to it."* I divine the words she is not saying. *"Our house in London is only small,"* I reply. Mrs. Harding brightens. *"You're better off with something you're used to,"* she says. The Hardings are part of that vast army of people who, taking society at its face value, have been made unsure of their place in the world, or who fear there is no place for them.

"*My Aunt never lets soap touch her face and she's got lovely skin,*" Doreen informs me. We are sitting on the settee, Mrs. Harding in the armchair, Sheila the other side of me. "*And her little girl wears lovely clothes. My Aunt's posher than us.*" Mrs. Harding, and Primrose, who is standing, listening, nod their agreement. They are proud of this connection for they see it as taking them a little way up the pecking-order. I am shy with this family. I do not know how to talk to them; not even with Primrose, who is my age. She is a quiet, withdrawn girl and I would need to take the first step towards any friendship. But I cannot make it. Therefore, I occupy myself in keeping Sheila amused for she is young enough not to have lost the spontaneity of early childhood. Maybe she has three or four years more before the iron sets into her soul. Sitting in the Harding living-room in the evening, I read comics to Sheila, play a card game or help her to dress and undress her dolls. The Hardings look at me in amazement. They think I am odd.

"*My friend's got an evacuee and she's a right caution!*" says Mrs. Harding, looking at me reproachfully: "*Real saucy and does a tap dance when she comes in here. She's a right lad!*" I couldn't compete with this, I was too lost and unsure of myself. This 'right caution', a pale, flabby girl, named Joan, visits the Hardings once while I am there. She comes into the living-room with a shuffle which passes for a tap dance, and in a loud voice talks nonsense which passes for humour. I envy her this ability to get past the Hardings' defences by bringing with her a kind of warmth. Later Joan is to become over-burdened and disorientated by the enforced role of perpetual comedian and this leads her to run away from the Convent and the Garden City. She takes with her a class-mate, Barbara, and the two girls are found by the police wandering in London. Joan is expelled from school and Barbara disciplined. The two adult sons take no notice of me and I am nervous of them. Harry, the son of Mrs. Harding's first dead husband, is in his twenties. His hair is brown and wavy, his face sharp. Mrs. Harding tells me that Harry's father had taught him to write with his left hand "*because my husband was right-handed and had that arm shot off in the war.*" This was WWI. I am awed for it seems to me that Harry has been made into a walking, living memorial to his father. *"What if Harry were to lose his left arm?"* I ask myself *"would he in turn make his son write with his right hand?"*

Johnny, the second son of about 18 years, is a little above average height, well-built, with a wide swarthy face and brown eyes. He is at home more often than his brother. He brings home his girlfriend. She wears a mauve dress pulled in tightly at the waist by a wide gold belt, her face brightly made up with lipstick and rouge. All my previous training tells me that she is 'common', especially as she sits on Johnny's lap, kissing and cuddling and allowing him to explore her body. My face feels hot and then cold, my limbs tremble, I want to be sick and to prevent myself from gagging, clench my teeth together and try to still my breathing. One evening, Johnny comes home drunk, staggering about the living-room, a silly grin on his face. While my father has been a heavy drinker, I have never seen him in this condition: out of control. I am terrified for the drunk, like the insane, are unpredictable. *"He's only joking"* Mrs. Harding assures me. *"He wouldn't dare come home drunk to this house!"* I don't believe her and thankfully run up the stairs to bed.

Doreen is a thin, nervous girl, her brown hair softly waved. Having left school at the age of fourteen to work on the assembly line of the spring factory means that she has jumped, or sprung, the threshold which separates childhood from adulthood. Therefore, while there is not much more than a year between us in age, the difference in experience and expectations makes us years apart. Doreen, if we happen to be walking up the road in the same direction, might speak agitatedly of the factory, but Primrose never talks about anything, not her school, her friends, her hopes. It is only later, not long before I depart from this billet under unhappy circumstances, that I become a little at ease with this pale-faced girl. She takes the initiative in asking me to accompany her up the road on an evening walk. Then she suggests that we knock at doors and run away, and throw bricks into gardens. Half-heartedly and unhappily I comply, for I realise that this is a gesture of friendship. At long last the 'walk' is at an end and it is time to return home.

It is while I am with the Hardings that a bomb falls across the road, failing to explode. The inhabitants of these houses, crowded one upon the other, are advised to evacuate and so the Harding girls go to stay with relatives. I am left in the house to face danger together with Mrs. Harding and her sons. In fear, I see myself lying asleep in bed, the bomb blasting its way through the night shooting out bricks and debris in all directions—a brick to crash onto the roof of my billet tearing it like paper to strike me on the head and kill me while I lie sleeping. I am angry at the Hardings, for it seems that evacuating the girls without me shows they do not care if I live or die. But uppermost is my fear, which must have shown in my face for Johnny says to me *"Garn! You're not frightened! Garn! You're a brave one, you come from London."* I am moved into the long back bedroom to sleep in one of three beds. For a long time I lie in the dark, my eyes peering towards the ceiling, but at last I sleep. When I awake in the morning to find myself alive and whole, I am almost light-hearted.

At the Convent, I have been put into the Lower Third. I sit at a single lidded desk, my text and exercise books, pens, pencils, ruler and rubber in the space under the lid. The other side of the narrow gangway which separates each line of desks, sits Colleen. The lesson is Latin. *"Take out your books and do the exercises from number 41,"* says the lay teacher, sitting at her desk in front of and facing the class, her black graduate cloak hanging over the sides of her chair like the wings of a bat. Although at St. Martins Convent, at Church and chapel, we had sung hymns in Latin, I have never learned it as a language, not even as a dead language. Therefore, Latin to me is no more than strings of letters put together without meaning. I copy from Colleen's exercise book, which she surreptitiously hands to me from under her desk. When the exam is held at the end of the term, I sit in front of a piece of paper, blank except for my name and the letters A.M.D. with which we head every page of our work books, and the words 'Latin Exam'. After that, I am dubbed a dunce at Latin and am excused lessons. Instead, I am told to tackle outstanding homework or work from my arithmetic text book. Fortunately, I have been free of asthma for some months, but the serious gaps in my education caused by absence from school have not healed. Later I am to be excused drawing lessons, for a hatred of the subject developed when I was at St. Martin's, has resulted in my hand refusing to hold a pencil firmly enough to mark a piece of drawing paper. Joan Fletcher, whom we call 'Fletch', a tall-built girl, short blonde hair, pale face, is also excused drawing lessons and for similar reasons. Later 'Fletch' and I are to live together in the Convent hostel.

Scholastically, I do no better than at the other schools, but as I have decided that, anyway, all school learning is gobblydegook, it seems unnecessary to expend upon it my energies, except in the case of lessons I find interesting, such as English Composition. Choosing the words to set down on the page, rejecting one word in favour of another, putting words together to make a statement; I have a measure of control over this. And yet the strict rule of adherence to standard English is to impede for the greater part of my life a fluency in writing, especially in reported conversation. This, together with the subjects deemed appropriate to write about, all others taboo, stilted my imagination and language. A condition from which I have spent the rest of my life recovering.

History is taken by Miss Murphy, a short, stubby figure, with carefully waved hair, and very deaf—except when a girl whispers a rude remark about, or to, her. Such a remark is usually uttered by Pamela Bloomfield, whom we call 'soapbox' (whose life I am later to help save). 'Soapbox' with her bright blonde hair, red face, wide turned-up nose and small blue eyes, is given her nickname because she harangues rather than talk to her class-mates, and is always ready with her views. Miss Murphy, a fanatical Catholic, is so incensed by the sins of Henry VIII that she never teaches us any other era of history. As soon as she comes to the end of this King's reign, she begins all over again from the beginning, for she cannot bear to let go of his iniquities. Much later, I am to view this as an advantage, for it means that I escaped establishment history. Therefore, when, as an adult, I become interested in the past, I have no preconceptions and choose to learn about the history of the common people in a political, social and economic context.

The geography lesson I loathe, for we are expected to spend the entire lesson tracing maps. Most of the girls do this easily, but for me the tracing paper always shifts, so that I cannot join the lines without changing the shapes of countries and Continents. If I do manage a reasonable facsimile and begin to draw around the faint outline with a wooden pen holder and nib, dipped into the inkwell fitted into the desk, a blob of ink is always sure to fall upon the page, obliterating countries, towns and ports. The only time I do any good at geography is when we are asked to find war maps in newspapers and magazines and stick them into an exercise book. *"An A-plus will be given for every map found,"* says Sister

Ursula, our geography and form teacher. We call her 'pussy-foot' because she has a habit of creeping into the class-room before we are aware of her presence. A-plusses are given for especially good work and go towards the sum total of the 'house' to which each pupil is allocated, a winning house being announced every month. There are four such houses, all of them referring to a shrine to Our Lady—Loretta (green); Walsingham (red); Senario (mauve); Lourdes (orange or yellow)—these colours appearing as stripes on the school scarf, on a background of navy blue. I have been put in Senario and wear on my navy-blue gym-slip, in line with my chin, a small shield contained within a mauve outline. The shield bearing the letters A.M.D. Generally, I am a dead loss insofar as Senario is concerned, for I never present the house with an A-plus. But now is my big chance. I write to my mother and ask her to send war maps from newspapers, I ask Oonagh for newspapers from her billet, I search the streets for newspapers blown about in the wind. I even spend my pocket-money on buying them. At last I present some eleven or twelve maps carefully cut out and pasted in my exercise book. Maps at which I barely glance, except to determine that they are what is required. I see nothing of the weaponry wielded by soldiers, tanks crashing their way through field and desert, the answering fire; nor do I smell the stink of blood and rotting corpses. Tobruk, Tripoli, Abyssinia, Benghazi, Libya, Mogadishu, Baghdad, Iran, Crete, Greece, Damascus; war maps to me are no more than black squiggly lines upon the pages of newspaper, each map representing an A-plus. Eleven or twelve maps—and all the other girls have dozens and dozens, many producing an exercise book filled to the brim with war maps. In fact, so phenomenal are the number of A-plusses awarded that the whole system of awards becomes unbalanced and begins to crumble. *"After today no more war maps are to be collected,"* announces Sister Ursula. She stands in front of the class, her mouth a grim line, from which we gather that our enthusiasm has rebounded to her discredit. And so we abandon the allied forces and from henceforth they are on their own.

Out of school, I continue my friendship with Colleen. However, she wants us to form a threesome, which includes Barbara Metcalfe who is in our form and also from St. Martin's. Barbara has become a pupil at the Convent in the Garden City some weeks before my arrival, this giving time for Colleen and her to become friends. Now I see this slim, dark-eyed girl, her hair short and a shining black, her clothing always neat, as attempting to supplant me in Colleen's affections; a girl whose mouth droops discontentedly and who lacks vivacity. Even at St. Martins Barbara and I had not been friends. She was one of the girls who had sneered at my clothing and untidy hair, but now Colleen is the friend of both of us. And so Barbara becomes an appendage to Colleen and me, although much of the time I feel that it is I who am the appendage. The Metcalfes have moved to Hatfield and so Barbara travels to school each day by train. *"Her mother's very strict,"* Colleen says to me, explaining her friendship with Barbara who is an only child. *"Her mother goes to work all day and leaves a glass of milk and biscuits for when Barbara gets home from school. Then she has to go to her room and finish her homework. If she touches anything she shouldn't, or doesn't finish her homework, she has to stay in her room all night."* I couldn't work up any sympathy for Barbara. I didn't like her and she didn't like me. Colleen accepts her invitations to tea, counter-signed by Mrs. Metcalfe, but I am never asked.

Every other weekend, Colleen and I travel home together on the green line bus to Barnet, where we catch the 134 to Wilton Road. Later, I am to cycle home alone, pedalling the miles which seem endless until I recognise the large Express Dairy on Barnet Hill. This is the first sight of home. On one occasion at least, my father cycles with me on my return, until he has completed the twenty miles allowed him under alien restrictions, then he must turn back. It is on one of these trips home by green line that I learn that the bookshop at 68 Red Lion Street has been destroyed, one of the casualties of the incendiary bombs which light up the City at night; an illumination which shows the way for the wraiths of Oliver Cromwell, Henry Ireton and John Bradshaw as their shades walk the path now lost. The lost river Bourne boils and hisses as through the inferno the condemned are dragged down the river banks on hurdles, to become Catherine Wheels, while their tormentors dance away from the scorched earth. Along Theobalds Road, Kings and Queens ride in their carriages on their way to their Hertfordshire Palace. They turn to watch the fiery red of the sky and complain of the heat while the horses whinny and the coachman struggles to maintain control.

My father had arrived home by the side entrance, banging the kitchen door behind him. My mother was in the scullery preparing a meal, for she had not long arrived home from work at the Standard Cable Works where she is employed on munitions.

"*You're home early!*" she says to my father in surprise, and then she notices the bandage on his left foot, the loosened straps of his open-toed sandals barely buckled together. "*What's happened! What have you done!*" she asks in alarm. My father shrugs and gives her a rueful smile; "*Mutchie, I got a splinter in my foot while climbing over the ruins of our shop!*" The bookshop described by Alan Steele, publisher, as "*Charlie's minute shop*," and H.E. Bates as "*a rabbit hutch.*" "*A bookshop,*" which, said Kenneth Hopkins, was "*so full of would-be poets and novelists between the hours of twelve and three that it was like a madhouse. In the middle of the melee would be Charlie, reading the stock or engaged in an animated discussion and greeting every request with the words, 'Christ! Get out of my shop can't you!' or simply 'Bastards! They steal my books, clutter up my shop, use my telephone'.*"[1]

My mother cries at the loss although its dream has long escaped her, and laughs at my father's manner of imparting the news. My father is full of plans. He has been offered a room by the bookmaker at No. 74 Red Lion Street. He will take the stock and shelves from the press room, from the bedroom, he will cycle round the secondhand stalls... It is this aspect of my father's character that my mother most admires. "*He won't let anything defeat him*" she says to me. "*He always picks himself up and starts again.*" My father moves into 74 Red Lion Street and a friend says to him "*a bookmaker and a bookseller, all you need now Charlie is a good bookkeeper!*" With superhuman energy he erects shelving, lines it with books and a few days later the Nazis burn his books once again, for No. 74 goes up in flames in a further raid on the City:

December 29th 1940, Sunday: *The beginning of what became known as the 'Second Great Fire of London'... The Civil Defence workers had their work cut out this night. Between 6 a.m. and 9:30 p.m. the Luftwaffe... dropped 127 tons of High Explosives and more than 10,000 incendiary bombs, starting a series of massive fires which threatened to turn the City into one huge conflagration. Using 2300 pumps on a night when the river was at its lowest, 20,000 fire-fighters assisted by countless soldiers and civilians fought until dawn to control the blazing City.*[2]

1. *The Book and Magazine Collector*, published Diamond Group No. 113, August 1993.
2. Maureen Hill, *The London Blitz*, Chapman, 1990.

But this does not finish my father as a bookseller. For during the war an important slogan exhibited on boarded-up windows, the glass having been blasted, read 'Business as Usual'. There was no remaining part of 74 on which my father could pin this notice so, instead, he rented a shop at 12 Little Newport Street, opposite to the back of the Hippodrome and off the Charing Cross Road, now part of Chinatown. It is here that he is to meet Bill Howley, an American GI from Newcastle, Pennsylvania; Bill, a former member of the Socialist Workers' Party (USA) and a book-lover; Bill, stationed in the South of England and for a time at Clacton-on-Sea, a plump, rounded man of medium height, in his early thirties, who is to spend his furloughs at Wilton Road until 1947 when he is returned to the States to be demobbed, by which time he had become part of our lives. However, it was not in the bookshop that my father met him for in 1981 when I visit Bill and his wife Sally in Washington, he tells me that on the fateful day he had consumed several pints of beer and was about to relieve himself by a lamp-post in Little Newport Street. My father, having spied his intention, runs immediately from the shop, taps Bill on the shoulder and says, *"you'll get arrested, use my WC."* Bill is delighted at making contact with a bookseller, and saw the humour in this unusual manner of introduction. Having relieved himself, he talks with my father and discovers that he has many interests in common with the Lahrs. It is then that he says to himself, *"this is for me."* Bill is good to Oonagh and me, taking us out for tea or to the cinema. He is a meteorologist in the Army and tells us about different cloud formations until I, becoming bored, or to tease, ask him if the cigarettes which he smokes, called 'Passing Cloud' are cumulus or nimbus! I enjoy joking with Bill and making him laugh. When at last he returns to America, for the following two or three years I make up a newspaper called 'Lahriana', giving news of the family in comic vein. Many years later, in 1995, when my parents, Bill and Sally are long lost in history, Bill's and Sally's older son, also Bill, and his wife Lorie, are to stay for a holiday with me and my husband at our home in Whetstone, Barnet.

However, at the Garden City, I have other problems uppermost in my mind. Although Primrose and I are a little more friendly, she takes every opportunity to complain about me to her mother. I am not a sibling, and yet she has of me a sibling's jealousy, without the usual loyalty. One morning, I am in the hallway preparing to go out when I hear Primrose speaking to her mother. No doubt she assumes that I have left the house for her mother is using the treadle sewing machine, at which she sits working furiously, the noise of which shut out any noise made by me. I hear Primrose say complainingly *"Joyce thinks her school's better than anyones. When it said in the paper evacuee girls were getting themselves pregnant, she said it wasn't her school."* I do not hear Mrs. Harding's reply, for I leave the house, banging the door loudly behind me. Therefore, it should have come as no surprise to me when one Friday afternoon I am called out of the classroom by a nun who hurries me to Mother Prioress' room. Mother Prioress, a nun of indeterminate age, a little above average height and broadly built, her long black gown adding to her width. Her way is never to sound harsh or threatening. Instead she reduces girls to tears by looking at them sadly and letting them know that of them she had expected better. Her great trust in them has been broken. Today, she says to me from behind the desk at which she is sitting and eyeing me seriously *"Mrs. Harding has phoned the Sisters' house to say that you have stolen from her a sixpenny piece left on the mantelpiece."* I am shocked. Me, a thief. How could she! *"She says you're not honest,"* the Mother Prioress continues earnestly, *"She says you took a bulb from your sister's torch, for your own torch."* I had mentioned this to the Hardings, more for something to say than any other reason, but Oonagh and I were brought up to share and I did not regard this as stealing. Now it is to be used against me. *"Why should I steal sixpence?"* I ask desperately. *"My mother sent me two shillings and sixpence last week and I've still got two shillings left."* Mother Prioress dismisses me and says she will look into the matter further. I leave her room miserably, for I am convinced that she does not believe in my innocence.

Outside the school at the end of the day, I wait for Oonagh and we walk together up the road. *"I won't go back to that house!"* I say fiercely. *"I'm going home. I'll catch the green line."* Oonagh doesn't argue and comes with me to the stop, to wait with me until I board the bus, when, as I take my leave, she pushes a bag of sweets into my hand. I arrive home in the late afternoon and wait at the gate to Wilton Road for my mother to return home from work. As her small, hurrying figure rounds the corner, her shopping bag loaded, much to her surprise, I rush up to her. I go with her indoors and recount the whole sorry tale, concluding *"I didn't take her sixpence,"* and I know that my mother believes me.

Having passed the matter into her hands, I relax and luxuriate for a week in my own home. Somehow, in spite of long hours at work, my mother clears my position with the Mother Prioress and I am allowed back to school in the following week. Colleen greeting me in the classroom, before the beginning of the first lesson, whispers *"all the girls are on your side—they don't think you stole sixpence—except for Pamela Bloomfield, but you don't want to take any notice of her!"* I am not to return to Mrs. Harding's house, but am given the address of a further billet.

Now I can understand Mrs. Harding's motivation. Her house was overcrowded and her life a constant struggle with money and housekeeping. There was no profit in the eight shillings per week paid by the government for each evacuee. And while some parents of evacuees supplemented this payment, maybe my parents could afford no more than Oonagh's and my school fees. For Mrs. Harding to welcome me into her household I would have had to become not only another daughter, but the liveliest and most helpful of her daughters, who in her cheerfulness and friendliness reduced the family's burdens. This I could not do.

The Hostel

I am to go to one more billet before it is decided that I should be taken into the school hostel. This billet is also on the Peartree side, with a Mr. and Mrs. Johnson and their twenty month old son, in a Council house so uniform with its neighbours that it is difficult to tell the houses apart. For the most part I check the numbers on the doors, but on one occasion I return home from school, walk into the back entrance and use the WC. Then I pass through the kitchen, noting the uniform aluminium bucket underneath the butler sink and enter the living-room. There, to my surprise, I see sitting stiffly in an armchair, a white-haired old lady, her startled eyes staring at me, her twisted hands grasping the arms of the chair. I am equally shocked, for the barrenness of the living-room of my billet has been turned to a room decorated by antimacassars, framed photos, chintz curtains and china ornaments. It is as if it is under an enchantment—and then I understand I am in the wrong house. And this is after I have lived at this billet for some weeks.

Mrs. Johnson, a youngish, nondescript woman speaks to me rarely and it is Mr., Johnson who attempts to joke with me and exhibit his dog training abilities. The Johnsons possess a medium sized brown mongrel and each evening in the living-room, Mr. Johnson puts it through its paces. *"Sit, come, heel, wait, beg!"* and at the end of the show, *"roll over and die."* I dread this last command on which the dog lies on its back, its paws in the air, its eyes closed. What if it really died? I wait in trepidation for Mr. Johnson once again to order the dog to *"come"* so that it jumps up, tail wagging. Sometimes the small boy copies the dog, lying on his back, thin, pale arms held in the air, his eyes tight shut in his pale wan face and I feel that I too am dead. At night I lie in bed in this strange house, holding my torch for comfort, the bulb covered in phosphorus paper so that when the torch is turned off it gives a green glow. This is a war-time economy measure to save the battery. When at an end, batteries are put into the oven for a short time, which provides them with a few more hours of light.

While I am at this billet, I am not much help to Mrs. Johnson, for I am unaware of the demands made by domestic work and the care of a young child, the day in and day out chores which are undone as soon as done, the continual call of a young child requiring attention. And, of course, in our inarticulate society, no one ever talks to me or begs for my help. Therefore, grudgingly I peel potatoes on a Saturday morning as asked, or indicated by this woman who rarely puts two words together. Then, before she can find me a further job, I go out to meet Colleen. However, in spite of my non-domesticity I might have lasted longer in this billet if unshed tears had not poured from my body at night, to leave the bedding wet and sodden. This shocks me for I have never been a bed-wetter. This is Oonagh's role. She has always suffered from enuresis and my mother had dosed her regularly from a large bottle of medically recommended belladonna. This to dry up all within her and leave her arid and barren. It is Oonagh's bed-wetting that had decided Mrs. James to ask for her removal, in spite of the fact that she worked hard in the house. In fact, Pamela Bloomfield had told me that her foster-father—her lady's husband—was a milkman, and whenever he delivered to the back door Oonagh was working in the kitchen. *"She's made a proper skivvy of her!"* he said to Pamela. Oonagh, like me, is to go through a number of billets. Later, I hear that Diane has taken my place with the Johnsons. She is in Oonagh's form and I know her also from St. Martins. The story whispered is that following his exhibition of dog control, Mr. Johnson had instituted a rough and tumble on the floor with Diane, during which he pulled down her knickers.

Dubbed a bed-wetter and difficult to place in a billet, my next move is to the school hostel and there, except for one disastrous period when I am moved out, I stay until I leave the Convent.

The school hostel is a three-bedroomed suburban house standing with others in a line in Attimore Close: *Det. Lge. Kit. 2 Rec. 3 B eds. usu. offs. Gdn. Des. Res.* Now, with twenty-four children in the house, all apart from the kitchen and one large room upstairs are used as bedrooms. Only Sister Agatha has a room to herself. The other rooms are so crowded with beds and children that many of us are forced to sleep together. Until, at last, the Convent introduces a sleeping-out policy for a few of the more reliable girls. This suits those local people who are willing to sleep an evacuee without becoming responsible for her welfare during the day. Each evening I accompany 'Fletch' and her sister Eileen (known as 'Dinkie') to their lodgings for the night, happily walking back down the road to return to the hostel on my own. For while they fear the outside world when it is dark, my only fear of the night is the complete blackness of a closed room.

The small garden slopes downwards towards a main road, the other side of which stretches a golf-course, in wartime no longer used for this sport. And so, we use it as a playground, hiding in the bunkers, running across the greens, exuberant as cowboys and Indians, chasing each other for the sheer heck of it. As for the occupants of the Hostel, its composition cannot be stereotyped. The first and original occupants are the two daughters of a family named Smith who own the house. Their two girls, eleven-year-old Edna and six-year-old Jean, have been left in the care of the Hostel Supervisor, Sister Agatha. Edna is a kindly, pleasant girl, resembling a Dutch doll with her skinny short plaits, tip-tilted nose and wide blue eyes. She is wizard at making beds, murmuring as she tucks in sheets and blankets to form perfect hospital corners:

> First the foot, and then the head
> that's the way to make a bed,

Jean, livelier than her sister, more demanding and sharper. A whizz-kid at draughts, beating girls much older than herself, including me. Possibly, it is the presence of the Smith sisters which prevents the Hostel from becoming a refuge only for those girls unable to settle into a private billet. There are a number of these, including myself, but others, such as 'Fletch', are considered to be stabilising influences and a potential help to Sister Agatha. There was also a policy to keep sisters together and, of course, if it had not been for Oonagh and my noisy disagreements at

Mrs. James' house, I am sure Oonagh would have joined me at the Hostel. Fletch's sister Dinkie is a pretty edition of her sister. Whereas Fletch's complexion is sallow and coarse, Dinkie's face is bright and her skin smooth, a bloom on her cheeks. While the manner in which her features are arranged give her face a piquancy instead of Fletch's plainness, her figure also is a refined edition of Fletch's large frame. 'Dinkie' is the nickname brought from home and no doubt this had first been given her in comparison with Fletch. However, there appears to be no jealousy between the sisters. Perhaps the loss of their father had brought them closely together, and their love of their three-year-old sister at home with their mother. Other sisters at the Hostel are the three Mongan girls. Margaret some two years younger than me, a clever, thoughtful, bright girl who writes short stories and poetry. I would have enjoyed her friendship, but it is not done for older and younger girls to become close friends. *"They'd say I've got a G.P. on you,"* Margaret remarks: G.P. stands for 'grand passion'. Margaret likes to tease and one day takes my diary from wherever I have left it and carries it into the dining-cum-living room upstairs (the room intended by the builder to be the master bedroom). In this room we eat, tackle our homework, play and pray. *"I've got your diary,"* she says exultantly, *"I'm going to read it out!"* She makes as if to open it. I rise quickly from my seat at the table where my work is laid out. My activities as such are of no interest, but in the diary I reveal my 'innermost thoughts' and I will not have these held up to ridicule. This apart, I am outraged that the privacy of a diary should be violated. In fury, I rush across the room and push Margaret who falls in slow motion, her arms flung wide, her mouth open to scream. THUD—her head catches the corner of a chair. She drops to the floor with a clatter. There is the high-pitched cries of children, their fingers pointing at me. I turn my face away in shame. Margaret's parents sitting among us, having travelled from somewhere in Hertfordshire to make sure that the stitches in their daughter's head have kept in place her mind. *"She read my diary, she read my diary,"* is all I can say. I apologise to Margaret, to Sister Agatha, to the Sisters at their substitute nunnery in Young's Close, to Margaret's parents, to everybody. At last I am forgiven and no more said on the matter.

'Happy' Mongan—real name Patricia—two years younger than Margaret, had been given her nickname when a baby. Evacuation has made of her a thin, nervous, wide-eyed serious child, and so the nickname sounds as irony. The youngest of the Mongan girls, four-year-old Brigid, wiry short straight hair, stolid build, is a great favourite with the older girls, for we treat the three or four year old infants as pets, vying to take them out with us, mounting a small child behind us on the saddles of our bikes. During my second year at the Hostel, an auburn-haired, two-year-old child arrives, alone and with no sister to watch out for her. The childless nuns have not considered the practical difficulties of accepting such a placement and soon Sister Agatha is in almost permanent ill-temper with the infant. *"She's vain! She looks in the mirror all the time!"* she says grimly, dragging the sobbing, screaming child across her knee and hitting at her bottom with a hairbrush. I am puzzled. Why shouldn't a small child look in the mirror? Surely she is wondering over her reflection, who is that in the mirror, who am I? Now I can understand the real cause of Sister Agatha's ill-humour. She has chosen one of the seven deadly sins with which to attack the child, but the infant's real 'sin' is in wetting, or even dirtying, herself; an offence not included in the catechism. As a consequence of this almost daily punishment, the infant becomes silent and cowed, showing none of the curiosity natural to a child of that age; an interest and energy which would have further enraged the nun, leading her to search for some other sin with which to cover the child's further 'offence'.

However, by and large, the Hostel suits me for I can hide among the other girls. Even better, Sister Agatha's determination to be no more than a matron, or warden, frees me from the responsibility of regarding her as a substitute mother. An organised woman, she has ensured the smooth running of the hostel by drawing up rotas for everything—bath nights, hair washing, domestic jobs, and so on, this rota pinned to the door of the dining-cum-living room. This we examine every day to ascertain our place in the world. The heavy domestic work is done by a local woman named Mrs. Paternoster. She is not a Catholic, but on applying for the job, her name had convinced Mother Prioress that she was sent from heaven. We girls, of course, call her 'Mrs. Pat'. She is a sturdily-built woman, permed brown hair, somewhere in her forties. At the weekend we older girls take charge of the cooking, for on a Sunday Sister Agatha spends the day in church and in prayer. We recite:

> *Dearly beloved brethren, is it not a sin,*
> *to peel potatoes and throw away the skin?*
> *For the skin feeds the pigs and the pigs feed you,*
> *Dearly beloved brethren, is it not true?*

By mistake, I mix the custard for more than twenty children from yellow Soya flour—I do not know that custard powder is pink until mixed with milk. Also, I burn 14 lbs of jam. I stir the large, heavy pot standing on the electric hot-plate until I sniff an acrid smell. I don't think to turn off the hot-plate and remove the pot, instead I hand the wooden spoon to Happy Mongan, relinquishing all responsibility. As during war-time food cannot be wasted, we have to eat both 'custard' and jam. To cover the acrid taste of the jam, Sister Agatha adds vanilla essence which together with the burnt flavour produces a pungent, unpleasant tang. Jam tomorrow, yesterday and today—for weeks and weeks and weeks. Every day, after dinner, Sister Agatha meditates, shutting herself in her room for an hour. I, and the other girls, creep about the hostel, our voices muted. I picture the short, stubby Sister on her knees before the crucified Christ, her long black gown trailing behind her, her round pale face confined by the starched bonnet, alight with passion. A crown of thorns pierces his head, his hands pierced by nails, a sword penetrates his side, blood flows, *he* groans and Sister Agatha cries out in ecstasy.

"She's having a lie down," Pamela Davidson says to me. "Or reading her book," I say. Sister Agatha has left her book on a fireside chair in the dining-room and I, on returning home from school, pick it up and idly turn the pages. I expect to find a religious or moral tale, but no, it is a 1940s equivalent of a blockbuster. And I am most surprised to peep into a bedroom scene of Hot Passion. This book, I know, my parents would regard as trash. I return the book to the chair only just in time, for Sister Agatha who has suddenly remembered her oversight, hurries to retrieve it, shooting at me a suspicious glance as she gathers the book to her breast. Several months later, I am found to have borrowed from the public library D.H. Lawrence's *Sons and Lovers* and William McCartney's *Walls Have Mouths*, the life-story of a Communist given a ten-year prison sentence in England for spying. Sister Agatha finds the books in my chest of drawers and all hell is let loose. I am sent to Mother Prioress where I undergo an inquisition. I lie, of course. What else can I do? I say that I have read neither book. In *Walls Have Mouths*, McCartney writes about the conditions in gaol, the last Chapter dealing with homosexuality. And so I must tell the Mother prioress that I had thought the McCartney book was about prison reformers, someone like Elizabeth Fry. *Sons and Lovers*, I say, I had borrowed only because my father had known Lawrence. I had not opened this book, and had read only a few pages of *Walls Have Mouths*. It was boring.

As it happens, the McCartney book had been recommended to me by a girl in my class named Sybil, *via* Colleen. *"She says it's a good book,"* says Colleen. But to the nuns the quest of adolescent girls for knowledge outside the school curriculum is regarded as prurience. In fact, the nuns do not recognise adolescence. Girls go from childhood to adulthood without any in-between. Because of this, even after I have left the Convent to return home, I am once more in trouble; this time for writing a letter to Pamela Davidson. She had written to me to say that she was feeling very depressed. *"Mrs. Pat says she gets depressed, but with her it's the change..."* I reply, jokingly, that the cause of Pamela's depression couldn't possibly be the change, and that it must be adolescence. My mother receives a letter from the Mother Prioress, in which she asks that I no longer correspond with any of 'their girls'. This because the Convent was intent upon 'their' girls remaining children until they went out into the world.

Physiology is on the curriculum, and taught by a lay teacher, the lesson given from a chart thrown over the blackboard. The chart showing the outline of a man filled in by different colours to indicate heart, lungs, liver, the stomach, kidneys, intestines, blood; green, mauve, yellow, orange, blue and red. It bears no relation to a living person. I feel nothing of the lungs struggling to breathe, the blood coursing through the veins, blood rising up into the face or down to other places, or expelled during injury, the kidneys straining to emit body waste, or the liver out of condition causing vomiting and spots before the eyes. Nothing of the effort and mess of everyday living. This illustration is scientific, hygienic, the body behaving as a machine, its environment having no effect upon its function. There is no uterus, no ovaries, no fallopian tubes. Only those physical attributes common to both male and female are included. And so, at the Convent, the sexual functions of the body are never mentioned. Fortunately, with regard to D.H. Lawrence and William McCartney, Mother Prioress appears to accept that my possession of the two books is accidental. And yet I am sure that it is my possession of these which determines my exclusion from the Children of Mary. This is when I am in the Upper Third, at a time when we are of an age to join this sodality. Only myself and a girl named Rosemary, but called 'Vee', are excluded. I can understand my own exclusion because both Sister Agatha and Mother Prioress have accused me of being too critical, I lack faith. But Vee's exclusion I can put down only to her untidy curly hair and unpressed uniform. Vee and I look at each other ruefully. We feel shut out, and yet at the same time glad to avoid boring religious meetings.

At the Hostel, once a week, Father Brennan from our brother school, St. Ignatius College, visits Sister Agatha and she entertains him with cake and ginger ale. The two of them locked in the kitchen against our intrusion. How we older girls snigger. *"I reckon they're kissing and cuddling in there and she's sitting on his lap."* We roll our eyes. Unfortunately, the door is locked with an inside bolt and there is no keyhole. The ginger ale poured out by Sister Agatha for Father Brennan, the flowing glass placed before him, is very weak, for every time I and one of the other girls are left in charge of the kitchen, we creep into the larder and pour ourselves a drink, replacing the amount taken with water. We like ginger ale, but this is also our revenge on the St. Ignatius boys, for when one of them comes with a message to the side-door leading into the kitchen, Sister Agatha makes much of him, plying the boy with biscuits and ginger ale.

In one of the downstairs bedrooms stands a piano and sometimes of an evening, the beds pushed back against the wall, Father Brennan entertains us by playing and singing. He has a deep bass voice and his favourite song is:

> Drake is in his hammock 'til the great Armada comes,
> Captain, art thou sleeping down below?

He is also an admirer of Bing Crosby and encourages us to sing Bing's latest hits. One of the girls has a sweet voice and Father Brennan encourages her to sing solo. She is named Betty Devine and we call her 'Divinity'. A little younger than me, she is pretty and freckled. Every night she punishes her light brown hair by pushing it into shiny steel curlers. Sometimes, I cycle with 'Divinity' to local towns—Hemel Hempstead or Ware, or Hertford, or Hoddesdon. Although younger, Divinity is taller than me and her body already forming into curves. And so, Italian prisoners of war, identified by the large patches sewn on their uniform shirts, cycle alongside and chat us up. They are allowed out to work on local farms. I am sympathetic towards these prisoners and tell them solemnly that we too are Catholics. With a *'ciao!'*, they cycle past us on their way back to their camp. Cycling on a warm summer day with Divinity to an outlying Hertfordshire town, we grow thirsty and knock on the door of a cottage, one in a row, to ask for a drink of water. A woman answers. She is dressed in a cotton frock, the colour washed out of it, her straight hair parted in the middle and strained back to be fastened by pins into a small bun. On her feet, a worn pair of slippers. She turns, beckoning us to enter and we find ourselves in a darkened room, the greater part of which is taken up by a double put-up-up in which a man lies sleeping. His red face and dark hair lying on a pillow, one bare, muscular arm thrown outside the covers. Betty and I look at each other; we are embarrassed and want to giggle, but the woman opens a door and leads us into an adjoining kitchen, a room into which the sun shines through a window over the butler sink, lighting up a plain wooden table and a shelf of crockery. Wordlessly, the woman pulls out chairs for us and we sit stiffly, in silence, while she makes us each a cup of tea and puts jam on bread. We eat and drink until, at last, the meal over, we make our way once more past the sleeping man and out into the street. Our appreciation of the woman's kindness overridden by the sight of a man asleep in bed, we giggle and pull faces at one another, going into flights of fancy as to what might have happened should he have awakened.

Every morning at 6.30 a.m. Sister Agatha collects all those girls she can find to attend Mass at St. Ignatius College Chapel. 'Fletch' goes to Mass willingly every morning, for she is into religion and we respect her earnestness, not holding it against her. The rest of us go only reluctantly, and when Sister Agatha catches us on her morning rounds; we hide in alcoves, under beds, or lock ourselves in the bathroom, holding our hands over our mouths to stifle giggles. With no time to spare, the good sister is then forced to proceed without us. On those occasions when I am trapped before I can hide, I give in gracefully, resigned to spending this time before breakfast on my knees. *"I'm in love!"* Pamela Davidson, kneeling alongside me, exclaims. She too has been caught by the indefatigable Sister. Pamela is not a Catholic, but having been a boarder since the age of five with the nuns of

St. Mary's Priory, Our Lady's sister school, she identifies with Catholicism. *"I'm in love!"* she whispers again, indicating to me one of the servers, a kneeling boy seen in half-profile, high complexion, head drooping as if he is half asleep, which he may well be. His legs jut out behind him in unpressed, shabby, long grey trousers. He does not interest me, but Pamela's face is aflame with excitement, her body tense at the idea of being in love. I am more interested in the other server, not as a boyfriend, but because he is the older of two brothers who went into a billet where they were fed on nothing but porridge: two or three months later they were found to be suffering from malnutrition and returned home to London to regain their health and strength. Although, once more at the Garden City and in another billet, both boys remain thin and pale. I wonder what it is like to almost starve to death and see these two boys as romantic characters. With Pamela 'in love' with one of the servers, now, in the morning at the cry *"time for Mass!"* if I am to escape, I must avoid her as well as Sister Agatha.

"I've told my mother I want to be baptised a Catholic," Pamela tells me, *"but she says the beauty of the ritual can be deceiving. The heady incense, the candles dancing in flame, the sonorous music, the sweet singing, the altar flowers, the priest in his white and gold intoning strange words in Latin. You know, Lahr,"* Pamela says solemnly, *"it can all combine to deceive. My mother says I must wait until I'm grown up before I decide."* Her words give me a jolt and I agree with every one of them. However, having hidden my secular background and family secrets for so long, I cannot reveal myself now.

Each evening, Sister Agatha gathers us together for prayers. We kneel in the dining-room while she leads us and gives a homily on 'Defending the Faith':

> *Faith of our fathers, living still*
> *in spite of dungeon, fire and sword;*
> *oh, how our hearts beat high with joy*
> *when e'er we hear that glorious word!*
>
> *Faith of our fathers! Holy faith!*
> *We will be true to thee till death,*
> *We will be true to thee till death.*
>
> *Our fathers, chained in prisons dark,*
> *were still in heart and conscience free;*

how sweet would be their children's fate,
If they like them, could die for thee!

We walk tall, seeing ourselves as soldiers ready to make war against an unknown enemy, only just out of sight! I have an odd relationship with God at this time. At school He takes hold of our lives. Night and day he is there, making His presence felt in all that we do. At home, my father claims to be an Atheist. There is no God. My mother has rejected the religion in which she was raised and has put no other theism in its place. Although, for a time when she was very unhappy, isolated at Wilton Road and plagued by economic and domestic problems, she had taken religious instruction from Sister St. Alban, the crosspatch nun at St. Martin's Convent. My mother had always said to me that religion was no more than a crutch and at that time she was desperate for some form of support. However, it went against the grain to take the further step of entering the Church. When it came to the choice, rationalism had upon her the stronger hold. *"Is there, or is there not a God?"* I had mused while at St. Martin's Convent. *"Prove yourself,"* I ask the God in my head. *"If you really do exist, let me hear a strange noise in reply."* Lying in bed that night, suddenly I become aware of a series of squeaks. Rather like mice, but we have no mice in the house. Can this be God? I am not convinced. *"God,"* I say, *"if you're real, let someone down here claim to be Jesus. Not like before, I don't want him crucified. Just let someone claim he's Christ."* A week or two later I pick up one of my father's Sunday newspapers—and he bought them all—to read in the *News of the World* that a man charged in Court with obstruction, had claimed to be Jesus Christ. I am awed. God did exist! But this newly found personal God bore no relation to the God I learned about in organised religion. He was more of a friend.

That is how I come to pray to God not to let me die from lack of a gland when I arrive at my fourteenth birthday. I pray at odd moments and at evening prayers in the Hostel. This worry over a possibly non-developing gland, I owe to Mrs. Sargie. On one of my weekends at home, Mrs. Sargie is sitting in our living-room talking to my mother. *"She were a lovely girl,"* I hear her say *"beautiful long blonde hair and such a sweet nature. Her parents were heartbroken when she died. I were upset 'cos I often saw her coming down Wilton Road from the top and she'd always smile. She died from a gland that should have grown when she were fourteen, but it didn't grow and the poor girl died."* She went on to describe the beautiful funeral and the lovely flowers, but I heard none of this for my mind was concentrating on my own predicament. I was nearly fourteen! Every day at the Hostel, I examine myself most urgently, pressing at the glands in my neck, watching myself in the mirror to determine whether my face betrayed the seal of death. I fully expect to drop dead on the very day of my fourteenth birthday, 18th March 1941; a month during which the Minister of Labour, Ernest Bevin announces plans for the conscription of women to ensure that shell-filling factories work round the clock; a month of a new Spring Blitz in the South East, one 500lb bomb hitting a crowded suburban dance hall; a month in which the BBC lifts its ban on employing Conscientious Objectors; a month in which Virginia Woolf drowns herself in the River Ouse. The 18th March comes and goes and I sleep that night to wake on the morning of the 19th March. The danger is past and I thank God for answering my prayers.

I have settled down happily at the Hostel, but one Friday on returning from school, Sister Agatha calls me into the kitchen. *"You're moving out tomorrow,"* she says abruptly. *"Put all your things together this evening."* As I pack my battered suitcase I wonder if this is a promotion, or whether Sister Agatha has lost patience with me. On the morning of the next day, Mary, a good-natured girl some two or three years younger than me, accompanies me to my new home, carrying one or two things I am unable to get into my case. I have been sent to a hostel run by a Mrs. Hazer, a squat woman with untidy hair. She has with her two daughters, one of whom is at Skinners Grammar School, evacuated from Stoke Newington, an older daughter and an 8-year-old boy. There are some twelve to fifteen girls in this hostel, most of them from Skinners, girls from other schools being accepted to make up the number. Eileen Martinelli, who sits two or three desks away from me at school, is also a resident. Because 'Martinelli' rhymes with smelly, her nickname is 'Sentez' the French for 'you smell'. We are not close friends, but from my desk in the classroom I admire her raven-black shining short straight hair, kept in place by a white Alice band, her dark eyes and pleasing features. She and her friend Joan Gatcum, whom we call 'Gak', and Eileen sing at school concerts, and Eileen's singing of 'Bless this House' produces floods of tears from the audience. I envy Eileen her talent and courage in standing alone on the stage.

Before being dumped at this hostel I had never heard of it, and only later do I learn of its occupants' proud boast that no Jewish girl sent there stayed for more than a week or two. Of course, in view of the area in which Skinners was situated in London, a large number of Jewish girls were pupils at the school. When I arrive at this hostel there are no Jewish girls in residence and I, although half-Jewish, am known only as a Catholic. The absence of a scape-goat has resulted in a certain boredom setting in and, therefore, when I show myself vulnerable to bullying, gleefully the girls set to work. As it happens, the ringleader is not a Skinners girl, but a Convent girl named Kathleen Webster. She is in Oonagh's class and they are fairly friendly. It is Oonagh who tells me that Kathleen has a chip on her shoulder because of a step-mother whom she dislikes and a disinterested father. I arrive home from school, to find Kathleen, small of stature, brown curly hair, green eyes, standing by my bed in the downstairs room which I share with four or five other girls. She grins at me spitefully while other girls stand and watch. My blue dressing-gown has been spread inside-out across my bed. "*What's that?*" Kathleen interrogates me, pointing to a small stain at the centre of the gown. The threatening atmosphere of the room makes me fear the worst. "*What is it?*" I recoil, mumbling weakly "*I don't know.*" Kathleen pounces, she is triumphant. "*Yes you do! You're filthy! No one wants to sleep in the same room as you. You're spreading germs.*" She acts out a shudder. I cannot defend myself because I hear my mother's voice grumbling at my having left a menstruation stain upon a bed sheet. "*You should be more careful,*" my mother had said, "*If you did that in someone else's house they'd be disgusted!*" She had told me of a woman, "*the lowest of the low,*" who had gone out into the street wearing a skirt the back of which bore a blood stain. "*Men despise women like that.*" "*When I get my periods,*" my sister had said sanctimoniously, "*I'll manage them better than Sheila.*"

Now, all this comes back to haunt me and I feel guilty and cannot make any reply to Kathleen. I do not know what this particular stain might be, nor whether my tormentors have placed it there, but I cannot defend myself. This, of course, encourages Kathleen and her cohorts to continue their persecution. On another day, I return to the hostel to find my frayed and worn underwear, knickers and vests, pulled out of the chest of drawers to be displayed on my bed. No doubt the other girls' underwear is in a similar condition, for this is wartime and we are away from home. But this does not occur to me. Once again I am a young child boarding at St. Martin's and despised for my family's poverty. *"You must live in a slum and your mother and father must be beggars!"* sneers Kathleen. Kathleen has cornered me in the bedroom, the girls once again watching me with their accusing eyes. *"Look at your hair!"* a girl says, pointing a finger, *"It's a disgrace! Where's your comb?"* She rummages in my bedside locker and flings the comb at me. With trembling hands I push it through my hair, tugging at tangles. *"It's no good—her hair's filthy! Like her neck! Go and wash your neck!"* I am given a slight push towards the stairs to help me to the bathroom, where I lock myself in and hope to stay until they tire of their game. I see myself creeping down the stairs, opening the front door and running down the street, to go where? Somewhere. They bang on the door, one after the other. *"We're waiting. Mrs. Hazer says you've got to come out."* I know this is a lie, but at last I emerge and my neck is examined. *"It's still filthy, it's been filthy all her life, it will never be clean. We ought to push her head in a basin and make her wash the fleas out of her hair."*

Recently, I have read *Cat's Eye* by Margaret Atwood, in which the main character speaks of being bullied at school.[1] This book bringing back to me all I had suffered:

> I worry about what I've said today, the expression on my face, how I walk, what I wear. Carol is in my classroom, and it's her job to report to Cordelia what I do and say all day. They comment on the kind of lunch I have, how I hold my sandwich, how I chew. On the way home I have to walk in front of them, or behind. in front is worse because they talk about how I'm walking, how I look from behind.

A Jewish girl named Marion is sent to the hostel. Not a pupil at Skinners, but attending at a local Grammar School. She is a girl of athletic build, bold brown eyes, curly black hair. She is soon sucked into the game on the side of my abusers, acting often as their mouthpiece. For they are having too good a time abusing me to interrupt my maltreatment and turn their malignity upon her. As I know of the anti-Semitism rampant in the hostel, and nurtured by Mrs. Hazer, I feel betrayed by this girl, a potential victim who ought to be on my side. But she, of course, is ignorant of her own vulnerability. I grind my teeth. *"Just you wait my girl!"* I

1. Margaret Atwood, *Cat's Eye*, Virago, London, 1990.

say to myself as if speaking to her, *"you'll get yours sooner or later!"* Eileen Martinelli does not join in with this bullying and yet she does nothing to stop it. Instead, she distances herself from my victimisation. Once, when at school I am crying to Colleen during the dinner hour, she calls Eileen over and asks for an explanation. *"It's only because they like you,"* Eileen says to me weakly *"they only tease people they like."* This makes me angry, for I know it is her excuse for standing on the sidelines.

At the Convent Hostel, I can remember only one incidence of bullying. This had occurred when Maureen Quinlan, while we were at dinner, was accused by one of her class-mates, of losing the form a netball match. Other girls sitting around the two tables arranged in an L-shape, begin to take sides and the argument gains momentum. Brickbats fly at Maureen who, half crying, tries to defend herself, until Fletch intervenes and the girls are told in no uncertain terms to stop picking on Maureen. The girls subside and loaded missiles fall harmlessly to the floor. Afterwards, I walk to school with Maureen, a girl some eighteen months younger than me whose sister Theresa sits behind me in class. Maureen's hair is in such tight curls that it is no longer than a boy's and in each ear she wears a small circular dangling gold earring. She expresses her anger at her accusers and I excuse myself by telling her, *"I didn't say anything about you."* She looks at me contemptuously: *"You never do. You always keep out of it."* I understand the justice of her accusation and am ashamed. And I promised myself that I would be like Colleen who, sure of herself, is always willing to stand up and be counted on behalf of others.

However, the verbal assaults at Mrs. Hazer's hostel continue to batter and damage me. If it had not been for this bullying, the hostel would have suited me fine, for Mrs. Hazer never objects if I go out in the evening or asks where I am going. One morning I decide to get up at 3 a.m. and go mushrooming with local sisters Madge and Betty Roberts, to whom Oonagh has introduced me. Like Oonagh and me, the Roberts girls are great readers and have organised their books into a lending library at 1d per book, although I don't remember ever paying this amount. Madge is a short girl with straight brown hair, pale complexion, tip-tilted nose and light green eyes. I recall her face more easily than that of her younger sister, thinner and potentially taller than Madge, and who wears her hair long. A few short years later, Madge is to reappear in my life in London, when I treat her badly. To go mushrooming, I creep out of the hostel in the early hours and cycle in the direction of the Roberts house. They live in a road on the outskirts of the Garden City, adjoining another street, the two streets running alongside the Cherry Tree/Pear Tree divide. In the half-light, I mistake the house and neither of the Roberts girls in evidence, I try to attract their attention by picking up some small pebbles from the garden path to throw them gently at the upstairs front window which I imagine to be Madge's bedroom. No response. I pick up and throw a further handful, and then I see a man's sleepy head at the window, his hands struggling with the catch. I am shocked and immediately realise my mistake. In discomfiture, I jump on my bike and pedal to the right address, by this time giggling over the whole episode. Madge and her sister are waiting for me and the three of us make our way over the fields, plucking out the light brown mushrooms as they push their heads out of the dark earth and above the green grass. Flushed with pleasure, my large paper-bag filled by fungi and stowed in my saddle-bag, I return to the hostel in time for breakfast. Timidly, I present the mushrooms to Mrs. Hazer who takes them without looking at me. She never looks at me, not even when I am helping in the kitchen by wiping-up while she washes-up. The mushrooms are never to appear on the table. Fearful that they are toadstools, she throws them all into the dustbin.

As the weeks go by at the hostel, I become more and more unhappy and yet it does not occur to me to complain of my treatment. For I have a sense of guilt. The fault must lie in myself. Then, one day, a Mrs. Bishop, a tall, dark-haired woman with a gentle manner, calls to visit her small daughter Josie, who is staying at the hostel temporarily. Josie had shared a billet with Oonagh, until the 'lady' became ill and was taken into hospital, Oonagh moving on to another billet. Mrs. Bishop finds me sitting in the living-room and I am weeping. My elbows on the table, my head in my hands. Concerned, she asks me, *"what's wrong? Why are you crying?"* I pour out over Mrs. Bishop my misery, my lamentations, to set the floor awash, lap against the walls, press against the ceiling, push the windows outwards. She is appalled and, unknown to me, immediately goes to the nuns at Little Young's, her small daughter bearing witness to my unhappiness.

Therefore, I am surprised, but happy, when on returning from school on the next day, Mrs. Hazer says shortly, *"you're going back to the Convent School Hostel.*" Mary helps me carry my belongings and soon I am at 97 Attimore Close. Happily, I embrace its wall-papered rooms, the furniture provided for use not ornament and the bare lino. This is a place I know well and all the girls are my friends.

Life Saving

The Welwyn Stores: Poetry: Pamela Davidson again: Messerschmitting: Scrumping apples: Valerie.

On a Saturday morning, after we have finished our chores, Sister Agatha turns us out with instructions to take a walk in the fresh air and not to return until dinner-time. No matter whether the day brings sunshine, rain or snow. While we might protest silently at the beginning of these enforced walks, once under way, we enjoy them. On the outskirts of the Garden City there is a park, or perhaps grounds, and I can remember climbing over the gates, the snow on the ground, to pick up sweet chestnuts fallen from the trees. We walk on another day along the top of a high grassy embankment. Margaret Mongan takes a false step and rolls down its length into the road. Edna Smith clambers after her to comfort the wailing Margaret. We pick watercress from a shallow brook and then throw it away because someone says it can give us typhoid if not treated. Shuddering, we wash our hands in the brook water, shaking them dry.

I convince myself that we girls at the Hostel are becoming welded into a family and, as my ties with Colleen weaken, I spend time with my 'foster-sisters'. Sometimes after school we form a Hostel netball team, playing on the Handside pitch, the team cutting across age. We offer to play all-comers and I fancy myself as a 'shooter' for I am too short to play in any other position. I practice shooting the ball into the net, balancing the ball on the hand of one outstretched arm, or copying those girls who raise the ball with two hands, shooting upwards to watch it fall into and down through the net. I have some success, but the taller girls hold the advantage. Not that games interest me, but in the schoolgirl books, the heroine always becomes the most popular girl in the school because—after a hard struggle—she wins the game for the school, whether it be netball, cricket, lacrosse or hockey.

With Colleen and other girls from my form, I spend time in the Welwyn Garden City Stores, an emporium in which many evacuees hide to get out of the cold. The manager's five-year-old daughter, Gillian, lives with us at the Hostel for her mother is ill. I seem to remember that the Manager was a Catholic convert and wanted his daughter to be brought up in the Faith. Gillian is a small thin child with lively brown eyes and short brown hair. I wonder how she must feel knowing that her parents live within walking distance and yet she cannot go to them. In the Stores, its wares spread out before and around us like an Eastern bazaar, we walk carefully to avoid knocking down and breaking centre displays of glass and china. I can recall moving too closely to a balanced glass jar and hearing it fall to the floor with a crash. Fortunately, I was not asked to pay for it. Sometimes I make a purchase in the Stores, and I have before me a paper-backed booklet, with maroon cover, of Shelley's poems. I bought this and also a John Drinkwater, both of them in a basket placed in the centre aisle and offered for sixpence each. The frontispiece of the Shelley declares 'Sheila Lahr, July 31st 1941'. Shelley at that time is my favourite poet and one of my old notebooks, dated 18th January, states 'Poetry Book: poems by Sheila Lahr (two by Shelley)'. This respect for Shelley, however, does not prevent me from writing parodies. I write in place of Shelley's 'Good Night':

> *Good night? Oh! no,*
> *The hour is ill*
> *Which keeps us in the shelter at night.*

And in parodying his 'A Dirge' write:

> *Siren that moanest loud,*
> *Too ugly for song,*
> *The Junker in the cloud,*
> *Groans the night long.*

One of my own poems, which I write in a fit of adolescent excitement and while sitting at my bedroom window looking out on a moonlit night, is dated 2nd March 1942:

The Moonlight

Dance all the night, dance and write,
By the misty shine of the pale moonlight.
I feel mad, gay, I could rush out in the night,
By the misty shine of the pale moonlight.

Another being have I become,
A gipsy now, a harum scarum.
My sense and soberness have taken flight,
And left me alone in the pale moonlight.

Pamela Davidson and I make up a nonsense poem, never written down, but committed to memory:

And so he faced the 'angman
With an awful 'acking cough
He sat down at the piano
And he played Rachmaninoff.

He gazed round at his children
For he knew that he was done
And he gathered them around him
Yes, every blessed one.

He called them all together
From his lips came forth a sigh
"I wish I knew if my horse came in"
he said "before I die!"

The last line of this poem is inspired by news from home. Twi's gaunt, cadaverous, distant father has died in hospital from cancer. He was a betting man and my mother has reported that Mrs. Carson had said that his last mumbled words were *"I wonder what came in at the 3:30."*

I begin upon stories which I am never to finish. I co-opt Pamela and Dinkie to write a book entitled *The Flying Island—Britain's Secret Weapon.* Each of us androgynously taking on the name of a man—I am Kit Derrick, Pamela is Jim Masters, and Dinkie is Michael Carter—the title page stating that the book is 'edited by Sheelagh Lahr' and dedicated to my co-writers together with the rest of the 'Servite Hostel, Welwyn Garden City who took an interest in the writing of the black book—as it was called'. I have covered thirty-five pages in this exercise book with its black shiny cover, my writings sprawling from page to page and the story showing the influence of H.G. Wells.

In those days of youth when energy seemed to be boundless, I flung myself into many activities and with so many girls at the Hostel we were able to play a variety of games. Sometimes, when Margaret is in bed, for our bedtimes are staggered according to age, I creep into the room with a pack of extra-sensory cards and either she, or I, shut our eyes tight to envisage a pattern upon one of the cards—a triangle, a square, a circle—the other concentrating on picking up on this mind pattern and draw from the pack the right card.

By this time Oonagh has left the Garden City and returned to Wilton Road. She has walked into my classroom between lessons, passing me by without a glance. Instead, she has deliberately crossed to the other side of the room where Colleen sits and said *"I'm going home, home to Muswell Hill!"* *"Oonagh, Oonagh!"* I call out after her as she crosses the classroom again, back to the door. She has snubbed me, exposed me to ridicule. She ignores me and exits from the room. During the break, I grumble to Colleen about this, and Colleen, flattered at Oonagh's favour says *"there must be some reason for it. You're not kind to her."* *Mea culpa.*

Pamela and I begin to hitch-hike during the holidays, or on a Saturday or Sunday. We stroll down Valley Road which runs between the back gardens of Attimore Close and the golf course, listening for the sound of approaching vehicles. We prefer to thumb down a lorry, for in a private car there is always the possibility of an over-zealous responsible woman who will question us too closely. The lorry drivers—some of whom are unshaven and covered in grease—are bluff and hearty, apparently believing our stories of being called to a dying Aunt, or a distressed mother, for we travel as sisters. Not that we look alike. She is some inches taller than me, long face, fresh complexion, electric blue eyes, black curly hair parted in the middle and falling to her shoulders. All her movements are quick and sudden, the toss of her head, the way she walks, even her speech is a kind of staccato. Her drill slip too short, the pleats lost and the back shiny. She seems to be discarding her uniform as if it is an old skin. Pamela has no sister, she is an only child and loves her parents wildly. They are separated and she sees them rarely, so she stores up in her mind every moment spent with either one of them. All the time, in and out of school, she conjures up their presence in words. I can remember meeting Pamela's mother twice. This is some time later when I have left the Convent and arranged to meet Pamela at the night-club her mother ran in the West End. The mother is a small, dark plump woman whose straight brown hair is parted in the middle and pulled back ballet fashion. We stand in the room in which there is a bar and several tables. One or two men sitting on bar stools. Pamela's mother greets me and says *"you haven't changed a bit!"* This doesn't please me, for I think of myself as 'grown-up' and am wearing lipstick, rouge and mascara! A year or two later I am to see both parents at Pamela's wedding, when she is eighteen, to an American Officer. The wedding taking place in a Greek Orthodox Chapel in Kensington, for Pamela has always claimed that the family are White Russians; a phrase not clear to me at the time. The bearded Patriarch places a golden crown on Pamela's head as a finishing touch to her long white dress, her groom in his uniform of beige-green coat and light beige trousers, also crowned. Downstairs, her father, a small grey man, mutters agitatedly *"It won't last, it won't last."* Pamela keeps in touch with me, but I throw away her friendship because, intent upon saving the world, I become involved in socialist politics. I reject the microcosm for the macrocosm, a decision which I regret often when I become old enough to understand that neither is totally exclusive.

At Welwyn Garden City, Pamela and I hitch-hike together to all the towns of Hertfordshire, on one occasion going as far as my home-ground, Barnet. I hanker to fly the short distance to Wilton Road, but if my mother were at home she would demand my method of transport. We give this hitch-hiking a code name: 'Messerschmitting'. Why, I do not know; perhaps we like the sound of the name. Certainly, we know it is a German fighter plane. 'Messerschmitt' named for its designer and manufacturer, Willi Messerschmitt (1898-1978). Held prisoner at the end of the war, first by the British and then by the US, until it was decided by an Augsburg Court that the 44,186 planes he had built between 1939 and 1945 had been produced against his will. This decision meaning that Willi survived to work in the 1970s on the airbus and the Tornado, a fighter, for NATO. Pamela and I know nothing about Willi, nor do we care. We enjoy saying casually at the Hostel during dinner, *"we've been Messerschmitting today"* and leave the girls at the tables to guess what we mean. My plate piled high with the swede which other girls will not eat, the platter swimming in brown gravy, for in my excitement I have forgotten to say *"when"* quickly enough to answer to Mary's demand while pouring the liquid from out of a jug to *"say when."*

We must not let Fletch hear of our adventures, for it was she who had put an end to our scrumping apples. Two or three of us would bike to a village and raid the orchards, climbing the fence, grabbing from low-lying branches three or four apples, scramble over the fence to stow our booty in our saddle-bags and pedal quickly to make good our escape. This was not stealing, it was warfare and the apples tasted all the sweeter. Fletch knows nothing of this until I decide to extend the operation into the garden next door to the Hostel. I creep through a hole in the hedge, crawl over the grass towards the apple tree at its centre, freeze for a moment to allay any suspicion from the house of movement, move forward to capture my prize and quickly return home, thrilling at my own daring and skill. I am Leslie Charteris' Saint, or The Thin Man, or a Commando. Somehow or other, Fletch finds out about this activity and calling my accomplice, Margaret, and me together in one of the bedrooms, makes us swear on the Bible that we will never, ever again steal an apple, if we do so, God to strike us blind. As he did for St. Paul on the road to Damascus. Blindness! While at the Garden City I am prescribed spectacles, ones with round lens and ugly wire frames for I am short-sighted and my sight is already impaired. But to be completely blind, to live in the blackness of a closed room! horror of horrors! Willingly, I take the oath and have never stolen an apple from that day to this.

Valerie Dundon arrives at the Hostel; a fresh-faced, freckled square-built girl, straight brown hair and blue eyes. She is my age, but has been placed in the form above, the Fourth Form. But it is me she chooses as a friend, vying with Pamela for my company and I cannot believe that I am so much in demand, so popular! Valerie, whose heart has not loosened itself from her life before the Convent and the Garden City, pours out to me her recent experience of being evacuated to the West Country with a local Paddington school. I am a good listener, because in merely listening I need not reveal anything of myself. *"My best friend was Betty and we were like twins, we never went anywhere without the other. One day I went up the road on my own and a man in a garden wanted to know if Betty was ill because he'd never seen us apart."* An argument had brought this relationship to an end, but Valerie continues to remember it with nostalgia. While with her previous school, she had attended the Methodist Chapel and, she told me *"I wanted to be a Methodist."* Fletch, on hearing this, bridles, for Valerie is a Catholic and has an Irish father, although he does not appear to live with the family; a matter on which Valerie is reticent and in my usual way I ask no questions. I am to spend several weekends staying with Valerie, her mother and sister in the ground-floor flat in a large house in Artesian Road, Queensway. The hustle and bustle of the cosmopolitan Paddington streets I find exciting. On my first night, sleeping on a couch in the front room, I listen to people passing by and then sweet voices singing part of a religious song, and then laughter and the sound of running feet. Some twenty-five years later when I, a mature student at a Teachers' Training College, have been sent out for the day on a project, I break the journey at Queensway underground station and walk to Artesian Road. For a time I stand and gaze at the old house where Valerie once lived, hoping against hope that somehow or other she would materialise before me. I stand there for some minutes, before shaking off a longing for the past, I make my way back to the station.

While at the Hostel, during the summer holidays, we go swimming at an open-air swimming pool, its water captured from the River Lea. On a warm day the baths are crowded with children, both in and out of the water, a constant melee of bare limbs, threshing bodies and bobbing heads. On one such day I luxuriate in the sunshine, for I am always a fair weather swimmer and spend more time out of the water than in. I have promised myself that I will learn to dive, firstly from a sitting position at the edge of the pool, and later from a standing position. This ambition is nourished by my dislike of jumping feet first into the water and feeling myself sink down, down, down, perhaps never to surface. It seems to me that in diving I will have a greater control over the process of hitting the water and that my face will hardly be engulfed at all. Sitting on the edge of the pool, my arms and hands raised above my head, I lean forward, poised to make the plunge, when I hear a voice calling me urgently. *"Sheila! Sheila!"* I turn to see Barbara Harris, a girl in the class below me at school. She runs towards me over the floor, her bare feet slapping the tiles, her brown eyes wide, her curly dark hair escaping from a rubber cap. *"It's Pamela Bloomfield!"* she blurts out, *"She's in her cubicle asleep, and she's making moaning noises."* I run with her to view Pamela and find her half sitting, half lying on the floor, the wooden wall of the cubicle partly supporting her back. Her wet, blonde hair hangs in spikes about her head. There is none of the usual pugnacity in this face, she is almost a stranger. Her mouth droops laxly. I shake her and call her name, but the only response is the lolling sideways of her head and an animal-like grunt. Barbara H. and I run for the baths attendant, a tall young man, sharp to exercise control over his domain if the children step out of line. He carries Pamela to the tiled floor at the side of the baths, lies her face downwards and begins upon artificial respiration. He turns her over, desperately calls her name, pats her face, instructs me to massage her legs and sends me for water. We are surrounded by gaping children as if this is an exhibition provided for their benefit, and I am centre stage. Suddenly, it dawns on me that for the first time in my life I am being treated as a responsible person—and I revel in the role.

At last Pamela stands up and the young man commands her to walk, *"take a few steps, turn and return to me."* She responds as if she were an automaton, her face blank, her limbs stiff. The man's voice reaches her to trigger off a response not of her own volition. At last, satisfied with Pamela's progress, the man instructs me to take her home and so Barbara and I, Pamela between us, each take an arm to urge her forward. She walks stiffly and then begins to lag, so that we are pulling at her. She stumbles, her legs buckling, and it seems that she will sink to the ground. When that happens, Barbara gleefully steps in front of Pamela to slap her face and shout *"stand up, keep walking!"* Pamela rubs her eyes with her hand. We make slow progress and we are only half-way to Pamela's billet when her 'lady' appears in front of us, for she has been alerted by someone running on ahead to the house. The woman is distraught and calls to Pamela, who even in her half conscious state, recognises a caring voice. She runs to the woman and throws her arms about her, sinking her face into the lady's shoulder. For a moment, I envy Pamela a billet 'lady' whom she can love, but then I remember that Pamela's mother lives also in the Garden City and she and Pamela are always at loggerheads. A day or two later, when Pamela is in hospital, we are told that her illness was a form of sunstroke and that the doctors were of the opinion that her life had been saved only because she had not been allowed to slip into deep unconsciousness.

When my involvement in the saving of Pamela is reported at school, the nuns and teachers can hardly believe that I have been so useful. *"Was it you who helped Pamela Bloomfield?"* asks Miss Tynan, the math's teacher, at the start of a lesson. She speaks softly and I can hardly hear her and so walk towards her to catch her words. *"Yes it was!"* shout all my classmates. The teacher looks at me in wonder. However, I cannot luxuriate in the role of heroine for long, for one morning I am called out of my class by Mother Prioress and one of the Sisters. We stand in the corridor while they gaze at me worriedly. A telegram has been received from the Standard Cable Works insisting that I be taken to a doctor and examined for signs of Scarlet Fever. I had been home to Wilton Road for the weekend returning that morning by an early green line bus. *"When you were at home did your sister or anybody else you came into contact with have Scarlet Fever?"* *"I don't think so,"* I reply. *"Take her to Dr. Miall-Smith,"* Mother Prioress instructs the nun, holding the telegram and looking at me in annoyance. Later, my mother tells me that seeing me off to Welwyn Garden City made her late for work and therefore called to account. In desperation, she makes the excuse that she had noticed spots on my back. She was worried that I might be starting upon an infectious childhood ailment. This throws the Management into consternation for the spreading of germs in war-time is an offence.

Dr. Miall-Smith examines the spots on my back—a rash which is always with me, no doubt due to one allergy or another. *"I don't know what it is,"* I hear the doctor say. She pulls down my vest. *"We'll send her in for observation."* Of course, the doctor is used to girls from the Hostel developing one infectious illness or the other. Because the Hostel is seriously overcrowded, we undergo a continual stream of infections—measles, chicken pox, scarlet fever, even scabies—when the children affected are taken into Wellhouse Hospital, a few of us cycle to Barnet to ask after them from a surprised nurse who answers the front door to our knock. Not only do we suffer from infections at the Hostel, but also from head parasites—nits, fleas and lice, Sister Agatha referring to them all as 'fleas'. Every other week she examines the heads of all of us and washes the hair of those afflicted with paraffin or a mild acid solution. My mother, aware of these risks from her own childhood, has presented both Oonagh and me with dust combs and so whenever I can snatch an unobserved moment, I push and pull the comb through my hair, leaning my head over paper spread out on a chest of drawers. I congratulate myself that up until now, I have escaped all the illnesses and Sister Agatha had found 'fleas' in my hair once only and this shortly before my admittance to Sisters hospital, St. Albans, a fever hospital.

"*Your hair's growing brown underneath,*" says a nurse. She is combing and washing out of my hair parasites missed by Sister Agatha. The nurse imagines that auburn is my natural colour. She does not know that Sister Agatha has washed it in an acid solution and turned my dark brown hair auburn. I do not disabuse her and remember my wish to resemble Colleen, but this does not seem so important now and, anyway, there is no way my hair will grow down to my middle back to form two fat plaits. For a few days, I am put into a side ward on my own, but then the Nursing Sister decides to put me in the main ward. "*If she hasn't got it now, she'll catch it,*" she says indifferently to a nurse. She speaks over my head as if the matter does not concern me. While in this isolated ward, I have written a complaining letter to my mother, on 8th November 1941:

> *I guess that was good of Sister Agatha, for at one discovered infection, all the children at the Hostel were forced to undergo an examination, this disrupting the usual routine.*

Now I am placed in a ward in which set out against the two long walls and opposite each other, are some fourteen beds. Not all of them occupied. The morning begins early with Matron visiting the ward, her straight-backed uniformed figure standing by each bed to note its tidiness: has it been made properly? are the covers crumpled? The children are not allowed to move until her visit has ended. Then both patients and nurses can relax.

Boredom is my main enemy, for I am not ill and there is no natural outlet for my energy. Opposite me is a thin ten-year-old girl named Maureen. Calling across the ward, she tells me that she is from the National Children's Home, but she lives with foster-parents. She has a thin, narrow face and straight light brown hair, its texture straw-like. "*They come from the Home every year to weigh me,*" she says self-importantly. "*They want to know if my foster-mother's giving me enough to eat.*" I see her standing on the scales while a male anonymous figure adjusts the weights. The foster-mother, a figure in dress and apron, hovers anxiously in the background awaiting a verdict. Maureen is a lively, argumentative girl and one day I find myself running across the ward, my hand raised ready to strike her. I cannot remember what she has said to me, but I am very angry. But I have forgotten the glass window at the end of the ward, behind which the nurses and Sisters sit. "*Sheila!*" a shocked voice calls and the Staff Nurse appears. I retreat in confusion, mumbling almost to myself my grievance and only half listening to the nurse's sharp words. I know that I am in the wrong in attempting to assault an orphan.

Sister Agatha sends me a small booklet of the Stations of the Cross depicted in black and white woodcuts. Every day I gaze at each picture in turn and try to think myself into Christ's suffering—bearing the heavy cross, falling under its weight, the crown of thorns digging deep into my head.

A secular activity is in teaching eight-year-old Verna handwriting which she calls 'big girls' writing, for at school she writes script. A round-faced child, straight brown hair and a long fringe, she progresses under my tuition and it keeps us both busy and interested.

Oonagh sends me two cushion covers to be embroidered, the pattern on each a regimental badge marked out in blue lines. One for the Royal Army Service Corps and the other for the Royal Electrical and Mechanical Engineers. I don't remember the badges in detail, but I can recall working in chain-stitch and back stitch around a vast number of laurel leaves. "*Are people in your family in those regiments?*" a nurse asks me. "*No,*" I admit, and add, "*my sister sent them.*" "*She probably has friends in them,*" remarks the nurse wisely. She is seeing me as having an older sister and I forbear to tell her that my sister is twelve-years-old. That there is neither rhyme nor reason for her sending cushion covers with these particular designs.

My main problem at the fever hospital is hunger. 'Feed a cold, starve a fever' says an old Wives Tale, which is all very well if one has a fever, but I do not. Therefore, the light diet provided does not satisfy my appetite. In fact, I begin to almost hallucinate on seeing a nurse carrying a tray, scalpel basins becoming pots of jam, the scalpel itself a knife with which to cut bread, cloths become serviettes. I write to my mother to ask that she bring me food for I am starving. And my letter frightens her, for since the day of my birth, my mother has been intent upon nourishing me, agonising over refused food, crying over my inadequate appetite. Her life has been marked out by soups, vegetables, meat, fish, eggs, gravies, pies, poultry, milk and cream.

She arrives at Sisters' Hospital with a small suitcase packed with sandwiches, fruit and plain cake, which she hands in at the desk, for there is no visiting at a fever hospital. The attache case and its contents are brought to me, but the Sister is angry. How dare I say I am hungry! how dare I say I am not being fed! I have given my mother a journey for nothing and made her look foolish. Thereafter, I understand that it is not for me to decide the workings of my body or mind, they are under the control of others.

The ward is being decorated in preparation for Christmas and we sit in our beds making paper-chains. My month of internment will be up in the first weeks of December, but glad of an occupation, I stick together the ends of the utility strips of coloured paper, taking one round the other to form a chain.

The day of my release arrives and I say goodbye to Verna, to Maureen and to a little blonde girl who should also be going home. Instead, she has developed a high fever and a very sore throat. She lies in bed barely conscious and it is whispered that she will be given a tracheotomy. I see the sharp knife entering her slender neck to make a gaping wound, a wound which trembles in and out, in and out, like a slight breath or pulse.

I am taken to a hut where my school uniform is returned to me. There I must wait until my mother arrives, for I must not come into contact again with the hospital infections. Parallel to the Scarlet Fever ward is a low-lying pre-fabricated building in which are incarcerated the diphtheria patients. I can hardly bear to look at it, for diphtheria is a killer disease, but I take swift glances and then look away quickly, never to see any sign of life. Perhaps everyone within the sprawling hut is dead.

Sitting isolated in the isolation hut I become bored and go out into the grounds. The day is bright, not at all cold, and I explore until I find a low wire fence separating me from the street. I am challenged for it says to me *"make a bid for freedom—if you dare!"* I pull myself over the fence and walk towards the town, a spring in my step at entering the world. Of course, I know that I must eventually return to the hospital, but in the meantime I am enjoying my liberty. However, as luck would have it, Matron driving a van sweeps around the corner, almost in my path. Our eyes meet and she stops the van to call out of the window; *"what*

do you think you're doing! Where do you think you're going!" Sitting in
the back of the van, I am returned to the hospital and isolation
hut in disgrace. My mother comes for me the next morning, having changed her shift at the factory to the afternoon. Of course,
Sister informs her that I had tried to run away. My mother says
to me reproachfully. *"you know I was coming for you. I wouldn't have
left you at the hospital!"* I give no explanation. Instead, I smile happily for I am returning for the holidays to Wilton Road.

On Tap

The school dinner strike: My classmates are stricken by adolescent calf love: I become very ill: I return to Wilton Road: My mother's work on munitions: The Girls' Training Corps and Madeleine McCormac: 'Aunt' Kitty and 'Uncle' Rex: Shorthand: Pitman's College: I make a new friend, Pat Moors: The Youth Employment Bureau: Hamburg is almost wiped off the map.

I return to the Hostel after Christmas, and at the beginning of the term, those girls who have school dinners call a strike. They refuse to eat at the school and instead bring in sandwiches or go out in the dinner hour to buy snacks. The strikers claim that the servers give preference to Handside girls, allowing them to go to the head of the queue and also in the portions handed out. I eat at the Hostel and regret that I cannot take part in this militant action.

I and a few other girls in my form, are interested in learning to type and we enroll at a local private evening class. Every Tuesday, after tea, Theresa Quinlan calls for me and we spend the evening learning the keyboard. At this class we are taught the keyboard finger by finger, the two index, the middle, the fourth, the little, in their turn travelling from the home keys up and down the keyboard: rut; tum; yum; rum; run; mut; deck; kid; low; pa; pap;, and so on. A method preferable to the usual which, I am to find later, is learning one bank of keys at a time. To accompany Theresa to the class is an added pleasure for me because she is popular in the class. each week, I worry that she will fail to call for me and go instead with someone else.

Nearly all the girls in my form are now 'in love' with boys evacuated from Hastings Central School. These are tall, muscular lads who put to shame the thinner, smaller boys from St. Ignatius. Only Pamela remains faithful to her St. Ignatius 'love' whom she admires from a distance. The Hastings boys in their black blazers, caps and grey trousers are seen in groups returning home from school. Aware of the girls walking together behind, or in front, the boys attract their attention by talking loudly, laughing, mock fights, until the girls either catch up with them, or the two groups meet. More jokes, more laughter, names exchanged and the girls parcel the boys out between themselves as their 'loves'. For that St. Valentine's Day I make some twelve cards, one for every girl 'in love', all of them apart from Pamela's reading *"from an admirer at Hastings Central"*. In the previous year I had passed through a stage of hero-worshipping an older girl, a prefect, good at sports, active and quick in all her movements, her hair short, her uniform smartly pressed. As I cycle along the road, I long for her to see and admire me. I see myself jumping off my bike to administer to a vague figure knocked down in a road accident. I am holding a hand, reciting the *De Profundis*, the prayer for the dead. This hero-worshipping I had kept to myself, and when it came to boys, I professed to no 'love' for I did not think that any of these boys would be interested in me.

During the past months, my health has been good, but suddenly I come down with a series of asthmatic attacks. Gasping in elusive air, soon lost. No air in my lungs, I am forced once again to move by supporting myself against walls, hanging on to furniture. I long to sit. It is summer and in the garden I sit on the ground, leaning forward, my head down, almost touching the slim trunk of a young tree as if I am making obeisance to its spirit. *"What's the matter with you?"* Sister Agatha has come up behind me. *"You should be running about, exercising, it would be good for you."* Healthy exercise, the cure for all ills.

Between bouts of asthma, which last maybe a week or more, I continue with my normal summer activities, cycling, playing games and swimming in the cold waters of the River Lea. The river which has almost killed Pamela Bloomfield. I have an asthmatic attack. At last my breath comes more easily, but I am left cold and shivery in the warmth of the day and I have no appetite. It is a Saturday and I sit close to the boiler in the kitchen. Sister Agatha bustles about, occasionally shooting at me dubious glances. At last she says *"why don't you go home for the weekend. Your mother would be glad to see you."* Home. Wilton Road. Of course. That is where I want to be.

"*You aren't eating!*" says my mother and I try to push down the plate of food put before me, food which has ceased to be pleasurable to the taste buds or sustenance for the body. Instead it is a mound. A pile which I must clear. To my mother, once again, I am the baby who had refused solids and whose skeleton softened and threatened to crumble. My mother is between jobs. Oonagh's arrival home had precipitated my mother into leaving the factory where for the past year she had worked permanently on the night-shift. Arriving home in the morning to creep into a warm bed vacated by my father. In the evening going out to work as my father arrived home. Turning night into day had played havoc with my mother's digestion, although she had enjoyed the factory. She had money in her pocket and the comradeship of the other women. She had worked in the Inspection Department, taking her work seriously, condemning those on piece-work who tried to get by with poor work. "*It's men's lives!*" said my mother, contemplating an inadequate part for a gun, or poor work which could mean that an aeroplane would fall apart. She had told me also of a chargehand nicknamed 'Gestapo Gertie' because, if a woman spent too long in the WC, Gertie shouted and banged on the door. However, apart from Oonagh's arrival home, it is also her union activities which have taken my mother out of the factory. With enthusiasm, she had shed twenty of her forty-four years and had organised the Department into the Transport and General Workers' Union, a union which—unlike the craft unions—accepted women and the previously unskilled, called dilutees. Of course, her union activities made her unpopular with Management. Whether pressure was put on my mother to leave the factory I do not know, and this is one of the many questions which I regret not having asked her. But she always claimed that her name was blacklisted by the Standard Cable Works. Certainly, my mother had been part of a great movement on behalf of women, for on 26th January, 1940 the newspaper had reported:

> *The government was today urged to give women workers the same pay and conditions as men. The call came at a special meeting of leading women's groups which condemned current practices. Speaker after speaker told of wage cuts and worsening conditions as employers tried to use the high level of unemployment among women to get skilled labour at unskilled wages.*

Now I am at home and unwell, although my mother cannot tell the nature of my illness. She is sure that if I eat a good meal I will soon be better. And so, on the Monday after I have accompanied my mother into London on an errand, she takes me into a restaurant. I sit disinterestedly in front of a plate of food. *"Why aren't you eating?"* my mother asks me, almost in tears. *"I'm not hungry,"* I snap. I am surly and resentful at this attempt to control my appetite. I pick at the food, but leave most of it on the plate and at last, unhappily, we return home. I go to bed and in the early hours of the morning awake to the pain of a knife striking into my lung, tearing me apart. Weeping, I run to my parents' put-u-up bed in the press room to lie between them while they comfort me. There I stay until morning. I have pleurisy and pneumonia, the cause of which, my mother insists, is immersion in the cold waters of the River Lea: a river which Heraclitus's dialectics insisted it was impossible to bathe in twice, while Cratylus, speeding up the process of change, said that it was impossible to bathe there even once.

My back and chest encased in kaolin poultices—for as yet there are no anti-biotics available—I lie in bed in the downstairs front room for a month or more. I am nursed by my mother and Mrs. Norah Taylor. The Taylors have moved into our upstairs flat as newly-weds, the Higgs having moved out. Mrs. Taylor, a slim, green-eyed woman in her early twenties, had been a nurse at the Colney Hatch Asylum, but now she is pregnant. John Taylor is in a reserved occupation, and so not called up for military service. Every morning, my mother calls upon Mrs. Taylor for help in lifting me into an armchair while the bed is made and my lungs replenished by warm plasters. And so the days pass. I am not to return to the Garden City for my mother is angry that I have been sent home in such a condition, alone and with no prior warning to my parents. She has sent an indignant letter to the Mother Prioress. This knowledge, however, passes over me without involving my thoughts for the future, for I am too ill and have only the present.

At last I am convalescent and must learn to leave behind me my life in the Garden City and become at one with Muswell Hill. At first reluctantly, for I miss the noise and bustle of the Hostel, of being part of a large family such that I never lack companionship. In contrast, Wilton Road is as quiet as the grave and I am friendless. *"Please,"* I ask my personal God, *"send me some friends."*

But I do not wait for his reply. Instead, I join the Girls' Training Corps, an organisation set up to involve teenage girls in the war effort. I join at a time when Rommel's offensive in the deserts of Libya has driven back the Allies, while the USA and Japan wage battle in the coral seas of the Pacific; in the Warsaw ghetto, following the rising, the SS slaughter the Jews; Allied troops assault Dieppe, with much loss of life; the British ship *Laconia*, carrying 1800 Italian POWs, is torpedoed by a German U-Boat and at least 800 drown; the Nazis slaughter a Czech village in reprisal for the murder of Heydrich; in Bombay, Ghandi heads fifty Indians arrested by the British in dawn raids; a mistaken order by the Admiralty dooms one of its own Arctic convoys to be picked off one by one by the German Fleet.

On one evening every week, I go to Holly Park School, off Friern Barnet Road, dressed in a uniform of navy blue skirt, tie, forage cap and black shoes. There we march—left, right, left, right, right wheel, left wheel, stand at ease, easy, form up and number from left to right—or was it from right to left?

> *We shall defend our island whatever the cost may be, we shall fight on the beaches, we shall fight on the landing grounds, we shall fight on the fields and in the streets, we shall fight in the hills: we shall never surrender.*[1]

At GTC, marching is not all we do. There are talks on the application of cosmetics, map reading, how to make a street oven, how to use a telephone, and much else besides. Some of us are sent on a Saturday to help at a Day Nursery in which children are cared for while mothers are at work; this is in a wooden building erected on a green space opposite the park in Oakleigh Road South:

WOMEN OF BRITAIN — COME INTO THE FACTORIES

Those who do war work locally will be backed up by a huge expansion in day and night nurseries and child-minding systems. Special welfare arrangements are to be made for women who have to leave home.

---

1. Winston Churchill, June 1940

Following a nurse, I take a line of toddlers across the road to the park, each child holding onto the coat tail of the one in front. *"Come on, eat up or you won't be fit for the next war,"* says a nurse, trying to feed a recalcitrant baby. I do not appreciate the irony of this statement, nor the cynicism learned over the years. I am young and idealistic. There must be no more wars, the world must become socialist, co-operative, an international society where everyone lives in peace. I had looked to make a special friend at the GTC, but before I can do so, Oonagh says to me *"Madeleine McCormac wants to go with you to the GTC—I told her you'd take her."* Madeleine McCormac—the girl responsible for Miss Stranger kicking me out of the Maypole dance. Madeleine had left St. Martins for some years, but now she has returned. *"I don't want to take her,"* I say crossly, but as I go out of the house on the following evening, I see Oonagh coming down Wilton Road with Madeleine. Madeleine, about my height, with an old-young squarish face and light blue eyes which have no depth. I cannot refuse to let her come with me and so, both of us lonely, we become friends of a sort.

At first, Madeleine and I meet once a week only, she calling for me to go to the GTC, but later I become involved with her family. The McCormacs, an Irish family, live in a flat above a motor-cycle shop on the Great North Road, the name on the shop stated in bold letters 'Percy Beecher'. The large, red wooden doors forming the frontage are permanently closed, for the shop had belonged to an Uncle killed in a motor-cycle accident. His widow, Aunt Kitty, has let the flat above to the McCormacs. This accommodation can be reached only by entering through a normal sized door cut through the large red doors and by walking over the concrete floor which had at one time contained row upon row of shining motor-cycles, their gleam long faded into the empty gloom. Rickety wooden stairs lead up into the McCormac flat, a dark place. Madeleine's parents prefer to make a second home in the lounge of the Green Man at Muswell Hill. They are not heavy drinkers, but are in need of the pub's brightness and its comfortable impression of bonhomie. One of their two sons, Madeleine's older brother, went down with the *HMS Hood*, sunk in the Atlantic by the *Bismarck* in May 1941. Only a handful of the 1,421 crew survived. Mrs. McCormac's son was not among them. In their grey, drab flat, the McCormacs see his white face, his water-drenched hair, his flailing arms, his hands in spasm searching for a hand-hold in the fluidity of the ocean, and hear his cries *"Mother! Mother! Mother!"*

Madeleine spends most of her time at Aunt Kitty's house in Grove Road, near to Alexandra Palace and that is where we usually meet. Unlike Mrs. McCormac, whose face is lined and whose tall spare figure is a little bowed, Kitty, her younger sister, is round of limb and on her cheek remains the bloom of late youth. As she and her two children live in a large house, she is able to maintain the family by letting rooms to gentlemen. Here she provides a happy home from home. One of these gentlemen occupies a special place in the household and is referred to as 'Uncle Rex' by six-year-old Patty, eight-year-old Christopher, and also by Madeleine and I. He spends much time with the children, and on taking them out is proud to be mistaken for their father. Uncle Rex, a man of middle height, dark hair and bright blue eyes, is a Special Constable often on duty at Highgate tube station, where he stands importantly alongside the ticket collector. The police uniform together with the specials' flat peaked cap bestowing upon him an unusual authority:

> *You can't trust the specials like the old-time coppers*
> *When you can't find your way home.*[2]

Spying his sturdy figure as I am lifted up to the final part of the escalator on my way home late at night, I greet him as an old friend. Unfortunately, I am to fall foul of Uncle Rex. Madeleine, I and the two children have been out with him for the day—to where I cannot now remember—and on the way home Uncle Rex begins to speak of a well-known building as standing in quite the wrong part of London. Tactlessly, I correct him—and that finishes me with Uncle Rex. I am too clever by half, especially for a girl. His blue eyes flash, his full mouth drawn into a straight line and from that time on he ignores me.

Aunt Kitty's large drawing-room, bright, comfortably furnished with armchairs, carpeted, large French windows leading out to the garden, holds a pianola. I am fascinated to watch the ivory keys rise and fall as they play a popular tune. It seems as if ghostly fingers, maybe those of the late Mr. Beecher, are drawing out the music. Aunt Kitty always makes me welcome, for everyone who enters her house becomes one of the family.

---

2. From the Marie Lloyd song, *"My old man said follow the van."*

However, one of her friends, a middle-aged loud woman named Stella, who has an eighteen-year-old daughter, takes a dislike to me. She tells me I am a Jew, but like St. Peter and the crowing cock, I will not admit to my heritage. *"I'm a Catholic"* I reply. *"No, you're a Jew."* She looks at me with her dark eyes, her plump, short body aggressive in its stance and says again, *"of course you're a Jew."* Aunt Kitty is not happy at Stella's attacks on me, and when Stella is no longer present says to me *"she's got no right to say such things to you!"* I murmur, *"I'm a Catholic."* *"What does it matter if you were Jewish,"* Aunt Kitty says, *"she'd still have no right."* I like her for that. She continues. *"Stella does it because a lot of people think she's Jewish. She's trying to prove she's not."* Maybe, I say to myself, she is Jewish. However, this is for the future and in the present these possibilities hover over me, waiting to see whether Madeleine is to become more than a weekly encumbrance.

While I am not to return to school, my mother does not propose to end my education at the age of fifteen. Failing a profession, I must have a trade, and so she enrols me at Pitman's Commercial College at North Finchley. My mother has always been fascinated by shorthand and as a young woman had attended evening classes in the subject. The diminution of words and phrases into light, dark straight and curved squiggles, to her was a miracle. In fact, during all my growing years, my mother had spoken of shorthand. Whenever she had the time and opportunity, she gathered together me, Oonagh, Twi, Colleen, Ena Macfarlane, Eva Willis, the Dawson boys into a class held in our living-room. Each of us provided with a page of lined paper and pencil, we sit at the mahogany table inherited from Grandmother Rachel, while my mother makes strokes in the air with an index finger: *p b t d chay jay kay gay eff vee ish zhee ess zee m n ing l r ray way yay aitch hay*. We make it into a chant as we do grammalogues:

> *Had do different or difference*
> *Much which each large*

Each of these grammalogues represented by one stroke only. And so I am no stranger to shorthand and, in fact, once I have mastered it at the College, words present themselves to me as shorthand outlines. As a person speaks, so the words appear before my eyes in light or dark strokes, curved or straight lines, above, on, or through the line, the vowel indicated where necessary. Dancing out of mouths, including my own. I can even think in shorthand.

The College at North Finchley is contained within a square, yellow building in Ballards Lane, North Finchley, and the headmaster, a Mr. Pirrie, is a short, dark, glum man who rarely comes out of his office on the ground floor. At the side of the College, iron stairs run from the first floor onto the concreted ground. These stairs are important, for at lunch-time, or at the end of the day, the boys wait underneath them and look up the girls' skirts as they descend. The boys grinning and the girls attempting to pull their skirts around their knees. All official connection between the sexes at the College is banned and the little red book with which all students are issued states this in no uncertain terms. Male and female students must not associate in the College or within its environs on pain of expulsion. This means that boys and girls must not be seen walking or talking together within the area of North Finchley.

I am enrolled for shorthand, typewriting, English, French, German and book-keeping, each change of class marked by the loud buzzing of an electric bell, at which we gather up our books and writing materials to filter through into another classroom. This organisation is new to me for lessons at the Convent have taken place in one room and it is the teachers who have changed. However, unlike present-day Secondary schools, we are without a 'home classroom and, therefore, our starting and ending point for the day is a metal locker and key in the corridor. Tap, tap, tap, tap, fingers at a manual typewriter, one of a number in a row down the middle of the room and on each long side wall. Our gas masks slung over the backs of the chairs, carried in their boxes or in the neater gas-masked shape bags. If we arrive at College without the gas mask, we are sent home again. I have an advantage, for at the Garden City I have learned to touch-type all the letters and I need only to learn the numbers and pick up speed. Tap, tap, tap, in time to the music in four-time playing on a record spinning on a turntable gramophone, wound up intermittently by the teacher, a sharp-faced sharp voiced Sergeant Major of a woman, for whom our fingers are squadrons of soldiers. *Marche Militaire*, Sousa marches, any bright lively tune which will drill our digits into marching swiftly and evenly over the banks of keys. Between our eyes and the keys a metal shield juts out to prevent cheating by peeping at the keys over which our fingers move uniformly. *"Keep your wrists up—fingers on home keys... axs aga fxf fcf axs sex (sex!) vex tax... We want a first-class employee." "The junior office clerks were quite amazed at the extra reward given by their generous employer." "Dear Sirs, Please send us a copy of your Invoice No. 246 dated 16th December for £5 (five pounds) the receipt of which we cannot trace. Your prompt attention will be appreciated."*

There is no time for levity in the typing class, or time to greet each other or our teacher, for she sees her pupils merely as class after class of sharply advancing digits. tap, tap, tap space tap, tap space tap wham! The front of the typewriter, four banks and space bar, has shot out at me. Sybil, who sits next to me, a madcap of a girl, has relieved the oppression of the class by playing a practical joke, pressing down on the two clips each side of the typewriter which holds the front of the machine in place. My fingers jump off the keys and I nurse the machine part in my lap. *"Miss Lahr!"* shouts the typing teacher. We girls are all 'Miss' at the College and the boys 'Mr.', for we are being prepared for the office. And yet to the teacher I remain a child. *"Miss Lahr! Leave the room and stand in the corridor!"* I, still imbued with the school-pupil prejudice against sneaking:

> *Tell tale tit*
> *Your tongue shall be slit*
> *And all the doggies in the town*
> *Shall have a little bit*

but smarting at the injustice, open the door to stand outside, the fingers tap, tap, tapping out my exit. I expect Sybil to own up, for this too is part of school lore and I wait to be recalled. However, Sybil's school was not mine and she says nothing. Instead, her fingers tap, tap, tap.

Shorthand lessons I attend at twice a day, morning and afternoon. The teacher is a short plump woman with a martinet, with a strict face and manner. She dictates and drills us in consonants, vowels and grammalogues which are now called 'short forms'. I am at home here, keep abreast of the class and pass the various tests held to check our progress and understanding. My father, who all through my growing-up years, and beyond, has provided the appropriate reading material for my activities, now brings me *Pitman's Office Training* magazine, the front page of which is written in shorthand, beautifully set out in its printed outlines. I glance cursorily at it, picking out the outlines easy to read and peruse the page given to the reading and typing of corrected manuscripts. Of this, 'stet' is the only instruction I now remember.

The bookkeeping class: Cash books, day books, ledgers; all to record the accretion or disbursement of money, and I am confused. Why an entry in this book rather than another? My penned figures lurch this way and that as if they too are not sure of their place. Blots appear, or I smear the ink over the page. It soon becomes clear that the teacher, Mr. Brooks, a broad, bespectacled middle-aged man, regards me as unpromising material. He reserves most of his interest for Patsy James, the daughter of the footballer Alec James. While others in the class struggle with 'income', 'outgoings', 'trial balance' and so on, he recalls with Patsy, Alec James' past exploits on the football field. Mr. Brooks' tone is so doleful at the apparent demise of professional football in favour of the war effort, that I interpret his hushed voice as an obituary for Alec James. I imagine that Patsy and her small brother have lost their father who can be restored to her only by the teacher's reminiscences. Eventually, I beg to be allowed to withdraw from the bookkeeping class in favour of an extra English lesson. To this, my mother acclimatised to my failure in math agrees. In the English, French and German classes we work at our own pace, for the classes are very mixed. Apart from those intent on learning office skills, there are a few eleven and twelve-year-olds enrolled for general education; the College provides secondary schooling, denied to the vast majority of children excluded from Grammar or Central Schools. Farther along Ballards Lane, and on the opposite side, Clarks College fulfils a similar role and, unlike the Pitman's students, the pupils wear a College blazer. "*They learn Greggs shorthand there,*" we say, wrinkling our noses, for we are convinced of the superiority of Pitmans.

Miss Cohen is the teacher assigned to the English class, and one day I am taken aback to hear her remark during a conversation with a student "*well, people like us are Aryans*"! "*Surely!*" I say to myself "*this plain, middle-aged woman with tightly curled hair as if the curlers are merely slipped out of their work each morning, must know that the word 'Aryan' is part of Nazi propaganda? And with the name 'Cohen' too!*" But maybe she didn't make the connection and like most people divided her life into separate compartments. In the English class I work from a text-book most of the time, but also begin to read Shakespeare's plays, and enjoy them. At the Garden City, each of the girls was given a part from a Shakespeare play and we read around the class. Invariably I was given the part of the Fool. This provided the other girls, and especially Pamela Davidson, with the opportunity to address me, with some glee, as *"Fool!"* I, of course, unable to make any reply except for the words set out for me on the page. Also, by concentrating on the words I must speak so that I do not miss my cue, I hear very little of the play. Now at Pitman's I can become involved with Shakespeare and renew the interest first found as a child on going to see the film of *Midsummer's Night Dream*. An interest developed also by my mother's habit of quoting odd pieces from Shakespeare, almost as if he were a member of the family.

When the electric bell sounds, I make my way to the German class to work from a text-book printed in Gothic lettering. *Das Büro, Die Rechnung, Die Stenotypisten, Der Chef...* Pitman's teaches language for commercial use only and the words remain on the page. We do not learn to speak them. Of course, this was the general method of teaching languages at that time, as if it were intended to inhibit the population from communicating too directly with their opposite numbers abroad. The German teacher is a refugee from Nazism, a large, dark-haired, dark-eyed woman, approaching middle-age.

It is in the French class that I am to make my first close friend from Pitmans, in the person of Pat Moors. On my first day at College, at lunch-time, a pair of girls ask me if I would like to come to lunch with them. They are aware that I am a new pupil and cannot bear to envisage my loneliness. I appreciate their kindness and each lunch-time accompany them to The White Heather, a small cafe then at North Finchley. During conversation, I learn that Betty Love and her friend Rose live at South Mimms, Rose having been billeted on the Love family and choosing to remain with them. Two very nice girls, a year or so older than myself and I am grateful to them, but they are without the 'edge' and vitality which I look for in a close friend. Pat Moors is the seventh child of a Flemish speaking Belgian couple who, in 1914, fleeing from the advance of the German army, came to England as refugees. Pat is some inches taller than me, with light brown hair, a heart-shaped face, pearly-white skin, slightly spread nose and green eyes. *"She's ruining you, that girl!"* Max says reproachfully. He is a boy of about my age who sits behind me in the French class. He is referring to the rouge and lipstick with which I have begun to improve my face, flaunting it as a badge of maturity. Pat, although some nine months younger than me, has used cosmetics for some time, the rouge bright upon her rounded cheeks. *"You'll go downhill"* Max says gloomily, regarding me as if I am a potential whore. Pat he has no hope for at all. I shrug in reply and continue to make up carefully each morning in the large mirror nailed to the side of our coalshed outside the kitchen window. Marking a wide cupid's bow around my mouth and, as I have been shown at GTC, brushing the rouge upwards on my cheeks. Max plays the straight guy to his brother Arnie, also at the College. Arnie is a handsome Jewish boy given to boasting of his female conquests (not, of course, within Pitmans or its environs) The majority of the students at the College are Jewish, and on Yom Kippur the building is almost empty.

In the French class, Pat and I work together under the tutelage of Miss Kennedy, a smart woman somewhere in her thirties, and Pat and I encouraged by one another build on our school-girl French, so that by the end of the year we can both read a French newspaper without difficulty. A few years later, Pat is to learn to speak French by finding a boyfriend among the Free French servicemen and attending at their Club. At the age of eighteen she is to marry her Free Frenchman, and I attend the over-long ceremony at Our Lady of Muswell. However, when I first become friendly with Pat we meet only at the College, or I might meet her occasionally for a specific activity, such as going to the cinema, which we call 'the pictures'. It is not until Pat and her family move from New Barnet to Muswell Hill Road that she becomes my out-of-school friend and I get to know her family. It is then that I meet her parents and her sister Hilda, nicknamed 'Goo'. Goo had returned to the parental home after her flat had been destroyed by a bomb. Half-conscious, half-alive, she lay for three days under rubble, a hard bed, on which she breathed in dust from broken bricks and debris which bore down and oppressed her yielding, but unmoving, body—until, at long last, she was found by rescue workers who dug her out of the grave, and once more she joined the living.

The Pitman's year passes quickly and I pick up a Pitman's Shorthand Theory Certificate and two English RSA Certificates: Second Class, and having re-sat the exam, First Class. My essay for this exam is on the subject of 'Your Favourite Historical Figure' and so I write about Wat Tyler, which fits in with the period's democratic aspirations and the promise that the era of the common man is about to arrive. This First Class Certificate is all but lost, for it falls out of my saddle-bag while I am cycling home. Fortunately, a kindly man in Sydney Road picks it up and phones the College and so I am able to go to his house and, with many thanks, collect my prize. I have always regretted that at the time I was going through a wish to experiment with my identity and so signed my exam form 'Sheelagh G. Lahr'. 'G' for Gemma which is not my name, but while at the Hostel I had translated my Hebrew name Simcha as 'Seema'. This was mistaken for 'Gemma' and, therefore, I had decided to be at one with Blessed Gemma Galgani. After all, who had heard of Seema?

The College year completed in September 1943 I am ready for the world of work: 70 wpm typewriting, 80 wpm shorthand (although I never admitted to would-be employers less than 100 wpm, or even 120 wpm). My mother would have enrolled me at the College for a further year if Mr. Pirrie had agreed to reduce the fees. I sit in his small office, alongside my mother, Mr. Pirrie at his desk attempting not to meet our eyes while my mother pleads. I hear only the halting tone of her supplicating voice and wriggle in embarrassment, for all my experience has taught me that poverty is the most heinous of crimes. A nervous giggle works its way from my diaphragm, into my throat, to explode from between my lips. My mother looks at me angrily and Mr. Pirrie who has barely replied to my mother, his pale flat face impassive, rises to indicate that the interview is at an end. My mother is humiliated. *"Laughing like that!"* she says to me *"you were very rude. No wonder the headmaster won't let you stay."* I am discomposed, but make no reply, for I cannot explain to her my hatred of being made to feel like a pauper.

Madeleine accompanies me to the Youth Employment Bureau at the Town Hall in Crouch End, run by a Mr. Kingswell, a grey-haired handsome middle-aged man of above average height. I had registered here in March on reaching my sixteenth birthday, cheerfully protesting that as I had been born three weeks prematurely I should not sign on until the following month. Sixteen-year-olds registered for the purpose of being asked to join Cadets, Youth Clubs or any other community activity. But, as I am a member of the GTC, a Youth Club in Colney Hatch Lane and a Youth Parliament, there is no need for me to join anything else.

Now that I am ready for work, Mr. Kingswell presents me with a form to apply for a junior post in the Civil Service. "*This is a very safe job,*" he says kindly, "*with good benefits.*" At the age of sixteen I am not looking for a safe job, I am looking for interest and excitement. The Civil Service to me spells Boring and Bureaucratic. Anyway, I know that to be accepted by the Civil Service both parents of an applicant must be British, and I do not want to reveal to Mr. Kingswell my unfortunate origins. So I take the form home to worry my mother about it. A few days later, I return to the Youth Employment Bureau where I muster a confident voice to tell Mr. Kingswell that I do not want to join the Civil Service. He shrugs and sighs, then he searches through the cards on file for an appropriate job to which he can send me for interview.

In the August, Hamburg had been 'wiped off the map' by air-raid. The US attacking by day, have poured more than 10,000 tons of bombs on the City in eight days. Seven square miles have been wiped out: a greater weight of bombs has fallen on Hamburg in this period than during the whole of the 1940-41 Blitz, new phosphorus incendiary bombs creating such intense heat that 'burning asphalt makes the streets look like rivers of fire'. A Danish consular official in the city has claimed that there are 200,000 deaths including 2,000 Danish workers.

Baptism of Fire

*I lose my first job due to asthmatic attacks: Oonagh and the library
books: I am delirious: More about the Misses Vernon: Celia, a survivor
from the Portsmouth fire: Mrs. Sargie and Guy again: The Youth Club:
Madeleine's disappointment: Again I go roller-skating: I join the Civil
Defence: Common Wealth: I get a job at the Law Society, Bell Yard.*

*I've worked in the law,
On divorce I'm proficient,
I've done shorthand and typed
And my work was efficient.*

*If you want to insure, yourself, or a bike,
It's a terrible bore, but I'll advise if you like.
If you want to know how to procure a house
I'll advise you now,
(The surveyor's a louse)*

*Worked in Wardour Street too,
For some little time,
The things film folk do!
Wouldn't make this verse rhyme!*

*I found farming too hard,
What with ricking and stooking,
And could only sit down,
When the man wasn't looking!*

*In politics too, I have had my fling,
'til the party went broke - An unforeseen thing.
I've worked under matrons,
And Sisters galore,
But I was not amused,*

And at last said, no more.

No more will I sell,
(You can see I've read Marx)
What is called 'labour power',
To capitalist sharks!

I write this in February 1946, the poem including some poetic licence. And, of course, the necessity to rhyme meant that I could not set out in correct order the jobs I was to undertake in the first two or three years of my work career. It was not difficult to find employment in those days, especially for typists. A joke going the rounds declared that if a job applicant could pick out the typewriter in a room in which there were also a sewing machine and a lawn mower, she got the job.

My first job, in the Summer of 1943, is at the New Realm Film Company in Wardour Street, distributor of such films as the *Old Mother Riley* series. The Company is situated on the ground-floor of an office divided up by filing cabinets, desks and piles of paper, so that I am fenced into a corner. From there I watch the passing show, people coming and going, calling out to one another, working at their desks. None of them exhibit the slightest bit of interest in me. I am merely a spectator. To take shorthand dictation I am called into a small side office and on one or two occasions sent farther up the road to another office to take dictation from one of the two brothers Fancey, Directors of the Company. I sit on a chair to the side of his desk and Mr. Fancey, a tall, dark, dour man throws dictation at me. Then I go to my typewriter in the same room to type his words into longhand. Psychologically, I remain at the College and cannot rid myself of the belief that all this typing and shorthand is merely acting, no more than exercises from a textbook to be marked up by the teacher. I cannot believe that my letters will be put into envelopes and posted to the addresses. Therefore, I do not take them seriously. Mistakes, or typographical errors, of which there are many, are merely blips that will reduce my test speed and I will do better next time. But, it is not the levity with which I greet the Company's correspondence, but a series of asthmatic attacks which are to take me out of the Film industry. I stagger up Oxford Street, holding onto the glass frontages of clothing stores. And those are my better days. On the others I cannot get into the office at all. At last I am sacked. A few months later the press reports a drama enacted at the New Realm Film Company, when an Accountant stabs one of the Mr. Fanceys in the leg with a paper-knife. I regret having missed the fun.

In the meantime, I am caught up in a drama of my own. I lie in bed in a high fever for bronchitis has become pneumonia and I live in the strange land of delirium. There, I stand still and will myself to fly into the kitchen, walls and closed doors melting away at my touch. I wish myself into the garden and find myself wandering down the path, on each side of me red, white and yellow roses. In front of me is the lily, Solomons' Seal, which leans across the pathway, and which when younger I liked to jump. Fruit trees, cherry, plum and apple spread their branches above my head and I see clearly the ripening fruit. Then I wish myself in bed and wake to find my mother beside me. She gives me the medicine prescribed, a new drug, M&B (named for the maker May and Baker). This is a large, white antibiotic tablet. I swallow it down with some water and wish myself into the street where I fly above the queues gathering at the shops, all of them intent upon obtaining the day's food, supplementing their rations with whatever is on offer. I fly above them, but none of them look upwards, their eyes are fixed downwards, firmly on the ground. This is like swimming in air. I say to myself, *"Why have I never done it before?"* I wake again to find my mother beside me. She is sitting on a chair. *"You've been giving directions to Muswell Hill Post Office in such a refined voice,"* she says chuckling. *"Oonagh and I have been laughing our heads off! Why don't you always talk like that!"* My mother dislikes the slang which I pick up from my peer group.

A nun calls at the front door. *"How is Oonagh?"* she asks my mother, who is surprised at this visitation. *"Oonagh?"* my mother queries. *"You must mean Sheila."* *"No, Oonagh"* insists the nun. My sister has not been at school for the past month or more, although each morning she has left the house at the right time for school, dressed in her uniform, and returned home at what was presumed to be the end of the school day. My mother is shocked. What has Oonagh been doing all day? She is soon to find out, for demands arrive from libraries, both public and private, for books Oonagh has borrowed and not returned. Books which have been lost to our view among the many hundreds already in our house. It was G.K. Chesterton who remarked in one of the *Father Brown* stories, that if something is to be hidden away, it must be stowed among its like. During the following weeks, my mother spends much time in tracking down drama, adventure, mystery, history, philosophy and comedy, and trudging as far as Crouch End to return books to the library marked on the inside covers; Friern Barnet, Hornsey, Boots, W.H. Smith, and many more situated in confectioners and stationers which displayed books for borrowing at threepence per volume.

Oonagh wants no more of the Convent. She has had her fill of the black and white nuns, the Acts of Contrition, the Catechism, the Lives of the Saints, the Confessions, the interminable Mass, the intellectual confinement, God watching her most intimate moments in thought and deed, Faith of our Fathers, *mea culpa* and *De profundis*. She refuses to return to St. Martins, so my mother pays for her to attend Woodhouse Grammar School in Friern Barnet Road, surrounded before the war by iron railings which have gone to assist the war effort. At that time 25% of Grammar pupils won scholarships from the State system, and the rest paid fees.

As for me, soon I have flown away from the mound threatening to engulf and bury me beneath the heavy weight of history. Convalescent, one afternoon I find myself travelling on a tube train to go to a job interview at a small publishing Company. Standing by the doors is a black American soldier, a GI, the Americans having entered the war in December 1941 following the bombing by the Japanese of Pearl Harbor. He is holding onto the shiny steel bar and resting his body gently against the glass and wood half partition separating the seats from the boarding platform. We pull into a station and an American Army officer dressed smartly in his light and dark green uniform and peaked cap, enters. With a frown he notes the blackness of the GI, and lifting one hand signals with a thumb *"OUT"*. The soldier, with no argument, obeys, and the train pulls out to leave him standing on the platform. The scene passes before my dazed eyes and part of me asks why I have not caught hold of the black man to keep him from stepping off the train. Why have I not shouted angrily at the Officer *"There's no Jim Crow over here!"* But that part of my inner core which would have prompted me into action remains hovering above the burial mound and has yet to re-join my body, a body which sits heavily on the train seat, unable to consciously participate in the world around me.

I am interviewed by a shock-haired man somewhere in his thirties, and a fair long-haired woman, of about the same age. I do not get the job. Perhaps I am thought to be too young, or I appear as only a wraith. My mother is to say, *"they recognised your name and know your father is a publisher. They looked upon you as competition."* My mother, no longer in receipt of the fifteen shillings per week I had paid her from my wages, once more must provide me with pocket money, for in the evenings I go to the Youth Club, the GTC or somewhere with Madeleine. During the day I catch up on all the news of our neighbours.

The Misses Vernon, Dolly and Nelly, had been evacuated to Ilfracombe at the beginning of the war. Dolly eagerly climbing aboard the charabanc stationed outside 14 Wilton Road. She turns to call to Nelly who, for once dressed normally in floppy small brimmed grey felt hat and long dark coat, moves at a snail's pace, clutching hold of the front door, the front gate, the hedge; clinging to these familiar static objects. Until, at last the driver, good-naturedly, but eager to be away, takes her firmly by the arm and pushes her gently into the coach. Apart from one or two hastily scribbled notes and a picture post-card from Dolly, my mother hears nothing of the two sisters for some months. And then Dolly arrives home alone. She is homesick for Wilton Road. Also, she is angry. Nelly has refused to return, for in Ilfracombe their positions have become reversed. Dolly is the quiet sister unable to cope with strange surroundings and circumstances. Nelly is in her element. The sea breezes whip into redness her pale cheeks and stir into being a long repressed vitality. They whisper to her of adventure on the high seas. She becomes outgoing, the much valued friend of the other evacuees in the boarding-house. She is invited to tea by the local ladies who are beguiled by her obvious pleasure in the delights of Ilfracombe. She goes for long walks, on her feet sturdy boots, and climbs hills which my mother reports to me as mountains. And the more extroverted and popular Nelly becomes, the greater is Dolly's retreat into her shell. She can hardly bear to speak to the other residents of the boarding-house, these people who are so fond of Nelly. *"Your sister's not very friendly,"* they whisper to Nelly, *"she's a little, well… odd."*

Eventually, Miss Vernon leaves behind the lively, born again Nelly and returns to Wilton Road. There she hopes to find the reclusive, semi-invalid who had for so many years occupied the second bedroom. In vain. Miss Vernon can do no more than write almost daily to Nelly. Letters which plead with her to return home. As it happens, while in Ilfracombe, Dolly has made one contact. This is Celia, my mother's niece, the older of my Aunt Flora's two children rescued from the Portsmouth fire and who had lived with my grandmother Rachel for some years. Celia, together with her two younger daughters had also been evacuated to Ilfracombe and lived in a house next door to Miss Vernon's boarding-house. Breaching the smoke in which Celia will walk to the end of her days, Miss Vernon in reply to a question, tells her that she comes from Muswell Hill. *"I was so surprised when she asked me if I knew anyone named Lahr,"* Miss Vernon tells my mother. She gives my mother news, eagerly received, of Celia's appearance, her interests, the ages of her children, their names, and so on, for it is many years since my mother and her niece have met. Later, my mother is to say to me, *"Celia has another child, her eldest, but she's brain-damaged. Such a pretty baby with bright red hair. They employed a nursemaid and she dropped the baby."* This was a popular conception, or perhaps, misconception, in those days, for a child born mentally handicapped was considered to be a blot on the family name. Their condition must be by accident. *"Celia worried so much she lost all her hair! Miss Vernon said she suspected her hair to be a wig."*

Years later, while I am staying in Southsea, I call upon Celia and her husband, taking with me my eldest child who is two years old. The family live in a large house and I walk through the front door into an environment of soft lights, soft furnishings, soft voices, soft people beautifully groomed from head to foot. I sit on a settee against the wall, my daughter next to me, in a sitting-room in which the warmth of the fire has been banished and only the smoke remains.

With respect to Miss Dolly Vernon, having returned from Ilfracombe bereft of her dependent sister, no longer able to carry out the terms of her father's will, she has lost the *raison d'etre* for her existence. She moves into a deep depression, passing through each day greyly and greeting each new day reluctantly. A greyness which blotches and darkens her mind, as if her soul is within her head and marked by sin; a blackness which will not be lifted or shaken away. In desperation, she turns on the gas oven, and lies her head, the offending part, on the hard metal shelf. The windows closed, unopened for many years, the door bolted, newspaper pushed into the unused keyhole and into the space under the door, Dolly prepares herself for death. Soon the room is filled by noxious fumes which permeate the newspaper under the door and makes its way into the Ridgeways' flat, where Mrs. Walker, Mrs. Ridgeway's mother, is home alone. She, an older version of her cadaverous daughter, sniffs at this invading odour and checks her own gas stove. "*Miss Vernon!*" she calls up the stairs, "*Miss Vernon! There's a gas leak somewhere, is it yours?*" No answer. She climbs up the stairs, calling all the time "*Miss Vernon, Miss Vernon, gas!*" The door to Miss Vernon's cluttered sitting-room is open, but the kitchen door is locked. Mrs. Walker bangs on it with her fists, pulls at the handle to shake the door backwards and forwards. No response from Miss Vernon. Thoroughly alarmed, Mrs. Walker runs to a nearby neighbour who has a telephone and the police are called.

I return home from the Youth Club just in time to catch sight of a black police car shooting backwards up Wilton Road towards Colney Hatch Lane, its tyres screeching. My mother is at the gate of No. 9 and neighbours are gathering at their front doors, or peering from behind net curtains. "*Miss Vernon's tried to gas herself,*" my mother tells me, her face white, her eyes large. The ambulance arrives and two attendants hurry into No. 14, the front door open, but Mrs. Walker is hiding herself away from painful memories. The ambulance men emerge, carrying a stretcher covered partly by a blanket under which lies the small form of Miss Vernon, her grey hair showing above the cover. My mother walks over to the men. "*Where are you taking her?*" she asks, "*She has no family, only a sister who's away. I'm her closest friend.*" The attendant hesitates and then almost whispers, "*the Whittington.*" The police contact Nelly, but she refuses to return. At that time attempted suicide was a crime, but perhaps in 1942 when the whole world appeared bent on suicide there seemed little point in prosecuting one ageing lady. And so Miss Vernon soon returns home, to make a further attempt on her life by gas a few months later. This time she is despatched to Napsbury Asylum at St. Albans, where my mother visits her regularly. But Nelly refuses to return home.

Coincidentally, Miss Vernon meets at the Asylum a girl named Jean whom I know from the Youth Club, where she had attached herself to me—against my will, for she has an intensity which makes me uncomfortable. A short, plump girl whose clammy hands grabbed at mine. She hates her mother; "*She's a Jew,*" she tells me. This puzzles me, for it means that Jean herself is half-

Jewish, but she does not see herself as part of her mother. *"My mother wants me to leave home"*, Jean continues, *"she says that if I don't go, she will."* Now Jean is in the Asylum. My mother has met Jean once only, when she called on me at a time when I was ill in bed and she fell asleep across my legs. Knowing that Jean is epileptic, I am afraid to wake her: what will I do if she thrashes about in a fit? At school we had been instructed to put a cork in the mouth to prevent biting of the tongue. Frequently, in my mind's eye, I had seen myself performing this heroic feat, but with the actual possibility before me, I am not so keen. At last, my mother enters the room and gently shakes Jean awake. *"Time to go home,"* she says, *"Sheila must sleep."* I breathe a sigh of relief on hearing the front door close behind Jean. The next time my mother sees Jean, she is in Napsbury, slumped in a chair, out for the count, in the same ward as Miss Vernon. *"She's very trouble-some,"* says Miss Vernon, *"The nurses don't like her because she argues, over the food, the beds, the arrangements for baths—everything."* When my mother visits again Miss Vernon tells her that Jean is dead. Having been tranquilised into pliancy, she had fallen asleep never to awaken.

Miss Vernon is proud of her own eagerness to survive by co-operating with the nurses, doctors and the regime. With or without Nelly, she now longs for the peace, security and freedom of Wilton Road; a goal towards which my mother is assisting her, for she has written to the Asylum authorities requesting Miss Vernon's release. My mother sets out on several sheets of note-paper the case for Miss Vernon's return to the community, stringent in its application to detail—my mother had always prided herself on her awareness of the exact language to use to impress authority—with the result that Miss Vernon is released into my mother's care. For some days she sleeps in a made-up bed in our living-room, but eventually returns to her own home to sleep and spends her days with my mother. Until, at last, Nelly returns home.

It is a much changed Nelly who comes home from Ilfracombe. The pleasure of companionship has banished the recluse and exercise has made her physically fit. No more halting figure, corset tied over dress, creeping down the garden path to the front gate, to walk along the pavement clinging to the hedge, and then to turn and scurry once more into the house. Now she walks sturdily up the road each morning, smiling at the neighbours as she passes on her way to a job in the kitchen of a small cafe. She has her own money in her pocket and is once more the elder sister.

Mrs. Sargie also continues to call upon my mother. Her son, Guy, has been called up for the army, his tall, thin frame enclosed in rough khaki. His medical had revealed that he was suffering from malnutrition, so the army had fattened him into fighting condition. *"She never cooked for him,"* laments Mrs. Sargie, sitting at the table in our living-room. She is talking about Guy's wife, Iris. *"He'd come home from work and have to see to himself. He lived on bread and marge."* Other facts are now emerging about the errant Iris. While Guy was at work, his wife took herself off to the West End, leaving their baby son Allan alone in the house, lying in a cot. Later, when he could stand, and then walk, she tied him to the cot. *"That neighbour of theirs, Mrs. Jones, told me about it a long time ago,"* says Mrs. Sargie, *"I wish I'd done something then, but I didn't know what to believe."* Allan is now evacuated to the countryside, and with Guy away as well, Iris is relieved of all family responsibility. She earns money by war-work and spends her leisure-time in dance-halls and pubs. Every evening she hurries home from the factory to put on her glad rags, rouge, lipstick, takes her hair out of the band into which it has been rolled to prevent it from catching in the factory machinery, and combs her dark hair into an imitation of the Hollywood star Veronica Lake's blonde hairstyle, her long hair brushed almost over one eye. And she removes from her finger the gold band which confines it.

At the Astoria Dance Hall, Charing Cross road, she meets Eddie Dunlop, a petty officer in the Navy, and within five years she is to give birth to three children. Iris wants to be free, but she is betrayed by her body. Mrs. Sargie knows the name and date of birth of each child, for these have been set out on Guy's divorce petition, filed under the government sponsored scheme '£5 divorces for the forces'—a department of the Law Society in which I am to be employed during 1943. Mrs. Sargie, sitting in our living-room, recites each name and date of birth as if she is recounting the facts of an extended family. She is especially fascinated by the first illicit child born, Emma, for Iris, in answer to Guy's divorce petition, had tried to claim him as the child's progenitor. But Guy had been able to produce his army pay book which proved that, at the relevant date, he had been on duties outside the British Isles. And yet, Mrs. Sargie sees Emma almost as a longed for granddaughter. Guy has custody of Allan, for his mother does not want him, and Mrs. Sargie has agreed to rear him when he is returned from evacuation.

Several times in each week, I go to the Youth Club which is situated in a large old house on the right-hand side of Colney Hatch Lane (walking up the hill from Wilton Road). There, I take part in the discussion group held in an upstairs room, to put the world to rights. I can remember speaking about 'vested interests', but when a boy asks me earnestly what that means, I do not know. I cannot reply. I am stupid. Sometimes I play table tennis on one of the three long tables at the end of the long ground-floor room, but I am not very skilled at the game. Years before, I had played regularly with Twi, either at her house, or mine, on makeshift tables, but the long, correct sized table is more of a challenge. Madeleine comes to the Youth Club only occasionally, for she is not much interested in any of the activities on offer. To this day she must have wry memories of this Youth Club, for it is here she is to receive a grievous disappointment; a disappointment, the roots of which began at the house in Grove Road, for Aunt Kitty had a new boarder, a tall young man named Arthur. He had shown an interest in Madeleine, taking her out for walks and to the pictures. Holding her hand, giving her chaste kisses. I had not met Arthur, but he was to call for Madeleine at the Youth Club. *"He says he'll be here at eight o'clock,"* she says proudly, looking at her watch. And she continues to look at it: 8.15, 8.30, 9 p.m. She becomes agitated, her face an unhappy mask. *"He'll be here soon,"* she assures me, but mostly herself. *"I expect he's had to go somewhere first."* At last he arrives, accompanied by Madeleine's younger cousin, Ruth. I had known Ruth at St. Martin's Convent as a small quick-moving little girl who we named 'twinkle-toes'. Ruth had also been evacuated to the Preston Park Convent and, like me, had temporarily lost much of her hair. This had been the only time during which I had seen Ruth unhappy, for she was a laughing, lively girl, a smile always ready on her round face, her blue eyes dancing with laughter. Now she accompanies Arthur into the Youth Club and from the first moment they walk into the hall, Arthur with a stride of his long legs and Ruth hanging onto his arm, it is clear that they are a couple. Madeleine makes an attempt to claim her boyfriend, to regain her territory, for she cannot bear to lose this pale, moustached young man dressed always in smart double-breasted suits.

Arthur is some years older than both girls, but certainly nearer to Madeleine in age, for Ruth is no more than sixteen. Until now, Madeleine had not thought of her cousin as a rival. *"You're late,"* she says waspishly, eyeing the couple standing close together in the Youth Club's long room. *"I've been waiting all evening."* Arthur makes no reply, but puts his arm around Ruth, who giggles. *"Ruth and I will walk you home,"* Arthur says carelessly. Arthur and Ruth become engaged and then married, and Madeleine is forced to swallow her disappointment. However, she cannot resist making the occasional spiteful remark about her would-be lover and her cousin Ruth.

The members of the Youth Club are offered a reduced fee for roller-skating at Alexandra Palace. I search out my skates, nailed to a pair of shoes and, accompanied by a tall, fair-headed boy named John, make my way to the skating rink; a place not frequented since the days with Colleen. Now I am to skate alongside a boy who seems to enjoy my company. We skate round and round the rink, talking and laughing, until our feet are blistered from an activity from out of the past. Next time I see John at the Youth Club a dance is in progress and he stands with his mates, a group of teenage boys, on the other side of the room. I walk past the swinging couples and go towards him, sure that soon he will greet me. Instead, he turns away. He ignores me.

Madeleine and I have tired of the Girls' Training Corps. For a short time we transfer from the Holly Park division, to a Catholic GTC meeting in Crouch End, but soon 'fall out' for the last time and do not return. I join the Civil Defence as a Messenger, attending for instruction in the garden of a house in Colney Hatch Lane. It is here that I learn that 'make-up' does not necessarily mean cosmetics. It can mean also winding, or unwinding, a stirrup hose pipe. I learn too that if a house is on fire it is best to mount the staircase on the inside, away from the outside wall. I learn that fire runs first along the joists. Many are the scenarios I picture in my mind of flames and billowing smoke against which I run lithely up the stairs away from the wall to rescue the screaming residents. Then I lead them to safety. Instead, once the siren sounds at night, I put on my tin hat and jump on my trusty steed, and cycle up Colney Hatch Lane to Friern Barnet Town Hall. Pedalling furiously, I pass the wall of the Asylum and the swaying trees, the ack-ack of the anti-aircraft guns above my head accompanying me as background music. Once at Friern

Barnet Town Hall, I sit on a chair in a corridor, ignored by the men and women in an office collating the state of the raid. There I wait to be sent to deliver a vital message. All communications down, only I can pedal through the streets, bombs falling around me, to deliver the message which will win the war. Instead, the raid over, I cycle home again. When, at the end of the war, I receive a Certificate from Civil Defence, stating that I have served my country in time of need, I am more than a little surprised.

My mother, miserable at beginning upon the menopause decides that before it is too late she must bear a further child. My father, who longs for a son, agrees, and night after night they go through the necessary performance. But my mother does not become pregnant. She has had an operation for appendicitis some years before and maybe this had finished her as a child-bearing woman. My mother had undergone this mutilation while James Hanley stayed at Wilton Road to care for both Oonagh and me. Eventually, my parents admit defeat and my mother takes a job as an orderly at the Colney Hatch Asylum where she tends the dying, gives blanket baths to the insane, geriatric, or senile, some of whom are deformed, and cleans up faeces. She has entered voluntarily into a place from which Cecil had escaped. and she regales me with tales of the hospital: *"When they've worked there a long time,"* my mother says, *"the nurses are as mad as the patients. It's the environment."* Her blue eyes large and serious, her mouth a thin line. She tells me also of amusing incidents; of a new orderly who, asked to bring the bier for a dead patient, whispers to my mother, *"why do they want beer?"* My mother chuckles at the macabre thought of the orderly returning with a crate of beer for a wake amidst the cries of the elderly, the insane and the hurrying nurses bearing bedpans. The Voices and the Visions.

For some months I have belonged to a Youth Parliament meeting in Crouch End. I had considered joining the Young Communist League in order to find a soul-mate interested in politics and wider social issues. My mother is sympathetic, but I am afraid of my father's reaction. Later, I am to joke that my father would never have turned me out of the house for bearing an illegitimate child, but he would have slung me out if I'd joined the Stalinists! Fortunately, the setting-up of a Youth Parliament is advertised in the local press, *The Muswell Hill Record.* And so, on a Sunday morning, I make my way to the stated address in the large back-room of a shop. There, young men set out chairs opposite one another to represent government and opposition. Two more young men are canvassing for persons to sit on the cross-benches for the Common Wealth party.

As it happens, no more than a week or two previously, my father, standing in the living-room, the newspaper open in his hand, has said, "*This Richard Acland must be genuine. He's donated all his Devon family estates to the National Trust, because he believes in public ownership.*" So, of course, I join the cross-benches. I put my name down also to join the party, expecting to be brought quickly within the fold, but months pass without me being called to the colours. At last, I write to the Headquarters in Gower Street—where I am later to work for a short time—and obtain the address of the local Secretary. She lives in Muswell Hill Avenue with her husband and here a few of us gather occasionally for a cup of tea and a chat. It is at one of these meetings that I meet Ann, who is to become my friend.

Common Wealth: *The Reference* books read as follows:

> *Sir Richard Thomas Dyke Acland, English politician educated at Rugby and Balliol College, Oxford. he entered parliament in 1931 and resigned from the Liberals to found with J.B. Priestley the Common Wealth Party (1942).*

Posters advertising Common Wealth appear on hoardings in London: 'Is It Expedient?' crossed through and 'Is It Right?' taking their place. Common Wealth breaks the electoral truce between the Tory, Labour and Liberal parties, putting up candidates against Tories in Tory seats. In three consecutive years, Common Wealth wins bye-elections. The *Longman Companion to Britain in the Era of the Two World Wars: 1914-45* states:

> *Common Wealth (CW), based its appeal on Christian morality, and its policy was of extreme socialisation, although it eschewed the term 'socialism' in favour of 'Common Ownership'. Its main appeal was to the middle classes.*

Common Wealth's main recommendation to me was its activity at a time when parliamentary political life was dead. Of course, the newspapers, angry at this breaking of the political truce, infer that like Oswald Mosley's 'New Party', Common Wealth could be the forerunner of a fascist organisation. How many people fall for this lie I do not know.

With regard to the job situation, in the Autumn of 1942 I am well again. My mother's nourishing broth has returned me to health and strength. My mother is proud of her soup. When we were children and sat at table, bowls of soup in front of us, she had often told Oonagh and me a fairy story of how, Once upon a time, the Queen had knocked at our front door for a bowl of soup, because my mother made the best soup in the Kingdom. Now I am recovered, but I remain without employment, for my previous experience has left me with employment shock. My mother must have wondered when, and if, I would work again. But, our tenant Mrs. Taylor introduces to her a Mrs. Parnell, who supervises a typing pool at the Law Society. Mrs. Parnell, a middle-aged woman who lives in Sutton Road, comes to visit my mother, who says to her, *"you've got a good name!"* Mrs. Parnell knows that my mother is referring to Charles Stewart Parnell, the Irish Nationalist Leader, hounded out of politics by his political enemies, his private life with Kitty O'Shea revealed to the censure of the world. Mrs. Parnell, proud of her name, is delighted that my mother makes this connection, for Parnell has been forgotten, except by the few. The two women talk politics, Mrs. Parnell pessimistically of the opinion that the establishment would never allow a Labour government to carry out its full programme. The end result of this visit is that Mrs. Parnell arranges an interview for me at the department of the Law Society, dealing with a £5 divorce for servicemen and servicewomen. And in December 1942 I begin upon employment at the Law Society at a wage of £2.10—a few shillings more than I had received from the New Realm Film Company.

In another place, Beveridge is proposing a Welfare State. The entire adult population to be brought within a comprehensive, compulsory insurance scheme to give protection against sickness, unemployment, old age and to provide support for families. Hailed by the press as *"Social Security from Cradle to Grave."* Or, as A.J.P. Taylor writes in *English History 1914-45*:

> The Liberal planner (Beveridge) took over the principle of flat rated contributions which Lloyd George had unwillingly accepted in 1911 and so perpetuated the retrograde principle of poll tax against which Englishmen had revolted as long ago as 1381.

However, because of my sickness record, I had been refused membership of a Friendly Society, which for a weekly payment provided benefit during illness. Therefore, I am to welcome the introduction of the National Insurance Scheme.

Abroad, the Nazis are planning the extinction of the ghettoes for Jews in Poland. Ghettoes which the Nazis themselves had reintroduced. Those living in the ghettoes were to be imprisoned in concentration camps or to be used as slave labour. The old, the sick and the children to be murdered and cremated in the ovens.

Love and Marriage

The Admiralty, Probate and Divorce Division: £5 divorces for the forces: The girls in the office: Pat Moors again: Doodlebugs: Ely Place: Lincoln's Inn's Fields and Sammy Marks: Going dancing: Ivy Benson's all-girl band: NO jitterbugging: The GIs: Lyons Corner House: The Norwegians.

The Law Society is in Bell Yard, off Chancery Lane, opposite the Royal Courts of Justice; the section for Services Divorces part of the Admiralty, Probate and Divorce Division—a designation we type at the top of each Petition and Affidavit—is situated on two upper floors. The offices are large and some dozen shorthand-typists, all about my own age, rising seventeen, sit in rows at desks in front of typewriters. Large, long dusty windows look out on the Law Courts. For dictation by the solicitors and Managing Clerks, we go to their offices or cubby holes outside the main office.

I sit at a typewriter allotted to me, files piled alongside on the desk. I open the first and immediately a scene pops up in 3D, a picture of the lives of the petitioner, the respondent, the co-respondent or, occasionally, when a service wife is suing for divorce, the Woman Named. A wedding scene outside the church, the bride in white, veiled and in a dress made by herself, her mother, or a local dressmaker. The bridegroom in his best suit, brushed and pressed; the bridesmaids, little girls in long dresses in a bright hue, flowers in their hair. These little girls tell themselves that they are princesses and one day they too will wear a white dress and be Queen. Relief shows upon the faces of the bride's parents—their daughter is married, she is respectable. The bridegroom wears a lop-sided grin. He has crossed the threshold from boyhood to manhood. He is master of his own home. He is the equal of his father.

The bride has dreamed of this day; dreamed while servicing a machine in the factory, serving in a shop, washing in a laundry, or filing in an office. Her eyes are dreamy, her thoughts far away with a handsome man, her hero, tall and dark, masterful yet gentle; a scene from any of the romantic novels, or stories she reads in magazines: *A Taste of Paradise; Passion Rekindled; A Wild Heart Tamed*:

> *He was close to her. so close that she could look into his blue eyes to see a small mirror image of her own face. It were as if she were part of him. He pressed her closer, lowering his mouth to cover hers, crushing her red lips and a shudder ran through her body, an excitement, a pleasure never known before, and one over which she had no control. He pulled her body closer to his and a deep, sobbing breath escaped her lungs. this was madness. "No!" she denied hoarsely, dragging herself free from his arms. "No!" She could not look at him for she knew that it was her fault that things had gone so far, so out of control. She felt ashamed. She could have slapped his face, if she had really wanted to.*

She is at the cinema and larger than life movie heroes—Clark Gable, Cary Grant, Gary Cooper—flicker across the silver screen of her mind, turning her into a Rita Hayworth, a Merle Oberon, an Ann Sothern, an Irene Dunne: films which reinforce the advice given by the 'Aunts' of the women's magazines: *"Save yourself for Mr. Right—and only for him. Avoid compromising situations which could give you the reputation of being a loose woman"*

> *I don't care what you used to be,*
> *I know what you are today!*[1]

To the married woman: *"Keep your man by being part wife, part mistress, otherwise he will stray. No matter how tired, or drab, from the day's toil, before He comes home, put the children to bed, tidy the house and for Him make yourself beautiful—a pretty dress, comb out your hair, replenish your make-up. Otherwise you will lose Him."* Memories of the bride's upbringing show in her face. Her father, respected as the main breadwinner, must have the best they can afford, and his wife and children only what is left over. By divine law the

---

1. From popular song.

position of man and wife are unequal. A law compounded by the revolutionary poet Byron who said:

> *Man's love is of a man's life, a thing apart,*
> *'tis woman's whole existence.*

A picture rises from the file in my hands of the bride and groom at the start of their married life, living in rooms. One day, the bride knows they will have a neat little house with front and back gardens, in the country perhaps, or at least in the suburbs. On marriage, she has had to give up her factory job, but she takes off her wedding ring and calls herself 'Miss' to find laundry work. At the end of a hard day, she runs home before He arrives, to cook dinner, tidy up, to make herself beautiful for Him. They are still in rooms when the first baby arrives, and the next. Her mother, who lives nearby, is her main support. *"You've got to put him first"* she says, emphasising the advice given by the magazine *Aunties*. *"Don't let him feel the children have taken over. You've got to give way to Him. He's the breadwinner for you and your children."* The bride finds a part-time job cleaning other people's floors, private homes and offices. Mother minds the children, both women making sure that He does not suffer from her absence from home.

In this manner, the weeks, months and years pass, with dreams of a happy family in a neat little house, roses around the door and hollyhocks in the back yard. and so it might have continued if the war had not intervened, to throw everybody's life out of kilter:

> *He was supposed to come home to her each day:*

> *You'd be so nice to come home to,*
> *You'd be so nice by the fire,*
> *You'd be so nice, you'd be paradise.*[2]

She was supposed to be able to flaunt her status of a married woman. Her marriage and her home were supposed to be all that mattered and the world outside an intrusion. Now, he has been called away to the Colours and home and family are no more than an interlude of photographs around which he can weave memories and dreams. Her man at war, her children evacuated, her value to society is her work at the factory on munitions and, as a poster announces, she is:

---

2. From popular song.

The woman behind the man who mans the gun

Can it be wondered at if the happy bride, in her white dress and veil, no longer feels that the old rules apply? What is more, she has some money in her pocket.

That the files at the Law Society contain sexual details comes as no great shock to me—although I close my eyes and do not look directly at the couple, for while my mother has been open with me about sex, she is of the opinion that couples deserve some privacy. Not so some of the girls employed on this work. It is as if after years of reading nothing but *The Girls' Own Paper*, they have been thrown the *Kama Sutra*, *The Perfumed Garden*, or at least *The News of the World*. They sit before those files like a rabbit before a snake, and one girl is sacked for reading files all day long instead of typing—red-headed Gladys, whose eyes pop out of her head and whose mouth gapes. Conversely, Madge Roberts, who has insisted upon joining me at The Law Society, commuting each day from the Garden City, reads only that amount of the file demanded by the work. She turns her face away from the cavortings of Petitioner, Co-respondent, Respondent or Woman Named. She does not want to know. Myself, I temper the reading with work, skimming through the files, but keeping my fingers moving on the keys. I note that when the husbands are first called-up, the wives write to them *"yours, 'til hell freezes."* *"It froze over pretty quick!"* I quip. Of course, in some cases, such as the young Sarginsons, the marriage has long been broken, or unsatisfactory, neither party able to live up to the stereotype of a happy marriage, but previously they had been tied together through lack of money and resources. In the Services, they grasp at the opportunity for a cheap divorce.

Opposite me in the office works Iris Irons. a small polyphoto of her in one of my albums shows her as forever wearing her blonde hair tightly curled, a stray lock over her forehead. Her nose snub, her mouth wide. Polyphotos were the fashion then, providing some forty sights of the sitter's face from every angle. The intention was that one or two would be enlarged. However, we were generally satisfied with the representation of our face from so many points of view and snipped out each snap to present to friends. Iris Irons' father is an Edmonton publican named Ian, who has married a woman named Irene, this setting up a family tradition, for when Ian Irons noted his matching initials and those of his wife, he decided that his children must follow suit. Therefore, in addition to Iris, there is Ivor, Ida, Igor and Iolanthe. Iris has a cousin, Eileen, working at the Law Society. She is also an Irons, but as her father is named William that part of the family are not concerned with the incantation of initials. Eileen, also blonde, but with finer features than Iris, works on the floor above, the cousins meeting during the dinner hour and also travelling home together. In fact, they are inseparable, until one dread day they have a falling out which sunders the relationship forever. I suspect the quarrel was over one boy or another, but I cannot now remember. But I still see Iris' closed face should Eileen come into the main office, and I see Eileen refusing to meet her cousin's eyes.

Also working in the upstairs office is seventeen-year-old Jenny, a slightly built girl 'five foot two, eyes of blue', long dark hair. She is married to Bob, her childhood sweetheart, not much older than herself, for, when he received his call-up papers for the RAF, in a panic they rushed to become one. He would have a girl to come home to, she would be supporting with her love one of our fighting men. What a dramatic parting as he leaves her to join his comrades-in-arms somewhere in Britain. They promise to be faithful forever and to write often. Now Jenny keeps a daily diary into which she pours out her feelings, crying out her adolescence, which she confuses with the absence of her husband. Sometimes, Bob's letters make her cry. He accuses her of going out with other men and in revenge for her imagined infidelities, of which he dreams as he lies in his hard, lonely bed, he describes girls he has met and whom he magnetises. When Jenny has received such a letter, her hands move wildly over the keyboard and she speaks of suicide. She will put her head in the gas oven, a facility which represents an empty symbol of the meals she would willingly cook for Bob. Lovers' quarrels by post without the satisfactory resolution of forgiveness and concupiscence.

I become friendly with one of the girls, named Margaret, also aged seventeen. She is a natural platinum blonde whose ruddy face, spread nose and light blue eyes do not fit the Hollywood stereotype of the blonde. A well-built athletic girl, she is a member of the Young Farmers' Club, which meets weekly at a church hall, this organisation having been set up to encourage young people to dig for victory. Margaret lives in St. John's Way at the Archway. Her father, a paper and magazine seller, a sprite of a man, sits against a building in Holloway Road, his wares displayed on wooden boxes. Both Jenny and Margaret are often on my trolleybus in the morning on our way to work, the 517 or 617, for if we have to change buses the ticket is interchangeable. The streets well aired, for the office does not open until 9.45 a.m. Sometimes, Margaret and I cycle to work, or else I meet her on a Saturday or Sunday and we cycle around the streets. She is engaged to a Petty Officer in the Navy, known as 'Writer', and he is stationed in Highgate Village. In such close proximity, it might be imagined that the course of true love would run smooth, but there are weeks when he makes no arrangements to meet Margaret, and does not phone her at work. Nor does the Writer, write. At time like this, the forthright Margaret shrugs and cheers herself with thoughts of the compensations of freedom: Pedalling along the road she leads me in singing:

> *Give me land, lots of land,*
> *Under starry skies above,*
> *Don't fence me in.*
> *Send me out forever,*
> *but I ask you please,*
> *Don't fence me in!*

The only other girl I can remember now is Jean. Neat, soft brown hair, brown-eyed Jean, who has the confident manner into which the middle-class are born and raised and which the working-class rarely attain. A confidence bred from a secure financial, professional background and a private income from investments in the working ability of others. Jean is friendly enough, but we are never her friends. She comes to work each morning in Mr. Jobson's car. Mr. Jobson, a lightly built man of medium height is one of the solicitors under the jurisdiction of the head of this department, Miss Eugenie Eulalie Spicer. Mr. Jobson and Jean and her family live near to one another in the Home Counties, the two families meeting socially. She sits at her work, tap, tap, tapping without taking part in our banter. A few years later, Jean would have been at University, and even then we knew that she was destined for better things with superior people.

I had corresponded with Madge Roberts on returning to Muswell Hill from the Garden City, and perhaps I made my job at the Law Society sound interesting. Or perhaps the bright lights of London beckoned. Or maybe Madge regarded me as a close friend. Whatever. One day she arrives at the Law Society for interview, she rushes into the general office, a wide smile on her broad face, to tell me excitedly that she is to start work on the following Monday. Some time later, I am to hear Mrs. Roberts say reproachfully to Madge, *"you wanted to work here, but they haven't been exactly friendly."* I continue to hear her voice stirring my conscience, but cannot picture the circumstances. I suppose that I regarded Madge's sudden appearance in my life as an intrusion. She belonged to another place and another time. Apart from which, she had remained very much the schoolgirl, in dress, hairstyle and interests. She had none of the sophistication adopted by me and my current best friend, Pat Moors.

Pat is working at Estates Gazette in Ely Place, not far from Chancery Lane. On some days, having eaten a hurried dinner in a cafe—for my mother insisted that a hot mid-day meal was essential for good health—I meet Pat, who brings sandwiches to work, and we roam the Holborn streets. In Hatton Garden we dream of sparkling diamonds hidden behind the facades of shops and offices. In Leather Lane we pass the market stalls. Or we go into Gamages, rival to Selfridges. When I was at St. Martin's Convent, other girls would boast of Christmas-time visits to Gamages or Selfridges. This was not part of my family's tradition, nor interest, and so I either listened without comment, or, not to be outdone, inferred that I too would be making a similar visit. Now, at last, I have the freedom of Gamages for part of each week-day. So why do I recall only the basement in which the hardware was displayed? Perhaps my memories passed along with the passing of the store itself. Quite often I accompany Pat back to the office buildings in which she works in Ely Place, for I find this cul-de-sac with gates and a lodge at one end, fascinating. H.V. Morton writes in *In Search of London*:

> It is just a short street of Georgian houses, tenanted now mostly by solicitors and business firms. Until recent times Ely Place was technically speaking not in London, but in Cambridgeshire. It did not pay London rates and taxes, neither did its one public-house observe London times of opening... The City police have no right of entry and the lodge gates are closed each night by watchmen who until the outbreak of the last War were in the habit of calling the hours of the night.[3]

3. H.V. Morton, *In Search of London*, Methuen, London, 1951.

In stepping through the open gates of Ely Place, it seems to me that I am flying out of London, over Counties, through space and time, into this quiet backwater in which an almost sunken medieval Roman Catholic Church stands. St. Etheldreda's is pressed between the surrounding London, in which Mass is celebrated, for this church, formerly the Chapel to the long vanished Ely Palace, was purchased by the Fathers of Charity in 1874. I creep down the steps into the low ceilinged, half-dark church, in reverence for the many generations who have entered there before me. A church now no more, for it was destroyed by an IRA bomb in recent years.

On some days of the week, I go to a cafe in Staple Inn where a good, inexpensive meal is served in a small space crowded by dining office workers. Pat would have loved this, she would have flirted outrageously with the men, testing her powers upon them, fluttering her large green eyes. But Madge would have eaten her meal as if she were alone. As it is, Madge, like Pat, brings sandwiches to work. On the morning I arrive at the office to find that a bomb had fallen during the night on Staple Inn, not only do I mourn this attractive, historic place, but I have to find another cafe. In fact, two bombs fall on Staple Inn during the same week.

Sometimes, a flying bomb, or buzz bomb, or doodle bug—call it what you will—flies over during the day. I can remember one of these chasing me along the Strand, the people in the streets watching its progress or hiding in doorways:

> *Buzz buzz buzz buzz*
> *Honey bee, honey bee*
> *Buzz all you want*
> *But don't sting me*[4]

A bomb falls during the night on the Law Courts, blowing in the Law Society's windows, the glass littering the floor and desks. Should an air-raid take place while we are at work, we are called into a windowless corridor to sit and wait until the All Clear sounds. Male law students hurry past us, ogling the prettier girls. Mr. Jobson chuckles proudly, "*law students don't change!*" he says, carried back to his own youth.

Sometimes, I spend my dinner hour in Lincoln's Inn Fields where I stand to listen to Sammy Marks, who speaks also at

---

4. Sung by Arthur Askey, comedian.

Speakers' Corner, Hyde Park. He is a small, thin, shabby man
of indeterminate age, black trilby hat pulled down over his forehead. He stands in front of the fountain, greenery and grass
forming a back-cloth. *"After the war,"* I hear him say, *"we won't
need bunting. No, there'll be no need for bunting. We'll hang a landlord on every lamp-post."* He is speaking of the perniciousness of
landlordism which pushes families into slums and leaves others
homeless. *"There was a time when the Britons were men,"* he tells the
few who have gathered to listen, *"and they met the landlords who
had stolen the land, with picks and staves. Now,"* says Sammy, looking round contemptuously at his audience, *"you poor mutts meet
them with rent-books—compounding a felony!"* He is at one with the
dispossessed and quotes a fellow Jew, Jesus:-

*The foxes have holes and the birds of the air
have nests, but the Son of man hath not where to lay his head.*

Matthew 8: 20, Luke 9: 58

Maybe he, the visionary, sees about him in Lincoln's Inn Fields,
the makeshift camps of the homeless of the 1980s and 90s. Cardboard boxes under which young and old crouch in a vain attempt
to keep from the cold, blankets and ragged materials arranged to
form crude tents. Do the homeless see Sammy Marks walking
among them? Do they hear his exhortations to resistance against
a society which throws away human kind as if it were so much
garbage? Sammy Marks, the patron saint of the homeless.

After work, on most evenings, and having eaten the evening meal cooked for me by my mother, I hurry to Pat's house
in Muswell Hill Road, where the Moors family now live in the
ground-floor flat of a house. Pat's parents always make me welcome, for they are glad that their youngest daughter has a friend.
Pat is an afterthought, a gap of some years separating her from
the nearest sibling. The Moors had tried to adopt a child as a
companion for Pat, but as Mrs. Moors states indignantly, they
had been refused because they were foreigners. She says, *"a child
can be starved and ill-treated in an English home, but not allowed into
a good Belgian home!"* Perhaps it is this sharing of a foreign background which has brought Pat and me together.

Mrs. Moors is short and plump, and her dark hair, speckled
with grey, is pulled back and parted in the middle. Mr. Moors is
above average height, but now a little bowed, and he has a mop

of grey hair above a rugged face. Unlike the Lahrs, who call the afternoon meal 'dinner', the Moors dine in the evening, the table laid out beautifully, with shining cutlery set out on a white cloth, in the dining room at the end of which are French Windows. Usually I arrive at the house after they have eaten, but should I ever be there earlier, Mrs. Moors lays a place for me. From the Moors I pick up a few Flemish words, such as '*Gloska*' for glass and '*Boska*' for boy—a name applied to the Moors long-haired terrier. Pat and I spend one evening a week at her house in 'beauty treatment'. We rub Cold or Nivea cream into our faces, we experiment with cosmetics, lipstick, rouge, powder, mascara, eye pencil. Pat has an eyelash curler, a machine resembling a safety razor, but the eyelashes are caught between two thick rubber bands which kink them upwards. I have always sprouted long lashes, my mother, when I was a child, often said to me, "*you have such lovely long lashes.*" Too modest to declare that, unlike Pat, I do not need the machine, I take my turn with it.

Several times a week, we go dancing—the Paramount in Tottenham Court Road, the Astoria in Charing Cross Road, the Lyceum in the Strand, Covent Garden where the floor tilts upwards at one end. A long line of girls and men in uniforms wait in the vestibule to be admitted. Dance-hall officials stand to one side to watch the line closely, and I am always called out to show my identity card, to show that I am seventeen, the minimum age for admittance, for I remain small, skinny and under-developed. Pat, who is nine months younger than me and for some time only sixteen, is never called upon to prove her age. Once inside, the bright lights beckon, the wide floor invites and we hurry to pass our coats over the counter into the cloakroom. For safety, we stow our handbags in a second cloakroom where we can request them at any time. The couples move around the floor in a perpetual dance, widdershins, many of the girls dancing together, but looking around hopefully to catch the eye of one of the men made handsome by uniform:

You dancin'?
You askin'?
Yeah
I'm dancin'

we joke. We call dancing 'cutting a rug': "*You wanna cut a rug?*"

I dance with Pat, she as the taller girl playing the male role, not too successfully: quicksteps, waltzes. Sooner, or later, she will be asked to dance by a serviceman—maybe an airman to whom Churchill referred to in a different context as 'one of the few', and I am left sitting against the wall with a row of girls. All of us trying to appear as if we are merely resting between hectic dancing and are certainly not wallflowers.

Wallflowers: *fully to half-hardy. Grow in any fertile soil in an open position. Short-lived species are best treated as biennials.*

If I am asked to dance, it is usually by a weedy youth not much taller than myself, not yet in uniform, possibly medically unfit. Stiffly, I move around the floor in a formal dance, worried that I might put a foot wrong and throw my companion out of step. Once more on my seat, I look across to Ivy Benson's all girl band, dressed in long frocks, breathing out into the room lilting dance music. The slow smoochy tune: *"I'm in the mood for love, simply because you're near me,"* or the quicker tempo: *"Don't go walking down lover's lane with anybody else but me, anybody else but me, anybody else but me, oh, no, no,"* or the waltz: *"I'll be with you in apple blossom time, I'll be with you to change your name to mine, some day in May, I'll come and say, happy the bride the sun shines on today,"* or the tango, *Jealousy*, which only a few can dance expertly, the rest of us watching couples bending and swaying: *"T'was all over my jealousy, my fault was my blind jealousy."* But we sing a parody:

> *T'was all over my S O P,*
> *He gave all his kisses to me*
> *He was my lover*
> *Now I am a mother*
> *T'was all over my S O P.*

(a S O P was a sleeping out pass for the services.)

Sometimes, an old-fashioned waltz to *The Blue Danube* or another Strauss waltz, quickens the pace and I close my eyes to see crinolines spinning and swaying as the dancers are swept up into the tempo. 'In the Mood' takes me into the jive age, when it is no longer necessary to sit out and wait to be asked to dance. Now I can dance alone, or perform at a short distance from Pat:

> *Mr. Whatyamacallit,*
> *What ya doin' tonight?*
> *Hope you're in the mood because*

I'm feelin' jus' right.[5]

NO JITTERBUGGING!, dance-hall notices command. Throwing your partner around, over your head, your shoulder: managements do not want such dancing taking up space, making their customers run for cover as arms, legs, heads, swoop among them. The newspapers speak of dislocated and broken limbs. Jive is OK, and is reintroduced some time after the war as 'rock and roll' as if only just invented.

And so I dance round and round and round, with Pat, a pimply youth, the occasional serviceman who picks me from the wall. Dance while the band plays on, and I swirl around the crowded floor, dresses of blue, green, yellow, pink, swinging in time to the music, trousered legs in khaki, Airforce or Navy blue, leading the way. a bright spotlight touches our heads, steadying every now and then to illuminate a dancing couple. Sometimes, during the interval, an appeal is made for a banana for a sick child, for this fruit has not been in the shops for a very long time and as if by magic, someone will always come forward to present this fruit to a good cause.

In Europe, Jews, gypsies and others shut into the gas chambers, twitch their limbs involuntarily in a dance of death.

After the dance is over, Pat and I take the tube to Highgate, climbing up the steep hill to Muswell Hill Road. If we have missed the last bus, the 11.20 p.m., we walk to Pat's house, where I leave her, and continue alone. Sometimes, I hear flying bombs overhead and listen to their drone, but I feel safe when I am on the move. I imagine that I can outpace them. On one of these evenings, I hear a landmine fall on Crouch End Broadway, the terrific crash and explosion shattering the night. However, when I lie helpless in my bed at night and hear the buzzing of a doodlebug overhead, I hold my breath while I wait for the engine to stop, for then it must fall. I stiffen in fear. I make the sign of the cross 'just in case' and pray, "*don't let it fall on this house*," adding guiltily, "*or on anybody's house. Let it fall on open land*":

> *When they sound the last all clear,*
> *how happy my darling will be.*
> *When they turn up the lights,*

---

5. Jimmy Kennedy, Michael Carr, *The Washing on the Siegfried Line*, 1939.

and the dark stormy nights,
Are only a mem-o-ry.[6]

None of the Lahrs use our Anderson shelter now, for I have better things to do in the evening than spend my time under its tin roof. And, anyway, the Pearce tragedy has shattered my faith in shelters. *"If your name's on a bomb, it will get you,"* is the general, fatalistic opinion. Make hay while the sun shines.

The brightness of the West End beckons to Pat and me— bright although the neon lights have been switched off and shine to me now only as a memory. My father, pre-war, having called to me to turn and look at the signs shining high up on Piccadilly, the words of their advertising lost to me, for the letters were no more than separate shapes of colour. Although Ann, who was to become my friend, always referred to Cambridge Circus as 'Damaroid' Circus, because of the large neon sign which lighted up had advertised this sexual stimulant. However, to Pat and me the West End remains bright even in the half-light, or dark, because of the crowds walking through, or gathering around its precincts. Some aimless, others going to, or coming from, theatres or restaurants. Pat and I join the throng, down Charing Cross Road and into Leicester Square, Shaftesbury Avenue, the Haymarket. We walk with the crowds, chatting to one another vivaciously, laughing a lot. Pairs of American GIs wander among us or lean against buildings as if holding them up. For the Yanks are not only in the war, but on our streets. Before Pearl Harbor and after the fall of France, the cry had been *"Britain stands alone!"* Then Hollywood offered moral support.

Chin up Tommy Atkins,
Be a stout fella,
Chin up, cheerio, carry on,
There's a whole world behind you shouting
Stout fella.[7]

I first heard this song at the Garden City cinema, having first waited outside to ask an adult to pretend that I was with her, and so take me into an 'A' film.

---

6. Hughie Charles, Louie Elton, *When They Sound the Last All Clear*, 1941.
7. Hubert Gregg, *I'm Going to Get Lit Up*, 1943.

Now that the Americans are over here, sooner or later, one of a pair of GIs will chat us up, walking behind us, talking loudly, their remarks obviously addressed for our hearing. Or sometimes they speak to us directly; *"hi ya gals, where ya goin?"* We allow them to walk with us. Sex is not part of the programme, for we are 'good' girls and, anyway, would not risk an illegitimate pregnancy. Looked at coldly, sex frightens me, the thought of being entered presenting itself as an invasion. No, all Pat and I want is the excitement of talking with men in uniform, to be admired, to be recognised as adult women. At the dance-halls we rarely meet Americans, for their method of dancing in their own space is not acceptable to British dance-halls where the object is to keep moving around the floor. The GIs, unable to adapt to our ways, and with no homes to go to, spend their leisure time in the streets, watching the passing show and calling out to girls.

British servicemen are piqued because the GIs, wrapped in Hollywood glamour, giving out largesse and dressed in smart uniforms, are able to snap up the girls. The British sneer: *"The only thing wrong with the Yanks is they're over-sexed, over-paid and over here."* To which the Americans reply: *"The British are under-sexed, under-paid and under Eisenhower"*; General Eisenhower, Commander in Chief of Allied Forces. The Americans said also—referring to the large, whale-shaped barrage balloons high in the sky and surrounding Britain—*"if you cut the ropes, the island would sink."* Of course, the Russians also are in the war, the Soviet Union having been invaded by the Nazis in June 1941. The Communist Party deciding overnight that this was no longer a capitalist war, but one against fascism. However, we never saw a Russian. They were not on our streets.

Sometimes, we go with two GIs into a crowded pub, but if we decide that they are not for us, that they might demand more than we are willing to give, might become difficult to handle, Pat, rolling her green eyes says, *"we're going to powder our noses."* Then we disappear towards the Ladies, only to exit quickly and run giggling along the busy street.

I guess my parents put up with a lot from me, and at times they must have worried that I would be caught by a bomb, or something almost as bad, and never come home at all. But I didn't understand how they must have felt until I had teenage children of my own. But there was one occasion in which, in their eyes, I went too far: Pat's older sister, 'Goo', her brother Douglas and

Pat are going to Lyons Corner House in Coventry Street, Leicester Square, for an evening meal, and they invite me to join them. 'Goo'—who obtained her nickname as a baby because, like Pat, she has large green eyes *"like gooseberries,"* says Pat—had been married. By coincidence, her husband was a son of the Gruhn bakery family, and Goo had met my Uncle Henry, also a baker. The marriage had failed and she is now walking out with a widower, Luigi Polessi, manager of the Savoy Grill. A further coincidence ordains that Polessi is to receive a bequest of £100 in the Will of my father's customer Sir Louis Sterling; Sterling, who, when we were children, had sent our family hampers of food on high days and holidays. The Sterling Library at University College, London, holding Hanley's letters and many others to, and from, my father.

The evening out at the Corner House may have been to celebrate Douglas' return home from war work in the Midlands, where he had been billeted on a family in Erdington. From there he had sent letters home exaggerating the strangeness of the environment in which he had found himself, and claiming that a girl, whom he insisted was named Faith Doom, was attempting to get him to the altar. Douglas, fair-haired and of average height, had failed the medical for the Services, due to a lameness in one leg. *"He cried when he was rejected,"* Pat says to me, her eyes big, her mouth drooping. The family's eldest brother is a Chindit in Burma with Major Wingate. Although our party at the Corner House consists of the four of us only, one table among the midst of many, the orchestra playing, the bright lights shining, the sound of crockery clattering and cutlery clinking, waiters bustling to and fro, our laughter, our merriment and expansiveness fills the space, to blend with that of the people at surrounding tables, and soon our party grows. To our table we attract two more girls, a young man and an older man named 'Jigger'; A funny ha-ha name, because at that time a loose three-quarter length coat, which I myself wore, was known as a 'jigger'. And as Lyons Corner House is open all night, the evening passes without anyone calling *"time!"*:

> *I cried for madder music and for stronger wine,*
> *But when the feast is finished and the lamps expire,*

Then falls my shadow, Cynara![8]

We have missed the last tube train and the last bus. We will have to walk home from Leicester Square to Muswell Hill. My alcoholic haze lifts for a moment and I say in consternatio,n *"what will my mother say! She'll be worried!"* *"You'll have to stay at our house"* says Goo. I look around for a phone. We are not on the phone at home—very few people were in those days—but a blue police box stands at the top of Wilton Road in Colney Hatch Lane. I find a phone box and somehow get through to ask a policeman to go to Wilton Road and tell my mother that I have missed the last train and will stay the night with Pat. At long last we arrive at the Moors' house, having sung and danced for the first part of the journey, linking arms like Judy Garland (as Dorothy), the cowardly lion (Bert Lahr, who shares my surname), and the tin man. *"Follow the yellow brick road, follow the yellow brick road, follow, follow, follow, follow,"* kicking our legs and feet forward. But soon we grow tired and the walk becomes a trudge. When we arrive at Muswell Hill Road some time after 2 a.m. I feel as if I have made the Long March. But, as we creep slowly down the hill, I spy the figure of my father waiting outside the Moors' house and as we draw nearer he begins to shout and gesticulate. When Mrs. Moors opens the front door, he growls at her. Unceremoniously and protesting that I can't walk a further step, I am dragged back to Wilton Road. No doubt, when the policeman had knocked at the door, for one dreadful moment my parents had feared the worst. I was lying somewhere injured, or even dead—or perhaps they thought that once again they were to be shipped away for internment. But my mother expresses her terror to me by saying, *"how could you tell a policeman you were spending the night with Pat! How could he know that wasn't a man! Everyone will think you're a bad girl!"*

This doesn't end my friendship with Pat and the Moors, but I am a little shame-faced when next I meet them. Pat is surprised at my parents' reaction and especially that they blame her for leading me astray. For, as she says, her own mother always puts the blame squarely on her, and not on her friends. of course, my mother is critical of my friendship with Pat, as she has been of all my friends, and now I am almost grown up, she wants me to be at the centre of a group of intellectual or talented people. She

8. 'Cynara', Ernest Dowson (1867-1900)

cannot bear for me to follow the frivolous pursuits of teenage girls, my peer group.

Pat and I go often during the day at a weekend to a Lyons Corner House, in Coventry Street, in Tottenham Court Road or at Marble Arch. These are truly people's palaces with their large rooms lit by chandeliers, an orchestra playing, the musicians in dress suits, their melodies blending into the chatter of people around the white clothed tables waited on by tail-coated waiters. *Table d'hote* or a set meal. Occasionally, we go into the Salad Bowl, where half-a-crown allows customers to help themselves to as much as they can eat from various large bowls of salads. Pat and I go back to snatch a second dessert of gateau also, although I suspect that this is not included in the price. Once we have been served with a meal, Pat looks around at the surrounding tables to spy out what is now called 'talent'. Having marked her quarry, she takes out a packet of cigarettes which she keeps for this purpose, and, holding one between two fingers, sways over to the young man to ask breathlessly, her green eyes flashing, *"have you got a light?"* Sometimes, this takes us into conversation with the man, at other times it wins Pat a smile.

In the first floor self-contained flat in the Moors' house lives Mrs. Mary Harris, together with a ten-year-old daughter Sylvie, brown-haired and brown eyed, and a blonde baby boy. Mary is somewhere in her thirties, has soft brown hair, an anxious expression, a retiring manner and the most crossed eyes I have ever seen. The pupils and irises twisted out of alignment. Her husband, a civil engineer, works away. *"She says we will meet him,"* Pat tells me, *"He does come home sometimes. But he doesn't like the baby because it's a boy."* Pat frowns. *"He only likes Sylvie and they have to keep the baby out of his way."* I envision this woman's dilemma. I see her moving a small child around from room to room, shushing his cries. What does she do if he cries at night? *"She says it's because her husband was married before and has two sons, horrible boys. that's why her husband doesn't like boys,"* says Pat seriously. To me this is drama, and in my head, behind my eyes, an emotional Hollywood script is played out leading to a reconciliation between father and son, or sons.

Mary Harris is acquainted with several Norwegians in the RAF and billeted together in a large house in Highgate. Each of them bearing the designation 'Norway' on their shoulder tags. These blonde, bluff Norwegians, escaped from their Nazi-occupied country, for whom there is no tomorrow, who do not know when, if ever, they will return to their native land and, therefore, console themselves with heavy drinking and womanising. Although, it might be thought that one precludes the other. Mary invites me and Pat together with Goo to a party at the Highgate house, but Goo maintains a sharp eye on our drinking and she warns the Norwegians of Pat and my ages. For a time Pat is enamoured with a Norwegian named Olaf, pronounced 'All off', so that I quip ,"*is it all on, or all off with Olaf?*" But she is never alone with him. She can flirt with him only in the company of others.

"*Olaf says how much Mary's baby looks like the children in Norway,*" Pat says innocently, and something goes click in my head. It is not until some time after the war that I meet Pat and she tells me that her family knew now that a Norwegian had fathered Mary Harris' baby son. The affair long over, the man returned to Norway. "*Her husband wasn't mean to her,*" Pat says. "*He was very good, he always gave her money.*" She is obviously annoyed at Mary's deception. I ask after Sylvie. "*Her father's sent her to boarding school,*" Pat says. A few years later, I see Mrs. Harris and her son, now aged about fourteen, at Muswell Hill Broadway, walking close together, as if they are the only people in the world.

Hyde Park

*I leave the Law Society for Insurance: My boss has an accident: The
horrors of the Royal Exchange: Pat Moors again: Madeleine lets
me down: Community singing: Speakers' Corner: Prince Monolulu:
Sammy Marks once more: Jean: The Hackney Empire: The
International Youth Centre, Pont Street: Youth House, Camden Road:
I try once more to learn the violin: I obtain a medical certificate in order
to change my job: I take a job with a Surveyor and cannot cope.*

After some ten months at the Law Society, having found
myself caught and imprisoned within mountains of files
and shut away in grey pop-up pictures, I struggle from
out of the miserable morass of lamentable human relationships,
breaking free by giving in my notice. On my leaving day the girls
present me with a silver charm bracelet. *"They must like you a lot to
give you that,"* says John Hicks admiringly. He is a British soldier
dressed in rough khaki, no more than twenty years of age, of
medium height, with light brown hair. I cannot remember where
we met, but we have taken to each other immediately. We go to
the pictures or for walks on Hampstead Heath where I make
him laugh by my antics of jumping up to touch the branches of
trees. We talk and we laugh a lot, but I treat him merely as a companion. I do not want him to think that I expect any more from
him than friendship. Employed at the Law Society on divorce, I
say airily that I don't believe in love or marriage, as if I mean it.
John murmurs that it doesn't have to be like that, but I pretend
to hold to my view of marital disharmony. Soon after I leave
the Law Society, John is moved out of London to another base,
promising to write. But he never does so, and each day I watch
for a non-existent letter on the mat, or picked up by my mother
and perched on the high mantelpiece in the living-room. Inside I
hurt. I am surprised at this pain with me by day and night should
I wake. I have never felt like this before. I have John's address in

Exeter, but it is not done for a girl to write first; he will think I am pursuing him. I will make myself cheap. This is what I have been taught. and so I work through my misery and it is some weeks before the pain of loss eases and in relief I return to my normal life.

I find a job with the British Equitable Insurance Society at an office in Piccadilly, on an upper floor of a building next door to the American Services Club, the Stage Door Canteen:

> *I left my heart at the Stage Door Canteen,*
> *I left it there with a girl called Eileen.*
> *A soldier boy without a heart,*
> *Has two stripes on him from the start,*
> *And my heart's at the Stage Door Canteen.*

I sit at a desk in front of a small peg-type switchboard and a typewriter. A little forward and to the right of me is a gated counter. Drawers of file cards are placed to the side of the counter and it is while looking through these that I come across the name of our family friend Ralph Hoddinott as an agent. He had, as a very young man, been a customer at the bookshop, and Oonagh had always said that when she grew up she would marry him. He had written to my parents once or twice from Greece while in the army, but after that we had lost touch, and I do not see him again until the day of my father's funeral. He had come in response to Oonagh's announcement in *The Times*, his face in middle-age folded in upon itself.

Following the funeral, we sit in the rose garden of the John Baird pub at Muswell Hill Broadway and Oonagh asks Hoddinott for his address. He hands her a card which we examine later, to find that it sets out his name only. No address. He has come prepared for a day of nostalgia for his youth and in memory of my father, but no strings.

The Manager at the British Equitable, Mr. Pearson, handsome, grey-haired and middle-aged shares an office with me, but he is out a good deal and so I am left to my own devices. In the building's communal washroom, I meet girls from other firms and with the solidarity of youth we are immediately friendly. In the office opposite mine, across the passage, is an Agent who finds work for Variety artists. Two girls are employed here, crowded together in a small space in the midst of files. Most of the artists registered with this Agency are minor performers, but occasionally Mavis, plump and with shoulder-length fair hair, mentions someone of whom I have heard. One of these is an Irishman, Pat something or other, famous for a song which goes:

> *tooralooraloora, tooralooralie,*
> *tooralooraloora, it's an Irish lullaby.*[1]

I have been working for British Equitable for a month or two only, when Mr. Pearson, driving his car to his home in Oxford, crashes into the back of a lorry. Crash! Bang! Mr. Pearson is flung forward onto the steering wheel which pierces his chest and pins him to his seat. Barely conscious, there he stays until the ambulance, bell ringing wildly, arrives to take him to Radcliffe Hospital. A day or two later, Mr. Pearson's wife arrives to hurriedly clear his desk. I know that note-paper in one of the drawers indicates that he is doing some insurance work for himself, and have determined to hide such evidence from the prying eyes of the parent company, located at the Royal Exchange, but Mrs. Pearson beats me to it.

Previous to Mr. Pearson's accident, it had been agreed that I go once a week to the Royal Exchange for training. Now, much to my dismay, I must work there on two days of each week. The way I see it, the best part of working at the Royal Exchange is climbing up the impressive stone steps and walking through the neo-classical columns on either side, for I imagine silent watchers impressed at my importance. Once inside this gloomy building I travel in the narrow lift, all mirror and gilt, to an upper floor, where I am confined in a drab office, the windows opaque. Here I sit together with several older women and a dragon of a supervisor. They pay little attention to me, but when one of their fellows leaves the room immediately, as if a signal had been given, the women begin to tear her character apart. Soon the footsteps of the absent friend are heard returning and in that instance, when she takes hold of the handle to the door, and without a second's hesitation or break, the conversation turns to other matters. The broken bits of her character kicked out of sight.

I am given schedules to type and now I must stay in my seat, no wandering around the building or talking to girls in other offices. If ever I do have a few minutes break, I express my frus-

---

1. *Too-Ra-Loo-Ra-Loo-Ral (That's an Irish Lullaby)*, composed by James Royce Shannon (1881–1946), later popularised by Bing Crosby in 1944's *Going My Way*.

trated imagination in writing poetry, with the result that later, when Mr. Pearson is well again, I must answer the small switchboard and, in putting the call through to Mr. Pearson at his desk, I hear the Supervisor exclaim, *"I found her writing a poem!"* She is obviously appalled. On a Saturday, I worked at the Piccadilly office until mid-day, and on one of these Saturdays Madeleine had arranged to meet me outside the building together with a GI and his friend, with whom she had made for me a blind date. I leave the office promptly and wait in the street, office workers hurrying by, couples sauntering past, their arms linked, GIs coming and going in and out of the Stage Door Canteen. Piccadilly, a hive of activity, in the midst of which the boarded up plinth on which Eros once stood, overlooks the Circus. I stand in the street for an hour, anxiously searching passing faces for Madeleine. Watching for two GIs either side of my short friend. I grow hungry and re-enter the office for a moment to consume a half pint of milk bought for tea, drinking it straight from the bottle, gulping it down in case Madeleine and the GIs arrive during my absence. The fat of the milk, together with my apprehension that Madeleine and the GIs have left me in the lurch, makes me nauseous and at last I go home almost in tears.

Later, in the afternoon, I decide to call at Aunt Kitty's house and there I find Madeleine and the two GIs sitting at a table in the living-room, talking, laughing and sipping tea. Stella and her daughter, Sybil, are at the house and it soon becomes clear to me that the GI assigned to me, named Bud, is interested in her. A girl of about twenty years against his twenty-six or twenty-seven and my seventeen. She is tall, almost of a height with Bud, slim and in my eyes, plain, but very lively. She plays the fool, as if she has based herself on one of the Hollywood comediennes, such as Joan Davis; a comedy routine perhaps first adopted to counter a commandeering mother. Sybil is given to little shrieks of laughter. She sits on a chair and acts as if it is about to collapse under her, grasping its sides and back, rolling her eyes; she jumps and grabs Bud's arm and says *"let's dance!"* steering him around the furniture, kicking her legs up behind her. She makes him laugh and he loves it. I have no feeling about Bud one way or the other, for he is a stranger, but I am chagrined that Madeleine has put me into such a situation and has also, with no thought, left me standing and waiting in Piccadilly. She could have at least phoned me at the office, to tell me of the change of plan. This incident was the beginning of the end of our friendship.

Pat works also in Piccadilly, for she has left her job at Estates Gazette. Now she works for a firm which makes military uniforms for Officers, both everyday and dress. Golden braid, gold buttons, epaulettes, reds and navy blues, tartans, smartly pressed trousers, shiny black belts, insignia designating different regiments—all line up stiffly on parade, their materials cut by Mr. Barnett, a small bowed tailor, whose real name is Tuschneider, for he is the father of Edith Tuschneider, whom Pat and I have met at the International Youth Centre in Pont Street, Knightsbridge. Mr. Tuschneider, overawed by the brilliance and authority of the work in which he is engaged, on first entering the workshop to take his scissors to cloth, had been challenged by the would-be uniform of a General, who raps out at him *"name?"* Mr. Tuschneider hesitates, his eyes taking in the uniforms of Majors, Captains and other Officers lining the walls, symbols of the might of the British Empire, and he cannot bring himself to reply *"Tuschneider."* Instead, as he is balding and regrets the loss of his hair, he replies *"Barnett."*

Pat's office is a small room off the workshop and she must use a three-bank Olivetti typewriter, instead of the normal four-bank. This makes a nonsense of touch-typing, but Pat doesn't seem to mind.

Pat and I go to Speakers' Corner at Marble Arch where we join in the Community singing, encouraged by the government as a morale builder. We sing our way through the war. Songs from the First World War—*Keep the Home Fires Burning; It's a Long Way to Tipperarary*—and songs from the Second World War—*Roll Out the Barrel* (changing the last line to *"The Yanks are here!"*); *The Quartermaster's Stores; Lords of the Air; Run Rabbit Run; Goodnight Children Everywhere; Bless 'em All; Kiss me Goodnight Sergeant Major; Mister Brown of London Town; The White Cliffs of Dover; Maybe it's Because I'm a Londoner,* and:

> *I'm going to get lit up when the lights go up in London,*
> *I'm going to get lit up as I've never been before,*
> *You will find me on the tiles,*
> *You will find me wreathed in smiles,*
> *I'm going to get so blooming lit up,*
> *I'll be visible for miles.*

And we sing sentimental songs about love and the moon in June:

> *Moonlight becomes you,*
> *It goes with your hair.*

One song following another, together a circle of men and women singing out their hearts, while around us speakers, on home-made stands, shout out their philosophies, religious or political. We are lost in our own voices. On one occasion, Pat and I join a group singing in Welsh and, as Pat had been evacuated to Wales at the beginning of the war, she sings:

> *Mae bys Meri Ann wedi brifo,*
> *A dafydd y gwas ddim yn iach,*
> *Mae'r baban yn y crud yn crio,*
> *A'r gath wedi sgrapo Joni bach,*
> *Sospan fach yn berwi ar y tan,*
> *Sospan fawr yn berwi ar y llawr.*

Airmen greet her as a compatriot. *"You can always tell a Welsh girl,"* they say, *"they're prettier than all the others!"* Pat's eldest sister is married to a Welshman, the only one of the Moors girls to marry a man from the British Isles, although Mrs. Moors' stated aim had been for all her girls to marry Englishmen.

Before returning home, Pat and I go into the Dorchester, walking through the foyer as if we belong there, and make our way to their swish Ladies, perfumed, soft lights, shiny mirrors. We use the WC, wash our faces, renew our make-up and comb our hair. In those days I was always combing my hair. Having renovated our faces, we walk nonchalantly through the hotel lobby, Pat hopeful of meeting a handsome millionaire.

Later, I am to go to Speakers' Corner with my cousin Seema, two years younger than me, and who has grown into a pretty round-faced girl. She is an apprentice hairdresser in a salon at Temple Fortune, and once a week I act as her model at an evening class at the Regent Street Polytechnic, where she washes and sets my hair. At Speakers' Corner we stand in a circle with some half-a-dozen others, including an American sailor:

> *Is you is or is you ain't my baby?*

A tall dark handsome boy leads us. Having sung our fill, some eight of us go across the road to a cafe. We sit around a table and exchange names. Seema looks at Dave, the dark youth; *"You're*

Jewish," she says smiling, *"so am I."* *"So am I,"* says the American sailor, *"so am I"* says a red-headed girl, and so it continues around the table, even I admit to having a Jewish mother. Until we come to a woman somewhere in her twenties, a little dowdy, a provincial accent. Desperate to remain one of us, she finds a Jewish forebear. *"I think my grandfather was a little Jewish,"* she says. Later still, I am to go to Speakers' Corner alone to listen to the speakers, and on 20th July 1946 *Forward* publishes an article I have written about Hyde Park. *Forward* is a left-wing newspaper published in Glasgow by Emrys Hughes MP, who is Keir Hardie's son-in-law. I wrote about Tony Turner, the Socialist Party of Great Britain speaker, who always has the highest platform and the biggest and most attentive crowd in the Park. He silences any would-be hecklers with wit. When, during the war, a soldier took exception to some of his remarks and shouted at him; *"I'm fighting for the likes of you!"* Tony replied calmly, *"I give you my full permission to stop fighting for me this instant."* Prince Monolulu, the West Indian race-course tipster who dresses in long clothes, sandals and a head-dress of red, white and blue ostrich feathers, appears in the Park carrying the Union Jack, the Stars and Stripes, Star of David, the Czechoslovakian flag and the French flag. He tells the crowd surprising facts about the countries these flags represent, for instance, that Anne Boleyn was really a Czech woman named Anna Poleyni. Monolulu punctuates his sentences with the word 'bleddy'.

Sammy Marks who declaims, *"you say the Jews run the black market. Well, even if it were true, they could never make as much money out of it as the Salvation Army, the Church Brigade, Bible societies, Church schools and millions of men with their collars turned back to front, have made out of one dead Jew—and a foreign Jew at that!"* There is also Mr. Norris, a right-wing speaker from the Individualist Society who attempts to prove the competence of private enterprise. But he gets a rough ride from the hecklers. The religious speakers are a hecklers' delight, most of them regarded as cranks. Mabel, a middle-aged grey-haired woman, who rails against the young women in her audience, shrieking at them, *"painted hussies!"* Or Daniel Forbes, who claims that America is the promised land, he knows this for a fact for he has spent time in almost every jail in the States. On one Sunday morning, while I am wandering at Speakers' Corner, a doodlebug buzzes its way across the park, above our heads. Everyone, including me, runs to shelter under a hedge. Later, I am to remark that the religious speakers ceasing their shoutings about the glories of heaven, had been the first to make for the bushes;

Everybody talkin' about heaven, ain't goin' there.[2]

Hyde Park is to become my University, for it is in the small 'seminar' groups, especially one led by a large man named Carpenter, a customer in my father's shop, that I become interested in reading Karl Marx. I push myself into the group, making my way to the front, fearful that otherwise I might miss some great truth which will lay the world bare for me. And yet this same interest means that I write no more for *Forward* and, in fact, give up writing altogether for a very long time. Emrys Hughes, a square-set, grey-haired man with a pleasant smile, had invited me to the House of Commons to take tea. He had offered me a weekly column, but I have become involved in Trotskyism, and am so blinded by names and theories of which I know nothing, thrown back and forth, dominant men forming the 'leadership' who appear to encompass all knowledge, that I convince myself that I am not competent to write anything worthwhile.

While I am wandering alone one day at Speakers' Corner, I meet Jean, a girl of my own age. She stands on the periphery of a crowd, a slim figure, a little taller than myself, dressed neatly, her brown hair forced into curls, her face carefully made up with a little lipstick and powder. I am alone, but her aloneness crosses over into loneliness. She is a waif and stray on the edge of the crowd. She speaks to me and I register a cockney accent; an accent of which my mother would disapprove. At this distance in time, I cannot remember what she said, probably something innocuous like *"do you come here often?"* and soon we are walking together across the park on our way to a cup of tea. It must be almost summer, for Jean insists on carrying my coat. Not in a bullying manner. Now that she has found a friend, she is eager to prove her worth. We walk along the Edgware Road and she tells me that she was brought up in the National Children's Home and is at Marble Arch to visit one of the sponsors of the Home; *"She weren't in."* I see a large well-kept middle-class house occupied by a couple akin to Mr. and Mrs. Shillan, who are proving their right to be wealthy by patronising the 'unfortunate'. We find a

---

2. 'Walk Over God's Heaven' by Thomas Dorsey.

cafe to sit at a small table in the corner and Jean tells me her story. She works in a factory. *"When I were fourteen and left school,"* she says, *"they put me in service, but I run away. They put me somewhere else in service and I run away again. So they asked me why I weren't happy and what I wanted to do. so I said 'I want to work in a factory'."* I am shocked that Jean had not first been asked her preference, and yet pleasantly surprised that the Authorities had at last seen sense. *"I don't like service,"* Jean adds, *"you're at their beck and call all day long. They never leave you alone. I like to be independent."*

I admit to Jean that I work in an office and hope that she does not think of me as a snob, but I need not have worried. At that time factory work was lauded as war-work. The old working-class/lower middle-class stratification of jobs had been eroded for the present, and the pyramid of factory work at the bottom, shop work slightly above and office work at the top, now lies on its side. Jean lives in Hackney, off Mare Street, in lodgings used by the National Children's Home for its leavers. *"Mrs. Adams is the landlady,"* Jean tells me, *"I'm all right with 'er because I don't get in late and I keep myself to myself."* She looks at me glumly. *"Shirley, who I shared with, was out with boys all the time and didn't come in 'til two or three in the morning."* As Jean speaks, the tone of her voice becomes censorious and I see behind her an army of stony-faced men and women, their mouths opening and shutting—you must not, not, not, not, not. *"So Mrs. Adams slung 'er out."* Jean tells me that she isn't going to let boys take advantage of her. *"They're only after one thing,"* she says, pulling a face. She is a 'good' girl.

I meet Jean outside her lodgings, a tall grey house, and we walk to the Hackney Empire. Jean points out some prefabs. *"One of the women in there come 'ome and found 'er husband and two daughters 'ad been killed by a bomb. The woman walked up and down Mare Street, up and down, up and down, no one could stop her."* I see the woman in a frenzy, walking jerkily up the street, turning to walk back again when too far from her destroyed home, moving quickly in the opposite direction, her perpetual motion oiled by shock and grief. We speak about the disaster at Bethnal Green tube station on 3rd March 1943 when hundreds of people had dashed down the stairs at what they thought was the beginning of a raid; a woman carrying a baby trips on the stairs, a man falls over her, and within minutes 178 people have been crushed to death. In 1993 it is revealed that the army testing new booming guns in a nearby park had caused the panic.

At the Hackney Empire, we sit on red plush seats, gilt and gilded mirrors on every side and it is there that I see the Cheeky Chappie himself, Max Miller, dressed in a colourful silk jacket, plus-fours and spats:

> I like a girl who says she won't,
> but looks as if she might!

I meet Jean about once or twice a month, and on one of these occasions she tells me of a boy she has met. He lives down the road to her lodgings and she thinks he likes her. He is joining up soon, but has promised to write and see her when on leave. Her whole face lights up and I rejoice that at last she will be happy. And then I lose touch with her and it is only by chance that I meet her some three years later, after the war, once again at Marble Arch. But this time I am outside the gates to sell *The Socialist Appeal*. Jean appears before me as if from nowhere and I, not at first recognising her, pull a paper out of the bundle, but she pushes it away. *"Sheila!"* she is delighted to see me. But this is not the Jean I had known—neat, anxious, reaching out for a handhold or foothold. This Jean is brash, flamboyant, over-made up, skirt short and revealing, her movements exaggerated. *"Come for a walk,"* she says to me and, tucking the papers under my arm, I accompany her along the Edgware Road. I walk hesitantly, Jean swaggers. Every now and then she greets a girl standing in a doorway and they exchange a few words which come over to me only as broad syllables. Jean is on the game, on the streets, a prostitute. At last I return to my sales pitch and Jean goes her own way. I am never to see her again and am left wondering what turn of fate had taken Jean into prostitution.

I join the International Youth Centre in Pont Street and occasionally Pat accompanies me there. However, it is not her scene, for most of the members are left-wing students, or young Jewish refugees from Nazi Germany or Austria, also politically minded. The fact that most of them confuse Stalinism with socialism does not detract from their idealism and hope for a post-war socially just society. But I have many an argument with these members over the role of the Communist Party during the Spanish Civil War, or on other matters. When I become friendly with Ann, we go together to the IYC. Ann comes from a political family. Her father had been a member of the Independent Labour Party and she had grown up with a framed photo of Keir Hardie hung on the sitting-room wall. I know little of Keir Hardie, for Marx and Engels are my parents' mentors. Although my father has a favourite story about Keir Hardie who, it appears, had not long after my father's arrival in England, stepped off the pavement in front of my father's bicycle. My father dismounts, brushes down the bowled over Keir Hardie and sends him on his way. *"I daresay that hastened his death,"* says my father, for Hardie had died a few years later in 1915. A pacifist, he was heart-broken by the advent of, and support for World War I.

Ann, for a few years following the age of nine, had been sexually abused by an older brother, but she had not told her parents. It was a secret between brother and sister. She had told a friend at school and wondered why she didn't get pregnant. *"Perhaps you can't have a baby with your brother,"* says her friend helpfully. Sex, therefore, has become no more than a part of Ann's everyday experience and she expects men and boys to crown their dates by entering her. Eventually, her older sister, Jenny, who has found out about these affairs, warns Ann that no one will ever marry her if she continues to offer her favours freely. Ann decides from then on to be more selective, but the first time she refuses a member of the IYC, a young sailor who usually 'makes out' with her on Hampstead Heath, he becomes very angry and never wants to see her again. *"Do you think I'd walk up here, all over the heath, with you for nothing? You've been leading me on!"* Some time later, Ann, who is lodging with a brother and sister-in-law, decides to strike out on her own, and asks me to share a flat with her. I am more than willing, but unfortunately, puzzled over the matter of sexual morality, I had imparted some of the details of Ann's lifestyle to my mother. Now my mother is convinced that, should I share a flat with Ann, I would end up 'on the game'. She becomes so angry and hysterical I have to tell Ann, shamefacedly, that I can't leave home. I am a Mummy's girl. Eventually, Ann finds a flat-share with two other girls.

The IYC is situated in a tall house built for the gentry and covers several floors. It is open seven days of each week, providing a myriad of activities—folk dancing, ballroom dancing, discussion groups, music appreciation groups, speakers on various subjects and there are many places where members can merely sit and talk together. There is a canteen on the ground floor and a bar on the first, where I think of myself as blasé for asking for *"half a pint of wallop."* I become active is producing the wall-newspaper, pinned to the wall immediately outside the open door of the bar; therefore, when a queue forms I am sure that someone must read it while waiting! The IYC is always a busy, lively place where I make acquaintances rather than friends. I can remember cycling to Hampton Court with Archie Moody, a red-haired boy, and Hermann Essinger, a Jewish boy from Austria who lives in Muswell Hill. The photos in my album show me standing together with Hermann Essinger, his arm about my shoulders, my hair arranged in a frontal bang which is achieved by a ribbon tied at the back of the head, the front hair being rolled round under the ribbon. I wear navy blue slacks, a bomber jacket and sandals. Hermann dresses in baggy trousers and jacket. Archie, who took this snapshot, now hands the camera to Hermann, and poses with me. Archie wears long shorts and a zipped up cardigan. He looks at me and I look ahead, my tongue in my cheek. In the background is foliage. The date of this photo is 5th May 1946. The war has been over for a year, but post-war organisation is slow to change. Only the bombs and threat of bombs are missing.

I can recall few of the myriad of persons I met at the IYC— except for Edith Tuschneider, the daughter of Mr. Barnett the tailor, who remains for me an 18-20 year old girl, attractive in face and figure, both of which have become shadowy in my memory over the years so that now I see only dark wavy hair, a round face and a figure taller than myself. There is also Naomi, whom I see always as a pale, slim girl with worried expression, for I meet her shortly before she commits suicide by gas. At the time I am working at Transport House for the Transport and General Workers Union, and by chance meet Naomi at a bus stop in Whitehall. I greet her and speak only of myself, ignoring her white face and agitated movements. I do not know enough of her life outside the IYC to ask her about herself, nor have I developed any great talent at drawing people out. Naomi listens to me, she always listens and expresses admiration for observations and knowledge which appear to be new to her. A week or two later I meet Edith, who tells me that Naomi's death had been announced in the *Jewish Chronicle*. I am left wondering whether the right word from me might have prevented her death.

Then, there was Amelia. A short, black-haired girl given to speaking without first thinking, always a little wild in her movements. On one occasion I call IYC while she is manning the phone: instead of answering "IYC," she gives an alternative phone number, which I do not recognise. *"Wrong number"* I say and hang up. Three times this occurs when, with astonishment, I recognise Amelia's gravelly, yet peremptory, voice. *"Is that you, Amelia?"* I ask. I am amazed that of all the phone numbers in London, I should choose by accident to call her at home. Fortunately, the mix-up is eventually sorted out.

There is the fair-haired Jewish boy who tells a group of us that as he could 'pass' he had joined the British Union of Fascists before the war, as a spy. Therefore, he was able to leak plans to the local Jewish Defence Force.

Together with Ann, I go also to Youth House in the Camden road, Islington. Youth House is situated in a solid Victorian house, stone steps leading up to the front door, and as I pass over the threshold I am caught up in a world outside time. The house is residential, and those men and women who live there seem to me to have no life outside it. Should they step outside the front door they would disappear, vanish. The members are in age from the 'teens upwards and yet their style is timeless—hair-styles and dress. It is among the residents that the Stalinists can be found, clinging to a dogma with the intellectual tenacity of the religiose. The only time when Ann and I see a resident of the House outside is one day while we are having tea at the Marble Arch Lyons Corner House. *"Look! There's Max,"* Ann says to me. He is waiting on a table dressed in waiters' tails. We are embarrassed for him because he is a well-read, well-educated refugee, and we are sure that for him such a job must be demeaning. We deliberately look away and never mention to Max that we have seen him at work.

Outsiders bring some life into the House, and many of these are African students, happy to find a welcome and a place to mix socially. Peter Abrahams, a slight yellow man from South Africa, is a member of Youth House and he is later to publish novels set in Western Africa and the Caribbean. He meets at Youth House his second wife, a dark, part-Malaysian girl. Peter's first wife, Dorothy, is a customer in my father's bookshop and one day she comes home from work to find that Peter has abandoned her. Sunday after Sunday she cycles over to Wilton Road to cry on my parents' shoulders. Dorothy is an ungainly plain woman, but she has worked hard to support Peter while he stayed home to write novels.

It is at Youth House that Ann meets a tall, dark young man. *"My name's Stan Johnson,"* he says. He is standing in the community room. I am lounging in an armchair. Ann squats on the carpet. Stan and Ann get into a bantering conversation and he remarks that his name wasn't always Johnson. *"It was unpronounceable, so we had to change it,"* he says, wrinkling his nose. *"I know what you mean,"* says Ann. *"I wish my father had changed ours."* Her surname is Pratt. Stan looks down at her with interest. Perhaps he thinks she is Jewish and by the time he finds this is not so, it is too late. I am working at the British Equitable when Ann phones to tell me that she and Stan are engaged. A pang of jealousy rips through me. Why does no one ask me to become engaged? Now my friend will rarely have time for me. My emotions are mixed and for a moment, manufacturing an excuse that someone is at the counter, I put down the phone to collect my feelings and confine them within the shell of expected response. *"I went to his flat,"* Ann's voice comes down the wire when I again pick up the phone, *"and went to bed. We just felt it was right. Both of us."*

I don't see Ann for some months and when I do, it is at a Common Wealth meeting at Hornsey Town Hall. The engagement is at an end and she is gaunt and very thin. She looks ill. Shortly following the engagement I had been on a bus with Ann's sister Jenny and other Common Wealth members. Jenny says casually *"Ann's got engaged."* *"When's the wedding?"* asks an interested woman. *"Never,"* says Jenny decisively. Now that her prophecy had come true, I felt nothing but sorrow for Ann, who barely speaks to me at this Common Wealth meeting. We are never again to resume the old friendship.

I am bored at British Equitable and unhappy on my days at the Royal Exchange and so decide to give in my notice. Now I remember with nostalgia my days at the Law Society: my wanderings into Lincoln's Inn Fields, Staples Inn, Leather Lane, Ely Place, Furnival Street and Bream Buildings. The brash impermanence of the West End and its crowds of restlessly moving feet cannot compete as a working environment with the dignity and tranquility of Chancery Lane and its environs. The West End is for the evening only. *"It's people you chase after, not places,"* my mother says angrily. My mother is worried by my restlessness and regards my friendships as distracting me from achievement. But back to Chancery Lane I go. This as a result of an evening class in Marylebone where I take violin lessons. I am attempting to build on what I can remember from the lessons given me by Mr. Franks. I dream of putting the violin under my chin, moving my fingers up and down the strings, drawing the bow across and releasing beautiful music, music so spellbinding that all within earshot are bewitched. In conversation with the tutor, a pleasant man in his forties, slim, kind brown eyes, I mention that I would like to find a job in the Chancery Lane area. His face lights up. He has a friend, a Surveyor, who is looking for a Secretary and so an interview is arranged. The Surveyor, a Mr. Stevens, has an office half-way down Chancery Lane, comprising two rooms on the first floor of an old building, so that I must enter by a side door and make my way up a narrow staircase. These rooms are cluttered with files, piles of papers, bound books and office furniture, among which sits the Surveyor, a tall, gruff, grey-haired man. He asks when I can start and I say in the following week, but first I must obtain permission from the Ministry of Labour. At that time, from the age of seventeen everyone in the world of work must be engaged upon work of National Importance. I attend at the Labour Exchange and the clerk refuses me permission to accept the job with Mr. Stevens, at which the job becomes ever more desirable and Chancery Lane a paradise. I burst into tears, much to the clerk's consternation and she looks at me in embarrassment. *"I'm asthmatic,"* I wail, *"not everyone wants to employ me!"* *"If you obtain a medical certificate to that effect,"* says the clerk woodenly, *"we'll reconsider the situation."*

I go to see my doctor at Muswell Hill, a Dr. Blackburn, a tall black-haired, black-eyed man, and he provides me with the necessary certificate. Permission is granted for me to work for Mr. Stevens, but this same certificate is to rebound on me at a future date. Once again I am in an office much of the time alone, for Mr. Stevens leaves me to cope with piles and piles of scribbled notes, the basis of letters, which lie beside my typewriter in this dingy, crowded room. Much of these scribbles date back to the weeks, or even months, when Mr. Stevens was without a secretary. I cannot cope. I do not have the relevant experience. A few years later, I would have sorted the scribblings into piles according to importance and dates etc., but at the time all I can do is plough through them, stumbling from one piece of paper to the next, often attempting without success to decipher Mr. Stevens' writing. I cannot explain my predicament to Mr. Stevens because I do not know how to speak to him. Persons of his age have always been in authority over me and in many ways I remain a schoolgirl, unable to meet adults on their own terms. On one occasion, when I return from lunch, I am aware that there are two men in the office, Mr. Stevens and a friend. Mr. Stevens speaks to me, but I cannot meet his eyes and so look down to the floor, nervously twitching my fingers. *"You didn't recognise me,"* says my tutor at the next lesson, and I blush.

Occasionally, Mr. Stevens dictates a letter to me and I must desert the never-diminishing pile. Some of these dictated letters are to the Conservative Party or to the Freemasons. *"He's a Tory,"* I say to myself crossly, as I start upon deciphering another scribble. Once or twice only do I call on my old work-mates at the Law Society or go for a walk during the dinner-hour with Madge Roberts, but my heart is not in it and I can enjoy my old haunts no more. I am failing, becoming more and more behind with my work and often, in despair, when the Surveyor is away, I leave the office early, shutting away the piles and piles of paperwork. At last Mr. Stevens gives me the sack. This ends also my efforts on the violin, for I am too embarrassed to return to the class. In tears I arrive at my father's bookshop in Little Newport Street. I do not want to work for the Surveyor, but at the same time to be given the sack has shamed me, striking at my already low self-esteem.

Sowing and Reaping

I go with Pat Moors to an agricultural camp: A pilgrimage by bike to Portsmouth, the scene of the fire: Pat and I get drunk: Characters at the camp: A journey to and from the Radcliffe Infirmary which almost ends in disaster: More agricultural camps: Barbara Smith of Walsall: The Laws (previously Lahrs) of Pelsall.

I could not have spent more than three months of my life at agricultural camps and yet they are printed indelibly on my mind. Certainly, I am surprised that no one has written a study of them or a Ph.D. thesis. Or, if someone has done so, I guess the method used would be to list the number of camps set up throughout the country, the percentage of the population attending, their ages, the class composition, the cost effectiveness, the rate of production, and so on. Maybe a few of the persons, now elderly, who had spent their holidays at them would be interviewed. They would be asked whether they had found the work hard, the living conditions spartan, the food adequate, the recompense welcome. Camp organisers would be approached and also those farming during the war. Such a study would have its place in the archives, but it is unlikely to tell my story.

The Ministry of Agriculture posters exhorted the people:

PLOUGH NOW BY DAY AND NIGHT
GROW FOOD FOR THE NATION
FEEDING STUFFS FOR YOUR FARMS
KEEP OUR SHIPS AND MONEY FREE
FOR BUYING VITAL ARMS

One of the few books which I have found to contain a page or two on agricultural camps, although a little biased against the 'townies' who worked at them, states:

> *Townspeople responded to the call to 'Lend a hand on the land' during their summer holidays. Farmers welcomed them during harvest when a great deal of heavy, but simple, work had to be performed in the shortest possible space of time. their value was, at other periods, arguable, to say the least. Girls turned up dressed as for a picnic and were incapacitated in a matter of hours. The countryside which looked so idyllic from bus or train provided the smelliest, hardest work most townsfolk had encountered in their life. Some stuck it out, glad of the chance to earn a few shillings' pocket money in the fresh air… Servicemen from camps in rural areas were considerably more useful. Released from the tedium of barrack life, they gave a good day's work in return, for the bad worker was simply returned to barracks. From 1941 onwards there was the exotic addition of prisoners of war dressed in their blue dungarees with large green patches. Italians were far more popular than Germans. Most actively glad to be out of the war and the guard over them was of the sketchiest. A working party of perhaps thirty or forty Italians, scattered over a wide area with a single soldier technically in charge, became a common sight.*[1]

I am sixteen years of age when I go to my first agricultural camp and Pat is only fifteen. We apply to go to a camp at Alton, Hampshire and are sent a railway warrant. However, we must pay for food and board and will receive from farmers one shilling per hour for our work. In high spirits, we board the train on a Saturday morning and on arrival at the station jump onto the platform, collect our bikes from the guards' van, wheeling them with one hand, lugging a case with the other. Four boys wait for us, watching as we walk along the platform. We have noticed them sitting in the next carriage of the Pullman train, but have ignored their stares whenever we pass along the corridor. *"Carry your case?"* a redhead asks Pat. His accent is London. And she gladly relinquishes its weight. The boys themselves are travelling very light, their belongings in small battered suitcases. A fair-headed boy is good enough to carry my case, and so we find our way to the camp, walking up a country lane until we spy a field

1. E.R. Chamberlain, *Life in Wartime Britain*, ed. Peter Quennell: B.T. Batsford Ltd. 1972, reprinted 1985.

set out with khaki coloured bell tents, as if it were a harvest of giant mushrooms. Later, I am to write carelessly to my mother: *"We got off with four boys at the station and they carried our suitcases."* Of course, I mean 'got off the train', but my mother takes 'got off' in its colloquial sense which is 'flirted' or worse. And so I am to return home to a tirade which is aimed at my scrawling writing and loose phraseology. *"Mr. Taylor says that if that's the result of a grammar school education, he doesn't think much of it!"*

Having reported to a Nissen hut used as an office, Pat and I are directed to a bell tent which we are to share with four other girls, the straw palliasses placed with one end against the centre pole and the other end against the circular canvas. Having dumped our cases on the mattress, we go over to the dinner hut. Most of the workers are girls like ourselves, but there are a sprinkling of teenage boys, and we sit with the boys we have met at the station. The boys' names are Gary, Stephen, John and Richard, and Pat spends the next half hour in calling them by the wrong names. This is one of her favourite ploys for when we are out with boys she calls her boy by every name she can think of, except his own. After he has corrected her for the fourth or fifth time and is showing signs of annoyance, Pat puts on her Scarlett O'Hara voice and says plaintively, *"poor silly ole me, I know so many boys I just can't remember all their names."* This drives the fellows wild for her, Pat says.

After the meal, we explore the terrain, walking with the boys over the fields to clamber to the top of a haystack. Pat returns to the tent for something forgotten, but the boys sit looking at me, and without Pat I am at a loss. I do not know what to say. *"Aren't you afraid to be alone with us?"* Redhead asks suddenly. He dangles one leg carelessly over the side of the stack. The fair boy sits with knees drawn up, his arms around them. The dark boy half sits, half lies. The youngest of the group lies prone. Should I be afraid? I don't know. *"No,"* I say, embarrassed, hoping that Pat will soon return. *"I expect you want to get married, like all girls,"* declares Redhead, *"and not have to work any more. Take your old man's wages."* *"Yeah!"* chimes in Fair head, *"grab his wages on a Friday."* *"I work,"* I reply defensively, *"I'm in an office."* *"In an office!"* they jeer: *"That's not work!"* I reply, desperately, *"when a girl's married she has to do all the housework and look after the children."* *"Housework!"* exclaims Redhead, *"that's not work!"* and the other boys agree with him.

At night I lie on a straw palliasse covered with rough army issue blankets alongside four to six girls on their mattresses. The boys' tents are in another part of the field. Our heads against the canvas, our feet against the centre pole. From above we must resemble the patterns of people shown in Hollywood spectaculars. In the morning we will find the ground damp from dew, so that clothing must be laid at night on the mattresses, or hung from the tent pole, although many a time I dress in the morning in cold, wet clothing. Morning comes too soon, for we have been to a local 'hop' in a church hall the night before, a dance which had not begun until 9 p.m., and it is not until after midnight that we fall into our beds. Clothing pulled on hastily for a run down the field in the fresh morning air to the communal washing hut in which basins and running cold tap water are provided. A quick wash and a comb pushed through our hair. This is in a large hut set out with trestle tables, the meals served over a counter behind which is the kitchen. Chattering, clattering, scattering, nattering: it is as if the Pied Piper has led us all to this place, a space filled by energy as we mop up our breakfasts and, between mouthfuls, spill out words about yesterday, today. The boys joking, engaging in witty exchanges aimed at impressing the girls; the girls listening and laughing.

After breakfast, we walk together across the field, taking in the smell of cut grass, warm hay and manure, until we arrive at the gate to tumble out onto the dusty road to await a tarpaulin covered lorry which will take us to the day's work at neighbouring farms:

> *There'll always be an England*
> *While there's a country lane,*
> *Wherever there's a cottage small,*
> *Beside a field of grain.*[2]

As we ride, we sing and sometimes the lorry is so crowded that I stand leaning out over its tail-board, to hold onto its tarpaulin roof. My voice stirring the warm air, passing over hedgerows, fields and herds of cows which moo in recognition:

> *What d'you know he smiled at me in my dreams last night.*

---

2. 'There'll Always Be An England', Vera Lynn (written by Ross Parker and Hughie Charles, 1939).

My dreams are getting better all the time.[3]

Too soon, we arrive at a field of golden uncut corn, stirring in the gentle breeze and beckoning us onwards, on and on and on. The tractor is travelling on the perimeter of the field, cutting the corn and throwing it out in tied bundles: round and round and round until, like a children's puzzle of lines leading to the centre of a drawing, it will turn on its own axis to sever the last of the grain. Our job is to pick up the bundles and stand them up to dry by leaning three sheaves against one another. Often, on reaching with relief the end of such a line, I turn to find that all the sheaves which I have stood up so carefully, have toppled over and lie this way and that on the stubbled ground. Then I must start all over again, and also catch up with the bundles thrown down since from the tractor. This work is called 'shocking up', or 'stooking'. In a short story about the camps which I am to write in the early 1970s while a student at Sydney Webb College of Education, I say: *"Pat never appeared to be working very hard, but her corn stood up as if by magic, and she ended the day as fresh and cool as she had begun it."*

After a while at this work, I tire, and when the tractor disappears up the field and out of sight, I sit down until the man on the tractor is seen above the corn, or I hear the noise of its engine. Then I jump up and make frantic efforts to catch up with my work.

Alton is in Hampshire, the County which holds Portsmouth, the scene of my mother's childhood in whose shadow I have been raised: the fire, Flora's frenzy, the children's screams, Harry escaping through a window as the building burns, the sailors, my mother's prescience of disaster, the family's grief—all this lives with me and now my own presence is demanded at the scene of the crime. Perhaps I will quench the fire, save the children, bring Harry to justice. And so, on a Saturday, when we are not working on a farm, I persuade Pat to cycle with me to Portsmouth, some fifty miles away by the circular route which we must take. However, I do not tell Pat this, for she is not a serious cyclist. My bike is a Raleigh, pre-utility, with low shining silver handlebars, spokes and inner wheel. It has also cable brakes. Pat obtained her bike only to keep me company, and it is an utility model on

3. 'My Dreams Are Getting Better All the Time', Doris Day (written by Mann Curtis and Vic Mizzy).

which all the chrome is painted black and the brakes are standard. And so we set out for Portsmouth. There are no signposts, for these have been removed with the intention of confusing German parachutists fallen from out of the sky. Therefore, I must find my way 'blind', having ascertained the general direction to the coast. Fortunately, it is unlikely that we will be mistaken for Nazi parachutists for they are said to generally disguise themselves as nuns. Therefore, every little while I climb off the bicycle and ask a passerby along a country road whether we are travelling in the right direction. *"Ask him how far it is!"* Pat calls. She is sipping water from a bottle, for by now she is complaining continually. Unlike me, she has no impetus behind her to drive her forward, and no vision just out of sight. All Pat knows is that the day is warm and she is weary.

Whatever distance I am told, I halve for Pat's ears. *"Only fifteen more miles"* I say, when the distance is actually thirty. The country through which we pass means nothing to me. Towns and villages are no more than places on the way to my goal, my place of pilgrimage. Downhill from Alton—nowadays coloured yellow on the map for it is 400 miles above sea level—our wheels whizzing round, the breeze through our hair, to Bentley, green and 200 miles above sea level. Following the road from Bentley we cycle on the flat to Thursley, through Kingsley, downhill again to Petersfield, uphill at Buriton and then free-wheel down through Sloughton to Waterlooville, Westbourne, Hayling and we are there—*Portsmouth*! The town spread out before us. We do not look for the sea, for at this time barbed wire separates beach and sea from towns built in their honour.

By now it is late in the afternoon and like it or not, we must cycle back to Alton. I look down and along the streets, gaze into shop windows, hoping to be led to the scene of the fire, but this is a town like any other and I do not know the name of the street in which the tragedy took place. *"Let's get something to eat,"* Pat says, *"I'm famished."* And so we find a restaurant over a shop and each order fish and chips. Then we mount our cycle for the long pedal home. Next day, at the camp, I boast that we have cycled 'one hundred miles!' This puts us into the advanced cycling class! But, my main pleasure is in having stood on Portsmouth ground. Perhaps on the very spot trod by my mother, my grandmother Rachel, my grandfather who died before I was born, my Aunts and Uncles, and the dead Flora and her dead children.

Sometimes we work with farm labourers, who treat us tolerantly and with some amusement. But they are not unfriendly, and I can remember a broad, weathered man sharing with me his dinner of fresh bread and cheese when I admit that I have forgotten to collect a packed lunch before leaving the camp. We are all sitting together in an open barn, the smell of the hay and the countryside around us. He asks Pat her name and when she tells him, the man laughs, *"you want to see our guv'nor—he'll pat you on the 'ask no questions.'"* The man chuckles and Pat bristles, but not seriously. I am impressed that the farmer and his men call each other by their first names, for I come from offices in which everyone is given the title of Miss, Mrs, or Mr., and only staff on the same level use each other's first names. But, of course, at that time in the villages, generation followed upon generation so that the children played and grew to adulthood together.

Pat has let the redhead and his mates know that they are too young and unglamorous for her, which they take badly. *"You think you'll find a soldier!"* jeers Redhead, *"Well, you're only little girls!"* *"I'm seventeen,"* says fifteen year old Pat. That evening, after work, we set out for Aldershot, Pat telling the boys that we have dates with two soldiers. Aldershot is wall to wall with soldiers, for it is a military town. The doors of pubs are open and through the doorways spill the sounds of soldier's voices and women's laughter. *"We'll go and have a drink,"* says Pat, pulling me towards a pub, and we push through the crowd to the bar. *"We'll drink beer or they'll think we're too young,"* she whispers, and so we drink the first of five half pints at one crowded pub after another, none of the soldiers exhibiting any interest whatsoever in such young girls, and by this time we are drunk. In high spirits we board the train back to Alton. *"Tell the boys we've been out all evening with soldiers,"* warns Pat. The boys are lined up at the camp gate, watching our progress up the road, Pat walking carefully and me hopping, skipping and jumping. We push past them. *"We've been out with soldiers all night,"* says Pat, *"We've just left them!"* The boys follow us into the camp and I, excited by drink, dive under a line of barbed wire, judging the distance badly and tearing my loose fitting blouse all the way down the back. At first, this makes me laugh, but then I burst into tears, throwing myself down on the ground, crying and crying and crying. Pat drops down onto the grass alongside me and we weep and we weep and we weep, as if we will never stop, not until the end of time.

"Soldiers got them drunk!" say the boys in awe. An older woman urges us up from the ground, taking first mine, and then Pat's, arm; a woman somewhere in her thirties, taking time out of her life to spend it in this camp, for there are rumours of some tragedy—a deserting husband, or a dead child. Pat and I have taken a dislike to her, for she represents the authority from which we have escaped momentarily and, therefore, generally we respond rudely to her remarks and advice. *"You can't tell us what to do"*, *"Mind your own business."* Her response to this rudeness is to show us only sharp edges, to become ever more censorious, so drawing from us even more insulting responses. Now, here she is kissing us goodnight, tucking us in under the blankets. I am touched by her kindness, but embarrassed by it in equal measure. I am relieved when morning comes and all returns to normality and our adversarial relationship with this woman once more resumes. We do not mention her kindness of the night before, nor admit that it is remembered.

Pat and I must have gone together to at least three agricultural camps before I begin to go on my own. At one camp, our job is to strip down the hop plants to make them ready for the growth of hops, a job hard on the hands. Perhaps it is here where a group of British soldiers pull up beside Pat and me as we walk through the village. *"Come for a ride up the hill, girls?"* the driver asks. We hesitate and the driver says earnestly, *"You'll be all right with us, that's a promise."* He looks first into Pat's face and then into mine. We climb into the truck which speeds, rattling up the hill, the ground sloping away on either side. On arriving at its plateau at the summit, the soldiers ask us to come to the radio station. One of the soldiers tunes into another base radio and says, *"we've found the spirits of the hills! Beautiful young girls, we'll ask one of them to speak to you."* Grinning, he calls Pat over and I hear a one-sided conversation, a soldier whispering to Pat to say she wears green garlands in her hair. Perhaps the soldiers know, or feel instinctively the buried centuries of history, myth and legend surrounding hills; that Scandinavian trolls dwell beneath small hills and fairies, dispossessed spirits, dwell under mounds which resemble the graves into which all must disappear sooner or later:

> *And all those airy shapes you now behold,*
> *Were human bodies once, and clothed with earthly mould;*
> *Our souls, not yet prepared for upper light,*

Till doomsday wander in the shades of night.[4]

A lean, dark-eyed soldier invites Pat to take a walk, but indignantly the others intervene, *"No, you don't! We all stay together. We know what you're like!"* The dark-eyed youth persists, more to tease his mates I think, than in lust. *"I'll take the girls home"*, says the driver firmly, and we climb into the truck to be sped down the hill and dropped outside the camp.

Perhaps it is this kindness and sense of responsibility towards us which later, while at another camp, is to allow us to flag down an American convoy with nearly disastrous results. For, after all, we have been raised in the belief that men are the natural protectors. Men are the guardians of this world and the next, the doers, the founts of all wisdom, the mainspring of art, music, literature, architecture, sport, politics; courageous defenders of countries and populations. We girls could emulate men only by becoming androgynous, and once grown into women even this escape is denied us. This we accepted, even in the face of plenty of evidence to the contrary. This I accepted, in spite of the feminism inculcated in me by my mother, who also had a greater respect for men than she did for women. As Professor Higgins asks in *My Fair Lady*: *"Why can't a woman be more like a man?"*

At agricultural camps, I meet people from all over the country, many of them finding refuge for a few weeks. There is a girl whose broken nose has mended badly, leaving the bridge dipped and flattened in her sallow face. She has escaped to the camps to hide from a violent husband and there has found a protector, a short, thin man, the expression on his narrow face, anxious. They walk together holding hands and sit opposite one another at the long tables for meals. They sit without speaking. There is no need for speech between these twin souls.

The fourteen-year-old boy who spends the term-time at boarding school and the holiday times at camps tells Pat and me that his father is an Army Officer who 'likes women'. *"I'd like to dress up as a woman one day and meet him, just to see what he does,"* he says, half-innocently.

There is also 'Blondie', a young man with curly fair hair, fresh complexioned, pudgy and shy. He assists at the camp, although whether voluntarily or on the pay roll, I cannot remember. Blond-

---

4. Dryden, *The Flower and the Leaf*.

ie welcomes Pat's and my teasing attention. *"You can't call a man 'Blondie'!"* Pat's brother Douglas tells her when we arrive home.

At Faringdon, Berkshire, we meet Lieutenant David Parkin of the Pioneer Corps who is spending his leave at the camp. Above average height, blue-eyed, fair-haired, he is attracted to Pat and she plays her usual game of calling him by the wrong name. We walk up a green hill, a blue sky enveloping us, the birds singing, the grass soft beneath our feet. *"John!"* Pat calls out to David. Her big eyes innocent. *"No, Andy! Oh, no, silly me; Michael!"* David's eyes become bleaker and bleaker and his mouth forms an angry line. He tells us that he has no family and before joining the army had lived in lodgings. *"I've never been able to vote,"* he says bitterly, *"because I've never been on an electoral register."* This takes us into politics, and while Pat looks at distant horizons, I speak socialism. But David is a Managerialist. He sees the world after the war as belonging to the technocrats and managers. Perhaps this is why he complains that the Canadian troops stationed in the village fail to salute him as he passes through. Discipline is lax. To myself I think, *"good for them!"*

Factory workers, clerks, shop assistants, manual workers, those awaiting University entrance and students—taking time out to 'lend a hand on the land'. As the banner headline of a Sunday newspaper announces, 'ALL HUMAN LIFE IS HERE!' Sometimes, two, or maybe more, cultures clash. My father, while I am away, sends me newspapers and magazines, writing a short note in the margins in his small, neat handwriting. He sends me *The New Statesman* and *Nation*, and I sit in the communal tent reading the more interesting columns, such as 'This England'. *"I thought people round here only read comics,"* sneers a young man, a University student. The day before I had been reading the pull-out comic section from an American newspaper and laughing over the *Katzenjammer Kids*. I look at the sullen face of the young man and say breezily, *"Oh I like to read serious magazines as well as comics. I like both."*

Apart from local hops, at one of the camps we are picked up on a Friday evening and taken to a dance at an American base. At the local hops we generally meet a few British servicemen. I will always remember the rear gunner in the RAF unable to keep still, over-exuberant, calling out loudly. His mates whisper *"he's flak happy."* Rear gunners are not expected to live for very long. when the planes are shot down they are the first to be killed. The tension of each mission accumulates in the souls of air crew, so that long before they have completed their expected number of missions, their minds and imaginations are flying into another sphere. However, at the village hops there are never more than half-a-dozen servicemen. The American base is a whole new ball game. At these dances there are hundreds of GIs. They push vinegary beer upon us, ask us to dance or go for a walk. After a time, and depending to some extent upon how much beer they have drunk, the GIs become very busy with their hands, reminding me of the old joke: *"We went for a walk in the moonlight, we sat down on a bench, he held my hand, and then I had to hold his."* Dürer's painting of praying hands receives international acclaim, but these hands can be said to be 'preying' and I am relieved when the coach calls to take us back to the camp. But this experience teaches us nothing, and so we are to meet GIs again in a more dangerous context.

I awake one morning with cramp in my left foot. I go to work, but limp all day and, at the end of the day, hobble. On returning to the camp I ask at the office if there is a doctor in the village, the man in charge shrugs in reply. *"Why don't you go to the Radcliffe in Oxford,"* he suggests eventually. We decide to hitch-hike, walking along the country lane until an RAF articulated lorry stops for us. Sitting in the back, we bump up and down while the lorry wends its way through country lanes, stopping at last outside Oxford. Pat tries to give the driver some money, but he refuses to take it. *"I'm only too pleased to help our British girls,"* he says, and Pat rewards him with a smile. We must have spent some two to three hours at the Radcliffe, and at last I emerge with my foot bandaged in crepe. I have pulled a tendon, a condition which occasionally plagues me to this day. We wander around Oxford and go into a cafe for spam and chips. At last, we decide we must hitch-hike back to camp, but no one will stop for us. Soon it is dusk and we have been walking for what seems like hours and my foot is beginning to hurt again. We are desperate, when suddenly a convoy of American Army trucks swings into view. Pat thumbs madly and I copy her, although I have some reservations. The first four trucks drive straight past us, but the fifth and last, stops. The driver leans out of the cab and shouts, *"get in the back, girls."*

A dozen pair of hands pull us aboard and we find ourselves in the midst of a truckload of GIs. *"Hey, isn't this all right,"* says one,

feeling for Pat, who slaps away his hand. I find myself sitting on
a soldier's lap, his hands exploring my body. "*Smoke?*" asks a soldier, holding out a packet of cigarettes. I don't smoke, but take
one, the soldier lighting it for me, and I press the lighted end
down firmly on the wrist of the soldier on whose lap I am sitting.
He drops me on the floor. The truck stops and the driver's mate
pulls down the tail-board. "*Hey! We want one of those girls in the
cab!*" he shouts, "*or we're not budging!*" "*There's safety in numbers*" I
tell myself and stay where I am. Past gets up and climbs out of
the truck, while I watch her go. When the truck starts up again,
several soldiers reach for me and I push the lighted cigarette
against one after the other. The cigarette as deterrent, as a weapon of war. But it doesn't stop them feeling me, and so I burst into
tears. "*Leave the kid alone,*" a soldier mutters. I can see him in the
gloom, a middle-aged man and, sensing sanctuary, I climb onto
his lap, to cling to him as if I were a child. Soon the truck stops
and the driver and his mate accompanied by Pat come round to
the tailboard. "*Where are we?*" I call out to Pat. "*In the American
base at Wantage,*" Pat replies. She is worried and pleads with the
driver. "*Let us go home, our mothers will be terribly worried. I promise
we'll meet you another day.*" "*OK,*" replies the driver, "*you can go
home soon, but we want you to come for a walk first.*" The soldiers
jump down from the truck and my protector gives me a hand. He
stands beside me and puts an arm around my shoulders. "*Scram!*"
says the driver, looking at him hard, and reluctantly my protector
withdraws his arm, muttering, "*they're only kids,*" and slowly walks
away. I watch him go. "*Come on,*" says the driver and Pat and I
follow him and his mate into a coach.

Pat and I sit close to each other on the long seats, the GIs
standing over us. The soldier pulls me down to the front of the
coach and tries to pin me down on a seat, but I struggle and
wriggle away, running across to a seat on the other side. The
soldier follows and takes hold of me again. I can hear Pat arguing, "*don't you respect women? Don't you have any sisters?*" "*Sure I
do,*" the driver replies, "*but what's that got to do with it?*" Suddenly,
the driver shouts "*duck!*" and the soldier throws me down on the
floor to lie behind me. A light shines along the coach, lighting up
the windows and seats one by one. "*All clear!*" calls the driver as
the light disappears. We scramble back onto the seats. Pat speaks,
and the tone of her voice is happier, relieved. "*You know you're not
supposed to be here!*" she says. "*You could get into terrible trouble. You*

could even be court-martialled." "I'll risk that," says the driver, "you
just get down on the floor when I tell you." I have taken the opportunity provided by the diversion to sit next to Pat, and now I cling
to her. The soldier trying half-heartedly to pull me away. "Duck!"
shouts the driver again, and we crouch down on the floor as once
more the searchlight shines through the coach. When we stand
up again, the Driver says "OK, I guess you girls can go home." He
sounds defeated. We follow the two men out of the coach. "It's
cold," Pat says, shivering, for we have on only thin cotton dresses.
"I'll get you a blanket," says Bud and he disappears into the hut to
reappear a few minutes later carrying an Army blanket. Before
handing it over he says, "If anyone asks you how you come to be here,
say some Officers brought you in. don't tell on us." Fervently, we agree.
"Cross my heart," we both say. The driver and his mate turn to
leave, but before going, the driver says wearily, "I don't know why
you girls thumbed down our lorry." "We wanted to get home," Pat says.

Walking close together, the blanket thrown over our shoulders, we follow the main path by the light of the full moon. "If
we're challenged by the guard on the gate, what do we say?" I ask Pat.
"Friend!" she says, decisively. But, when we arrive at the gate there
is no soldier on duty, gun over shoulder, and so Pat puts out her
hand to operate the catch. "Hey!" a voice shouts behind us and
we turn to see a short, fat, middle-aged GI striding towards us.
"Where did you come from?" he asks. A promise is a promise and so
Pat says dutifully "some Officers brought us in here." the GI looks
us over. "What were their names?" We can't remember. "Was one
dark and the other with red hair?" he asks. "I think that's them" Pat
says, and I know that she has her fingers crossed. "Well, you're
stoopid gurrls" the GI says "young kids like you should be at home
with your mothers." Pat and I stand shivering under the blanket,
which keeps slipping from our shoulders, and so the soldier steps
forward and ties the two ends under our chins. "That's better," he
says and opens the gate to let us out.

We find ourselves in a country lane. "How are we going to get
home now?" I ask, peeved. Tiredness and coldness are making me
bad-tempered. "If it wasn't for your stupid foot, we wouldn't be in this
mess!" Pat snaps. "It was you who thumbed down the lorry," I accuse.
"I didn't notice you refusing," Pat says, sarcastically. For the first time
in our friendship we are quarrelling, and I want to cry. We walk
across a field, finding our way by the light of the moon and at
last come upon a house, the moonlight shining upon a garden

seat at the side of a neat garden. *"Let's sit down for a moment,"* I ask timorously and Pat, without replying, flops down, pulling me, in the blanket, down with her. Involuntarily we close our eyes and the next time we open them it is morning and the sun is shining. Tied in our blanket, we make our way down the garden path to a gate to struggle through one at a time. *"Let's take this off,"* I say as we reach the road, and Pat pulls out the knot binding us and folds up the blanket, which she hands to me to carry. We are looking along the road, wondering which direction will lead us to Faringdon, when a mail van comes into view and we run to meet it. *"We want to go to Faringdon, can you give us a lift?"* Pat gasps, breathing hard. *"Hop in,"* says the mailman, a young fresh-faced fellow, as if picking up two girls at six o' clock in the morning is all in a day's work.

The camp is silent, for this is Sunday and all are allowed a long lie-in to recover from the week's work. We creep into the tent, put on our pyjamas and get into bed, my palliasse having become as soft as feathers during my absence. When I awake, the tent is empty and my throat is sore. The whole camp knows our story and I emerge sleepy-eyed to fame and notoriety. Pat might as well have announced the whole sorry tale over the camp loud-speaker. An older man asks us, concerned, *"did they do anything to you? Should we make a complaint?"* Hurriedly, we reassure him. *"All's well that ends well."* I would not risk my mother hearing of my stupidity.

Towards the end of our stay at Faringdon, Lt. David Parkin becomes very ill and is put onto the relatively new anti-biotic drugs. Day after day he lies on his palliasse, alone in a tent, while the rest of the camp goes about its daily business. On returning home from work, I creep into his tent and try to talk to him, but realise that he cannot reply and I am wearying him. When the time arrives for Pat and me to leave the camp, he is not yet recovered, and we leave him lying in sickness upon his straw mattress.

When Pat begins to go about with Goo's step-daughter to be, Yvonne, for the most part to the French Officers' Club, I go alone to agricultural camps. And while for the most part I stand, like Ruth, *"amidst the alien corn,"* I can recall also harvesting potatoes, that staple food whose failure in Ireland from blight in the 19th Century helped to populate America. For the most part, we followed behind the tractor as it lifted the furrowed black earth to reveal beneath the pale potatoes. But at one farm, the efficiency mad farmer had ploughed up before we arrived and the potatoes, in lines, warmed in the sunshine. Each of us are given a row and we must race each other to the end, lifting potatoes as we go, as if this is a team game. The farmer, a sinewy, weather-beaten man urging us forward. In the next field, a group of German prisoners-of-war are on the same task, but at a more leisurely pace. *"We're working harder than the Germans,"* a young man complains to the farmer. *"We've got to work harder than them if we're going to win the war,"* he replies.

After I lose my job with the Surveyor, I spend six weeks at an agricultural camp. I had been assisting my father in the bookshop at 12 Little Newport Street, moving between the dusty piles of books placed haphazardly on any and every available surface, including the floor, moving carefully between them so as not to send books tumbling about me. But it was not easy to help my father, for he was unable to delegate or explain to me the basics of a trade which he had learned empirically, gleaning knowledge almost unknowingly from the buying and selling of books over many years. Therefore he was unable to impart to me in a structured manner a trade which he had learned piecemeal. Added to which he would brook no interference in the disorganisation of his shop. Sometimes he sends me on an errand, or to HM Stationery on High Holborn, to pick up an order. I walk down Long Acre, through Covent Garden where the market men wear flat caps and unload vegetables—potatoes, cabbages, carrots— or fruit, carrying them in baskets balanced on their heads. All is bustle, the men moving backwards and forwards, pulling their burdens from the back of open lorries. They smile at me kindly and one time, when something, maybe a mote, or even a beam, flies into my eye, a market man jumps down from a lorry and taking from me the handkerchief with which I am pulling at my eyes, extracts the irritant. Perhaps this kindly experience among the fruit and veg encourages me to volunteer for an agricultural camp at Banbury, Oxfordshire.

Two of the girls with whom I share a bell tent at this camp are named Barbara Smith and Joan Hicks. Barbara is the quieter of the two, taller than me, a long face, soft brown eyes and hair and a milky complexion. She works in a shop. Joan is smaller and slightly cross-eyed, but her liveliness, the manner in which she tells a story, the fleeting expressions across her face, hide her plainness. She tells me that when she and Barbara first left school at the age of fourteen, the Labour Exchange had sent them for a job in a mortuary. She rolls her eyes, her body movements indicating surprise and fear, tinged with later appreciation of the humour of the situation. *"The smell of the disinfectant knocked us back,"* she says in her Staffordshire dialect, *"and there were all those bodies."* Her eyes open wide and I see marble slabs on which body after body lies as if in sleep. *"We didn't stop there,"* Joan says. Instead, she took a job in a factory.

We go into Banbury, and I am delighted to find that there really is a Banbury Cross; *"Ride a cock horse, to Banbury Cross."* Someone tells us that the lady in the nursery rhyme came from a local family named 'Fines'. I go with Barbara and Joan to the cinema to see *Oliver Twist* and together we make fun of the film's mawkishness.

Some time later, I am to stay with Barbara and her family in Walsall. The *Shell Guide Book to Staffordshire* by Henry Thorold (1978) states:

> One of the pleasant surprises of Walsall is to find… shady streets lined with great plane trees, early 19th Century stucco houses and terraces and especially to discover the great Doric stucco portico of the County Court, which was built for the Walsall Literary Society in 1831.

But this is not the Walsall which I see, for it is not the Walsall to which the Smiths belong. They live on a Council estate on the outskirts, an estate on which each house is a copy of its neighbour. Pete Seeger sang *Little Boxes* in which he referred to middle-class housing, but I have always thought the song more applicable to accommodation built for the working-class. Hemmed in by the estate, the Smiths are unaware that Walsall received its first Charter from Edward III and that a tablet in Bradford Street records the birthplace of Jerome K. Jerome. Nor do they care. They have troubles of their own. The Smiths are of that community ministered to by 'Sister' Dora who 'in the absence of medical care for the working-class' devoted her life during the 19th Century to caring for the impoverished of Walsall, whose health had been stolen by industry, poor living conditions and malnutrition. Sister Dora died in 1878 and now her statue gazes out over the 'better' part of the town, for the middle-class are always willing to honour those who, by their charity, screen the worst excesses resulting from policies advantageous to the middle and ruling class.

Barbara has two younger sisters. Their father had been killed while working on the railway. Recently, Mrs. Smith had remarried a man named Smith, also widowed, and his teenage daughter and young son have joined the family in their three-bedroomed house. I share a bed with Barbara and her step-sister Eileen, a bright, lively girl with a mass of dark hair and we laugh and talk each other into sleep. The Smiths make me very welcome and take me to the pub and to the fair. At the fair, I am imprisoned in a seat many feet above the ground, the gig wheel having stopped in mid-motion. I am terrified, clutching at the restraining bar, my knuckles white. I am convinced that my feet will never again touch ground. Gritting my teeth I control my fear, for I cannot admit this lack of nerve. At last the wheel swings round and I, somewhat shaken, climb out onto the ground.

While staying at Walsall I cycle to Pelsall to visit my father's second cousin, Harry, and his family. They had changed their name from Lahr to Law, during WWI, because of anti-German prejudice. At that time, my father had lost sight of Harry. Harry's father had died, leaving a widow and three young children, and Harry had been taken into the German Orphanage at Dalston. His sister Ida had been taken by her mother to relatives in Germany, and only the youngest, Adelheid, remained with her mother. My father had visited Harry at the orphanage, but while my father was interned for four years in WWI, Harry left school and the Orphanage and my father did not know where to look for him. It was not until WWII that Harry traced my Uncle Henry, who brought him and his wife Florrie, to the bookshop. Henry, himself, standing a little way up the road, just out of sight, because of the quarrel with my father which had sundered their relationship.

The Laws, who had been bombed out from Birmingham, rent two adjoining cottages in Pelsall, set in a half-acre of ground. One cottage for Florrie, a Birmingham woman, Harry and their only son Howard, and one for Florrie's elderly mother and Aunt. Florrie is tending the garden when I arrive and she turns as I walk up the garden path. I see a middle-aged woman, grey hair pulled back, a long plain face, clumsy frame, large hands. She is delighted to see me and I enter the cottage for tea. I do not meet Harry on this occasion, for he is a long-distance lorry driver, travelling the length and breadth of the British Isles, bringing back with him plants for his wife's garden from every part of the country. However, their son, Howard, a boy of fifteen, appears. He is a fair-haired, gangling boy and he takes me for a walk around the village, without speaking. Howard, for all of his short life—he is to die at the age of forty-two—lacks words. Perhaps the non-stop talkativeness of his mother had locked him into silence. Florrie is some years older than her husband. She had been working at a hostel into which came Harry, a boy who was in obvious need of care and attention. At first she had mothered him, for she was a kindly soul, and then she had married him. In those days he had welcomed her continual chatter for it returned him to a lost childhood. Now, he could bear with it only because her continual spillage of words formed no more than an interlude between his travels alone in his cab.

In the following year, Barbara comes to stay with me at Wilton Road, but I refuse to give up my normal activities and take her to a demonstration in Trafalgar Square. It is a demonstration like all those I have been to over the years, crowds milling about, sellers of political newspapers shouting their wares, banners, the speakers high on the rostrum, police maintaining a stringent eye, for an assembly of the people is a concession, not a right. Barbara is confused by all this demonstrating and the meetings to which I take her. But, fortunately, my mother fills the gap between Barbara's expectations and my interests by taking the girl with her to the shops and out on the domestic round. By this time I am employed and so while I am at the office she takes Barbara to St. Paul's Cathedral and the Tower. When Barbara returns home, we correspond for a while, but our letters become fewer and fewer until they dwindle away altogether.

Endings

I work for Common Wealth: Peace breaks out: VE Day: Labour is elected to government: I go to a further agricultural camp and meet with anti-Semitism: The A-bomb vaporises Japanese cities: VJ Day.

On 6th June, 1944 the Allied troops have landed at Normandy and are fighting their way across Europe. While (contrary to received opinion) I don't remember where I was, or what I was doing when President Kennedy was assassinated, I do remember that I first learned of the D-day landings while standing on a tube platform. People hurry down into the station, several brandishing an evening paper, the headlines announcing D-DAY. A whisper travels along the platform "*D-day, D-day, D-day…,*" and I am electrified by the tremor of excitement which shoots sparks along the track, rushing through the darkness of the tunnels; "*D-day. D-day D-day.*"

For months, if not years—certainly since the Soviet Union had been invaded by the Nazis is 1941—the Communist Party had been holding rallies in Trafalgar Square, 'Open A Second Front Now!'; rallies which filled the Square, for the middle-class had poured into the Communist Party in support of the Soviet Union, whom the press presented at that time as 'our gallant ally'. And it goes almost without saying that this sudden mass party was also an indication of the country's move leftward politically. With regard to the Second Front, a middle-aged French prostitute who was a customer in my father's shop, a good-natured woman who always returned magazines to my father for resale, on hearing the above slogan, told my father that business was so good, she wished she too could open a second front! Having survived the war, and served the troops and others, after the war she is to throw herself underneath a lorry which, under its bulk, crushes her to death.

On the 50th anniversary of D-day 1994, the *Evening Standard* runs a headline **ON THIS DAY AT THIS HOUR** and continues:

> *it is 6.20 a.m. on 6th June and at the exact time that the invasion landing began half a century ago, soldiers hit the beach again at Arromanches, in the swirling mist of a grey dawn. But no guns greet the men who bear the standards in the surf. Only history.*

A large photo shows two soldiers carrying Union Jacks, wading through the sea. an inside page story is headlined **WHERE THE SEA RAN BLOOD RED.**

The *Observer* issues a replica of their 6th June, 1944 edition:

FRANCE REVOLTING AS ALLIES ADVANCE—TANK BATTLE NEAR CAEN— NEW GAINS ALONG WHOLE FRONT

Stories in other newspapers and on radio tell of how Normandy villages were destroyed in the mistaken belief that they housed the German army. Some 15,000 civilians were killed, their houses collapsing upon them, masonry falling, chunks of macadam bursting upwards, peasants in the field exploding with their crops: earth, stone, brick and flesh darkening the villages. What is now called 'collateral damage'. *C'est la guerre.*

In September 1944, British and American paratroopers drop from the skies in an attempt to seize the bridges over the lower Rhine. A mission which is to end in defeat, for the troops are cut off at Arnhem by the German army and forced to retreat over the Rhine. Of the 10,000 Allied troops involved, only 2,400 return.

Now, as the war draws to an end, one Allied victory follows another, an impetus that has been put into motion and feeds upon itself. But I myself continue to be caught up by daily living. For during these months, I am working at the offices in Marylebone of the Royal College of Nursing. This, because on returning from the Banbury agricultural camp, I have volunteered for the Women's Land Army, an organisation which functioned during both World Wars. Entrants received training in farm or horticultural duties, following which they were sent to work for individual farmers or market gardeners. The uniform consisted of belted breeches, green pullover, buff shirt, green tie, long woollen socks, sturdy shoes, topped by a hat with a small brim. I volunteer because I feel fit and well from my work in the countryside and the catarrh always with me in the City, has dried up. But in the meantime, I must find a temporary work. I am sent to the College of Nursing by Fines Agency in Praed Street, Paddington for a temporary appointment as a shorthand-typist.

When I try to recall the general office, I see it as a church where I sit in a pew with others, none of them speaking to one another—we are all strangers. Of course, I must have sat at a typewriter, for I remember an angry boss—an ex-Matron—a large middle-aged, middle-class woman calling me into her office and shrieking at me a stream of invective as she tears up a letter I have translated from my shorthand notes. She has always behaved abruptly towards me, but this is something else. At the back of my mind lurks the suspicion that someone has reported to her that I read 'Commie' literature during the dinner hour—*Wage Labour and Capital* and *Value, Price and Profit*, both by Karl Marx—for I know there is nothing wrong with the letter which she is attacking so violently. Here, at the Royal College of Nursing, the military tradition of Florence Nightingale prevails; left, right, left, right, right, right, right, turn, sit, type. There is no stand easy. That is not part of the prescription. At the end of my three-month temporary employment, I am not asked to stay on, nor would I have wanted to do so, in spite of the fact that I have been turned down by the Land Army on the grounds of poor health. Dr. Blackburn has submitted a medical certificate similar to the one he provided for me previously, at the time when I had wanted to take the job with the Surveyor in Chancery Lane and escape work of 'national importance'. But, on leaving the RCN, I am at a loose end and once again 'assist' my father in the bookshop. I have continued to be involved in Common Wealth, manning a Committee Room during a bye-election. Now I reply to an appeal for volunteers in the office at 4 Gower Street, and on reporting for duty I am sent across the road to two rooms on an upper floor, managed by Arthur Carr and his future wife Jo Dalliston. Arthur, short, dark, Brylcreemed hair, black eyes, a square face which wears a brooding expression. Jo, tall, slim, auburn-haired.

I have typed a few letters and dealt with some filing, when Mr. Carr asks me why I am not in employment. I murmur about working for a Surveyor, a Tory... and Mr. Carr jumps to a conclusion. *"He sacked you for being a socialist!"* I do not disillusion him. *"We've got jobs going here. Go across the road and see Mr. Barham. I'll phone him while you're on your way over."* That's how I come to work for Arthur Carr and Common Wealth in a department maintaining contact with members in the Services. Common Wealth had played a part in the Cairo Parliament at which servicemen and women had met to discuss their hopes for the peace, until the parliament was disbanded as 'too left-wing'. Arthur Carr is not an easy man to work for. He believes in keeping employees on their toes and then treading on them heavily. I don't think that I ever typed a letter he didn't criticise. Arthur is a working-class lad who had grown up in Hull; joined the Royal Navy, sailing the seven seas and a couple of oceans, the whole time resenting the imposition of discipline by Officers who had no other recommendations than their haw, haw, haw, voices. It makes him angry when he reads a statement of a Director, or a Minister, *"we are building,"* or *"we are mining"*—*"they're doing nothing of the sort!"* he says *"It's others who are on the site, or down the mines, doing the work!"*

Back to the war. In February 1945 Dresden is reduced to rubble by day and night bombing by the American and British Air Forces—Lancaster bombers deluging the city with tons of incendiaries and high explosives. Their work is continued by over 400 American B17s, which appear over the smoking ruins to resume the destruction. Estimates of the dead vary from 60,000 to 130,000, many of them refugees; for Dresden, famed for its 17th and 18th Century baroque and rococo art and architecture, had presented itself as a safe haven. Later, Kurt Vonnegut, who is a prisoner-of-war in Dresden during the fire-storm, cowering within an abattoir together with other prisoners, is to write *Slaughterhouse Five* about the destruction of Dresden, and yet not about it. For it is not possible to set out on paper the shattering and terrible events of those days, and so Vonnegut contents himself with a story of science fiction. In the streets of London, or in the queues for vegetables or other comestibles, women shake their heads at the sound of British and Allied planes overhead on their way out over the Channel. They remember the London blitz and say sardonically, *"some poor devil's going to get it!"*

The Allied troops cross the Rhine. From my cousin Woolfie, in the RASC, we receive letters which give graphic descriptions of the Battle of the Rhine; letters in which we can hear the booming and the clatter of gunfire, the roar of explosions, the heavy movement of tanks, hear the crackle of fire, be overcome by its acrid smell and blinded by its orange flame and thick concealing smoke, hear the cries of the wounded and the dying. All take their toll on my cousin and, on his return to England, he joins a number of his fellows, all dressed in blue overalls, reminiscent of the RAF uniform, in the military wing of the Colney Hatch Asylum. A blue uniform which Woolfie would have preferred to wear if he had not failed the eyesight test for pilot in the RAF. Now he is dressed in hospital blues. Sadly, these letters to my parents are long lost, but the battle and Woolfie's experience of it, was kept alive for many years in letters sent to my cousin Flo, until some time during the 1990s she committed them also to the flames.

The Soviet troops take over the Balkans. They march into Austria and also into Berlin. The Soviet Union has lost 20,000,000 of their people during the war. Hitler shoots himself, and his mistress, Eva Braun, takes poison. The Duce and his mistress, Clara Petacci, are shot by Italian partisans and strung up by their legs in a public place. Italy had signed an armistice with the Allies in September 1943, following which, it had not become an ally, but a co-belligerent. As a result, Italy had been occupied by the German army.

The Third Reich having crashed about his ears, General Alfred Jodl, German Army Chief of Staff, surrenders in a Rheims school which has been made into General Eisenhower's HQ. Count Schwerin von Krosig, the German Foreign Minister, has broadcast over Flensburg radio that to continue the war would *"only mean senseless bloodshed and futile disintegration."* The Germans had delayed signing in order to allow as many soldiers and refugees as possible to give themselves up to the Western Allies, rather than to the Russians. Three days earlier in Field Marshal Montgomery's tent on the desolate Luneburg Heath, south of Hamburg, 'Monty' had received the surrender of all German forces in North-West Germany, Holland and Denmark.

VE-Day: 12th May 1945: During the past week high wooden gates have been erected around the West End in order to control the expected crush of merry-makers:

> *Mother may I go and maffick*[1],
> *Dash around and stop the traffic?*

Now, a public holiday has been declared. Pat and I travel by tube from Highgate to Leicester Square, where we join the drifting crowds. Newspapers report:

> *Britain took to the streets to celebrate the victory. By mid-day Whitehall and the Mall were packed with a crowd. 50,000 people went wild with joy, shaking hands at first then kissing and hugging strangers, dancing, blowing whistles, throwing confetti and forming impromptu parades, a massive 'hokey-cokey' snaked round Queen Victoria's statue.*[2]

The *Daily Mail Golden Jubilee Book 1896-46* shows a photograph taken from above, the packed crowd in Trafalgar Square, the plinth of Nelson's column covered on the two sides by large placards: **VICTORY OVER GERMANY 1945** and **GIVE THANKS BY SAVING**. Pat and I, caught up in the crowds, move slowly. At one time we are in Piccadilly Circus, where a drunken American sailor and a girl stagger in an attempt at jive. The crowd gathers around them, hoping to be entertained and, when the sailor and the girl at last stop their antics and collapse against each other, their eyes glazed, the crowd wanders off to find other amusement. We pull out of the crowd into Little Newport Street, where I find that the window of the camera shop, next door to our bookshop, has been smashed, the remaining glass forming a jagged hole. Again with the crowds, we find ourselves at the front of a building on the balcony of which American GIs trumpet out jazz. *"Play Land of Hope and Glory,"* shout one or two voices, and the cry is taken up, but the band do not know the tune. A man in the crowd starts the hymn and it is taken up by the crowd, the band doing its best to improvise a backing:

> *Land of hope and glory,*
> *Mother of the free*

---

1. Maffick: to celebrate with boisterous rejoicing and hilarious behavior; a back-formation from 'Mafeking Night', English celebration of the lifting of the siege of Mafeking, South Africa, May 17th, 1900.
2. If this in fact took place, it must have been a conga, not a hokey-kokey!

Now we are in front of Buckingham Palace, hemmed in on every side, the statue of Queen Victoria scaled by several youths whose legs dangle from her head. A call goes up, *"We want the King! We want the King!"* The cry ripples through the crowd until far above us on the balcony, several figures can be seen, at which the cry changes to a roar of approval.

Later in the evening, Pat and I are on the tube, the Northern Line to Highgate. Every seat taken by other foot-weary passengers, we, with many others, sit above the seats on the window-sills, feet hanging behind the backs of those on the seats. No one remarks on this arrangement. It happens and is accepted. At Highgate we struggle up the steep hill leading out of the exit and once on the pavement take off shoes from our hot and aching feet to walk home in the dark barefoot, the paving stones cool beneath our feet. I have mixed feelings about the end of the war. My mind is split into several directions.

During the last year of the war, Ann and I, within the political atmosphere of the International Youth Club, have become anti-war. Fascism, which we agree is endemic to capitalism, cannot be ended by it. Workers of all lands must unite to bring about co-operative socialism under which poverty and racism will be a thing of the past. And yet, I do not want the Nazis to win the war and destroy the Labour movement and all the vestiges of democracy. And, apart from these considerations, their victory would mean a concentration camp for me and my family. But, of course, if the Nazis invaded Great Britain, the people would fight for their freedom and defeat the Nazis on the streets, or would our government capitulate and leave us to form partisan groups as had happened in France? So the argument goes back and forth:

> *Myself when young did eagerly frequent,*
> *Doctor and Saint, and heard great Argument,*
> *About it and about; but evermore,*
> *Came out by the same Door as in I went.*[3]

Now the war is coming to an end with victory to the Allies, and I wonder how I will adjust to peace. After all, as I say to Ann, we are the true children of war, for we have grown up in its shadow. What would take its place? The siren might come as a threat, but

---

3. Omar Khayyam, Stanza XXVII, tr. Edward Fitzgerald..

it was also exciting, when on the street, to respond to its warning by hurrying into a tube station to join those almost permanent residents bedded down on the platforms; an underworld, a
world within a world, a shelter community. Entertainment and
sing-alongs part of the nightly terror. For my generation the war
had become a way of life. A security of insecurity. Such are the
vagaries of our psychology, which changes more slowly than political, economic and even personal fortunes.

Also, I know that during WW2, for the first time in living
memory, or perhaps since WW1, the working-class have been
given a sense of importance. No longer are we the lower-classes,
the uneducated, the great unwashed. We are essential to the war
effort, brave fighting men, munitions workers; *"the woman behind
the man who mans the gun!"* No longer merely persons employed
until employers consider us as expendable. We are heroes and
heroines of labour and, what is more, we stand firm under nightly bombing, our morale unbroken. Radio, newspapers and government all tell us what wonderful people we are, us, the British
working-class. How will we be pictured once the war is ended?

The first General Election since 1935 is held on 5th July 1945
with a resounding victory for Labour. Common Wealth had cam-
paigned for the updating of the electoral registers, and in 1943,
as a result of the Vivian Committee, this had been agreed. At
the age of eighteen, I was not entitled to vote. At that time it
was necessary to be twenty-one. Out on an errand for Arthur
Carr, I return to the office, walking across New Oxford Street,
to read the placards proclaiming a **LABOUR LANDSLIDE**. I am
happy, for the Tories have been rejected, this in spite of the massive campaign to thank Churchill for winning the war by voting
Conservative. His picture, many times life-sized, and complete
with cigar, is on every hoarding; an advertising campaign which
is counter-productive, for many people, praised for so long by
government and media, bridle and ask *"What! On his own? What
were we doing?"* Of course, the *Daily Mirror* had struck a blow for
Labour by issuing its now historic edition calling, in large black
headlines on the front page, for the population to support 'the
boys' by voting Labour. The population has returned to Churchill his own 'V' sign, but the fingers turned the other way around:
"Up yours!" The people do not want to return to pre-war unemployment and poverty and even the middle-class are willing for

the working-class to have a greater share in the fruits of their labour. Labour has won 393 seats against the Tories 213.

But it is the Labour victory which is to lose me yet another job. For the elected and re-elected Common Wealth MPs, now that the political truce has ended with the election of a Labour government, decide to join Labour. Finances are tight and I suspect that financial backers had withdrawn. Mr. Barham calls the staff into the main office, in which one woman is sitting with a hessian sack upon her lap. The room is crowded in this well-appointed building, carpets upon the floor, light pouring through the large windows. I sit down on a wooden chair and listen to Mr. Barham who is humming and ha'ing, but in the end we get the message. Common Wealth is retrenching. It can no longer afford to maintain a large office and large staff, *"but the movement will go on"*, Mr. Carr declaims with fervour, a statement which does not impress the majority of the staff, for whom this is merely a job. A brave soul enquires why Common Wealth had been taking on staff up to a fortnight previously and Mr. Barham hums and ha's once again.

I leave almost immediately, but it is some weeks before others go and later, when Arthur Carr has left his office and opened a Personnel Service Bureau to provide secretaries for Labour Members of Parliament—a bureau for which I am to work occasionally, unpaid—he tells me that staff had walked out with typewriters and other office equipment. When he had attempted to intervene, he was told to mind his own business. Now only two small offices, once occupied by Arthur, remains to Common Wealth, and Arthur's and Jo's places are taken by two young men recently discharged from the Services, a young woman acting as Secretary. She calls these young men by their first names which, when on a visit, takes me aback, for Common Wealth had maintained the traditional formalities and titles between bosses and staff.

Common Wealth limps on and I am a nominal member, attending at the odd meeting or rally, where I sometimes see Ann. By now she is working for a middle-aged, wealthy, silver-haired man who is a member of Common Wealth. He owns a bookshop in Victoria Street and, I seem to remember, another in Crouch End. His bookshop is the antithesis of my father's, for it is a book store, the shelves tidy, all labelled neatly. When I had first met Ann, she was a cub reporter on a North London newspaper and I envied her this job. I saw her work as exciting and varied and, after all, it was writing. But she found court work boring, and often induced a male reporter to take notes for her while she slipped out with a friend for coffee. Now, she works as a bookshop assistant at very low wages. She doesn't win any medals from me when she says *"if Mr. Wilson paid better wages, the shop might have to close."*

Temporarily out of work, I decide to go again to an agricultural camp. For the life of me, I cannot recall in which part of the country this camp was situated, all I can remember is that we shared it with a group of Royal Marines, a body of troops trained to serve on land or sea. Each morning and evening, we line up outside an outbuilding to receive over the counter our meals from Marine cooks who smilingly ladle out whatever is on that day's menu. We collect our sandwiches from the same hatch before setting out for the day's work. I expect to hear trumpeted *"Come to the cookhouse door boys—and girls!"* There is a saying during the Second World War, *"tell it to the marines,"* meaning that only they will be stupid enough to believe it. A popular song at the time ends:

> You can tell it to the navy, tell it to the army,
> and tell it to the marines!

Well, I guess there's always a section of the population picked out to be stupid, it convinces the rest of the populace that they have the exclusive right to intelligence. Maybe this is a spin-off from imperialism and colonialism, for the conquered are always said to be more stupid and less human that their conquerors. The marines whom I meet are a cross-section of the conscripted male population; short, tall, thin, broad, young, nearing middle-age, bright, dull and, for the most part, friendly. They share with us a recreation hut lit by a paraffin lamp which has to be pumped up whenever the light dims. Also we are amused to see adult men sparring like little boys. We go out dancing to the local hop with the marines and I can remember, on the way home, a short, but handsome marine, black hair and bright blue eyes which look into mine, standing with me by the hedge outside the camp and putting the argument as to why I should go to bed with him, although, to this day, I am not clear as to whether he truly desired me, or was merely going through the motions of what a man has to do. I refuse. I am not aware until later that the cooks are in the cookhouse cleaning up and hear every word. A bluff, hearty cook compliments me on being a 'good' girl. He tells me also that from the camp there had been marriages between Marines and campers. In fact, only the previous week a Marine had married a widow with six children.

"*They shouldn't have dropped those Atom bombs on Japan,*" says a Marine to me hesitatingly. Tall and fair, he is a shy boy, not an easy talker, and his face is red with the effort to express his feelings. We have been together to the cinema and are returning to the camp by bus. "*I don't agree with it,*" he says, troubled.

A-BOMB VAPORISES
JAPANESE CITIES

shout the headlines. Shadow towns, the outlines of formerly living, breathing people, men, women and children, burned onto walls. Illnesses, mutations to the end of the century and beyond.

> *Aug 9th: For the second time an atomic bomb fell upon Japan today, obliterating Nagasaki, the shipbuilding centre on the Japanese island of Kyushu. Smoke and dust clouds completely covered the town and rose five miles high in a giant mushroom shaped cloud. Japan claims that 70,000 perished and more are dying daily.*

The Japanese had tendered their surrender seven weeks previously, but the Cold War was under way and Truman wanted to impress the Russians with the weapons of annihilation held by the West. The Cold War, which was to be used to crush dissent and demands for social justice. A world predicted by Orwell, who warned that governments would always keep the populace under control by building up belief in a supposed foreign enemy—or the enemy within.

I am to hear the sentiments of the Marine voiced by many when I return home, which is to be shortly, although I had intended to stay until October. As it happens, I am almost thrown out of the camp, for the Manager has taken a dislike to me. Whenever I pass the caravan used as an office, or have to go to this office for any reason, he glowers at me and answers my queries shortly, as if he cannot bear to waste words upon such as me. The young woman, formally his assistant—a tall, fair-haired woman—barely glances my way, and yet her disregard is tangible. Soon I am creeping past the caravan in the hope that if I make no sound and close myself down as small as possible, I will not attract attention.

By now, we girls have moved out of the bell tents into a long wooden hut, to sleep, dormitory fashion, in two long lines, a passage between us. On one morning, having been out late, I cannot face getting up for work. Suddenly, the Manager appears with his girlfriend as chaperone. He stalks down the centre gangway. *"Why isn't she up and ready for work?"* he demands. Two girls with whom I have become friendly, both of them students at Nottingham University, do their best to defend me. *"She's not been well,"* one says weakly, *"she's got a headache." "She's been feeling sick,"* said the other, backing up her friend. I keep my eyes tight shut and pretend to be asleep. I hear the Manager muttering and my friends assuring him that I am *"a very heavy sleeper."* At last he, and his girl-friend retreat from the hut. However, when a day or two later, in answer to my application for an extension of my three week stay, the Manager calls me into the office, he sneeringly refuses my request. *"People of your race always want everything,"* he says. This leaves me confused. Is he referring to my German surname, or does he assume that I am Jewish? I have been attending the local Catholic Church on a Sunday for Mass, for it provided a toehold on my childhood, but the Manager is not deceived. He knows I am a Jew. This at a time when the horrors of the Nazi concentration camps are opened to the world. Great heaps of naked rotting corpses, skeleton survivors, gas chambers, the ovens. Buchenwald, Dachau, Belsen. I am thrown off balance. I do not know how to defend myself and my anger does not begin until I return home a day or two before VJ Day. And then other concerns take over.

15th August: VJ Day is a repeat of VE Day—the crowded West End surrounded by high wooden gates to control the crowds, the drifting together with masses of people from one place to another, the ride home in the over-crowded tube train.

While VJ Day signals the end of the war between the Allies and Japan, it does not signal the end of war in China, where Chiang Kai-shek has been fighting the 'Communists', leaving the Communists to fight the Japanese. And this war between Chiang and the Communists is not over until 1949, when Chiang and the Nationalists are forced to retreat to Formosa. But, as a result of the Cold War, it is not until 1971 that the Communist government is recognised by the West as the government of China. Chiang having been backed by America and the West. And it goes without saying, that the 'Communists', having forged their government by warfare, continue to maintain a martial control over the population; a totalitarianism which is to lead in June 1989 to students being mowed down by tanks in Tiananmen Square. A technological advancement over the severing of heads by the broadsword in the year of my birth, 1927.

As World War Two comes to an end, my father says, *"Peace has broken out!"* and I know that I must learn to live with it. But the changeover from war to peace happens slowly, so for some two or three years men in uniform form the majority of men on the streets, or in the dance-halls. It is only gradually that the civvies appear among them and at last take over. The youth clubs flourish, as does the International Youth Centre, where I continue to spend much of my time. From an ethos of enthusiasm for winning the war, we are now enthusiastic to win the peace by the introduction of the Welfare State, the National Health Service, secondary schooling for all, decent housing and full employment. A consensus exists between the political parties that this is what the people deserve and Councils, whether Labour, Tory or Liberal, vie with one another to build the greatest number of Council houses, while out in the countryside, new towns of rented housing rise from out of the fields. Not that I ever deceive myself that this is socialism, but it is a beginning—better than what went before. And, in this way, something of the urgency of war-time continues to imbue our daily lives.

Agricultural camps also continue to be held every year, and it is while I am spending a fortnight's holiday at one of these in 1947, before starting a job with the Independent Labour Party journal *The Socialist Leader*, that I receive a note from my father that Bill Howley is to return to America for demobilisation. I write Bill a very sad letter, for he has become part of our lives, and in those days America seemed to be so far away. Of course, in the interim, the development of modern means of travel has brought other countries and continents ever closer. But it is some years before we are to meet again.

Afterword

Reflections

When I was a child, a favourite poem of mine was by the time-obsessed 17th Century poet Robert Herrick, the words of which were set out under black notes in a music book which we had at Wilton Road, and although I could not read the tune, I often recited:

> *Gather ye rosebuds, while ye may,*
> *Old time is still a-flying:*
> *And this same flower that smiles today*
> *Tomorrow will be dying*[1]

A warning of which I have remained aware, but in spite of ourselves we pass through time, or time passes through us, and the events recorded in this book for the most part took place fifty years ago and more. So many pages to illustrate the first eighteen years of my life, when it is possible that the remainder could be telescoped into a similar number of pages. Perhaps a partial explanation can be found in the third verse of the above poem.

> *That age is best which is the first,*
> *When youth and blood are warmer,*
> *But being spent, the worse, and worst*
> *Times still succeed the former.*

---

1. *To the Virgins, to Make Much of Time*

But, my intention in writing this book was to speak of my origins and the influences which continue to dominate my life. The child comes into the word an alien, and is fitted into society where it has been decided by culture, tradition and economics how s/he should grow, a society in which there is a pretence that stability is the norm. On the other hand, history is a record of change and upheaval from the beginning of time, bringing with it displacement and a great migration of peoples from one place to another, from one part of the world to another, across seas and continents. And so the streams of displaced persons throughout the centuries maintain their exodus, yesterday and today. For all of us in our time have been 'driven from the Garden' and the golden age, as the perceived promised dream of stability, has remained elusive. Hopefully, this book will indicate my own part, and that of my family, within this maelstrom.

It is said that 'the past is another country' and perhaps this applies more so today because of technological invention within the past fifty years and more the extension of the global economy. In comparison, the world in which I grew up appeared to be more simple, and innocent. And yet this is an illusion, a surface impression, which I hope this book will show.

Finally, I hope that within these pages I have told something of my family history, and have made the world of my childhood live again. An especial pleasure for me has been in raising from the dead my parents (even though my father continues to appear before me in autobiographies, or biographies, of his writer friends), my grandmother, relatives, neighbours and friends, so that for a short time they push aside the vast heap under which they have been buried and take their places upon the stage. I, and those who have grown old with me, have relived our youth in these pages, while those still living, but whom I have not seen for fifty years or more, remain forever young.

Sharon Borthwick: Afterword

W hy do people trace back their family trees? I think it's because such research personalises history—something too often deemed the preserve of academics and pundits. Four years ago, Unkant published Ray Challinor's book about the Second World War, *The Struggle for Hearts and Minds*. In this volume, a Trotskyist historian contested what we're told about the conflict at school (and in countless magazine articles and TV documentaries). Here, Sheila Lahr—in the late 1940s a member of the Revolutionary Communist Party, the Trotskyist split from the Communist Party of Great Britain—contests ruling-class narratives by setting down her own memories as a child in pre-war London, then as an evacuee and finally as shorthand typist in London during the war years.

We are often told that Marxists and Trotskyists, in trying to understand global issues, cauterise immediate sympathies and become heartless 'politicos'. Sheila's account defies such slurs. She makes history reachable to us: its smells, its tastes, its quaint phrases. She does this through her own very personal—and very brave —account of the pains and joys of growing up. In writing *Yealm* she used her own diaries of the time, whilst also looking back with adult eyes, reconsidering what was motivating the grown-ups. Her mother sent her to a Roman Catholic boarding school run by martinet nuns, and you can still feel the hurt and indignation of a child facing cruelty and dogma. However, she now writes about her mother's fears of a Nazi victory against the Allies, how she thought she was hiding her Jewish daughter in a safe place.

Sheila's mother, Esther, is tiny of frame and indomitable in personality. She is fighting stupid times. Married to a German emigré, she laughs at her husband's retort to being handed a white feather (message: *"Join the army, you coward"*): *"They won't let me join the British army, I'm German"*. Esther is well read, political, but being a girl was denied further education: *"You can start at the factory for making cigarettes"* she was told aged thirteen. My own mother, born in 1935, begged her father to stay on at school after the age of fourteen, but was disallowed as a female. The brothers made good. So *Yealm* is necessarily a feminist book: women, the stupid and ignorant as well as the inspiring, wonderful ones, have the major roles. Esther, although more competent than her husband at running their bookshop, is assigned to the domestic sphere. Charlie is spending too much time in the pub, and the shop has gone to pot. It is Esther who digs them out of their financial woes.

Sheila, away at school, notices boys. They seem so exciting, allowed to be physical and boisterous, climbing trees. Sheila, by comparison, when unexpectedly slipping out a fart in chapel is humiliated and punished by being forced to eat alone. These nuns are the very worst of the women in *Yealm*: ignorant and cruel, forcing a little girl to eat spinach till she is sick, suspicious of small children going to the toilet in pairs. What a contrast to these warped, shut-in minds was a figure like Valentine Ackland: a writer friend of her mother's, decked out in a man's suit, collar and tie, with cropped hair and in a long-term relationship with Sylvia Townsend Warner. Of course, these women were well-off. Away from long shifts in factories and launderettes, it's much easier to live 'experimental' life styles.

Sheila looks in on a home economics lesson: *"girls industriously plying irons back and forth"*. If these girls deck themselves in lipstick and rouge, they are sluts. If they are careless enough to have an accident with menstrual blood, as did Eileen Martinelli, they're told: *"Men despise women like that"*. While experimenting with make-up, Sheila is admonished by a censorious boy: *"You'll go downhill"*. It is 1932, and capitalism has yet again proved a failed and useless method. The National Unemployed Workers Movement march from all over the country to Trafalgar Square:

"WE REFUSE TO STARVE IN SILENCE". The times change and they don't. The protestors are charged by police on horses and beaten with batons, bundled into Black Marias and given prison sentences. Maybe that will ring a bell with anyone who was a student in the UK in December 2010.

Incarceration and restrictions on living are an abiding theme in *Yealm*: from being told how to dress, how to behave, that you must marry, have babies, not go out to work, be clean demure and pretty... all the way to Sheila's father, Charlie Lahr, being expelled from the Communist Party for 'levity' (asked by a fellow member what an abstract painting on the bookshop wall 'meant', he shot back: *"It's the comrades on the barricades... all six of them."*). Then there was cousin Cecil, locked up in Friern Barnet lunatic asylum, there's the Jews in the death camps, and Jews escaping the Nazis in Germany only to be locked up by the British as 'aliens'. Charlie, despite 35 years in England, is deemed an alien, and locked up on the Isle of Man: *"In Britain you have to realise every German is an agent. All of them have both the duty and the means to communicate information to Berlin,"* pronounced the *Daily Mail* (the times change and they don't). Esther is married to an alien, so at 6:00am the knock on the door comes for her, and she is locked up too. Her two daughters accompany her to the police station. Witnesses to her despairing tears, the pair do a daft song and dance routine to cheer her up; the only power they have left.

The Daily Mail does its usual number on the oppressed and incarcerated: *"Ooh, it's luxury in there, they're whooping it up, dining on the best fare, sunning themselves, while we are at war!"*. During this time, Sheila and her sister Oonagh are living with foster parents, who if they don't read the *Daily Mail*, certainly share its views. Sheila comes into her own at this point, gaining in confidence and answering back. Her foster-carers, Mr and Mrs Shillan, are 'working class made good'. They are not accepted into the farmers' club of their chosen village, but they fill up their house with objects they think they ought to own, including a great library full of books (*"obviously bought by the yard"* sniggers Sheila to herself). While Mrs Shillan contains their reading to fifteen minutes a day, their parents' letters from the internment camp are restricted to 24 lines. Rationed reading, rationed writing... while the Nazis burn books outside the universities. Meanwhile, using all their ingenuity, refugee German artists ring fenced on the Isle of Man make art. For Kurt Schwitters, anything can be made of use: ink is made by mixing crushed graphite with margarine, paint brushes are constructed from the tough bristles of Samson Schames' substantial beard.

Eventually the family is reunited. But Charlie Lahr's movements are restricted and there's a midnight curfew. Nazi bombs are dropping on London. Charlie Lahr bought and secured an Anderson Shelter in the family garden. It's taken over by neighbours; but with his alien status he doesn't dare make a fuss of the matter. Two bombs hit Wilton Road, their road! Sheila details a family's tragedy and all its repercussions. Much writing reduces the world to the wants and needs of an individual; in contrast, Sheila Lahr's sympathy for others extends the world, making us see it as it is, infinite. Sheila's details make the times real for us. Like the horsemeat dyed green that the cat eats. Dyed green so you can tell it isn't fit for human consumption. Sheila slings her gas mask over her chair before lessons. She fills us with the songs, the films, the slang, the brand names, the nursery rhymes of the time; but most of all with the people. And we meet so many who live again in the pages of *Yealm*: Pamela George; broken biscuits; Gracie James; Force Cornflakes; Sister St. Clare; coconut 'tobacco'; Herman Nonnenmacher; potatoes, cabbages, beans; Pamela Davidson; Welwyn Garden City Stores; Father Brennan; Betty Devine; White Heather Café; pianola...

> *Land of soup and water*
> *Mother wash my feet*
> *Father cut my toenails*
> *Give them to baby to eat.*

Sheila was born in 1927 and by the time the book ends is merely in her late teens. We have a special opportunity here of looking in, of actually living with Sheila through her growing-up years—she makes it so vivid you feel with her those times/her times. This isn't history perfect, closed off, merely factual: in reopening the diaries she kept, Sheila relives the moments as she writes, but also applies the wisdom of age and of her later political education—filling us in on what other things were at large in the world. For instance, whilst she is ailing in bed as an infant, she acknowledges that other children were dying of starvation in China. She researches the histories of those places she was evacuated to, seeking out the stories behind what you observe on the surface.

Sheila is a child of World War Two. By the time 'Victory' comes for the Allies, she's working in an office, dreary work only alleviated by dressing up and attending dances in the evenings. She notes how whole German cities are vengefully, or for show, annihilated: 'collateral damage', it's called today, as adults, children, prisoners of war, talking, playing, going about their business, are blown up, or burnt up by incendiary bombs. Unlike Westminster, there are no monuments to Bomber Harris in *Yealm*.

Weeks after conceding defeat... Atom Bomb drops on Hiroshima... Cold War... Show... collateral damage... In *Yealm*, political imagination does not mean denying subjective experience, it means taking it seriously. Sheila's scrupulous observation allows us to revisit our own childhoods. Affection is expressed for a particular tree she used to climb. Suddenly I remember my own favourite tree as a child. We both read books in their branches; different trees, different times, different getaways, but all so familiar. *"It was a high day"*, when Sheila was allowed to catch a bus on her own. And I remember my own struggle to let me be and do as I am. The powerlessness of childhood is so palpable in *Yealm*. We are, after all, born into a world indecipherable, set up by previous adults, so many of whom accept the previous set ups and do not think beyond. Oh, for more Sheilas who do.

Sharon Borthwick
2015-vi-21

Index

The Assassin

Michael Tencer and Andy Wilson (eds)

ISBN: 978-0-9926509-2-6
Published: Dec 2014, 518pp

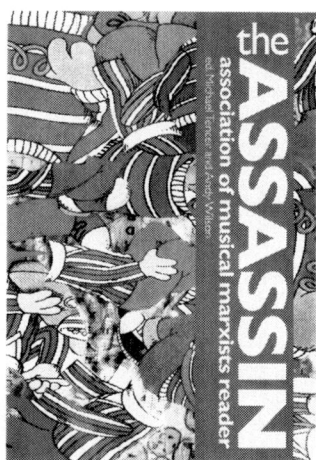

Unkant Reader: The Assassin includes excerpts from all the Unkant publications released since we started out in 2011: Ben Watson, *Adorno for Revolutionaries* ✦ Sean Bonney, *Happiness: Poems After Rimbaud* ✦ Ray Challinor, *The Struggle for Hearts and Minds: Essays on the Second World War* ✦ Dave Black & Chris Ford, *1839: The Chartist Insurrection* ✦ Ben Watson, *Blake in Cambridge* ✦ Jim Higgins, *More Years for the Locust: The Origins of the SWP* ✦ Ken Fox, *Azmud: An Oily Saga on the Surface of the Word Bath in 5 Expired Generations* ✦ Dave Renton, *Socialism From Below: Writings from an Unfinished Tradition* ✦ Andy Wilson (ed), *Cosmic Orgasm: The Music of Iancu Dumitrescu* ✦ Esther Leslie, *Derelicts: Thought Worms from the Wreckage* ✦ Rob Dellar, *Splitting in Two: Mad Pride and Punk Rock Oblivion* ✦ Dave Black (ed), *Helen Macfarlane: Red Republican*.

Priorlectics: Also within are the complete pamphlets: Ian Land, *The SWP vs Lenin* ✦ Ben Watson, *Music, Violence, Truth* ✦ and an extract from Andy Wilson's, *Faust: Stretch Out Time*.

AMM Journal: There are also 100s of pages of scores, photographs, poems, paintings and images, essays, comics, reviews, notices and manifestos from the AMM, its friends and supporters. Featured articles include essays on Comic Book Marxism ✦ Jeff Keen Flix ✦ Critique of the Situationist Dialectic ✦ Wilhelm Reich and Class Consciousness ✦ The State of Scripts ✦ Cartoon Trumpets and Horseshit ✦ The 60s Counterculture, and the Culture of the Left, and more.

Contributors: Jules Alford ⋆ Ana-Maria Avram ⋆ Derek Bailey ⋆ Dave Black ⋆ Sean Bonney ⋆ Sharon Borthwick ⋆ Sky Budgen ⋆ Dunya Bueler ⋆ Marie-Angelique Bueler ⋆ Stuart Calton ⋆ Eugene Chadbourne ⋆ Louise Challice ⋆ Ray Challinor ⋆ Sophie Clare ⋆ Ged Colgan ⋆ Eleanor Crook ⋆ Rob Dellar ⋆ THF Drenching ⋆ Iancu Dumitrescu ⋆ Evil Dick ⋆ Simon H. Fell ⋆ Keith Fisher ⋆ Chris Ford ⋆ Ken Fox ⋆ Richard Hemmings ⋆ Jim Higgins ⋆ I'd M Thfft Able ⋆ Stefan Jaworzyn ⋆ Asger Jorn ⋆ jwcurry ⋆ Jeff Keen ⋆ Ian Land ⋆ Daphne Lawless ⋆ Esther Leslie ⋆ Johan Lif ⋆ Steven Lowery ⋆ Manchester Left Writers ⋆ Len Massey ⋆ David Mills ⋆ Elkka Reign Nyoukis ⋆ Dan O'Donnell ⋆ Guillaume Ollendorff ⋆ Out To Lunch ⋆ Harvey Pekar ⋆ Ed Piskor ⋆ Michel Prigent ⋆ JH Prynne ⋆ The Psychedelic Bolsheviks ⋆ Tom Raworth ⋆ Dave Renton ⋆ Jenny Russell ⋆ Peter Shield ⋆ Andy Shone ⋆ Sonic Pleasure ⋆ Verity Spott ⋆ Luke Staunton ⋆ Michael Tencer ⋆ John Tursi ⋆ Ben, Iris and Mordecai Watson ⋆ Andy and Huxley Wilson ⋆ Susann Witt-Stahl.

Derelicts: Thought Worms From the Wreckage

Esther Leslie

ISBN: 978-0-9568176-9-3
Published: Mar 2014, 254pp

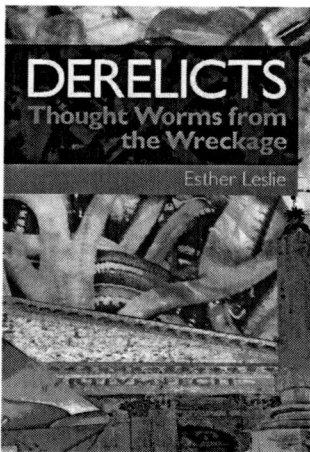

Philosophy and art with the imagination to actually change the world: this is the unfinished dream of history and the heart of the revolutionary modernism of the early 20th Century, which globalised war and exploitation managed indefinitely to defer. Esther Leslie reopens the cold case on filmmakers, artists, thinkers and other animals, exiled or otherwise Disneyfied, and finds still-warm fertile ground for a wild future as yet unfulfilled. From ideal homes with traces erased to utopian rivers drawn back to their source, the alienated subject of history discerns its rightful place in the present tense, with no room for buts or half-measures. The derelicts of history find new life beyond commodified thought: would that the same could be said for all their readers.

Michael Tencer

Cosmic Orgasm: The Music of Iancu Dumitrescu

Andy Wilson (ed)

ISBN: 978-0-9568176-5-5

Published: May 2013, 406pp

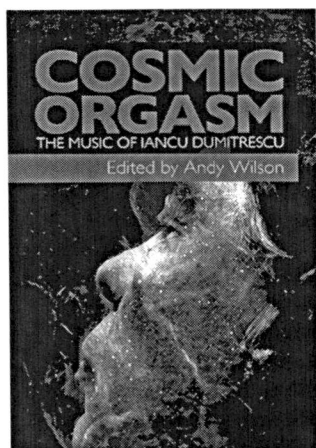

"As a creator of radical music that breaks convention, riding on the edge of the classical avant garde onto realms more closely associated with the likes of Nurse With Wound or The Hafler Trio, Iancu Dumitrescu has the talent to lure you in, mystify and startle with unnerving ferocity."

Alan Freeman

"Iancu Dumitrescu stands at the cutting edge of the whole range of new tendencies, representing a musical avant garde uncorrupted by compromise—in which the taste for invention merges with intellectual speculation in the philosophical sense of the word. As the outstanding figure in Romanian composed music, Iancu Dumitrescu developed from the 1970's the concept of acousmatic—a pre-Socratic term that refers to the art of concealing the sound source to render a message more mysterious "

George Astalos

"Of all living composers, Dumitrescu is the one who has most exploded sound. Dumitrescu's work is a negation, from the depths, of everything in contemporary music symptomatic of distraction, of banalisation, and of a radical loss of purpose. His music is not a new convolution in the knot of modern music, but an unravelling of the curse."

Tim Hodgkinson

Azmud

Ken Fox

ISBN: 978-0-9568176-4-8
Published: Mar 2013, 270pp

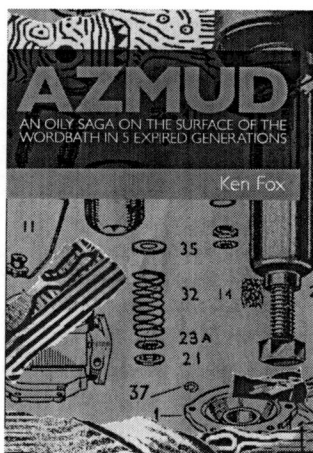

Drifting in & out of sense as in an interrupted dream, Azmud is a novel contribution to literary art as political allegory. In each of its five sections—'expired generations'—it attempts to retell the tale of the human psyche, the damage it has undergone under capitalism, in the form of a wandering work tribe searching for value in the spectacular flow of mass communication, on behalf of various severe 'generals' who demand a quota of abstract accumulation. But each of Azmud's industrial adventures in turn become allegories for the act of the text's own creation. But what happens in Azmud? Under orders, a human herd wanders thru the dense miasma of mass communication, hunting for precious ox-ore to stash in their air-ark or fuel their ancient steam engine. A vagrant crew invades the broken dreams of a drowsy industrial tycoon, stealing baskets full of his precious sleep. A homeless hoard combs thru post-industrial litter, searching for burnable rubble. A fake engineer captures a team of lost work-horses & four mammoth protozoans to help boost the energy yield of his toxic currents. A cargo ship collects a crew of stranded industrial outcasts with their precious ark full of ore & its tyrannical captain subjects them to relentless injections & many unwanted adventures.

Association of Musical Marxists

More Years for the Locust

Jim Higgins

ISBN: 978-0-9568176-3-1
Published: Jun 2012, 330pp

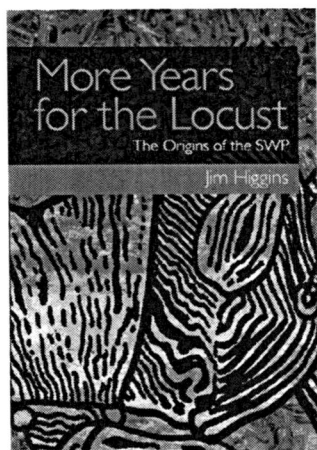

"*There is a human scale to the story so often missing in the more staid accounts of the left and its history which often create an artificial barrier between readers and the activists being written about, who were after all, people much like them. This dimension of the book which, to put it bluntly, makes it such a good laugh, also provides a great store of what Aristotle would have called practical wisdom. The laughter and the nous are here very closely related and impossible to summarise, they must be read...*

The trouble with Higgins is ultimately our own trouble. The reward for recognising this is to be able to rehabilitate and nourish a part of ourselves. The IS tradition is broader than the latest line or missive from the latest CC. This may seem a problem to some but it ought to be seen as a great resource. Revolutionaries too have traditions. Perhaps we are now in a position to learn from Higgins even if we were sadly a bit too stupid to do so before."

John Game, *Foreword*

Blake in Cambridge

Ben Watson

ISBN: 978-0-9568176-8-6
Published: Apr 2012, 168pp

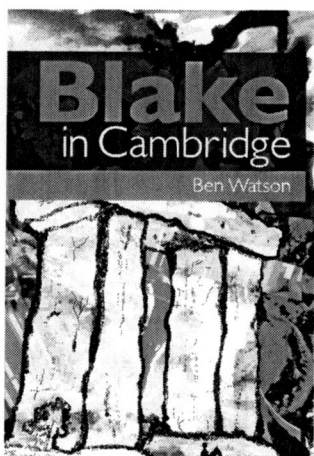

Blake in Cambridge was written after reading William Blake's visionary epic *Milton* during extended bouts of childcare in Coram's Fields in the summer of 2010. *Blake in Cambridge* is the Marxist critique of Eng. Lit. Christopher Caudwell was meant to write, but screwed up due to a CPGB sociology which denies literature the chance to answer back. In Marx's polemic, the jokes of *Tristram Shandy* and *Don Quixote* became weapons in class struggle. This, argues Watson, is how Blake can and should be used.

The **Association of Musical Marxists** says: A revolutionary party would not be paranoid about its members' proclivities. It would not try, like the Lindsey German-era SWP, to insulate members from avant garde extremes and bathe them, infant Cleopatras, in a dilute milk of inoffensive, politically-correct culture—soggy crumbs from the bosses' table. We need to pierce the veil of moralism and fear which protects the bourgeois racket. Blake for the masses! Start here...

1839: The Chartist Insurrection

Dave Black and Chris Ford

ISBN: 978-0-9568176-6-2
Published: Apr 2012, 268pp

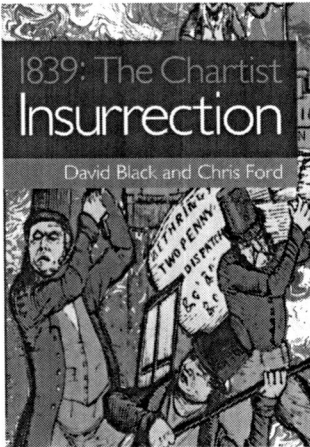

"With its meticulous attention to detailed sources, its comprehensive scope and its exacting research, this book doesn't just address the neglect of this important and interesting episode in Labour movement history, but more importantly it also challenges us to think again about the revolutionary potential of the British Labour movement."

John McDonnell MP, *Foreword*

In retrieving the suppressed history of the Chartist insurrection, David Black and Chris Ford have written a revolutionary handbook. Without romanticism or condescension, they track the difficulties of unifying local revolts without selling out to the 'representative politics' favoured in the parliamentary charade. As today's anti-capitalism faces the problem of anger without organisation, the lessons of the Chartists become crucial. Dialectics is not something to be derived from pure philosophy: by looking at the political problems of an insurgent working class, Black and Ford resurrect the true One-to-Many dialectic.

Association of Musical Marxists

Adorno for Revolutionaries

Ben Watson

ISBN: 978-0-9568176-0-0
Published: May 2011, 256pp

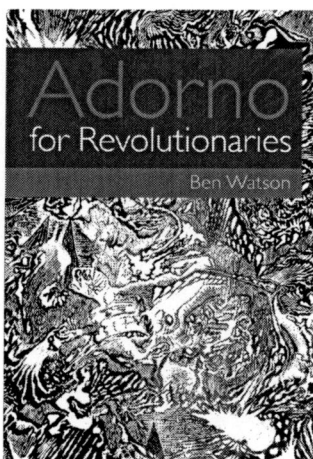

Starting with the commodity form (rather than the 'spirit' lauded by everyone from Classic FM retards to NME journalists), Adorno outlined a revolutionary musicology, a passageway between subjective feeling and objective conditions. In *Adorno for Revolutionaries*, Ben Watson argues that this is what everyone's been looking for since the PCF blackened the name of Marxism by wrecking the hopes of May '68. Batting aside postmodern prattlers and candyass pundits alike, this collection detonates the explosive core of Adorno's thought.

The **Association of Musical Marxists** says: Those 'socialists' who are frightened of their feelings can go stew in their imaginary bookshop. For us, great music is a necessity. To talk about it is to criticise everything that exists.

"For those who have the ears to hear I strongly recommend Adorno For Revolutionaries *as a substantial and very readable effort."*
Dave Black, *Hobgoblin*

Lightning Source UK Ltd.
Milton Keynes UK
UKOW02f2342030816

279937UK00001B/44/P

9 780992 650940